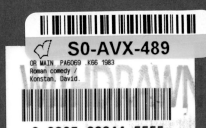

PA
6069
.K66
1983

Konstan, David

Roman comedy

223252

ROMAN COMEDY

ROMAN COMEDY

David Konstan

Cornell University Press

ITHACA AND LONDON

PA
6069
Kbb
1983

First published 1983 by Cornell University Press.
Published in the United Kingdom by Cornell University Press Ltd.,
Ely House, 37 Dover Street, London W1X 4HQ.

International Standard Book Number 0-8014-1531-4
Library of Congress Catalog Number 82-22112
Printed in the United States of America
*Librarians: Library of Congress cataloging information appears
on the last page of the book.*

*The paper in this book is acid-free and meets the guidelines for permanence and durability
of the Committee on Production Guidelines for Book Longevity of the Council on Library
Resources.*

88 - B1973

To my children,
Eve (called Tupi) and Geoffrey

Contents

Preface

The things that people do, they normally do for reasons, and reasons, which by their nature must suffer an account of themselves, are never wholly private. So it is that stories, which are narratives of purposive actions, necessarily project an image of a social code, though not always a simple or harmonious one. Indeed, conflicting values or impulses are the source of narrative tension, and in comedy such tension must be resolved through those conventional turns of events which we identify as part of the form. The very essence of comedy is social, therefore, and in the complex movement of its plots we may be able to discern the lineaments and contradictions of the reigning ideas of an age. In the following chapters we shall examine Roman comedies in the context of the institutions and ideology of the ancient city-state.

Many friends and colleagues have read all or part of this book in manuscript, and I have greatly benefited from their suggestions. I am happy to thank my colleagues at Wesleyan University, Richard Slotkin, the late Catherine Rhorer, Marylin Arthur, Andrew Szegedy-Maszak, Duffield White, James Truscott, and Stephen Dyson, for their kind help at various stages of the writing. I am especially indebted to Eleanor Winsor Leach of Indiana University for many discussions and ideas and to my friend Barbara Smith Canham for the opportunity to air and clarify many notions that, at their inception, often took the form of nagging obsessions. Cynthia Dessen of the University of North Carolina shared with me a manuscript copy of her paper on the *Truculentus,* and also com-

Preface

mented in detail on my chapter on that play. My wife, Barbara Harlow, shares in all with me. To Susan Potter and Clare Johnson I am grateful for their patient typing of the manuscript. Many others—students, colleagues, and friends—have contributed to my thinking in one way or another, and though I cannot neatly discriminate the individual debts, I am deeply aware of the fruitful process of intellectual exchange at Wesleyan and elsewhere; I single out UCLA, Connecticut College, the University of Connecticut, Colby College, the University of Maine, Smith College, and the Classical Association of New England, at which I read early versions of various chapters of this book. I also thank the National Endowment for the Humanities, which awarded me a research grant for the summer of 1978, during which I completed the draft of the book. Earlier versions of the chapters on the *Aulularia, Asinaria, Hecyra,* and *Captivi* were published, respectively, in *Arethusa* 10 (1977); *The Classical Journal* 73 (1976); *The Far-Western Forum: A Review of Ancient and Modern Letters* 1 (1974); and *Ramus* 5 (1976). The last appears by permission of Aureal Publications. Finally, I am grateful for the careful comments of five anonymous readers and to the editors of Cornell University Press who encouraged the final revisions of the text.

DAVID KONSTAN

Middletown, Connecticut

Abbreviations

AJA	*American Journal of Archaeology*
AJP	*American Journal of Philology*
CJ	*Classical Journal*
CP	*Classical Philology*
CQ	*Classical Quarterly*
CW	*Classical Weekly* or (after 1957) *Classical World*
Class. et Med.	*Classica et Mediaevalia*
HSCP	*Harvard Studies in Classical Philology*
LSJ	H. G. Liddell, R. Scott, and H. S. Jones, *A Greek-English Lexicon* (Oxford, 1940)
OLD	*Oxford Latin Dictionary* (Oxford, 1968–)
RE	A. Pauly, G. Wissowa, and W. Kroll, *Realencyclopädie der classischen Altertumswissenschaft* (Stuttgart, 1894–)
REL	*Revue des études latines*
RFIC	*Revista di filologia e d'istruzione classica*
Rh. Mus.	*Rheinisches Museum*
SIFC	*Studi italiani di filologia classica*
TAPA	*Transactions of the American Philological Association*
TLL	*Thesaurus Linguae Latinae* (Leipzig, 1900–)
YCS	*Yale Classical Studies*

ROMAN COMEDY

Introduction

The twenty-six Roman comedies that survive today are adaptations in Latin of Greek originals produced in the latter part of the fourth century B.C. and the first part of the third. This body of drama is known as "new comedy" (the early form is also distinguished as "middle comedy"), as opposed to the "old comedy" of the fifth century B.C. represented by the works of Aristophanes. Precursors of new comedy may be identified in the late plays of Aristophanes, composed after the Peloponnesian War, in such romantic tragedies of Euripides as the *Ion,* and undoubtedly also, if the record were complete, in the mythological travesties called satyr plays, as well as in popular mimes and folk tales.[1] This book, however, is not concerned with origins, but rather with that stage at which new comedy "attained its natural form," to borrow the expression Aristotle applied to the development of tragedy in the *Poetics* (1149a). We shall be interpreting new comedy as a genre, on the basis of the laws or conventions which define its specific nature.

Among the features that constitute new comedy, we may first of

[1]The debt of new comedy to Euripides and the dramatic technique of the late fifth century is exhibited brilliantly in Wolf Friedrich's *Euripides und Diphilos: Zur Dramaturgie der Spätformen* (Munich, 1953) [Zetemata 5]. See also T. B. L. Webster, "Menander and Earlier Greek Drama," in *Studies in Menander* (Manchester, 1950), 153–94, for the background in tragedy and old comedy. Materials for the debt of new comedy to folktales or minor dramatic genres are widely scattered: Examples are Jocelyn Penny Small, "Plautus and the Three Princes of Serendip," *Renaissance Quarterly* 29 (1976), 183–94, and William F. Hansen, "An Oral Source for the *Menaechmi,*" *CW* 70 (1977), 385–90.

Introduction

all observe that it is a species of verse drama. This means in antiquity a form of popular entertainment, in contrast, for example, with the learned compositions that characterized other branches of poetry in the epoch following the conquests of Alexander the Great. The comic playwrights exploited a more or less common cast of characters, such as the young lover, the straitlaced father, the wily slave, braggart soldier, in limited situations and story types, so limited, in fact, as to incur from many readers the charge of monotony.[2]

With a certain shift in perspective, we can look at the narrow range of plots not as an inhibition on the form but as its condition: The recurring story patterns or paradigms define the genre. Within the overall homogeneity is extraordinary room for variation, and some examples seem to lie at the outermost boundaries of the form. In all these respects, the closest analogue to new comedy may be in the various subgenres of the modern cinema, such as the western or the detective movie, or, to take a comedy type that is a true descendant of the ancient, the television situation comedies.[3]

What Aristotle observed of the nature of stories of course applies to the ancient comedies: They have a beginning, a middle, and an end. That is, they exhibit closure, a completion in the conclusion of the action initiated at the opening of the drama.[4] In comedy, closure takes the form of a resolution, by which the tension or disequilibrium that establishes the plot is abolished.[5] Normally, this tension is embodied in a conflict among the characters, as when a father opposes some passionate but unrespectable affair pursued by his son, or two rival lovers—one rich, one poor—contend for the same woman. The aims and actions of the dramatic personalities, however, are always an expression of certain values. The traditional father, for example, defends a public conception of a legitimate or proper marriage when he forbids his son to court a

[2]For example, Philip Whaley Harsh, *A Handbook of Classical Drama* (Stanford, 1944), 317.

[3]For criticism concerning such forms, see Richard Slotkin, *Regeneration through Violence: The Mythology of the American Frontier 1600–1860* (Middletown, Conn., 1973); John G. Cawelti, *Adventure, Mystery and Romance: Formula Stories as Art and Popular Culture* (Chicago, 1976): Bruce Merry, *Anatomy of the Spy Thriller* (Montreal, 1977).

[4]See Frank Kermode, *The Sense of an Ending* (Oxford, 1966); also Terry Eagleton, *Criticism and Ideology* (London, 1976), 87.

[5]On the form of comic closure, see Northrop Frye, *Anatomy of Criticism* (Princeton, 1957), especially the section "The Mythos of Spring: Comedy."

woman of inferior status; in the case of rivals, their competition is interesting precisely because the sides are not identical: The audience is thus permitted to take the part of the hero against his antagonist, who is usually foreign and of a class, such as the mercenary soldier, that stands outside normal social relations. We may understand ancient comedy, therefore, as an enactment and resolution of conflicts generated by the system of values itself.[6]

Prominent in the Roman ethical vocabulary are such concepts as loyalty or good faith (*fides*), dutifulness (*pietas*), consistency of behavior (*constantia*), and a sense of obligation for benefits received (*gratia*).[7] These notions are procedural, so to speak; they govern interactions among members of the community, but do not in themselves indicate the basis on which an original action is deemed right or wrong. Obedience to parents is a simple virtue, for example, when it is assumed that the father enjoins what is socially correct. Similarly, the Roman ideas of trust or gratitude presuppose an honorable standard of conduct. The procedural values refer implicitly to rules that define social relations. The moral authority of the father over the romantic impulses of the son assumes the premise that the parent's wishes or interests are consistent with the conventional protocols of marriage, while those of the boy are not. This situation is not always the case in ancient comedy, to be sure; but, when it is not, this fact itself becomes an element in the disequilibrium that drives the plot, and is resolved in the denouement.[8]

[6]See Pierre Macherey, "The Problem of Reflection," trans. S. S. Lanser, *SUBSTANCE* 15 (1976), 18–19, and the same author's *Theory of Literary Production,* trans. Geoffrey Wall (London, 1978); James H. Kavanaugh, "'Marks of Weakness': Ideology, Science and Textual Criticism," *Praxis* 5 (1981), 23–38. It is important to discriminate the *social* analysis employed here from a *political* approach, in which themes or references in comedy are understood as allusions to contemporary party conflicts or specific, articulated programs and problems. For such an interpretation, see Enrico Flores, *Letteratura latina e ideologia del III–II a.c.* (Naples, 1974), esp. 67–68, for a summary of Plautus's presumed connections with the party of Cato; contra, Donato Gagliardi, "Aspetti del teatro comico latino: La 'politica' di Plauto," *Le parole et l'idée* 5 (1963), 167–74, esp. summary, 173. Compare also D. C. Earl, "Political Terminology in Plautus," *Historia* 9 (1960), 234–43, and "Terence and Roman Politics," *Historia* 11 (1962), 469–85.

[7]Many useful works deal with Roman value terms as a semantic and ethical system; see above all Donald C. Earl, *The Moral and Political Tradition of Rome* (Ithaca, N.Y., 1967); Viktor Pöschl, *Grundwerte römischer Staatsgesinnung in den Geschichtswerken des Sallust* (Berlin, 1940); Hans Drexler, "Die moralische Geschichtsauffassung der Römer," *Gymnasium* 61 (1954), 168–90, repr. in Richard Klein, ed., *Das Staatsdenken der Römer* (Darmstadt, 1966).

[8]See particularly the chapters on the *Asinaria* and *Phormio*.

Introduction

The rules and values of ancient city-state society constitute a cultural system.[9] The system may be said to define, by the operation of inclusion and exclusion, the several groups or statuses of the society. As an example, we may consider the marriage code of Athens. At least since legislation initiated by Pericles in 451 B.C., and continuing into the third century B.C. and perhaps beyond, only the offspring of two parents of citizen status were entitled to full civil and political rights in the community. Classical Athens was thus what is called a consanguineal descent group. The perspective can be reversed, however: Instead of regarding kinship as the principle by which citizenship was transmitted, we may take the right to contract a recognized and legitimate marriage, whose heirs have title to citizen status, as constitutive of the citizen community. Citizens were precisely those who had connubial rights. From this point of view, we may identify Athenian society as a closed conjugal group.[10] The impulse to marry outside the group, common among the youths of ancient comedy, thus threatened to dissolve the boundary that separated citizens from strangers. The tension between father and son, which as a personal problem might find expression in the conflict between passion and duty, reflected on the social level an ambiguity or ambivalence in the status system itself.

We may consider another important feature of the marriage code: the prohibition of incest. Socially, this taboo is best understood as the obverse of an affirmative rule: Marriage must involve the union of two distinct households in the community. Rodney Needham, in a discussion of incest as an anthropological concept, remarks: "The regulation of access to women is . . . just like any other kind of regulation; access to certain categories of women is permitted, and to certain others is prohibited. These rules, positive and negative, compose in any particular instance a coherent set and

[9]On the idea of a cultural system, see Leslie A. White, *The Concept of Cultural Systems* (New York, 1975): Clifford Geertz, "Religion as a Cultural System" and "Ideology as a Cultural System," in *The Interpretation of Cultures* (New York, 1973).

[10]This perspective informs the structuralist approach to society, according to which social identity is a consequence, not a cause, of difference. The social other is identified by the operation of a rule whose ultimate justification or ground is the mere capacity to generate a distinction. See Claude Lévi-Strauss, *The Elementary Structures of Kinship,* trans. James Harle Bell, John Richard von Sturmer, and Rodney Needham (Boston, 1969), Intro., ch. 1, "Nature and Culture," and Pt. 1, ch. 3, "The Universe of Rules," esp. 32: "The *fact of being a rule,* completely independent of its modalities, is indeed the very essence of the incest prohibition."

should be comprehended as such, i.e. correlatively. It is methodically defective to consider only prohibitions, apart from permissions and prescriptions, and it is yet more invalid to consider only isolated prohibitions as though these alone were definitive or essential."[11] The positive rule provides a clue to the social function of the taboo. Leslie A. White offers a crisp formulation: "Incest was defined and rules to prevent or punish the commission of incest were established in order to require interfamilial marriage and to prevent intrafamilial marriage. . . . This was done because interfamilial marriage promoted the formation of the all-embracing web of kinship, providing society with connective tissue among all family groups, thereby increasing the cohesiveness of the society and the strength and power of the cultural system."[12] From this point of view, the danger met by the incest taboo is the disintegration of the community into discrete autonomous families.

The prohibition against incest also helps to articulate the internal organization of the family, differentiating the relationship between parents from that among brothers and sisters, for example, while it sustains the hierarchical principle of authority. This has enormous consequences for the formation of the human personality, which will vary from society to society. In ancient Rome, paternal power was very great, and could extend well into the adult life of the sons and daughters. This authority doubtless caused the children some anxiety, which may have been relieved in some measure by the spectacle of stern old men tweaked and outwitted by youths and slaves and marginal members of society.[13] Such a hypothesis might account for the apparently greater prominence of farcical episodes

[11]"Remarks on the Analysis of Kinship and Marriage," in Rodney Needham, ed., *Rethinking Kinship and Marriage* (London, 1971), 29.

[12]White, 29–30. Lévi-Strauss makes the same point, 45–51, 481; it is endorsed by Claude Vatin, *Recherches sur le mariage et la condition de la femme mariée à l'époque hellénistique* (Paris, 1970), 4.

[13]Erich Segal makes this feature the essential or defining characteristic of Roman comedy, above all that of Plautus, in *Roman Laughter: The Comedy of Plautus* (Cambridge, Mass., 1968; repr. New York, 1971). It is probably a part of the popular heritage of mime and farce, as Alan McN. G. Little points out in "Plautus and Popular Drama," *HSCP* 49 (1938), 205–28; see also Anthony Caputi, *Buffo* (Detroit, 1978), where Plautus is compared with dramatists of renaissance Europe whose comedies developed out of carnival traditions. Certainly, a comparison of Plautus's *Mostellaria,* on which Segal's analysis works best, with the same playwright's *Trinummus,* to which, as Little points out, it is "recognizably akin," though "its tone and emphasis are absolutely different" (221), reveals at once that Plautus's own conception of comedy was indifferent to the presence or absence of this farcical or carnival element.

in Roman comedy as compared with the Greek originals. From such considerations one might be tempted to interpret the conflict between father and son as a displaced version of the Oedipal complex, in which the forbidden woman stands in symbolically for the mother; and this thesis might seem to find confirmation in such plays as the *Casina* and *Mercator,* where father and son are rivals for the same young woman.[14] The explicit issues of ancient comedy, however, point to a different analysis. The competition between father and son is always the result of paternal encroachment, never of incestuous desires in the youth. By violating the connubial code himself, the father implicitly gives sanction to the son's impulse, and thereby weakens the status boundaries that are his obligation to uphold. A dovetailing or mutual equilibrium exists between the internal structure of the household and the outer articulation of the community over and against strangers. This system defines the basic roles and preoccupations that characterize ancient new comedy.

The sexual code is only one, albeit the most important set of rules in the ancient community. There were also protocols involving economic exchange, as well as varying degrees of civil and political rights, which functionally distinguished the several statuses and classes of the city-state society. In the chapters that follow, each devoted to a single comedy by the Roman playwrights Plautus and Terence, a variety of boundary problems will be examined. In the *Aulularia,* the focus will be on the forms of exchange that bind the individual household to the community at large. The proper relationship between father and son will emerge as the theme of the *Asinaria,* which concludes with the domestic erotic rivalry mentioned above. The *Captivi* centers on the complex question of Greek national identity, which began to challenge the exclusiveness of city-state society; for this issue is behind the abiding controversy over the enslavement of Greeks by Greeks. The *Rudens* brings heaven and nature under the city-state dispensation. The

[14]Northrop Frye, in "The Argument of Comedy," *English Institute Essays* 1948–1949 (New York, 1949), 58–59, adopted this point of view squarely. It is developed in greater detail with respect to Plautus's *Casina* by W. Thomas Mac-Cary, in "Patterns of Myth, Ritual, and Comedy in Plautus' *Casina*," *Texas Studies in Literature and Language* 15 (1974), 881–89. For a different account of the *Casina,* which is more in line with the present work, see Walter E. Forehand, "Plautus' *Casina*: An Explication," *Arethusa* 6 (1973), 233–56.

Introduction

Cistellaria investigates the ambiguous station of the Greek metics, resident aliens with severely limited rights, and applies the lesson of the Greek original to Rome's own relations with her allies. In the *Phormio,* the figure of the parasite stands forth, the landless citizen with only a marginal tie to the ancient community of agrarian smallholders. Other themes are present subordinately in the plays: the condition of women, city versus country, rich against poor, the humanity of slaves, the role of greed, and money as a solvent of traditional social relations. Old motifs are subjected to ironic inversions, as in Terence's *Hecyra,* or to satiric transformations, as in Plautus's *Truculentus.* Taken together, the dramas of ancient comedy map out the ideology of city-state society and reveal to us the sensitive areas where the borders were vague, weak, or changing under the pressure of new historical circumstances.

The world in which new comedy came into being, both in Greece and at Rome, was under intense social stress. Politically, this condition was manifest at Athens in a succession of tyrannies, persecutions, and foreign and civil wars which ensued upon the death of Alexander the Great. The conspicuous issue behind these upheavals was Athens's independence with respect to the Macedonian hegemony over Greece, but international politics in many ways was a mask for Athens's domestic crisis. "Fundamentally," writes F. H. Sandbach, in his handbook *The Comic Theatre of Greece and Rome,* "the people were divided between those who wished for security, which they expected to maintain by loyal acceptance of Macedonian protection, and those who hoped to regain independence by allying themselves with others among the powers who disputed Alexander's inheritance. The former party had the support of most of the wealthier members of the community, the latter that of the poorer and of the supporters of democracy, or equal rights for all citizens."[15] The struggle between landlords and smallholders had shaped Athenian history for the past three centuries at least; throughout this period, however, the centrifugal pressures of class tension had been in part concealed and contained by communal traditions, which bound the citizens together as a status group over and against foreigners, slaves, resident aliens, and other dispossessed elements in the society. The fourth and third centuries B.C. saw the weakening of those traditions, just as the collapse of

[15]F. H. Sandbach, *The Comic Theatre of Greece and Rome* (New York, 1977), 68.

Introduction

Athens's imperial power and the rising influence of Macedon in Athenian affairs exacerbated internal conflict.[16] The boundaries between metics and strangers on the one side, and citizens on the other, began to blur. Claude Mossé concludes a study of these populations at Athens with the following observations: "The distinction between metics and transient strangers tended to become attenuated, as a result of the weakening of the juridical definition of the metic"; and "among the more or less temporary resident aliens, the richer aspired to be absorbed into the bosom of the ruling class. The others were no longer very different from citizens who had lost all real power in political decisions."[17] Marriage customs and restrictions too were apparently undergoing a gradual relaxation in this era.[18]

Because new comedy centered on scenes of private life, it has frequently been taken as escapist. Sandbach, for example, remarks: "Because politics has so little part in the plays, some have supposed that they also had little in most men's lives." He goes on to refute the implication: "Athens was no longer a major power, and the politics of Athens were no longer such as to be of prime interest to the historian of the Greek-speaking world. But they did not lack importance for the Athenians whose lives they determined. They were bitter and sometimes deadly. They were not a suitable subject for entertainment on a holiday."[19] But the political turbulence of those years, as we have seen, accompanied changes in social life, and personal problems of love and authority, status and class were the locus of anxieties that were sharpened by the relative instability of traditional institutions. Comedy did not ignore these anxieties. Rather, it took them as points of departure, resolving them, to be

[16]Claude Mossé gives a general survey of the period in *La fin de la démocratie athénienne* (Paris, 1962). On communal traditions versus class divisions, there is a considerable literature; see esp. Robert A. Padgug, "Classes and Society in Classical Greece," *Arethusa* 8 (1975), 85–117, and my own rather different appreciation of the question in "A Comment on Class and Labor in Ancient Society," *Marxist Perspectives* 7 (1979), 124–31.

[17]Claude Mossé, "Métèques et étrangers à Athènes aux IVᶜ-IIIᶜ siècles avant notre ère," in Hans Julius Wolff, ed., *Symposion 1971* (Cologne, 1975), 213. Compare David Whitehead's section "The End of the Metoikia" in *The Ideology of the Athenian Metic* (Cambridge, 1977), 163–67.

[18]Mossé (above, n. 17), 210; Evanghelos Karabelias, "L'épiclérat dans la comédie nouvelle et dans les sources latines," in *Symposion 1971* (Cologne, 1975), 219; Vatin, 115–31.

[19]Sandbach, 68–69.

sure, in happy endings, as is the nature of the genre. The themes of comedy were serious.

The earliest Roman adaptations of Greek new comedy date from the years following the first Punic war, but the form reached its zenith during the second war with Carthage, when the Romans multiplied the festivals at which dramatic performances were given to entertain the population and "keep up civilian morale"[20] during the grim years of Hannibal's activity in the Italian peninsula. Naturally, changes occurred in the Latin versions: Plautus's language, for example, is more extravagant than the Greek of his models, his meter is more varied, whole scenes are compressed or excised, others, often farcical, are elaborated. Terence combined in his adaptations episodes drawn from more than one Greek original, and Plautus may well have done the same. Perhaps they took still greater liberties on occasion. We cannot tell, but we should recall that Roman playwrights did compose original comedies situated in Italian towns, although none has survived.[21] Whatever the degree of native invention in the comedies that have survived, the world they represent is clearly of a piece with Menander's. Like the Greeks a century earlier, the Romans returned to the theater again and again to watch the unfolding and ultimate resolution of a few familiar complications. The same stories spoke to the citizens of both cultures, and yet the destinies of Athens and Rome were vastly different in the century or so during which the genre of new comedy enjoyed in each its creative phase. For Athens dwindled to a satellite, now of one, now of another of the great Hellenistic empires, while Rome, a hundred years later, was engaging in the wars that brought supremacy over the entire Mediterranean world. Beside this, the institutions of the Roman *urbs* differed in important ways from those of the Greek *polis*. The class of metics or resident aliens did not play a significant role in Roman social life; women were not

[20]Sandbach, 107. For the theatrical festivals at Rome, one may consult such standard handbooks as W. Beare, *The Roman Stage,* 3d ed. (London, 1968), 162–63; the table (p. 162) indicates that three dramatic festivals were established during the second Punic war; the number of days devoted to dramatic performances increased from one to seven or eight in the period of the first two wars with Carthage. I am advised by an anonymous referee that this increase was a phenomenon especially of the later years of the second war and reflected the availability of booty, the patronage of proud generals, and a confident mood in the populace.

[21]For the general characteristics of Roman comedy, the most comprehensive survey is George Duckworth, *The Nature of Roman Comedy* (Princeton, 1952).

sequestered in the house; slaves might achieve citizenship upon manumission; political power had resided for at least a century securely in the hands of the landed aristocracy. These and other crucial points of divergence, however, do not obscure the underlying identity of the city-state as the dominant social form in early Greece and Italy; what is more, the successes of ancient Rome challenged the traditions and institutions of the city-state even more severely than the defeats suffered by Athens. These social transformations have been amply described by the great historian Arnold J. Toynbee in two volumes entitled *Hannibal's Legacy*.[22] At the threshold of the second century B.C., Rome was still a community of landholding citizens, who manned the armies that destroyed Carthage and were bound to one another by ties of kinship and legal rights that together were summed up under the formulas of *ius conubii,* the right of marriage, and *ius commercii,* the right of trade. A century and a half later, the city of Rome had become an imperial metropolis, inhabited by citizens and noncitizens drawn from three continents, propertied or not, free to trade or marry across boundaries of status which had stood as barriers to the ancestral population. The citizens of this new world might still, as we do, enjoy the revival of a comedy of the past, but no comedies would be freshly composed or adapted in this age.

In an epoch of social stress and change, new comedy represented on the stage a world where tensions evanesce through the mechanisms of the plot. The typical story in which a young man, against the wishes of his father, falls in love with a woman who is a slave, foreigner, or otherwise ineligible as a legitimate partner in marriage, is commonly resolved by means of a recognition scene, in which she is revealed to be a citizen of suitable status. With this device, the conflicting claims of private passion and social responsibility are neatly reconciled, for the waywardness of desire proves to be illusory. The impulse that aspires to the forbidden is domesticated, gratified without danger to public conventions, and thus the

[22]London, 1965. See also Peter A. Brunt, *Italian Manpower 225 B.C.–A.D. 14* (Oxford, 1971), and *Social Conflicts in the Roman Republic* (New York, 1971). A concise and sophisticated review of the social and economic factors in the transformation of late-republican Rome is in Keith Hopkins, "Economic Growth and Towns in Classical Antiquity," in Philip Abrams and E. A. Wrigley, eds., *Towns in Societies: Essays in Economic History and Historical Sociology* (Cambridge, 1978), 35–77.

threat to the city-state ideal of a closed conjugal group is averted. Conversely, the ideal itself is thereby affirmed. In a period when foreign campaigns, the rise of slavery on a mass scale, and growing class divisions among the citizens threatened the solidarity of the Roman community, comedy portrayed a natural harmony in the society, in which its members, despite contrary impulses, were ultimately united through the fundamental bond of kinship. This structure, already only the vestige of a communal past, thus came to serve an ideological function, if we understand by ideology an idealized system of social relations which appears to unify the actually diverse interests in a complex community.

The stories of ancient comedy are intricate and various, however, the resolutions often delicate, while the subversive passions may be portrayed in a vivid and sympathetic manner. Comedy is a subtle instrument, which may emphasize or exploit different meanings latent in the paradigmatic plot forms. The standard type of son–father conflict, for example, can be a vehicle for asserting the rights of the youthful lover against the repressive restrictions of the parent, who represents the prevailing social conventions. Such an intention seems to inform Terence's *Phormio,* in which the usual initial conditions of comedy are strikingly reversed: Against his father's wishes the young man has married a girl who is in fact a citizen, while the father has planned a different marriage for the boy with the purpose of covering up his brother's adultery. Quite the opposite is the lesson of Plautus's *Asinaria,* where the complex plot is designed to exhibit the vicious consequences of sentimental leniency in the father. Only by detailed analysis of the structure, imagery, and language of each comedy is it possible to establish its ruling ideas and significance, which reside not in the archetypes of the plots as such but in the specific articulation of divergences from the norm. The sympathy of the Roman dramatists with the themes of their Greek models is revealed by their coherent symbolism and terminology which reproduced or embellished the style of the originals in a specifically Roman guise. The Latin of Plautus and Terence could carry and even enrich the tenor of their Greek predecessors. To take but a single illustration, the Latin *fides,* or "good faith," had a different semantic range from the Greek *pistis,* as Polybius was obliged to observe, but in several plays, and notably in the *Captivi,* occurrences of *fides* serve as a register of the thematic moments in the action. Within a common set of narrative para-

Introduction

digms, such figures mark the embeddedness of new comedy in the Roman civic vocabulary.

The notion of archetype or plot paradigm requires some explanation. I do not intend by these terms a set of timeless and universal narrative forms, although a relationship between such forms and the story patterns of new comedy is not excluded. There are good reasons, for example, to associate the plot of Plautus's *Menaechmi* with a widespread folktale theme involving twins, while the motif of the foundling, so characteristic of the plays involving a recognition scene, may be interpreted as a variation on an archetypal myth of the hero.[23] Any such abstraction of types is an endeavor in theory, whose virtue is to reduce the bewildering variety of phenomena to a limited number of generative principles. My analysis of the story types of new comedy is such an endeavor, but its scope is confined to the patterns that inform the single genre. What is more, I claim for the forms no special ontological status, but regard them as inferred structures, which may be confirmed by the common consensus of informed critics and by certain indications within the plays themselves. The following argument may illustrate the process by which such structures are derived.

Sidney G. Ashmore, in the introduction to a school edition of the plays of Terence, gives us a synopsis of the characteristic plot in new comedy: "The central theme was usually the course of true love, and the action depicted the efforts of a youth to obtain possession of his mistress—often in the face of the determined opposition of a parent or guardian—and with the assistance of a tricky slave. The heroine, who at the start was supposed to belong to the class of courtesans or *hetaerae* (regarded as aliens), was eventually discovered to be a well-born maiden and an Athenian citizen, and her marriage to the hero of the play was the necessary and suitable conclusion."[24] The reader will recognize in this précis a version of the story we have just treated as exemplary. Ashmore's description applies to only a small percentage of the surviving Roman comedies, however. It is undoubtedly a mistake to reduce all the plays to manifestations of this basic form. All the same, the pattern he identified is a fundamental one, as we can confirm by analyzing its

[23]Hansen (above, n. 1); Joseph Campbell, *The Hero with a Thousand Faces,* 2d ed. (Princeton, 1968), 329; compare also Richmond Lattimore's analysis of *Oedipus the King* as a version of comic plot in *The Poetry of Greek Tragedy* (New York, 1958), 82–93.

[24]Sidney G. Ashmore, *The Comedies of Terence* (repr. New York, 1967), 5.

role in a drama where it does not control the primary movement of the action. Plautus's *Miles Gloriosus* is based on an altogether different paradigm, that of two rivals in competition for a girl. The task before the young lover and his allies is to trick the soldier into giving up the girl, whom he has abducted and possesses against her will. They accomplish this by seducing him with the pretended wife of his neighbor. The soldier himself acknowledges that to accept this latter lady he must dismiss the former, but he is at a loss how to reconcile her to this rejection (1094ff.). His slave, who is actually in the service of the rival lover, suggests the excuse: "Tell her that you have to marry, that your relatives insist on it, your friends demand it" (1118–19).[25] Thus, the soldier pretends to be in the position which defines the plight of the hero in the paradigm outlined above. He invents the customary conflict between love and obligation, in order to justify his renunciation of the girl. This excuse or any other will work, of course, since the girl is eager to escape him. It is Pyrgopolyneices' decision to give her up, however, that is implausible: there is no reason why he must rid himself of a concubine in order to conduct a secret affair with a married woman. No reason, that is, beyond the requirements of the plot, which must effect the union, actually the reunion, of the girl and her young lover. But Plautus, or his source, was able to motivate the soldier's behavior by casting him momentarily in the role of a lover caught between two mutually exclusive and irreconcilable claims. The audience or reader recognizes the familiar paradigm, and any doubts about the necessary exclusiveness of the soldier's new attachment are stillborn.

In the chapters that follow, several different paradigms are defined. At the most general level of abstraction, they may perhaps be regarded as versions of a single type. Thus T. B. L. Webster, speaking of the work of Menander, and borrowing the terminology of Claude Lévi-Strauss, observes: "We can consider the sixty plays rather as an anthropologist considers a group of myths related to meet a common need. They all have a common armature, union of youth and girl in spite of obstacles. But the common armature is clothed in sixty different ways to produce sixty different plays."[26]

[25]The text of Plautus used throughout this book is W. M. Lindsay, *T. Macci Plauti Comoediae* (Oxford, repr. 1959), 2 vols. The text of Terence is Robert Kauer and Wallace M. Lindsay, *P. Terenti Afri Comoediae* (Oxford, repr. 1961). Translations are my own.
[26]T. B. L. Webster, *An Introduction to Menander* (New York, 1974), 21–22.

Introduction

C. R. Post reduced the formula for new comedy to a mathematical equation,

$$w \left(\frac{x - y}{z} \right) = x + y,$$

where $x - y$ represents the separated couple, $x + y$ the united couple, z the obstacles to their union, and w the mode of overcoming the obstacles.[27] Webster inaugurates his own typology by attending to the nature of the union: "The sixty plays of which we know or can guess the storyline fall into a number of subtypes. The union of lovers which is achieved after surmounting obstacles may be union with a *hetaira* (i.e., courtesan), or reunion of a divided married pair, or marriage." The last category is the most numerous, and Webster further subdivides it as follows: "The young man may or may not have had intercourse with the girl before the play. If he has, the child may have been born before the play or may be born during the play or there may be no mention of a child."[28] Such a list appears to cover the field, but has about it something mechanical and arbitrary. No particular reason is offered for classifying the plays with respect to the time of conception and parturition, and many other details might serve as well. E. M. Forster makes sport of such systems in his delightful and irreverent book, *Aspects of the Novel*. He begins with "classification by chronology. Books written before 1847, books written after it, books written after or before 1848."

> "Classification by subject matter—sillier still. The literature of Inns, beginning with *Tom Jones;* the literature of the Women's Movement, beginning with *Shirley;* the literature of Desert Islands, from *Robinson Crusoe* to *The Blue Lagoon* . . . , novels relating to industrialism, aviation, chiropody, the weather. I include the weather on the authority of the most amazing work on the novel that I have met for many years. . . . The writer's name shall be concealed. He was a pseudoscholar and a good one. He classified novels by their dates, their length, their locality, their sex, their point of view, till no more

[27]C. R. Post, "The Dramatic Art of Menander," *HSCP* 24 (1913), 112.

[28]Webster, 14, 15. Compare the much wider typology of comic plots, in which new comedy figures as a single form, in Gerald Mast, *The Comic Mind: Comedy and the Movies,* 2d ed. (Chicago, 1979), 4–9.

seemed possible. But he still had the weather up his sleeve, and when he brought it out, it had nine heads.[29]

The typology in this book looks to the nature of the obstacle. If we take this interference to be merely a function of relations among the dramatis personae, the list is a matter-of-fact one. The blocking character may be the father of the young man, as in the *Phormio* and, partly, in the *Cistellaria;* these plays represent the paradigm I have treated as exemplary and have illustrated in reference to a minor moment in the *Miles Gloriosus.*[30] Again, the obstacle may be the father of the girl, as in the *Aulularia;* in the *Cistellaria,* the foster mother of the girl plays such a role. The obstacle may come in the form of a rival, as in the *Asinaria,* or an agent, such as a brothel keeper, who has power over the girl, and can sell her to the highest bidder—the *Rudens* has an obstacle of this sort, and it functions as a subordinate element in several of the plays we shall discuss. Through a complex turn in the plot, the obstacle may even prove to reside in the lover himself, as we shall discover in the *Hecyra,* or in the beloved, which is the source of the satirical mood in the *Truculentus.*

The above description leaves out of account the meaning of the opposition or tension in the play. I have already indicated that objections to a union on the part of the father of the boy are normally associated with issues of caste or class, although not inevitably. Opposition from the girl's father, however, is generally a different matter, expressing the old man's unwillingness to participate in the exchange that defines the life of the community. The threat to communal values posed by foreign power and wealth is the common theme of those plays in which a rival is the chief complication. A brief examination of this type will furnish the opportunity of contrasting my method with the important contribution to Plautine studies made by Erich Segal.

Segal has suggested that the spirit of Plautine comedy is saturnalian, the temporary abolition of convention, of prudish mores, or rather their inversion, in which the lowest emerge on top, tweaking their masters, indulging their lusty impulses in a celebration of spontaneous freedom and the appetites of the body. In Segal's own

[29]E. M. Forster, *Aspects of the Novel* (New York, 1927), 11–13.
[30]On the notion of the "blocking character," see Frye, 166–69.

words: "The festive feeling, as Freud described it, is 'the liberty to do what as a rule is prohibited,' a temporary excess which implies everyday restraint. Comedy, likewise, involves a limited license, momentary breaking of society's rules."[31] Yet in rival plays—Plautus's favorite type—the lover and his entourage have no particular concern to abrogate social rules. Their opponents, the blocking figures or agelasts, as Rabelais calls them, are only marginally members of society. The bombastic general is not a citizen-soldier, like the Roman who fought when armies were mustered and then returned to his estates. Rather, he is a professional mercenary, a stranger serving alien principalities.[32] Similarly, that other standard obstacle to a young man's passion, the pimp or procurer, has a most dubious status as a dealer in slaves and pander to illicit lusts. To turn a trick against such agents is not to shatter the social code. Furthermore, the element of intrigue, so prominent in these plays, may also be understood as an affirmation rather than a defiance of customary restraints. For the victim is fooled fairly and squarely. He may have made a wager that looked certain, or been inveigled by flattery or a devious appeal to his greed. Nevertheless, he has committed himself, and when the ruse is exposed, he is no longer in a position to back out. He has put himself in the wrong and lost moral authority; should he then threaten or bluster, the lover may bring him to law or join ranks against him with right-minded members of the community.[33] To be outwitted does not mean that

[31]Segal, 9. The quotation from Freud is from *Totem and Taboo,* vol. 13, 140, of *The Complete Psychological Works of Sigmund Freud,* ed. James Strachey et al. (London, 1953—). Compare also C. L. Barber, *Shakespeare's Festive Comedy* (New York, 1963; orig. 1959), esp. the introduction entitled "The Saturnalian Pattern."

[32]Contrast Segal, 124: "[Plautus'] soldiers, like his statesmen, are merely authoritarian types; and, like his comic senators who contrast so sharply with the real bulwarks of the Roman state, the military characters embody the Roman ideal turned topsy-turvy"; and John Arthur Hanson, "The Glorious Military," in T. A. Dorey and Donald R. Dudley, eds., *Roman Drama* (London, 1965), 51–85: "The impact of the returning hero, whether general, centurion, or common soldier, on Roman society is clearly revealed in Plautus" (61). The observation of G. T. Griffith, *The Mercenaries of the Hellenistic World* (Cambridge, 1935) 323, is still just: "The mercenary's manner of life must have been unsympathetic to the quiet and orderly citizen, and this is the most probable reason . . . for the series of unsympathetic portraits which has survived from the New Comedy." See also Leo Salingar, *Shakespeare and the Traditions of Comedy* (Cambridge, 1974) 107, for a contrast between the role of the citizen general in old comedy and that of the foreign mercenary in new comedy.

[33]Compare the trial of the pimp Labrax in the *Rudens,* the shame of Pyrgopolyneices in the *Miles Gloriosus,* and the ways in which the brothel keepers play into their own humiliation in the *Pseudolus* and the *Poenulus.*

the rules have been set in abeyance, but that they have been turned against one who normally was capable of exploiting them in his own interest.

Erich Segal writes: "Jean-Jacques Rousseau's angry objection to the inversion of status so frequently presented by Molière serves well to describe the technique in Plautus, who provided the precedent." Here is the passage from Rousseau's *Lettre à d'Alembert sur les spectacles,* in Segal's translation: "Observe how, to multiply his jokes, this man disturbs the entire order of society, how scandalously he inverts all the most sacred relationships on which society is based, how he mocks the well-respected rights of fathers over their children, husbands over their wives, and masters over their slaves. True enough, he does evoke laughter from this technique, but this makes him all the more guilty."[34] Segal concurs with this account; he differs only in that he approves what Rousseau condemns, for he is on the side of laughter. But Rousseau is wrong about the nature of comedy, and changing the minus sign to a plus does not correct the error. The braggart soldier and the pimp do not participate in the commerce and family ties that constitute the community: Their wealth and power are signs of the erosion of traditional social bonds, based on well-defined modes of exchange which exclude the sale of sex and military service. This is not to say that the lover's passion is socially respectable, for it is not. But in realizing the object of his desire, the lover simultaneously defends his community against the unequal advantage of the rich interloper—the mercenary stranger, the avaricious dealer in slaves. By his victory, he reaffirms the integrity of the citizen group.

A specific content subsists as well in the *Cistellaria,* in which the locus of opposition is the girl's foster mother; in the *Hecyra,* where the inhibition is in the mind of the lover himself; and in the *Truculentus,* where the beloved, for reasons of her own, withholds her favors.[35]

The meanings of the plays, however, are not reducible to a function of the blocking character. Plot forms are combined or varied in extraordinary ways, and the dramatic issues and conflicts

[34]Segal, 101–2.

[35]In plays in which father and son are rivals, the young man's mother normally plays the role of blocking figure to her husband. The *Menaechmi* is perhaps a distant variant of this type; Eleanor Winsor Leach provides a superb interpretation in "*Meam quom formam noscito:* Language and Characterization in the *Menaechmi,*" *Arethusa* 2 (1969) 30–45.

are correspondingly transformed. To identify the obstacle or blocking figure in such cases as these is itself an interpretation. Form and meaning are codetermined, and a typology of new comedy is, in the final analysis, indissociable from an investigation of its substance. In this dialectical spirit the chapters to follow are conceived.

Aulularia
City-State and Individual

In the characteristic story-type of new comedy, a young man's passionate infatuation with a girl who is ineligible for marriage is fulfilled in a respectable way through a turn in the plot—a recognition scene, for example—which reveals the maiden's citizen status. It is discovered, then, that the wayward passion had all along aspired to a permissible object, and the original tension turns out to be illusory. In plays of this type, the prohibited passion drives outward beyond the limits of the community. Love fastens in its willful way upon a stranger, and thereby threatens to violate the exclusiveness by which the community is defined. But a special class of stories, relatively rare in new comedy, looks not so much to urges that push across the boundary as to figures who withdraw into isolation from their fellow citizens. These are the tales of the misanthrope and the misogynist, the miser and the prude.[1] Their challenge to the community manifests itself as a secession, rather than as the pursuit of a forbidden relationship. Characters of this sort bear a certain affinity to the stern fathers who are typically the obstacle to love. By his withdrawal from society the misanthrope or miser may for example block a romantic alliance involving his daughter. Nevertheless, the differences between the two types are essential. In the amatory plays the "blocking characters" prevent or

[1]Compare the *Dyscolus* ("Grouch") of Menander; his *Misogynēs* ("Woman-Hater") and *Psophodeēs* ("Noise-Shy") must also have been of this type; see Günther Jachmann, *Plautinisches und Attisches* (Berlin, 1931), 139.

oppose the romantic union, but they do so as representatives of the claims of marriage, that is, of legitimate social communion. The recognition scene is an essential part of a plot of this kind because it permits the fulfillment both of the erotic impulse and of the social requirement of marriage among citizens, which had seemed to be opposed in their demands. The misanthrope and the miser, on the contrary, have themselves severed their ties with society. It is they who will not marry or allow their daughters to marry, they who will not engage in commerce with their fellows which is the right use of wealth. Consumed as they are by a private passion, they are more akin to the lover than they are to the conventional morality of the blocking character. Where the lover threatens to defy the boundaries of the community, the miser and the misanthrope dissolve its inner bonds and encyst themselves within society as internal exiles. They cannot be brought back into society by a dramatic coincidence or revelation. They must rather be made to realize the insufficiency of their isolation, so that they turn back of their own will to the community of men. Hence such plays depend essentially upon a change in character. The recusant foregoes his specious autarky, recognizes his insufficiency and the insufficiency of the ideal or symbol which he had made the sole object of his desire, whether it is the miser's gold or the misanthrope's virtue and sincerity. In a word, he gives up his fetish, which, from the point of view of community, consists in the worship of an abstract value at the expense of the social relationship that its function is to mediate. This paradigm defines the general form of Plautus's comedy, the *Aulularia*.

E. J. Thomas begins the introduction to his commentary on this play: "The Aulularia stands alone among the comedies of Plautus as a character piece." He continues: "The character of the miser is developed in connexion with a simple plot dealing with middle-class life, but it is the picture of the avaricious Euclio that gives unity to the whole."[2] I shall begin my analysis of the *Aulularia* by undoing its apparent unity to reveal the separate strands, woven together to compose a plot that in fact is double or complex. The initial conditions of the drama are these. Euclio has discovered buried in his hearth a pot of gold, which his grandfather had concealed, and with it his native stinginess grows into a grand passion.

[2]E. J. Thomas, ed., *T. Macci Plauti Aulularia* (Oxford, 1913), v.

The Lar—the household deity who speaks the prologue and gives
the mise-en-scène, explains that he has revealed the treasure so that
Euclio may arrange a proper marriage for his daughter Phaedria,
whose generosity and devotion have touched the god. The Lar also
relates that the unfortunate Phaedria has been raped. The offender
is Lyconides, the nephew of Euclio's wealthy neighbor Megadorus.
Finally, the Lar declares that, to induce Lyconides to marry Phae-
dria, he will inspire Megadorus to propose to the girl himself. The
prologue thus introduces two distinct components of the story,
which for convenience I call the theme of avarice and the romantic
theme. The discovery of the gold and the violation of the miser's
daughter are not logically related events. Only the intention of the
Lar that the gold be used as a dowry for Phaedria (27) brings the
themes together at this point.[3]

In the first act, Plautus exhibits the character of the miser and the
significance of his obsession as a withdrawal from social life. The
action neatly lays bare the difference between the miser's passion
for his gold and ordinary acquisitiveness or parsimony, which the
Romans regarded as a virtue.[4] Despite a paranoid anxiety for his
gold, Euclio is obliged to leave it unguarded while he goes to the
forum to receive a handout which the head of his *curia* or political
unit has advertised. Now, Euclio does not want the dole, inasmuch
as his trip to the forum puts his treasure in jeopardy, but he fears
that if he did not go out to get it, the danger would be worse, since
others would suspect him of harboring some hidden wealth. Be-
cause his hoard is secret, Euclio is caught in a double bind: If he
stays home with his pot of gold, he may arouse the curiosity of his
neighbors, so he must, however reluctantly, engage in public life in
order to keep up appearances. All of the miser's social activity is a
sham—even commerce or, as here, a petition for a free bequest.
The miser wishes not to make money but to have it, and to keep it
out of social circulation. The irony in Euclio's behavior is that, in
his obsession with his gold, he would reject, if he dared, even the
minimal public commitment involved in receiving a donation.

[3]The distinctness of the two themes is discussed sensibly by Walther Ludwig,
"*Aulularia*-Probleme," *Philologus* 105 (1961), 44–46.

[4]I differ here with the interpretation of Erich Segal, *Roman Laughter* (Cambridge,
Mass. 1968), 55, 76–79, who sees in the miser only an exaggeration of Roman thrift;
Franz de Ruyt, "Le thème fondamental de l'*Aululaire* de Plaute," *Les études classiques*
29 (1961), 376, also supports the view that Euclio is parsimonious as opposed to
fixated on his treasure.

Before he sets out, Euclio torments his old servant, Staphyla, with suspiciousness and orders her to extinguish the fire in his hearth, lest anyone enter his house with the purpose of borrowing a light (91–92). Perhaps he is particularly worried about the fire because the pot of gold, as we have noted, was buried in the fireplace. Nevertheless, the quenching of the hearth fire in Greece and Rome, as in all communities before the invention of matches, was a serious matter. More than this, Euclio also orders Staphyla to deny that she has any water. Now, the symbol of banishment in Rome was the *aquae et ignis interdictio,* the prohibition on the lending of water and fire.[5] Fixated on his private treasure, Euclio has in effect estranged his society from himself. The scene abounds in farcical humor, and Euclio extends his interdiction to knives, hatchets, mortars and pestles, and jugs of any kind. But the elements of parody or exaggeration do not conceal Euclio's attempt, in abolishing the commerce in fire and water which define symbolically the mutual ties of community, to exile the whole community from himself.

The romantic theme is brought to the foreground in the second act, in which Megadorus bids and wins consent for the hand of Phaedria from her father Euclio. In anticipation of the wedding, Megadorus arranges for a troupe of slaves and retainers to prepare the festivities. Congrio, a cook, is dispatched to Euclio's house, because the old miser is too niggardly to provide for his daughter's marriage celebration. Euclio himself, who has been out shopping

[5]On the interdiction of fire and water at Rome, see Cicero, *Philippics* 6.4; Caesar, *Gallic War* 6.44; Pauly-Wissowa, *RE* 6 (1909), 1683–84, *s.v. exilium;* Daremberg-Saglio, *Dictionnaire des antiquités grècques et romaines* 2.1 (1892), 943, *s.v. exsilium.* Lending fire and water was an important civic obligation also in Athens; cf. the *Appendix Proverbiorum* 1.61; *Xen. Oecon.* 2.15. On fire specifically, cf. *LSJ s.v. enauō.* (I have cited the *App. Prov.* according to the quotation in T. Kock, *Comicorum Atticorum Fragmenta* (1880), 2.561 on Diphilus fr. 62.) No secure evidence exists of a comparable interdiction in Greece, I believe, despite the confident assertion of Fustel de Coulanges, *The Ancient City,* trans. Willard Small (New York, n.d.), 199 and n.1 (in chap. 13, "Patriotism, Exile"); the sources cited by Coulanges do not support his thesis. In the passage in Menander's *Dyscolus* where Knemon refuses to lend any of his wares, there is no comparable mention of fire and water (lines 505–7; the context is a request for a pot, 470–73). On the other hand, Plautus appears to signal Daemones' moral inclusion in the Attic polity, despite his remote habitation in North Africa, by specifying that he freely lends fire and water—again listed first among an assortment of other goods—to the priestess of a neighboring temple; see the later chapter on the *Rudens.* Also at Rome the marriage ceremony, or at least the reception of the bride at the groom's threshold, was accompanied by some form of an exchange of fire and water from earliest times; see Alan Watson, *Rome of the XII Tables: Persons and Property* (Princeton, 1975), 13–14.

but has found everything too expensive except some incense and flowers, returns to find his house wide open and Congrio hollering for a larger pot (end of Act II). "Pot" is all the miser hears, and he rushes in to drive the poor cook from his house under a storm of blows. Suspicious of Megadorus and everyone else, he decides at last to remove the pot of gold from the house and conceal it in the temple of Fides, good faith (end of Act III). While Euclio is in the temple, a slave of Lyconides marches on stage. He has been sent to reconnoiter the wedding preparations on behalf of his master, who, he tells us, is in love with Phaedria (603). Plautus does not explain Lyconides' sudden feeling for the girl he raped nine months before. Presumably he is anxious lest, thus violated, she should become his uncle's wife, and Megadorus's interest in her may also have awakened a slumbering passion of his own. The Greek original, if it at all resembled Plautus's play at this point, may have accounted more clearly for Lyconides' change of heart. However this may be, Lyconides' slave is on hand to overhear Euclio's injunction to Fides to preserve his gold. With a vow of his own to Fides, the slave enters the temple to search out the gold, but is violently driven out by Euclio, whom the cry of a crow had sent scurrying back to check on his treasure. Euclio thoroughly frisks and abuses the slave, who in fact is empty-handed. He then reenters the temple, repossesses his pot of gold and, charging that Fides has not kept faith and that it took a crow to save him, announces that he will hide it outside the city walls in a thick and lonely grove of Silvanus, the woodland god, whom he trusts more than Faith herself (674–76). Lyconides' slave, quite angry now and determined to cheat the miser of his gold, has been eavesdropping. He beats Euclio to the grove, conceals himself in a tree where he can watch the old man bury the gold, digs it up himself, and steals home with it. The next words we hear are Euclio's after he discovers his loss: "I'm dead, finished and done for" (713).

As to the plot alone, the concealment of the gold twice, first in the temple of Fides and then in the grove of Silvanus, is plainly a doublet, a redundant repetition of a single act. Lyconides' slave could as well have found the gold in his first attempt. But to the theme of the play, the pairing of the actions is crucial. It is in the character of the miser, we have said, to exempt himself from the bonds of community. For the Romans, the spirit of these bonds was represented above all in the concept of *fides,* which variously

meant good faith, trustworthiness, and, most concretely, the war-
ranty on a pledge.[6] *Fides* was the basis of all contracts, the soul of all
honest exchange. From this spirit of collective good faith, Euclio
withdraws his confidence. We must observe that, despite Euclio's
ingratitude, his gold had been kept safe in the temple of Fides. The
miser's trust did not betray him; he thought more of a crow's
cackle than the personified force of social ties and rejected the good
faith of his community. Instead he went beyond the city walls,
which for the Romans especially represented the sacred boundary
of the civilized community where law and honor reigned, and
trusted his gold to the uncultivated precinct of a god of the wilder-
ness.[7] Euclio has deliberately and explicitly abandoned the city and
committed himself to the chance concern of nature. And there,
outside the city, he is treated like the outcast he has made himself.
Beyond the rule of Fides, his gold is appropriated by cunning and
theft. There is no injustice here: Having withdrawn from society,
the miser endures the fate of the stranger.

Thematically, then, the theft of the miser's gold is a function of
secession from society. At the same time, it exposes his lack of self-
sufficiency and establishes the conditions under which he may elect
to be reintegrated into the community, and thus to satisfy the
dramatic demands of comedy. To return to the romantic compo-
nent of the plot, the rape of Phaedria represents exactly the same
kind of assault on Euclio as the stealing of his treasure. The twin
principle upon which citizenship was constituted in ancient Rome
was the *ius connubii et commercii,* the right of marriage and of com-
merce. These two rights have in common that both are based upon
the sanctity of the contract and therefore rest upon the communal

[6]Cf. Eduard Fraenkel, "Zur Geschichte des Wortes *fides,*" *Rh.M.* 71 (1916),
187–99; Richard Heinze, "*fides,*" *Hermes* 64 (1929), 140–66: *TLL s.v.;* Wolfgang
Kunkel, "Fides als schöpferisches Element in römischen Schuldrecht," in *Festschrift
Paul Koschaker,* vol. 2 (Weimar, 1939), 1–15, esp. 5–7, 13.

[7]The *pomerium* in Rome, which was a sacred boundary more or less coincident
with actual mural structures, marked the division between civic and military author-
ity. A general was required to lay down his *imperium* before entering the city
precincts; symbolically, the axe, denoting the power of capital punishment, could be
carried with the rods of authority (the *fasces*) only outside the *pomerium.* The city
auspices could only be taken within the sacred perimeter; the dead must be interred
outside it; and foreign cults could not in general cross it, that is to say, be established
within the civic territory. Cf. *RE* 21.2.1871–72; Daremberg-Saglio 4.1.544: "La
condition du territoire *intra pomerium* diffère profondément de celle du territoire *extra
pomerium.*"

principle of good faith.[8] Outside the citizen community, the rule of violence, of *vis et violentia,* holds sway, except where special agreements may be mutually recognized. Where the *ius commercii,* the right of commerce, is abrogated, there robbery, a relationship of force alone, prevails. Similarly, rape is the mode of sexual appropriation where the right of marriage, the *ius connubii,* ceases to prevail. Because of his withdrawal, the miser is no longer sheltered under the laws of the community. Despite the absence of a causal connection between Euclio's obsession with his pot of gold and the rape of Phaedria, thematically the two facts are intimately related: The rape is the expression in the sphere of sex of the miser's isolation, just as the theft is its expression in the sphere of property. The rape and the theft are all the closer, in that women were not in Roman society so far removed from other forms of property. Phaedria's dishonor is thus her father's loss.

The love story is advanced through the proposal of Megadorus which, for reasons that Plautus's version does not make very clear, kindles or rekindles in Lyconides the desire for Phaedria. After his change of heart, Lyconides tells his mother, Eunomia, of the rape, and begs her to intercede with her brother Megadorus, who apparently retracts his offer of marriage: He is not seen again in our text. In this brief scene of nineteen lines (682–700), Phaedria is heard offstage to cry out in the agony of her labor pangs, and Lyconides wonders out loud where his slave might be, possibly a reminder of the connection between the theft and the rape. In the following scene, the slave appears with the stolen pot of gold, and in the next, Euclio bursts in with the vehement lament over his loss. Lyconides hears the howling, recognizes Euclio, and concludes that he has found out about the birth of Phaedria's baby (729). After a moment's hesitation, he decides to confess outright to the crime. An extraordinary exchange for some twenty-five lines follows, in which Euclio mistakenly believes that Lyconides has admitted to the theft of his gold. Without giving details of the misunderstanding, which accommodates even Lyconides' plea that love (*amor,* 745) was the cause of his offense, we note that the scene demonstrates the essential equivalence, from Euclio's point of view, of the rape and the robbery. Both are violations of his proprietary rights.

[8]Compare A. N. Sherwin-White, *The Roman Citizenship,* 2d ed. (Oxford, 1973), 33–34.

When Euclio at last dispels the ambiguity with an explicit mention of his pot of gold (763), Lyconides vigorously disclaims any part or knowledge of the theft. Then, just when he has persuaded Euclio of his innocence he discloses the rape. Finally, he mollifies the old miser, who by now is utterly overwhelmed, by reaffirming his wish to marry the girl, which the laws require (793), and he assures Euclio that thanks to him the old man can attend the wedding as a grandfather.

From this point on, the play moves into the phase of reintegration. Lyconides learns what has happened to the gold from his slave, who expects a liberal reward but instead is ordered to return it to Euclio. Thus, the recovery of the treasure too is predicated upon Lyconides' change of heart, which was poorly motivated if we look only to the plot. Thematically, however, it is exactly right, and probably Plautus's dramatic instinct assured him it would work. For having refused the mutual exchange which is the basis of the communal bond, the miser has been humbled. He has been dealt with as an outsider, plundered and stripped without regard to the laws of fair dealing which he himself had set aside by hoarding, which only those who give and take may invoke. He has learned the lesson of his insufficiency, the same way Menander's misanthrope discovers his need of others when he falls down a well. In accord with the comic convention, he can now rejoin society, renew the rites of exchange that define the group. In a stroke, the violation of Phaedria and the plunder of the gold are undone. Made wiser by his losses, Euclio is once more granted the chance of giving his daughter in marriage, and of using the gold as was intended, for a dowry. In the dowry, in fact, are symbolized and joined both terms of the *ius connubii et commercii*. In the relations of the community, the dowry is the exemplary use of wealth, for it represents the exchange of kin and property on which the solidarity of the several clans, of the society as a whole, is based.[9] The giving of the dowry, Euclio's ultimate assent to the mutuality of the communal bond, must have been the culminating action of the *Aulularia*. Unfortunately, the conclusion to the final act has not survived. Nevertheless, we may be quite certain about the disposi-

[9]See, for example, Claude Lévi-Strauss, *The Elementary Structures of Kinship* (Boston, 1969), 478–80, for the social function of exchange, and marriage as the chief process of exchange. Lévi-Strauss's view is critically summarized by Edmund Leach, *Claude Lévi-Strauss,* 2d ed. (New York, 1974), 114–16.

tion of the treasure. We know the Lar's intention in the prologue; the last line of an acrostic argument prefixed to the play reports the transfer of the gold; and finally, a fragment of our play preserved by the grammarian Nonius and undoubtedly to be attributed to Euclio reads: "Night or day I was never at rest. Now I shall sleep."[10] The miser's hoard is at last restored to use, its abstract value is reembodied in the practical relations of social life.

I turn now to the discussion of Megadorus; no treatment of the *Aulularia* can be complete without an analysis of his role, which brings out some of the most complex and challenging aspects of its theme. Back in the second act, after Euclio's initial scenes with his servant, Lyconides' mother, Eunomia, appeals to her brother Megadorus to take a wife. Nothing in particular motivates her intervention, but we sense the influence of the Lar. When Megadorus learns what she wants, he replies: "Aii! I'm dead!" (150). Megadorus may at once be recognized as a type: the inveterate bachelor, rich and contented with his lot, and loath to undertake either the responsibilities or the expense of a wife and family, like Micio in Terence's *Adelphoe*. Megadorus thus stands aloof from one of the bonds of community and neglects the obligation to continue his line (cf. 147–48). He does confess, however, to a special passion for Phaedria, despite her poverty, and declares his intention to ask Euclio for her hand. Because Megadorus was already infatuated with Phaedria before Eunomia's intervention, her advice to her brother serves no function in the plot, but again is a significant contribution to the theme. The dialogue between Eunomia and Megadorus underscores that Megadorus's interest is not in marriage as such, but has its source solely in desire. In terms of popular Roman psychology, he is motivated by irrational passion rather than by customary duty which, as Eunomia makes clear, would enjoin him to contract an advantageous alliance. Megadorus's desire thus resembles that of the young lover in the amatory plots—so characteristic of ancient comedy—to which we referred earlier. In those stories the erotic impulse usually attaches itself to an object outside the limits of the community. The same is true of

[10]I have fully presented the evidence that the gold was used as a dowry in the final act because this has been denied by some scholars, such as Jachmann, 138, on the grounds that it would be inconsistent with the characterization of Euclio; see also Ernst R. Lehmann, "Der Verschwender und der Geizige," *Gymnasium* 67 (1960), 88–89, who suggests that the miser parted with only a portion of his treasure.

Megadorus's passion, for Phaedria, because she has been raped, is according to the conventional taboo in ancient comedy ineligible to marry anyone but the man who assaulted her, and so she is removed beyond that circle of potential kin which defines the boundary of society. As we know, when Megadorus learns of the rape he will repudiate her. On the most general level, the stigma on Phaedria may be regarded as a sign of Euclio's voluntary withdrawal from social relations which is implicit in the fetish of his secret hoard. Of course, Megadorus is in complete ignorance of both the rape and the pot of gold. But his motive, which is erotic rather than connubial, and the relationship he is prepared to establish not between members of a common group but as a personal tie beyond communal sanctions, are reflected in the circumstances that Euclio and Phaedria are of an inferior social order, and that Megadorus, whose name literally means "Great-Gift," is willing to remit the dowry.[11]

When Megadorus approaches Euclio, the old miser immediately suspects him of being after his gold. He distractedly mumbles threats to his servant; when Megadorus asks him what he is grumbling about, he claims it is his poverty that prevents him for want of a dowry from marrying off his daughter (190–92). The connection here is overt between the hoarding of wealth and the denial of conjugality, the double abrogation of the *ius connubii et commercii* which isolates the miser. After a further display of Euclio's paranoid antics, Megadorus makes his proposal. Euclio, who has all along been leery of this untoward regard of a rich man for a poor one, at first acuses Megadorus of mocking him. Assured of his neighbor's earnestness, he laboriously expounds his concern that for a poor man to join himself to a rich is like an ass consorting with bulls: His own order will reject him, and Megadorus's will never accept him, the asses will tear him with their teeth while the bulls will attack him with their horns (226–35). Euclio's analogy between the different orders and different biological species points to the extreme separation of social classes in Plautus's Rome, whether or not the language goes back to the Greek original of the *Aulularia*. The wealthy and the poor constitute distinct communities within

[11]Eunomia's is also a significant name, meaning "good order," the condition in which traditional customs are sound and respected. For an interesting analysis of the symmetry among the scenes involving Euclio and Megadorus, see Ludwig, 67–68, and, on Megadorus's role, 53.

the society, not to be crossed by ties of marriage. Euclio then stipulates that there will be no dowry, lest Megadorus imagine that he has found some hidden treasure, as he says (240), and at last the nuptial agreement is struck, even though Euclio's fears are not altogether allayed.

If we look to the theme of the *Aulularia,* clearly Megadorus's proposal cannot possibly resolve the tensions of the play. If the miser is to be reintegrated into society, his treasure must be revealed and put to use in an exchange that confirms the communal bonds among families. Thus the dowry is crucial, and for Megadorus to waive it is to block the redemption of Euclio and leave him estranged by his obsession. That marriage to Megadorus is no solution is made all the clearer by Phaedria's pregnancy, which Staphyla proceeds to lament. To put it another way, marrying off Phaedria without a dowry is no better than giving her away to a total stranger. This point is developed at considerable length in acts II and III of the *Trinummus,* where the young, impoverished Lesbonicus expresses his anxiety to his friend Lysiteles that "they will spread the report that I have given my sister to you in concubinage, rather than in marriage, if I give her without a dowry" (689–91). The dowry is the sign of the communal sanction. Without it, marriage is not a bond but an appropriation. We have seen that Megadorus's offer is prompted by an erotic impulse rather than by a sense of civic obligation, and that his class is socially discrete from hers. In the plot as a whole, Megadorus's involvement is not so much the cause of Lyconides' reversal as a foil to it. Where Lyconides is in a position to convert the rape of Phaedria to marriage and the stolen gold to a dowry, Megadorus can do neither. He reaches out but cannot mend the breach created by Euclio's self-imposed exile. The class distinction between Megadorus and Euclio only mimics the separation between the miser and his fellows and may thus be regarded thematically as a metaphor for Euclio's isolation. Structurally, Megadorus's appeal across the barrier of class is only another manifestation of Euclio's being beyond the pale, as the erotic nature of Megadorus's attraction also suggests, and thus at bottom his proposal but reiterates the theme, albeit in a more gentle way, of the rape and the theft. Megadorus's proposal, then, is not the answer; it is rather another aspect of the problem of the play.

In the context of the play's dominant theme, the difference in

order between Megadorus and Euclio may be interpreted as a representation of Euclio's estrangement from society. Once it has been introduced, however, Plautus takes up the theme of class distinctions and develops it for its own value. We have already noticed indications of its seriousness in the first interview between Megadorus and Euclio. After Euclio drives Congrio the cook from his house, a scene occurs with Megadorus and the miser in which many critics have seen the hand of Plautus himself at work.[12] Sandwiched between Euclio's hostile complaints against his neighbor's suspected machinations (462, 551ff.), Megadorus delivers a soliloquy, overheard and heartily endorsed by Euclio, on the faults of the dowry system and the manners of contemporary women. Megadorus makes the following points: Dowries are the cause of discord between and among the social orders (481); they contribute also to the prodigality of women, who regard the money they bring into a marriage as their own to spend on luxuries as they choose (498–502); and finally, as a corollary of the preceding, women are becoming, thanks to the dowry, freer of the authority of their husbands (534). Scholars have in fact arrived at an approximate date for Plautus's *Aulularia* by interpreting this speech of Megadorus as a protest against the repeal of the *lex Oppia* in 195 B.C., which regulated the sumptuary expenses of women.[13] The most important feature of Megadorus's soliloquy, however, is that this intrusive condemnation of dowries and above all of their corrosive effect on the solidarity and harmony of the community runs exactly counter to the role of the dowry in the entire play. We have to do here with an independent set piece, in which the divisive social forces are represented not as the withdrawal of the individual householder from a community of equals, but as a general disintegration of social ties consequent upon the corruption of the dowry system by the qualitative but unequal increment in the wealth of the citizen

[12]Eduard Fraenkel, *Plautinisches im Plautus* (Berlin, 1922), 137 = *Elementi Plautini in Plauto* (Florence, 1960), 130, argues that the scene in Plautus is a very considerable expansion of its Greek model. The idea that the scene is Plautus's own is implicit in attempts to associate Megadorus's speech with the repeal of the *lex Oppia* in 195 B.C.; see, for example, Wilhelm Wagner, *T. Macci Plauti Aulularia* (Cambridge, 1892), 132.

[13]The chronology of Plautus's plays has been studied many times. Besides Wagner's comment (see preceding note), the reader may consult Charles Henry Buck, Jr., *A Chronology of the Plays of Plautus* (Baltimore, 1940), 37; Francesco della Corte, *Da Sarsina a Roma* (Florence, 1967), 54.

body.[14] The contrast may be put more pointedly: The extravagance of the aristocracy is precisely the opposite of the miser's retentiveness. To be sure, these contrary causes have a like effect, the weakening of the conjugal bond. But in the one case, this enfeeblement is due, as Plautus sees it, to the growing independence of moneyed matrons, whose subservience may be restored by the abolition of the dowry, while in the case of the miser the dowry is the substantial symbol of the communal relationship. What Plautus has added to the *Aulularia,* if indeed the scene is his own invention, is a piece of social criticism which violates the thematic coherence of the drama.

Yet on the deepest level Plautus's inclusion of Megadorus's complaint may not be misguided. After all, the archetypal story of the miser is, like all archetypes, abstracted from the realities of social life. The miser's gold is not real wealth, it is a pure symbol. Euclio's grandfather never bought a thing with it, but buried it, as he thought, for all time in the earth from which it had come. No more is the miser's withdrawal from society an expression of true autarky or power. In his helpless isolation, he is easily brought low and as easily regenerated. His is a docile defiance, perfectly suited to a moral tale exalting the ideology of community. No such character ever seriously threatened the solidarity of society. But what, then, is the real danger which the miser represents, and which is imaginatively overcome in the reconciliation with which the comedy must end? At the heart of the miser's nature is the priority he assigns to money over the actual human relationships with other members of his community. In the creation of the mythic imagination, this character worships the inert form of gold, as may in real life occur with the pathological personality. But the truly destructive manifestation of this spirit is not miserliness but materialism, which dissolves the ties of traditional obligation and restraint and leaves in their place the naked aspiration to wealth and power. The ostentatious spending of the aristocracy and the weakening of the marriage relationship are early symptoms of this spirit. The dowry was its victim: It ceased to be the material token of the communal identity of the clans, and became mere money. In this aspect, the dowry was a sign not of social integration but of fragmentation,

[14]Compare Plato's argument for the abolition of dowries as a means of reducing class divisions in the *Laws* 742C, 774C-D.

both within the aristocracy and between the orders. In attacking it, Plautus did what the comic temper and the ultimate theme of the *Aulularia* itself demanded. He disdained the consistency of the formal idea of the dowry and reaffirmed the claims of community against the real centrifugal tendencies of his day.

Asinaria

The Family

Four-fifths of the way through the play, the plot of Plautus's *Asinaria* takes a sudden and surprising turn. Briefly, what happens is this. Argyrippus, the young lover in the comedy, is madly infatuated with a *meretrix,* a harlot, whose name is Philaenium. Unfortunately, there is also a rival called Diabolus, who plans to hire the girl exclusively for himself for an entire year. To forestall him, Argyrippus has to produce twenty minae before Diabolus can, and thereby preempt the contract. He himself is destitute. At the beginning of the drama we discover that his father, Demaenetus, has learned all about the affair and the role of Libanus, a household slave, in abetting it. Libanus is in a state of great anxiety, since he expects to be sent to the mills, but Demaenetus is at pains to calm him down. "Listen to me," he says. "Why should I want to do a thing like that? Why should I threaten you just because you kept me in ignorance? And really, why should I get angry with my son, the way other fathers do?" (46–50). Demaenetus has, of course, answered his own question. Roman fathers typically disapproved of such liaisons, which could prove both costly and embarrassing. At all events, this was certainly the comic stereotype, and Demaenetus is a character in a comedy. When Libanus replies, "Now this is something new, isn't it?" (*quid istuc novi est?* 50) he would seem to be bearing a message from Plautus to notice a novel departure from the familiar pattern.[1] Demaenetus soon expounds his philosophy:

[1]Another such departure from the standard format in the plays of Plautus occurs in the *Persa,* line 25, where Sagaristio, upon learning that his fellow slave Toxilus is

"All parents, Libanus, if they will hear me out, will indulge their children, and will treat their sons with sympathy and friendship. This is what I try to do, I want to be loved by mine, I want to be like my father, who dressed up like a merchant for my sake and managed to steal the woman I was in love with from her pimp. And he wasn't ashamed in spite of his age to play tricks like that and buy me, his own son, with his kindness. I've decided to follow in the ways of my father. Just today my boy Argyrippus begged me for the money he needed for this romance, and I want passionately to help him out. I want to be loved for helping him, I want him to love his father" (65–77). For all his good intentions, however, Demaenetus is not in a position to grant his son the money, for it is his well-endowed wife—this expression is meant in the literal sense—who controls the purse strings. As Demaenetus himself puts it, "I took the money, and for a dowry I sold my authority" (*argentum accepi, dote imperium vendidi,* 87).[2] She, moreover, keeps her son neatly under control, he observes, "as fathers normally do" (79). Therefore he enlists Libanus and Leonida, another slave, to find a way to defraud his wife, Artemona, of the twenty minae so that Argyrippus may have his girl.

This basic information is presented in the first scene, which takes up slightly more than a hundred lines. Most of what follows simply exhibits the situation of Argyrippus and the rival Diabolus, and dramatizes the intrigue by which Demaenetus and the slaves obtain the money. Then, suddenly, at line 735, without warning, without so much as a hint to prepare the audience, comes the startling turn mentioned above: Libanus and Leonida, on the point of granting the silver to Argyrippus, speak of a stipulation which Demaenetus has imposed, that he have the privilege of a night, that very night with Philaenium. Argyrippus suffers agonies of jealousy, but at last Artemona is summoned on stage by the enraged Diabolus to wit-

in love, exclaims: "Do slaves fall in love here nowadays?" (*iam servi hic amant?*). Locating the action among slaves entails a substantial variation in the conventional paradigm, coordinate with a shift in the social meaning of the erotic impulse: There is no threat as such to the status of the citizen population, and class is represented in the play by an unusually virtuous and civic-minded young virgin whose role is unparalleled elsewhere. See Maximilianus Meyer, *De Plauti Persa* (Leipzig, 1907), 152–54.

[2]The type of the wife with a large dowry is examined by Elisabeth Schuhmann, "Der Typ der *uxor dotata* in den Komödien des Plautus," *Philologus* 121 (1977), 45–65, esp. 64.

ness her husband's debauchery, whereupon she unceremoniously drives the old lecher home, leaving Argyrippus in sole possession of his paramour. Two questions immediately suggest themselves. The first is, how did Plautus motivate so extraordinary a transition from Demaenetus's sympathetic support for his son's affair to the sordid competition with which the play concludes? The second question is, why?

The first step toward understanding the transition is to recognize that the change in the character of Demaenetus, which appears as the critical discontinuity in the play, is in fact a secondary phenomenon, a function of an alteration in the plot.[3] In the first scene of the *Asinaria,* Plautus planted certain expectations for the unfolding of the story. The expectations are based on the audience's familiarity with the standard paradigms of plot forms in ancient comedy. Toward the end of the play, he switched from one paradigm to another. This entailed some adjustments in characterization, and also left visible seams at the critical juncture. I shall indicate the chief anomalies presently, but first I shall briefly review the basic story patterns used by Plautus in the *Asinaria,* in order to show the sequence.

First there is the triangle involving a father, a son, and a girl, which I have taken as the characteristic situation of new comedy. The son is torn between passion for the girl who is at least to all appearances ineligible as a partner in marriage, and fear of his father, a stern paterfamilias of the old school. The *Asinaria* opens with an evocation of this type: The confrontation between the deceived and irate *senex* and the clever and intriguing slave belongs to the denouement of such plays as the *Mostellaria* and the *Epidicus,* for example. No sooner does Plautus suggest this paradigm, however, than he dismisses it, as Libanus shrewdly observes, for a different pattern.

[3]Compare the remarks of J.-P. Vernant on Eteocles in *Seven against Thebes,* "Tensions et ambiguïtés dans la tragédie grecque," in Jean-Pierre Vernant and Pierre Vidal-Naquet, *Mythe et tragédie en Grèce ancienne* (Paris, 1973), 29; an earlier version of this essay was published in English under the title "Tensions and Ambiguities in Greek Tragedy," in Charles Singleton, ed., *Interpretation: Theory and Practice* (Baltimore, 1969), 105–22. Compare also Richmond Lattimore, *The Poetry of Greek Tragedy* (New York, 1958), 91, on *Oedipus the King:* "Stories such as these have shapes of their own which force action rather than shapes which are forced by reason or character; and hence, romantic comedy tends to refine plot at the expense of personality."

Roman Comedy

Plautus's favorite story type is based on the competition between two rival lovers for a single girl. This pattern, familiar from the *Miles Gloriosus* and the *Pseudolus,* is built essentially on the struggle between two contending factions or parties. On one side are the supporters of the young lover, on the other the satellites, parasites, cooks, and other hangers-on of the rival. The rival himself, as we have observed, is generally a stranger, a foreign soldier, for example. He is full of bombast but not powerless: Either he already owns the girl or he is in a position to purchase her, in which case the procurer is his natural ally. Against such an enemy the lover requires guile, as well as the cooperation of loyal friends and advisers. No moral inhibitions operate here: The problem is essentially strategic. In plays of this sort the *senex* may have the role of an indulgent, humane, and even libertarian figure who encourages the intrigues of the lover, rather than that of the severe and conservative father in the first paradigm. The urbane Periplectomenus in the *Miles Gloriosus,* Callipho in the *Pseudolus,* and Micio in Terence's *Adelphoe* are representatives of this figure.[4] In the *Asinaria,* Demaenetus appears to have shed the usual patriarchal persona for the part of the sympathetic elder of this second paradigm, to assist Argyrippus against the superior resources of his rival, Diabolus. Yet it is extraordinary, even unique, that a paterfamilias should assume this latter role.

Another crucial difference exists between the situation in the *Asinaria* and the usual type of the rival play. The deception by which the *meretrix* (courtesan) will be won has for its victim not the rival himself or the procurer, but Artemona, Demaenetus's own wife. As we have seen, Artemona, by virtue of the large dowry she controls, has actually been playing the role of the paterfamilias, while Demaenetus has been reduced to a status of dependency. Demaenetus's position is essentially similar to that of the young lover in the first paradigm who struggles against the restrictions of traditional authority, although there is this difference, that Demaenetus's passion is so far vicarious. This circumstance necessarily casts some suspicion on the character of Demaenetus's sympathy for his son. He is not simply a knowing old gentleman lending a helping hand to a passionate adolescent. His desire for the

[4]The character of the urbane *senex* has been studied frequently; a recent treatment is Eleanor Winsor Leach, "The Soldier and Society: Plautus' *Miles Gloriosus* as Popular Drama," *Rivista di studi classici* 28 (1980), 199–200, and the literature cited there (n.29).

boy's affection in place of respect is dubious, because he does not have the title to respect: He sold it, as he confesses. This situation really presents two problems. First, Argyrippus must win his girl; second, Demaenetus must be put in his place, which means not only that his deception of Artemona must be exposed—this would merely leave Demaenetus where he was to begin with—but that he must somehow reassume his proper position in the household. The surprising conclusion to the *Asinaria* is designed precisely to accomplish both these objectives simultaneously.

There is a third kind of story, employed by Plautus in the *Mercator* and *Casina,* which may be described as a blend of the first two: In it the father is cast as the rival to the son. In the first type, the father is the obstacle to the son's affair, while in the second, the obstacle is the rival. In the third or hybrid form the father as rival is the obstacle to the son. But the passionate paterfamilias has an obstacle of his own in the person of his wife, from whom he must conceal the intrigue. Thus the wife becomes a natural ally of the son. The exposure, or threatened exposure, of the old man's infatuation simultaneously restores him to his family and leaves the field of love to the boy. Despite a certain indelicacy inherent in this plot form, it actually achieves a splendid reconciliation of passion and duty. The success of the son's affair is contingent upon restoring the social integrity of the father.

The sudden turn toward the end of the *Asinaria,* we now see, may be described as a shift into the third paradigm. In many ways, it is an excellent move. The tension between husband and wife, which is a basic feature of this type, had been built into the initial conditions of the play, because of Demaenetus's resentment of Artemona. Best of all, it solves at one stroke the problem of Argyrippus—who triumphs over Diabolus and then over his father—and also the matter of Demaenetus's abdication of his paternal responsibilities: He must now, according to the conventions of this story, mend his ways and take up his proper position in his house. To be sure, Artemona still has her dowry, if we wish to be sticklers on the point. But Demaenetus's weakness was really a moral fault in any case. His humiliation is intended to bring him to his senses and make him play the role, at least, of a Roman head of household.[5]

[5]Not that the play concludes in a tone of moral severity. Demaenetus begs his wife to let him stay with the harlot for dinner, since it's already cooking. When she tells him he'll be dining on crow today, he observes that his bed is likely to be none too soft either: "My wife is taking me back home a condemned man" (935–37).

Roman Comedy

So abrupt a switch in the story form, nevertheless, was bound to leave its mark on the text.[6] We can see the signs of strain in the way the intrigue develops. Saurea, the chief steward of Artemona, had sold some asses to a dealer (from whom the play apparently derives its name) at a price of twenty minae, and the dealer has sent a young man to render payment. Leonida meets the man in a barber shop, catches wind of his purpose, and at once pretends to be Saurea. Leonida then rushes home, enjoins Libanus to fall in with the ruse, and the two put on an elaborate act to induce the merchant boy to deposit the money with them. This action takes up slightly less than a third of the entire play. Nevertheless, it comes utterly to naught. The boy will surrender the silver to no one but Demaenetus, who is the only member of the household he knows by sight. The slaves pursue him from the stage. Then, after a brief interlude, Libanus and Leonida return. They engage for a while in comic banter, which Libanus at last cuts short with the remark, "Enough of this, answer what I ask you." "What would you like to know?" replies Leonida. Libanus gets right to the point: "Do you have the twenty minae?" "You're a prophet," answers Leonida. "As a matter of fact, old Demaenetus was as tricky as could be. It was hilarious the way he went along with the game that I was Saurea. I could hardly keep from laughing, when he hollered at the poor foreigner because he wouldn't trust me in his absence. He never once forgot to call me Saurea the steward" (578–84). It is easy to see the awkwardness here. If the merchant will pay the

Finally, the assembled players take up the banter: Who is so firm and stern he wouldn't do the same, given half a chance (942–45). But by this same token, that Demaenetus is no different from anyone else (943), we get the message that for the future he will have to learn to behave himself. His weakness was only a lapse; in the end, things must return to normal.

[6]It has been argued several times that the *Asinaria* was composed from scenes of two different Greek originals. See especially John Newbold Hough, "The Structure of the *Asinaria*," *AJP* 58 (1937), 19–37; Francesco della Corte, "La commedia dell' *Asinaria*," *RFIC* 79 (1951), 289–306; Giuseppe Rambelli, "Studi Plautini, I: *Asinaria*," *Dioniso* 19 (1956), 45–81. Franco Munari argues on the side of unity, "La composizione dell' *Asinaria*," *SIFC* N.S. 22 (1947), 5–32. The various positions are surveyed by F. Bertini in his copious edition, *Plauti Asinaria* (Genova, 1968), 48–59. I am in sympathy with the analytic tradition; I agree that elements derived from different story types have been welded together, but this procedure, as I understand it, represents Plautus's dramatic intentions. Thus the results of analysis are not in contradiction with the fundamental hypothesis of the unitarians, that the play is a coherent and intelligible work of art.

money only to Demaenetus, why do the two slaves go to such trouble to impersonate Saurea? Why not just take him straightway to Demaenetus and be done with it? As it is, a great portion of the drama is sacrificed to a useless action, while the twenty minae are acquired in an offstage transaction, effortlessly and without deceit. Finally, Demaenetus's connivance in his slave's imposture has no point whatsoever. He has only to receive the money in his own name; Artemona's steward has nothing to do with it. Clearly, there is patchwork here, and the seams are showing. I do not wish to speculate about Plautus's methods of composition, whether he freely invented certain episodes in the *Asinaria,* or welded together two Greek originals, or found the contamination of the plot already present in his model. I have no doubt, however, that at some time a joint was made. The reason for it, moreover, is obvious. Through-out most of the play—so long as it conforms to the simple rival paradigm—all that is required is that Libanus and Leonida obtain the money intended for Saurea, who was responsible for the sale of the asses, and then make it over to Argyrippus so that he may anticipate Diabolus and hire the harlot. But to effect the transition to the concluding paradigm, in which the father appears as the rival, Demaenetus has to be the actual possessor of the silver. Only thus is he in the position to attach the cruel stipulation to his gift to Argyrippus. Accordingly, he was made the direct recipient of the twenty minae, despite the dramatic and perhaps also ethical im-proprieties that this action entailed.

Up to now I have examined how the transformation in the plot of the *Asinaria* works. I conclude this chapter by briefly discussing what it means. To be sure, the transformation may be there for its own sake, as an ingenious new combination of the standard forms, although at the cost of a serious dislocation in the plot. But the sequence of paradigms described above is not without significance. Demaenetus is presented to us at first as a man who has voluntarily given up his claim on the strict obedience of his son—which was a father's due in Rome—and in its place established the ideal of a bond of pure affection, purchased by indulgence. But, as we have seen, Demaenetus's philosophy has something sham about it. He sold his authority in the home. The avuncular role is only a dis-guise. In truth a paterfamilias has abandoned or been driven from his position as guardian and representative of the Roman moral tradition and is now guided wholly by sentiment. But nothing

prevents his uninhibited feelings from fastening on the paramour of his son. This is in the nature of passion: It is indifferent to social customs and constraints. And when this happens, the sentimental bond with his son dissolves. All that remains is selfish desire. In a pathetic and rather touching scene between Demaenetus and Argyrippus in the presence of the girl Philaenium, the father insists upon his privilege. Argyrippus professes to be moved by *pietas* (831). This is a stroke of Plautine irony: It is not the duty of a son to promote his father's debaucheries. Demaenetus then appeals to Argyrippus' affections: "I don't want to be feared," he whines, "I want to be loved" (835). Nevertheless, Argyrippus is unable to conceal his anguish. At last, Demaenetus bares his teeth: "Put up with this one day," he orders; "I gave you the power to have her for a year, it was I provided the lover with his money." Argyrippus's answer is revealing: "Yes, that's what you bound me to you with" (*em istoc me facto tibi devinxti,* 849). The father who sold his right to respect now relies on the naked power of cash to bend his son to his will. Thematically, then, this scene recapitulates the movement of the drama as a whole.

Earlier in the play is a scene between Philaenium and her mother—also her procuress—Cleareta by name, which is analogous to the confrontation between Argyrippus and Demaenetus. Cleareta accuses the girl of defying her mother's authority (*imperium,* 505, 509) by yielding to her love for Argyrippus rather than respecting her mother's orders as filial piety requires. The dialogue here is plainly a parody of the commonplace comic situation in which the tension between youthful infatuation and parental authority is exhibited. It is unusual, however, in two respects. First, the lover is not a young man but a woman, and a prostitute at that. Second, and more important, Cleareta's appeal to her daughter's sense of duty has nothing to do with the communal norms of behavior; she objects to the irregular liaison only when it brings no profit. The ethical content of the *pietas* (509) or filial duty which she demands is wittily perverted. Philaenium is for her mother no more than an instrument of her avarice. To cloak this exploitation in the guise of filial virtue is an ironic travesty of the moral basis of relations in the family. The entire scene is a comic exposé of the materialistic abuse of conventional values, from Cleareta's opening demand for reverence to Philaenium's closing words: "Mother, you have raised an obedient daughter" (544).

Cleareta has made no secret of her materialism. A long scene between her and Diabolus is devoted to the expression of her acquisitiveness, which she defends as a matter of principle against Diabolus's appeal for gratitude and fairness (Act I, Scene 3).[7] The image of corrupt and selfish authority is represented also in two other scenes in the *Asinaria,* and in both the source of power is money. When Leonida masquerades as Saurea, in his attempt to inveigle the merchant's boy out of the twenty minae, he affects a blustering rage, in order to display his high position in the household and thus impose upon the boy to render up the money, if for no other reason than out of pity for the cringing and whining Libanus (371ff.). The humor of Leonida's despotic posturing derives in part from parody or inversion of the strict and repressive discipline of the Roman family. But his arbitrary and violent imperiousness is wholly different from the moral ideal of *patria potestas.* Saurea's status in the household is, we may recall, a reflection of that of his mistress and thus rests ultimately upon the power of her dowry. We may perhaps then understand the caricature of Saurea as another example of the corrosive effect of money on the natural order of the household, as the Romans perceived it.

After Libanus and Leonida have obtained the twenty minae, through the intervention of Demaenetus himself, a saucy burlesque follows in which the two slaves subject Argyrippus and Philaenium to outrageous indignities. They force embraces from the girl, piggyback rides from her lover, and demand to be beseeched by both as the very gods of Providence and Salvation, before they consent to surrender the silver (Act III, Scene 3). There is perhaps no better example in Roman comedy of sheer Saturnalian perversity, the elevation of the slave and humiliation of the master. Again, the only motive for this groveling is cash.

The theme of materialism pervades the play. Where money is the

[7]That the youth in Act I, scenes 2–3, is Diabolus, and not Argyrippus as the manuscripts have it, was argued persuasively by L. Havet, "Etudes sur Plaute, *Asinaria* I: La seconde et la troisième scènes et la composition générale," *Rev. Phil.* 29 (1905) 94–103, and endorsed by Bertini, 48–49. Bertini may also be consulted (57–59) for a review of the problem of Plautine authorship of the *Asinaria* which was challenged by L. Havet and A. Freté in their edition entitled *Pseudo-Plaute, le prix des ânes* (Paris, 1925). We can comfortably accept Plautus as the author of our play, I believe, although some stylistic anomalies may be due to later interpolations, as F. della Corte suggests, "Contaminatio et retractatio nell'Asinaria," *Dioniso* 35 (1961), 30–52.

basis of authority, customary moral restraints are swept away. This effect is exhibited in the first instance in Demaenetus's sentimental or vicarious attachment to his son's love affair. The audience may sympathize for a while with the posture of Demaenetus, because his liberal attitude seems to offer a reprieve from the oppressiveness of patriarchal authority. Argyrippus would have an ally in his father. But the development of the plot—the switch to the final paradigm—gives new meaning to the traditional ethical restraints. Sentimentality is exposed as the other side of self-interest and materialism. At the heart of the problem is the disorder introduced into the household by the abuse of the dowry system, about which Plautus expressed his concern also, as we have seen, in the *Aulularia*. The *Asinaria* is indeed an ingenious variation on the comic archetypes, but their sequence—the logic of their development—is controlled by an implicit structure of values, just as, in the *Aulularia,* the juxtaposition of the themes of rape and theft expresses a specific conception of social exchange. In each case, the significance of the general structure is supported and amplified by local devices of style, such as the imagery evoking exile by interdiction of fire and water in the *Aulularia,* or the reduction of filial piety to a mask for greed in repeated scenes of the *Asinaria*. In this way, the social meanings latent in the archetypes of new comedy are discovered and developed by the genius of individual playwrights.

Captivi
City-State and Nation

Plautus's *Captivi* is a play of discovery rather than of action. Its plot is a situation, which is misperceived at first but gradually revealed to the characters in the drama. The chief complications of the plot are all given as part of the initial conditions, which are described in the prologue as having occurred prior to the time of the dramatic action. There had been a war between two Greek communities, Elis and Aetolia.[1] The event itself is strictly and explicitly banished from the stage as befitting tragedy, not comedy (58–62). The prisoners taken on either side in the war were sold as slaves, as commonly happened.[2] Among these was a young Aetolian named Philopolemus, son of Hegio, who fell into the possession of a doctor in Elis called Menarchus. As a result, Hegio, though a man of excellent character, has begun to purchase slaves on the slave market, not with an eye to profit, however, but in order to acquire an Elean captive whom he may exchange for his own son. On the day before the date on which the play is imagined to take place, Hegio has succeeded in buying, at considerable cost, a distinguished citizen of Elis named Philocrates, along with his personal slave, Tyndarus. The doctor Menarchus, we shall learn (335), is in fact a client or dependent of Philocrates' family, and so the

[1]Aetolia is in fact not a *polis* but a territory, whose cities were, at the time of middle and new comedy, associated in a league. Plautus, however, appears to be thinking of Aetolia as a town: cf. *Aetolia haec est,* 94. Whether the same name stood in the Greek original there is no way of knowing.

[2]For the grim record, consult Hans Volkmann, *Die Massenversklavungen der Einwohner eroberter Städte in der hellenistisch-römischen Zeit* (Mainz, 1961).

trade will be easy to effect. In all this, there is little on which to build dramatic suspense—the revelation of Menarchus's connection with Philocrates comes as no great surprise. The comic tension is introduced, as usual, through an intrigue (*dolum* 35, 47; *fallaciam*, 40, 46). Philocrates and Tyndarus have exchanged identities, so that Hegio, thinking to send the slave back to Elis to negotiate the exchange of prisoners, will in fact be sending the master (36). The first important turn in the plot is Hegio's discovery of the deception, which he learns of accidentally through the testimony of another of his captives, Aristophontes, who was well acquainted with Philocrates and Tyndarus back in Elis (Act III, Scene 4). In a rage at the conspiracy, Hegio consigns Tyndarus to the quarries, where his life will be bitter and short. A second discovery awaits him, however, upon the return of Philocrates, who lives up to his promise and brings back with him Hegio's son, Philopolemus. For Tyndarus, as the audience knows from the prologue, is by birth neither slave nor freeman in Elis, but a second son of Hegio, who had been stolen and sold abroad into slavery at four years of age. With an extraordinary recognition scene the play is brought to its conclusion.

The two-stage revelation of the identity of Tyndarus is the fundamental feature of the structure of the *Captivi*. In fact, Plautus seems singularly inattentive to the devices by which it is brought about. Nothing is said, for example, about why Philocrates and Tyndarus decided to exchange roles in the first place, which they must have done before Hegio's plan to make a trade. Then again, the intervention of Aristophontes, who exposes Tyndarus's masquerade, seems quite arbitrary and unmotivated. But the most outrageous implausibility of all is the way Tyndarus's true identity as the long-lost child of Hegio is discovered: Philocrates, when he returns from Elis, just happens to bring along Stalagmus, the very slave who had abducted Hegio's infant son, and under cross-examination the full truth is finally revealed. All these coincidences may be and have been called technical improprieties, with the result that many critics have found the play a dramatic failure, although others have regarded it as a masterpiece of moral instruction, ever since the time when Gotthold Lessing described it as the best comedy ever written.[3] It seems best to view these features not as defects in

[3]See Eleanor Winsor Leach, "Ergasilus and the Ironies of the Captivi," *Class. et Med.* 30 (1969), 268; G. van N. Viljoen, "The Plot of the *Captivi* of Plautus," *Acta classica* 6 (1963), 38–63.

plotting but as economies which leave the fundamental situation of the play prominently visible and do not encumber it with distracting ramifications.[4] To understand the *Captivi*, then, we ought not to look so much to the dramaturgical technique as to the meaning and implications of the broad scenes or tableaux which constitute the play.

If we consider the initial situation in its most abstract lineaments, we see a similarity in one respect to the basic story-type of new comedy, the conflict between a stern, conventional father and a son driven to defiance by the irresistible force of erotic passion. A common figure in these plays is the household slave, who risks the displeasure of his senior master, the paterfamilias in the Roman versions, in order to advance the amatory interests of the junior.[5] Tyndarus likewise takes the part of his nearer master, Philocrates, against the authority of Hegio, who has all the legal power over both his captives. In the amatory plays, of course, the slave's problem is merely a by-product of the erotic complication, while in the *Captivi* his dilemma takes center stage. This difference is of great significance for the theme of the play. For instead of a conflict between duty and desire, social responsibility and private impulse, we are presented with a tension within the realm of morality itself. Tyndarus must choose between two obligations, loyalty to Philocrates and obedience to Hegio, and he is bound to violate his responsibilities to the one in acknowledging the claims of the other.

The ethical tension is brought out with great clarity in the dialogue between Hegio and Tyndarus which follows the exposure of the identity switch. Though the passage is long, it is worth quoting a substantial portion. Hegio has ordered several of his slaves to bind the hands of Tyndarus. Tyndarus interjects, "I belong to you (*tuos sum*, 668), you can have them cut off if you want. But what's the matter? Why are you angry with me?" Obviously, the question is disingenuous, and Hegio is prompt to indicate his reasons: Tyndarus' evil, lying treachery (*scelestis, falsidicis fallaciis*, 671) has wrecked his plan to ransom his son. Tyndarus persists in his pose of naive incomprehension: "I admit it, everything is just as

[4]There are analogous economies in Sophocles' *Oedipus Tyrannus*, whose form bears some resemblance to that of the *Captivi*. See A. J. A. Waldock's discussion of Sophocles' "finesse" in *Sophocles the Dramatist* (Cambridge, 1966), 160–66.

[5]For example, compare Terence's *Andria*, 209–11, where the slave Davus meditates aloud: "I'm not sure what to do, to help Pamphilus or obey the old man. If I abandon him, I have fears for his life. But if I assist him, there's the menace of the other one, who is hard to deceive."

you say, you've lost Philocrates treacherously thanks to my efforts and my brains. But, really now, is that why you're angry at me?" Hegio is naturally driven into a rage by Tyndarus's irony; "You'll be tortured to the limit for this!" At this point, Tyndarus drops the banter and with grandiloquent earnestness defends his innocence: "As long as I didn't do anything wrong, I don't care if I die. Even if he doesn't return, and I die here, what I've done will be remembered when I'm dead: When my master was captured, I restored him to his father and his country a free man, saved from slavery and his enemies. I preferred to risk my life than let him die." Hegio is unimpressed: "Go enjoy your reputation in hell." Tyndarus replies with a proverbial appeal to aristocratic values: "Who dies for virtue has not wholly perished." Hegio ignores the ethical implication: "They can call you dead or perished. Let them say you're alive, for all I care, as long as you're dead." Nevertheless, Hegio cannot resist a try at self-justification. "Didn't I forbid you to lie to me today?" "Yes," replies Tyndarus, "but the truth would have hurt the man I served, while lies have helped him." "But not you," observes Hegio. "So much the better," is Tyndarus's bold reply. "I saved my master, and I'm glad he's saved, because the old master made me his guardian. But do you think I did wrong?" "Bad as can be," comments Hegio. "But I say I did right," persists Tyndarus. "Think about it, how grateful you'd be if a slave of yours did such a thing for your son. Wouldn't you free him? Wouldn't he be your favorite slave? Answer me." "I suppose so," says Hegio. "Then why are you mad at me?" "Because you were more loyal to him than to me." Hegio has trapped himself, for he has put his claim to Tyndarus's obedience on the same level as that of Philocrates. Tyndarus is quick to catch him on it: "What's this? Did you really expect to train a prisoner in a day and a night, new, fresh and recent, to care more for you than for a man I lived with since I was a child?" Since there is nothing for Hegio to say to this, he once more takes refuge in his wrath: "Go ask him for thanks, then. Get him out of here, men, and into the heaviest, thickest shackles around." And with a few last noble sentiments on his lips—"This peril to my life is at your peril!" "In death I fear no evil!" "Farewell, though little you deserve it!"—Tyndarus is led off to the quarries.[6]

[6]Pierre Grimal, "Le modèle et la date des *Captivi* de Plaute," *Latomus* 101 (1969), 394–414, finds evidence of Stoic philosophy behind these and other ethical pro-

Tyndarus's selfless constancy has won the praise of centuries, and I have no wish to quarrel with this judgment. The question I wish to raise concerns the justice of Hegio's response. To be fair to Hegio, we shall have to look more closely at Tyndarus's defense. Tyndarus argues that long association obliges him to side with Philocrates against Hegio. More than this, it excuses his treachery to Hegio, which in no way diminishes his virtue. The moral basis for Tyndarus's view is not difficult to find, for it is rooted in the ethics of the ancient city-state. Moral responsibility ended with the borders of the community. The alien or enemy might hope for mercy, but this was a gift, not a right. A most interesting Greek epitaph illustrates the point. It reads: "This memorial is set over the body of a very good man. Pythio, from Megara, slew seven men and broke off seven spear-points in their bodies. . . . This man, who saved three Athenian regiments . . . , having brought sorrow to no one among all men who dwell on earth, went down to the underworld felicitated in the eyes of all."[7] A gravestone is an unlikely place for irony, and we may suppose that the author saw nothing contradictory in this tribute. The enemy is by an unconscious reflex excluded from the lists of those entitled to moral recognition. Similarly, Tyndarus's virtue is to have preserved his loyalty to Philocrates; that he lied to Hegio and cheated him in doing it is ethically indifferent.

Let us now consider the case from Hegio's point of view. As prisoners-of-war sold into slavery, Tyndarus and Philocrates have no rights. They were delivered to Hegio in chains. In spite of this, Hegio ventured to deal with them in a spirit of mutual confidence, asking honesty and good faith in the negotiations for the return of his son Philopolemus, while on his part releasing them from their bonds (354–55). Plautus's language at this point leaves no doubt that a moral relationship has been established between Hegio and his two prisoners. Tyndarus, posing of course as Philocrates, exclaims, "May the gods give you everything you want, for the great honor you have honored me with and for freeing me from chains" (*quom me tanto honore honestas quomque ex vinclis eximis,* 356). "When

nouncements in the play (see esp. 395–98); I am inclined rather to view them as paratragic moralizing.

[7]The translation is that of K. J. Dover, *Greek Popular Morality in the Time of Plato and Aristotle* (Oxford, 1974), 280; text in W. Peek, ed., *Griechische Versinschriften* (Berlin, 1955), vol. 1, no. 630.

you put a worthy man in your debt," replies Hegio, "his sense of obligation will bear you good returns" (*quod bonis bene fit beneficium, gratia ea gravida est bonis,* 358). The terms *honor, beneficium, gratia,* and *boni* have, like *fides,* a central place in the Roman ethical vocabulary. In acknowledging the moral existence of Tyndarus and Philocrates, in return for their pledge of good faith (cf. *fide,* 351; *fideliter,* 363), Hegio has in effect admitted his captives, with their consent, into a certain status, however dependent, within his own household and therefore his own society.

Tyndarus and Philocrates remain slaves, to be sure, but this does not automatically exclude them from moral consideration, for the slave had an essentially ambiguous position in the ideology of the ancient city-state. On the one hand, he was beyond the communal pale, a stranger to the human rights which derive from membership in society, and therefore a mere thing, a speaking instrument in the notorious definition of Varro.[8] On the other hand, he was a member of the household or *familia,* under the absolute dominion of the master, of course, but in this little different, at least in Rome, from the freeborn sons and daughters of the family, who were equally dependent on the sole authority of the paterfamilias. This latter, essentially patriarchal relationship is the basis of the ethical respect which slaves and masters may mutually enjoy, in comedy as in life—witness, in our play, the feelings that exist between Philocrates and Tyndarus.[9] If, however, by an act of deception or dishonesty the slave should violate the bond, then the moral relationship is utterly dissolved, and the master is free to discharge his indignation by means of the lash or the cross, or with their more protracted equivalents, labor in the mill, the mine, or the quarry.

At this point, the issue between Hegio and Tyndarus can be summed up in this way: Tyndarus escaped the dilemma of conflicting obligations to his new master and his old (cf. *novus erus,* 362; *veteri domino,* 363) by denying it, claiming to be bound only by loyalty to Philocrates. On these same grounds, however, Hegio is

[8]Varro, *On Agriculture* 1.17: *instrumenti genus vocale;* cf. Aristotle, *Politics* 1.4.1253b32 (OCT): "The slave is an animate article of property" (*ktēma ti empsuchon*).
[9]This ambiguity in the status of the slave—a necessary ambiguity, corresponding to the contradiction entailed in the very definition of the slave as human property—is exhibited with the greatest clarity and elegance for American slavery by Eugene D. Genovese, *Roll Jordan Roll: The World the Slaves Made* (New York, 1976; orig. ed. 1972), 25–47. Compare my discussion of the Greek ideology in "A Comment on Class and Labor in Ancient Society," *Marxist Perspectives* 7 (1979), 126–27.

equally justified in his punishment of Tyndarus who, beyond his having no right to better treatment insofar as he is an enemy captive, has also deceived Hegio and, to all appearances, wrecked the possibility of recovering his son. I say all this in defense of Hegio because many critics have charged him with inhuman harshness and found fault with Plautus for an inconsistent representation of his character.[10] And yet, one may nevertheless wish to agree with them that Hegio has dealt unjustly with so good a man as Tyndarus. What are the grounds for this judgment?

Tyndarus himself seems to base his appeal to Hegio on the premise that his loyalty to Philocrates is not a matter of parochial ties but a duty demanded by virtue as such, which anyone, even an enemy, should be able to recognize and respect. If he has deceived Hegio, this was warranted on objective grounds as the only way, and therefore the necessary way, in which to save Philocrates from slavery, and thus to meet a natural obligation. The interests of Philocrates have precedence not so much because Hegio is an Aetolian, while Philocrates is a fellow Elean, but because Philocrates is a friend, another self, as the ancients had it (cf. 249), and because redeeming a good man from slavery, when it is in one's power, outweighs the evil in a harmless lie.[11] For Hegio to acknowledge this ethical imperative, however, means nothing less than granting to his slave, a captured enemy, the right to disobey him, deceive him, and act against his interests in the name of a higher and universal morality. Such an idea runs counter both to the city-state ethic and to the moral foundation of slavery. Is it legitimate for us to interpret the *Captivi* in terms of this conception?

To respond to this question, we must now turn to one crucial and obvious factor in the scene between Hegio and Tyndarus: The audience or the reader knows what the dramatic characters do not know, namely, that Tyndarus is really the son of Hegio. Throughout the episode this knowledge decisively inclines our sympathies toward Tyndarus. Hegio's vindictiveness seems intolerable when it is directed not against a slave and alien, but against his own family which it is his whole purpose in life to preserve. There is a disturb-

[10]See Francesco della Corte, *Da Sarsina a Roma* (Florence, 1967), 252; also Leach (above, n. 3), who explains: "The anxiousness and inconsistency of Hegio are also the result of assuming a new role: that of slave trader" (280).

[11]Grimal, 397–98, cites Quintilian 12.1.38 for the principle, accepted even by the Stoics, that under certain circumstances telling a lie may be a praiseworthy action.

ing confusion of categories. The distinction between citizen and stranger, free man and slave, is blurred and as a result, we perceive the actions of Hegio ironically, even if they are in accord with the conventional morality of the *polis*. The old communal code cannot function if it is impossible to discriminate friend from enemy. It becomes necessary to judge a man not on kinship or association, but by a general standard of virtue, applicable to all alike. Citizenship and slavery appear as mere accidents, and therefore ought not to affect the criteria of right conduct. What would be lauded in a free man—the rescue of his compatriot—cannot be held blameworthy in a slave. In a word, the secret of Tyndarus's identity compels us to deny the legitimacy of Hegio's behavior, and hold him accountable to a transcendent concept of justice by which he must concede the legitimacy of Tyndarus's cause.

If we look only to the plot of the *Captivi,* the matter of Tyndarus's identity is a rather minor and detached element. The recognition scene, which hangs on the coincidental return of the evil slave Stalagmus who had stolen the infant Tyndarus, is postponed to the last fifty or sixty lines of the play and constitutes a coda to the action. The release of Tyndarus from the quarry, which is the important reversal so far as the plot is concerned, is independent of and precedes the revelation that he is Hegio's son. Here again we may observe how the dramatic design of the *Captivi* serves the structure of its fundamental situation, wherein lies the meaning of the play.

The basic tension of the *Captivi* goes deeper than a mere conflict of interest between Philocrates and Tyndarus on one side and Hegio on the other, deeper, too, than the moral dilemma of Tyndarus, who must choose between his obligations to two masters. It rests ultimately in the clash between two opposing ethical systems or world views, the communal ethos of the city-state and a universal humanism. The roots of this tension lay deep within the consciousness and the traditions of the Greeks in the era after the death of Alexander the Great, when the model for Plautus's comedy was undoubtedly composed.[12] The history of this problem and the

[12]Attempts to attribute the original to a specific date or author have not met with success. Most recently Grimal has put forward the name of Poseidippus, arguing from alleged resemblances between the *Captivi* and the *Curculio*. This evidence is extremely tenuous.

underlying causes of the change cannot be summarized here. A few illustrative examples of the attitudes involved, however, may provide a context for the issues under discussion.

Even within the individual city-state there were pressures to interpret the bond between citizens not as kinship so much as a common commitment to certain ideals grounded in temperament or character. The funeral speech of Pericles which Thucydides reports is an eloquent statement of this idea, which served, I think, to bind together an increasingly large and diverse population, much the way the notion of Americanism has worked to forge an ideological unity in the United States.[13] Another challenge to the communal ethos came from an incipient sense of panhellenic or national identity, which had its sources in the common language and culture of the several city-states and was greatly advanced by the threat of common enemies. One of the clearest statements of this sentiment in fifth-century literature may be found in the words with which the Athenian spokesmen, at the end of the eighth book of Herodotus's *Histories,* reassure the Spartans that they will not betray the Greek cause and make a separate peace with the Persians:

There are many and powerful reasons which would prevent us from doing such a thing, even if we wished to. First and most important are the statues and temples of the gods which have been burnt and destroyed and which we are obliged to avenge to the limit rather than come to an agreement with the agent of it all. But there is also the fact that the Greek people [*to Hellēnikon*] are of the same blood and the same tongue, that we have in common the edifices of our gods and our sacrifices, and that our traditional ways are all alike, and it would not be well that the Athenians should be traitors to all this. Know then, if you did not already know it, that so long as one Athenian survives, we shall never make a pact with Xerxes.

This ringing declaration comes as the conclusion to a series of episodes revealing the selfish rivalry of the Greek states which can be compelled only by bribery or tricks to stand united against the Persian invaders; Herodotus possibly set it down on the eve of the

[13]Thucydides 2.40–44. That there were contradictory currents in Athens is illustrated by Pericles in 451 having proposed the law restricting Athenian citizenship to the offspring of two citizen parents. See David Whitehead, *The Ideology of the Athenian Metic* (Cambridge, 1977), 42–43.

Peloponnesian war.[14] Clearly, then, the speech is more a pious hope than a reflection of political reality. Nevertheless, it was a step in the direction of the vigorous panhellenism and humanism propounded in the fourth century by such figures as Isocrates, and which later, in the wake of the conquests of Alexander, would inform the systematic cosmopolitanism of the Stoic and Epicurean philosophies: The true community, they proclaimed, was the community of the good and the wise, and they admitted no distinctions of nation, class, or sex.[15]

A natural consequence of the developing spirit of panhellenism, moreover, was the denunciation of the enslavement of Greeks by Greeks, as witnessed, for example, by Socrates' famous condemnation of the practice in Plato's *Republic*.[16] To justify this distinction in the treatment of Greeks and barbarians, Aristotle grounded it in racialist assumptions about the natural inferiority of certain non-Greek populations (*Politics* 1254b–1255a), although he admits that his argument was controversial, and that some held that slavery derived solely from the conventional right of the victor over the vanquished. The controversy did not end with Aristotle, of course. Neither did the practice of reducing prisoners of war and sometimes whole populations of conquered Hellenes to slavery, no matter how much it might be thought to offend against nascent feelings of Greek solidarity. The story of the *Captivi* is set within that world of internecine war and subjection among the Greek city-states; it serves to expose the ambiguities in the ideology that supported it.

The clash of values exhibited in the *Captivi* demands a resolution, according to the requirements of the comic genre, and immediately after the discovery of Philocrates' and Tyndarus's ruse the plot turns to the preparation of the denouement. Hegio announces that from now on he will never trust anyone again (*nulli quicquam credere*, 756), since he has twice lost a son through the treachery of a slave. Hegio's reaction is an extreme one. It was not enough to punish his unfaithful slave, but he must break the bonds of trust

[14]Herodotus 8.144.2–3; compare Henry R. Immerwahr's discussion of Herodotus on Athens and panhellenism in *Form and Thought in Herodotus* (Cleveland, 1966), 210–25, 234–35.

[15]An excellent, concise review of the tradition of panhellenism and its role in the plays of Menander is given by T. B. L. Webster in *Studies in Menander* (Manchester, 1950), 22–25; see also the section on Menander in H. C. Baldry, *The Unity of Mankind in Greek Thought* (Cambridge, 1965).

[16]*Republic* 469B–471C; cf. Adam's notes *ad loc.*

with everyone, friend and stranger alike. "I've decided to pity no one, since no one has pity for me" (764–65). This posture of Hegio's casts him now in the role of the misanthrope, who withdraws entirely from the community of mankind. This figure belongs, as we have seen, to a plot type with its own characteristic shape, in which social relationships are reestablished with the secessionist by means of outside gestures of generosity and good faith. This requirement to mend the breach with Hegio will govern the development of the story almost to the end of the play, and so will displace the ethical focus from the dilemma raised by Tyndarus's noble deception. The problem of the clash of values is relegated to the wings.

The undoing of Hegio's cynical withdrawal begins at once. No sooner has he voiced his loss of faith and shipped the unfortunate Aristophontes back into chains than Ergasilus, a parasite on Philopolemus's erstwhile generosity whose quest for the old bounty punctuates the action of the *Captivi,* bursts upon the stage in search of Hegio, broadcasting his transports of joy. The news he bears is that Philocrates has returned with Philopolemus, although a hundred lines of antics intervene, concerned mainly with Ergasilus's prandial expectations, before he comes to the point.[17] The still embittered Hegio supposes at first that he is being mocked (877), although he gives over his suspicions when Ergasilus swears his good faith (cf. *bonam fidem,* 890; *fides,* 893). He hastens off to the port to check this information with his own eyes, where at last the evidence that Philocrates has acted honorably toward him, despite the trick he played, overcomes his negativity. Hegio makes the point emphatically in a brief prayer of thanks to Jupiter and the other gods at the beginning of Act V when he returns to the stage with Philocrates and Philopolemus: "this man's faith with me proved steadfast" (*haec reperta est fides firma nobis,* 927). Philocrates strikes the same note: "What now, since I kept faith with you (*tecum servavi fidem,* 930), and brought him home to freedom?"

[17]The chief function of Ergasilus is to provide a coarse and comic symbol or echo of the fortunes of Hegio's family. With the capture of Philopolemus, he is reduced to meager fare at the table of Hegio, while all his former providers give him the cold shoulder. Correspondingly, when Philopolemus is finally brought home, Hegio grants him license to a perpetual feast (897), a prodigal iteration of the festive repast which commonly marks the restoration of community at the conclusion of a comedy.

Hegio acknowledges his debt of gratitude (*gratia*, 932, 941) for Philocrates' services (*beneficium*, 935; cf. 933, 941 *bene fecisti*) in the quid pro quo formulas of traditional Roman morality. Philocrates requests the return of his slave Tyndarus, so that he may reward him for his good offices (*bene factis*, 940). Hegio explains apologetically how he mistreated Tyndarus (*feci male*, 943) when he caught him in the lie, and at Philocrates' exclamation of distress he is prompt to make amends by giving Tyndarus his liberty free of charge. Philocrates graciously accepts the favor (*faci' benigne*, 949), and, with their obligations mutually acquitted, confidence is restored and the episode of Hegio's withdrawal from community is ended. We may observe that as a symbol of the bond of good faith, Jupiter, the sanctifier of oaths and supreme guarantor of *fides*,[18] reigns as the tutelary deity over the action of the play from the moment when Ergasilus brings on the news of Philocrates' return. With the invocation *Iuppiter supreme* the first scene of the fourth act commences, and the name of Jove is echoed in Ergasilus's identification with *summus Iuppiter* as the savior of Hegio's household (863), in a slave boy's cry *Diespiter* (Jupiter) with which the last scene of Act IV begins, in the initial word *Iovi* of Act V—Hegio's thanksgiving prayer—and once more in Hegio's appeal to *Iuppiter supreme* (976) when he first divines that Tyndarus may be his other son.

The return of Philocrates resolves the major complication of the play. True, the real identity of Tyndarus remains to be discovered, but we have already seen that this mystery is a subordinate element in the plot, which affords a dimension of irony but does not substantially influence the course of the action. The ethical problem, however, has not been solved, but merely evaded. The liberation of Tyndarus is not in recognition of his virtue. He is freed only because his dishonesty to Hegio proves to be inconsequential, and because Philocrates's faithful execution of the pledge to restore Philopolemus, after the deception which cast Hegio into despair, appears to Hegio as a voluntary or gratuitous kindness to which he must respond with like beneficence. Whether Tyndarus's loyalty to Philocrates was right is immaterial, since Hegio does not absolve

[18]Compare 426–27, Philocrates (as Tyndarus): *Iovem supremum testem laudo, Hegio, me infidelem non futurum Philocrati* ("I swear by almighty Jupiter, Hegio, that I will not be unfaithful to Philocrates").

him; he simply foregoes the punishment as an expression of his gratitude to Philocrates. Tyndarus's redemption is not a function of his own values or character, but is brought about accidentally as a by-product of Philocrates' decency. Thus, the moral issue is deflected or sidestepped, after the fashion of comedy, where a general contradiction in values tends to be resolved by an arbitrary or contingent circumstance which serves for the given instance but fails to meet the problem as such. To make the issue vivid, it is worth reflecting what the fate of both of Hegio's captives would have been, had Philocrates returned, as honor bound him to do, but unsuccessful in the bid to ransom Philopolemus.[19]

Philocrates, it will be recalled, had brought back with him from Elis not only Philopolemus but also Stalagmus, the slave who had abducted Hegio's infant son, and Hegio, having given word for Tyndarus to be released, undertakes the examination of the kidnapper. Stalagmus is brazen and unrepentant. One critic remarks: "Without doubt he is the most churlish and unregenerate of Plautine villains."[20] He proclaims his knavishness with proud bravado, like the procurer, Ballio, in Plautus's *Pseudolus*. When Hegio orders him "Over there, my good man, my charming chattel," Stalagmus parries, "Now what am I supposed to do, when a fellow like you can't tell the truth. Cute, charming, yes. A good man, never, not even an all right one, and I never will be" (954–57). He admits unashamedly that he stole and sold Hegio's son and recollects the buyer as the father of Philocrates, although beyond this he is ignorant of the boy's fortunes: "I took the money and didn't give a damn about the rest" (989). As the awareness dawns on Hegio that Tyndarus must really be his son, he is torn by warring emotions. "I

[19]On a very general level, the issue of the *Captivi* may be subsumed under the problem of the right treatment of a captured enemy. Two popular Roman tales illustrate the extreme alternatives. The first is the story of Regulus's torture at the hands of the Carthaginians after the defeat of his army in Africa in the first Punic war. Regulus himself, according to the tradition, persuaded the Senate not to ransom the captives. The second is the famous magnanimity of Pyrrhus after the battle of Heraclea, when he ventured to restore the Roman prisoners without ransom. Pyrrhus's grand gesture was recorded with eloquent embellishment by Ennius in the sixth book of his *Annals* (frr. 194–201 Vahlen). The destruction of Regulus is best known from Horace, *Odes* 3.5. The story goes back at least to the second century, and is probably historical, despite the silence of Polybius; Hildegard Kornhardt gives a full discussion in "Regulus und die Cannaegefangenen," *Hermes* 82 (1954), 85–123.

[20]Leach (above, n. 3), 293.

feel sick and I feel blissful, if what you're telling me is true. Sick since I abused him (*male feci*), if he is my son. It's horrible, I did more and less than I should have. I'm dying for how I abused him. If I could only undo it. Look, he's marching in, but hardly fitted out according to his virtues (*ex suis virtutibus, 997*)." Only in this phrase, when he has just surmised the true identity of Tyndarus, does Hegio appear to concede that Tyndarus did not deserve the punishment he received. The word *virtutes* signified in the time of Plautus both great accomplishments and the subjective qualities by which they were achieved.[21] That his deceiver is revealed as his own son has opened Hegio's eyes to the worth of both his conduct and his character. But this intimation of a larger ethical vision, of a standard of conduct independent of clannish bonds and interests, vanishes without a ripple in the finale of the play. Hegio's sorrow remains, after all, a response not to what he has done to a good and loyal man as such, but to a son. The extraordinary coincidence that the noble slave and stranger in his house is his kin permits a fortuitous harmony of sympathy and judgment. The contradiction between two systems of value is dissolved by the strategy of merging the abstract virtue of Tyndarus with his status in Hegio's household. In other words, the good man proves to be a member of the community, thereby abolishing or at least masking the tension in the concept of good faith or loyalty. The fate of Tyndarus, had Philocrates not returned, is best forgotten.

Or rather, not forgotten, but displaced on to a character created as the perfect foil for Tyndarus: Stalagmus. We may recall that the similarity between Tyndarus's treachery and Stalagmus's did not escape Hegio; each slave's wiles had cost him, as he thought, the loss of a son. Of course, what Tyndarus had conspired out of selfless fidelity to a worthy master, Stalagmus is represented as having done for vicious greed alone. He is an utterly evil man, and when we hear in the closing words of the drama that the shackles will be taken off Tyndarus and given to Stalagmus, we are not allowed much sympathy for the man, especially since he is still snappy enough to reply with a wretched joke about how good it is to give to the poor (1028). Here is none of the ambivalence that attached to the punishment of Tyndarus: The enemy is bad; the

[21]See D. Konstan, *Catullus' Indictment of Rome: The Meaning of Catullus 64* (Amsterdam, 1977), 41; Donald C. Earl, *The Political Thought of Sallust* (London, 1966), 28.

good man is a member of the community. The potentially tragic conflict is conjured away by an illusion of natural justice and the reconciliation of moral demands.[22]

The conclusion to the *Captivi* thus obliterates the ironic perspective on the communal ethos of the city-state which the secret of Tyndarus's identity had made possible. This is only to be expected in comedy. Plautus felt that he was skirting close enough to tragedy with the very mention of a war between Elis and Aetolia. Comedy prefers the appearance of reaffirmation and rebirth: The time of the drama is Ergasilus's birthday (174); for Tyndarus, his hours at the quarry are a vision of hell, his release by his father a second birth (1006–8). The recognition of Tyndarus is a readoption, a restoration of natural relations which shrinks from moral ambiguities. For all that, the glimpse which the *Captivi* provides into the problem of virtue and slavery is not canceled. Slavery and the communal ethic are two sides of the same coin, for communal exclusiveness necessarily denies the full humanity of strangers, and the slave is the stranger in one's power. The example of Tyndarus gives the lie to the essential premise of slavery, that the slave is different from oneself. Slavery is an accident: All men—at least, all Greeks—are essentially alike. The institution of slavery therefore necessarily rests upon a contradiction. The law of nations is opposed to the law of nature (*ius gentium contra naturam,* in Gaius's phrase). Within this contradiction lie the seeds of tragedy, "the rejection of all normal standards of success, of all comforting moralities, the naked exposure of the fault in things."[23] Custom cannot be reconciled with morality, the enslavement of war prisoners is ethically on a par with the lawless violence of the kidnapper. Eleanor Winsor Leach, whose sensitive interpretation of the *Captivi* proceeds from an idealistic sympathy with the character of Tyndarus, calls attention to the "relative joylessness" of the recognition scene with which the play concludes (293). "The Tyndarus who emerges from the stone quarries," she remarks, "is embittered and reproachful, hardly enthusiastic in hearing that he is Hegio's son."[24] For Leach, the cause

[22]Nevertheless, the dignity of the characters is to a degree compromised by this easy resort to coincidence. "How petty a thing is man" (*homunculi quanti sunt,* 51) exclaims the prologue.

[23]Bernard Knox, "Euripidean Comedy," in Alan Cheuse and Richard Koffler, *The Rarer Action* (New Brunswick, N.J., 1970) 87; reprinted in Bernard Knox, *Word and Action* (Baltimore, 1979).

[24]Leach (above, n. 3), 286; compare 295–96.

of this somberness is the weakness of Hegio, who "is pathetically cut off from the generous and provident man he had wished to be" (285). Because I see Hegio as a good man, after the standards and expectations of the culture of the ancient city-state, I venture to lift from him the blame for any gloom that attaches to the conclusion of the *Captivi*. The weakness is not in Hegio, but in the morality of his world, which was still fettered by a parochial exclusiveness that helped to sustain the ideological foundations of slavery. This morality was essentially incompatible with the panhellenic and cosmopolitan tendencies of the Hellenistic world. In the tone of the conclusion Plautus has perhaps betrayed the hint of an inexpungible flaw within the ethos of the ancient city-state. It is no more than a hint: The exuberant defiance of Stalagmus makes him a fit scapegoat through whom the ethical tensions of the drama may be exorcised.

Rudens

City-State Utopia

The scene from which Plautus's *Rudens,* or *The Rope,* derives its name turns on the tug-of-war between two slaves for a chest that has been tossed up from the sea. One of them has snatched the rope by which the other, who fished the chest out, has been dragging it. The fisherman is Gripus, whose name means "fishnet"; he is a slave of Daemones, a poor Athenian citizen living on the shore of Cyrene (modern Libya), where he and his wife took up residence some time after their only daughter was kidnapped. The intruder is Trachalio, owned by Plesidippus, a young Athenian visiting in Cyrene. Plesidippus is in love with a girl, named Palaestra, who is in the possession of a pimp called Labrax. Plesidippus had made a down payment toward the purchase of her, but Labrax, on the day the balance was due, secretly boarded a ship, at the urging of his companion Charmides, with the intention of cheating Plesidippus of his deposit and selling the girl more dearly in Sicily. While at sea, just off the shore where Daemones dwells, the ship was wrecked in a severe storm. Palaestra and her friend Ampelisca escaped in a boat, Labrax and Charmides were washed up as well, and finally the chest, containing the fortune of Labrax and also a small box belonging to Palaestra, floated in during the night, when Gripus recovered it. Palaestra's little case contains some personal jewels and tokens from her childhood, before she was sold into the possession of the procurer. On two of these are inscribed the names of her parents, who are, as the reader may have surmised, none other than Daemones and his wife. The recovery of the chest from the sea is

thus the vehicle for the discovery of Palaestra's identity, her reunion with her family, and her legitimate marriage to her lover and fellow-citizen, Plesidippus. Though the chest is undoubtedly of great significance, however, the struggle between the two slaves— Gripus, belonging to Daemones, and Trachalio, Plesidippus's man—for possession of it may seem peripheral to the action, a good bit of horseplay, perhaps, and not inappropriate to the farcical spirit of Plautine comedy, but essentially extraneous in the development of the plot. Frank O. Copley, in the introduction to his translation of the play, observes that "the incident in itself is relatively unimportant," though "it is, to be sure, the occasion for some hilarious pulling and hauling" between the two contenders for the treasure.[1] I shall begin my discussion of the *Rudens* with this scene, which I believe pertains directly to the central issue of the play.

First, the setting. We are introduced to Gripus by Daemones, who comes on stage to deliver a brief monologue, in which he informs us of two things: that his wife is likely to be jealous of the protection he has offered to two such young and attractive girls as Palaestra and Ampelisca; and that his slave Gripus has been behaving strangely, going fishing in the middle of the night in the midst of a storm, wasting his efforts and perhaps his lines when he would have been wiser to stay in bed.[2] When Daemones leaves the stage, Gripus enters, dragging the chest and pronouncing a prayer of thanks to Neptune, whom he calls his patron (906). His elaborate song or canticum is in three major movements. First, there is a brief conceit concerning the new kind of fish which the sea god has put into his hands (906–13).[3] The question whether a chest is like a fish will turn up again in the dispute between Gripus and Trachalio, where it is central both to the farcical wit and to the serious mean-

[1]Frank O. Copley, ed., *Plautus, The Rope* (New York, 1956), vi; John Herington, writing *in persona Gnaei Naevii*, calls such scenes "by-play," "Rudens," *Greece and Rome* 12 (1943), 78. The scene in which Gripus and Trachalio turn to Daemones for a judgment of their dispute inspired the title of Diphilus's Greek original, the *Epitropē* or "Arbitration."

[2]The tension between Daemones and his wife (cf. 1204) is probably a dramatic convenience: Appeal to a commonplace topic or pattern in comedy provides plausible motivation for removing Palaestra and Ampelisca from Daemones' house. Compare the function of lines 1118–19 of the *Miles Gloriosus*, as analyzed in the Introduction.

[3]Fish (*piscis*) is the key word here, and forms of it occur in 907 (*pisculentis*), 911 (*piscatu*), 912 (*piscatus*), and 913 (*piscium*).

ing of the scene. In the middle section of his song (914–26a), Gripus boasts of the energetic drive for profit to which he owes his luck.[4] Finally, in the third movement Gripus takes up the uses to which he will put the treasure: He will purchase his freedom, invest in land, then in shipping, until at last, a king among kings (*apud reges rex,* 931), he will fortify a great city and endow it with his name, a monument to his fame and the seat of his empire (*regnum,* 935a). Such are Gripus's dreams, and they characterize the man. His acquisitiveness is not the normal parsimony of the Roman. Gripus's fantasies carry him beyond the status of citizen in a commonwealth to that of tyrant, the usual signification of *rex* in this epoch. The best commentary on Gripus's heady ambitions, I believe, is the twenty-first idyll in the Theocritean corpus, a dialogue between two fishermen, of whom one relates a dream in which he caught a golden fish, to which the other replies with sober counsel, "hunt the fish of flesh and blood, lest starvation and your golden dreams prove the death of you."[5]

At this point, Trachalio comes upon the stage and seizes the rope to which the chest is bound (938). As the exchange between Gripus and Trachalio is a lengthy one, I shall give here only the general outlines of the argument. Having demanded, and received, a pledge of good faith (*fidem, fidus,* 952–55), Trachalio puts a hypothetical case to Gripus: Does the witness to a theft have the right to half the loot, if he knows the victim and can report the crime? Gripus agrees he does (961–62).[6] Trachalio then applies the tale: He knows the owner of the chest which Gripus has retrieved and demands half the spoils not to tell. Gripus's defense is that he is now the owner; the man Trachalio knows used to be (967). He then enunciates the fundamental premise of his defense, to which he will adhere throughout the play: What is captured in the sea is the

[4]No lazy man (*piger*) he, and forms of this word occur throughout the passage: *impigre,* 914–15; *piger,* 920; *inpiger,* 924; *piger,* 925; synonymous words and phrases abound. His object, he says, is profit (*lucrum*), which he puts before sleep and rest (916), for those who sleep without profit (*sine lucro,* 923) lie with misfortune.

[5]Cf. Eleanor Winsor Leach, "Plautus' *Rudens:* Venus Born from a Shell," *Texas Studies in Literature and Language* 15 (1974), 919, n.6.

[6]Obviously, Trachalio is not referring here to an actual law, least of all a Roman law; we have here a case of legal parody, which should be a signal that even where an allusion to enacted legislation may be suspected, the terms may be significantly altered. Compare Ugo Enrico Paoli, *Comici latini e diritto attico* (Milan, 1962), 46; William M. Green, "Greek and Roman Law in the 'Trinummus,'" *CP* 24 (1929), 188.

property of the fisherman. It is the law of the chase (*venatu*, 970): the sea is common to every man (*mare commune omnibus*, 975; cf. 976, 977, 981); its yield belongs to him who appropriates it.[7] Trachalio ventures a counterploy: If the wealth of the sea is common property, then the chest belongs as much to him as to Gripus. To this Gripus quite properly replies that under such a dispensation, all fishermen must starve, since potential buyers would merely claim their share in the marketplace (977–81). Trachalio then submits his fundamental distinction, which is the basis of his position throughout the discussion: Chests may not be compared to fishes (982–83). The dispute is embroidered with comic extravagance: Who, Trachalio inquires, has ever seen a chest-fish on sale in the forum? He challenges Gripus either to explain how a chest can be a fish, or to give up possession of an object which was not born in the sea and has no scales (991–92). Gripus takes the cue, explaining that chest-fish are indeed rare, especially in such a color and size, but they do turn up now and then. Trachalio impatiently demands that the case be submitted to arbitration (1002). After an exchange of threats, Gripus reiterates his postulate, that what he has caught in the sea by his own efforts is his (1019–20). Trachalio tries a last device: Inasmuch as he has been a witness, he is party to the crime (1020–23)

[7]Friedrich Marx, *ad v.* 975 (p. 181), cites Phoenicides, *Com. Att. Fr.* III, p. 335, 5 Kock, from Athenaeus 8. 345 E, and refers also to the Digest 1.8.2: "Et quidem naturali iure omnium communia sunt illa: aer, aqua profluens, et mare, et per hoc litora maris" (And indeed by natural law these are common to all: air, running water, and the sea, and by virtue of this the coasts of the sea); 47.10, 13, 7: "Et quidem mare commune omnium est et litora sicut aer, et est saepissime rescriptum, non posse quem piscari prohiberi" (And indeed the sea and the coasts are common to all, just as the air is, and there have been many decisions that no one may be prohibited from fishing); 43.8, 3: "Maris communem usum omnibus hominibus ut aeris iactasque in id pilas eius esse qui iecerit" (Use of the sea as of the air is common to all men and balls thrown into it belong to him who threw them). This last would apply to Labrax's case, though whether the law was elaborated thus in Greece or in Plautus's time at Rome is moot. See also Antonio Garzya, *Note al Rudens di Plauto* (Naples, 1967), 51, *ad v.* 975, and 52, *ad v.* 1025; A. R. W. Harrison, *The Law of Athens,* vol. 1, "The Family and Property" (Oxford, 1968), 244–45: "Aristotle (Pol. 1256[a,b]) recognizes fishing, hunting, and war as distinct sources of property, but he is not, in that passage, concerned specifically with Athens, nor with the juristic aspect of the matter. For objects found we have a law attributed to Solon reserving the ownership absolutely to the depositor, if there were such a one. We do not know what the rule was when the depositor could not be identified. . . . Menander (*Arbitr.* 64 ff.K.) and Theophrastos (*Char.* 30.9) assume that ownership could pass to the finder of a thing not deposited"; and "Plaut. *Rud.* 971–5, if it represents Athenian law, establishes the fisherman's legal ownership of his catch" (245, n.1).

and hence deserves his share of the proceeds. Gripus here tacitly concedes that his deed is thievish, though he ignores the implication of Trachalio's complicity: "I don't know those city laws of yours," he says (*neque ego istas vostras leges urbanas scio,* 1024). In the end, at Trachalio's suggestion, Gripus agrees to submit the issue to the judgment of Daemones, who, he thinks, must certainly decide in his favor, when the property of his own slave is at stake (1037–39): "right in my own back yard," says he (*hic intra praesepis meas,* 1038).

Let us begin our interpretation of the scene with Gripus's fundamental premise: *mare commune est,* the sea is common. The riches of the sea are the common property of all. Of course, Gripus does not mean this in an unqualified sense, as Trachalio's sophistical ploy makes clear. Once beached, hauled in, the gifts of the sea become subject to the law of private property, which reigns upon the land. The shore is the boundary between two domains. On one side, or within, is the civic polity, a community of possessors among whom the territory is discretely parceled (save, perhaps, for the commons, the *ager communis*). On the other side, beyond the frontier, is the wilderness, or, as here, the sea, where nothing is owned till it is captured and safely brought back home. The sea and the land are complementary regions: The rule of culture, that is, private ownership, is defined against the realm of nature. Without the land, there could be no appropriation of the sea's bounty; the sea, in turn, is the abiding symbol of the natural source of wealth, preceding the determinations of property, a reminder of the frailty of custom and civil order, and of their basis in a human sense of justice. This polarity of sea and land, nature and culture, common bounty and individual appropriation, is not in dispute between Gripus and Trachalio. The product of the sea belongs to him who has secured it, risking effort, toil, net, and boat, in the words of Gripus (1020). The point of contention concerns rather the rights over legitimate property that has been lost or abandoned at sea, beyond the perimeter of the polity. Does the sea wash away the tokens of possession, return appropriated wealth to the state of nature, there again to be claimed in the chase and pass in lawful ownership to its new proprietor?

For insight into the essential lineaments of the problem, we cannot do better than to adduce the brilliant and ironical explication in that masterwork of English prose literature, Herman Melville's

Roman Comedy

Moby-Dick, chapter 89, entitled "Fast-Fish and Loose-Fish." I quote in extenso, for Melville's argument is subtle, and it is difficult to compress or hasten the rhythm of his narrative. "It frequently happens," he begins

> that when several ships are cruising in company, a whale may be struck by one vessel, then escape, and be finally killed and captured by another vessel; and herein are indirectly comprised many minor contingencies, all partaking of this one grand feature. For example,— after a weary and perilous chase and capture of a whale, the body may get loose from the ship by reason of a violent storm; and drifting far away to leeward, be retaken by a second whaler, who, in a calm, snugly tows it alongside, without risk of life or line. Thus the most vexatious and violent disputes would often arise between the fishermen, were there not some written or unwritten, universal, undisputed law applicable to all cases.

This law, so obviously germane to the litigation between Gripus and Trachalio, has by the native wit and experience of American fishermen been enunciated in two general principles, "a system which," says Melville, "for terse comprehensiveness surpasses Justinian's Pandects and the By-laws of the Chinese Society for the Suppression of Meddling with other People's Business," to wit:

"I. A Fast-Fish belongs to the party fast to it."

"II. A Loose-Fish is fair game for anybody who can soonest catch it."

"But," Melville observes, "what plays the mischief with this masterly code is the admirable brevity of it, which necessitates a vast volume of commentaries to expound it." We begin with the definition: "What is a Fast-Fish? Alive or dead a fish is technically fast, when it is connected with an occupied ship or boat, by any medium at all controllable by the occupant or occupants,—a mast, an oar, a nine-inch cable, a telegraph wire, or a strand of cobweb, it is all the same. Likewise a fish is technically fast when it bears a waif, or any other recognised symbol of possession; so long as the party waifing it plainly evince their ability at any time to take it alongside, as well as their intention to do so."

Melville cites a case of a harpooned whale, which broke away from its pursuers with the harpoon, line, and boat itself in tow. The crew of another ship, which subsequently killed the whale, laid claim as well to all the appurtenances with which it came encum-

bered. The counsel for the defense illustrated his position, says Melville, with an allusion to a recent "crim. con." case—criminal conversation—"wherein a gentleman, after in vain trying to bridle his wife's viciousness, had at last abandoned her upon the seas of life; but in the course of years, repenting of that step, he instituted an action to recover possession of her. He then proceeded to say that, though the gentleman had originally harpooned the lady, and had once had her fast, and only by reason of the great stress of her plunging viciousness, had at last abandoned her; yet abandon her he did, so that she became a loose-fish; and therefore when a subsequent gentleman re-harpooned her, the lady then became that subsequent gentlemen's property, along with whatever harpoon might have been found sticking in her." The case was decided in favor of the defendants, save that the boat was restored to the plaintiffs. Can we not equally say that Labrax, under constraint of the storm, abandoned his chest to the high seas, whereupon it subsequently became the property of Gripus, who harpooned it, together with its incidental contents, that is, the box of tokens belonging to Palaestra? For those who might question the verdict of the judge, Melville appends a gloss, explaining the universal currency of the two principles, those of Fast-Fish and Loose-Fish, on which the decision was based.

Is it not a saying in everyone's mouth, Possession is half of the law: that is, regardless of how the thing came into possession? But often possession is the whole of the law. What are the sinews and souls of Russian serfs and Republican slaves but Fast-Fish, whereof possession is the whole of the law? What to the rapacious landlord is the widow's last mite but a Fast-Fish? . . . What to that apostolic lander, Brother Jonathan, is Texas but a Fast-Fish? And concerning all these, is not Possession the whole of the law?

But if the doctrine of Fast-Fish be pretty generally applicable, the kindred doctrine of Loose-Fish is still more widely so. That is internationally and universally applicable.

What was America in 1492 but a Loose-Fish, in which Columbus struck the Spanish standard by way of waifing it for his royal master and mistress? What was Poland to the Czar? What Greece to the Turk? What India to England? What at last will Mexico be to the United States? All Loose-Fish.

What are the Rights of Man and the Liberties of the World but Loose-Fish? What all men's minds and opinions but Loose-Fish?

What is the principle of religious belief in them but a Loose-Fish?
What to the ostentatious smuggling verbalists are the thoughts of
thinkers but Loose-Fish? What is the great globe itsefl but a Loose-
Fish? And what are you, reader, but a Loose-Fish and a Fast-Fish,
too?[8]

Melville has borne us a good deal further into the metaphysics of
ownership than we might have wandered ourselves. Whence the
original deeds and hereditary properties, whence the right to shave
a ransom in the form of interest off the earnings of the poor? By
what title does Labrax own the money in his chest, acquired in the
sale of kidnapped girls to satisfy the lusts of a chance buyer? What
right has he to possession of the girls themselves? Is there a moral
basis to ownership, or shall we say, with Proudhon, that property
is theft?

Plautus does not delve so deeply in the scene between Gripus and
Trachalio. Labrax's original title to the chest is not brought into
question, only whether its loss at sea entitles Gripus to it now. This
itself is a significant fact. Even in so obvious a case as the misbegot-
ten earnings of a pimp, Plautus does not and will not challenge, in
this play, the rights of property. It is not his purpose to uncover the
flaw in ownership itself. On the contrary, his argument presup-
poses a legitimate and equitable order of possession, guaranteed by
juridical sanctions. These are the "city laws," the *leges urbanas*
(1024) for which Gripus expresses his contempt. To be sure, the
term *urbanus* has the connotation of slick and sophisticated, reflect-
ing the peasant's distrust of urban cleverness and exploitation of the
countryside.[9] Gripus means that Trachalio is out to cheat him of his
due, with some fast and dubious reasoning. But Gripus is wrong; it
is the true laws of the city to which Trachalio has been appealing,
the legitimate rights of possession which are the basis of good faith,
fides, between citizens, and without which the civic bond would be
dissolved. The *fides* which Trachalio demands of Gripus at the
beginning of the scene (952–55) is echoed, albeit ironically, in
Gripus's consent, at the very end of it, to submit the case to
Daemones' arbitration: "Although you are summoning me to an

[8]The text of *Moby-Dick* follows the Norton Critical Edition, ed. Harrison Hay-
ford and Hershel Parker (New York, 1967).

[9]On *urbanus,* see Edwin S. Ramage, *Urbanitas: Ancient Sophistication and Refinement*
(Norman, Okla., 1973) [Univ. of Cincinnati Classical Studies], 24–34.

unknown arbiter,'' he deceitfully concedes, "if he will bring to bear good faith (*si adhibebit fidem,* 1043), then, though unknown, I know him; if not, though known, I know him not at all."

Far from relying on *fides,* however, Gripus's confidence is based, as we have seen, on his belief that Daemones will judge in favor of his own slave, that "he'll never give away in judgment two cents of his own today" (1039). When the case is brought before Daemones in the following scene, Gripus is indignant that his master consents to hear Trachalio first: "Will you give a stranger the floor before your own man?" (*alienon prius quam tuo dabis orationem?* 1063–64).[10] He expects Daemones to look to his private interests, not to the abstract and universal claims of justice. What he has found, what by chance has come into his possession, should be kept. The rules and trust of the community do not avail against the vagaries of loss and theft. To put it another way, the law of the sea, of the world beyond the walls of the city, has penetrated the order of the commonwealth. The rule of nature, where the rights of property are conferred by seizure, has overridden, in Gripus's mind, the authority of urban civilization.

In the arbitration scene that follows, the question of the chest itself is postponed; the issue centers rather on the little case belonging to Palaestra. The girl accurately identifies the tokens contained therein, and the scene ends with father and daughter falling into one another's embrace, Trachalio and Ampelisca rejoicing in their happiness, since, as Trachalio says, it was the consequence of their piety (*volup est quom istuc ex pietate vostra vobis contigit,* 1176), and Gripus, still unreconciled to his loss, muttering about hanging himself, at least until his present irritation passes (1189–90). The moral, of course, is clear. Daemones has respected the rights of ownership, and not taken advantage of an accident of possession to make himself the master of a treasure that was not his. In turn, the daughter who was stolen from him is restored to him from the sea. The virtue of the citizen is rewarded by the restoration of his household.

[10]From the order of speeches here, among other evidence, Wolf H. Friedrich, *Euripides und Diphilos* (Munich, 1953) [Zetemata 5], 197–99, concludes that the plot of the *Rudens* may be traced back through the original by Diphilus and through Menander's *Epitrepontes* to an ultimate archetype in tragedy. Ingenious as it is, Friedrich's formalist method is unconvincing; see W. Thomas MacCary, "The Comic Tradition and Comic Structure in Diphilos' Kleroumenoi," *Hermes* 101 (1973), 202–3.

Roman Comedy

The scene is excellently contrived to exhibit the working of a moral law, by which Daemones is tested and proved worthy. With the wonderful economy of new comedy, the chest which Daemones yields up to the claims of its rightful owner contains the evidence which reunites him with his child. This visible confirmation of poetic justice leaves Trachalio exultant, since his only purpose was, as he says, to salvage the box for Palaestra (1077–79). "Behold the crimes of Gripus!" he exclaims, vindicated by the result in the eyes of all.[11]

The recovery of his daughter is, as we have seen, the reward of Daemones' justice. More than that, her redemption is analogous to the fate of the chest. She too was borne away on the high sea, then cast up upon the land by the mysterious mercy of the storm where, despite her long residence beyond the communal pale, she may still be recognized and claimed by her own on the basis of signs of identity which neither the sea nor strange lands have stripped away. Like the chest, she reverts to original owners. Daemones' judgment in the matter of the chest enacts the basis in principle of the restoration of his child. But the story does not end here, and the reason why resides in the very nature of Daemones' decision. For the chest, by his own decree, belongs to Labrax, the most recent legitimate owner despite the dubious trade in which its contents were acquired.[12] By strict analogy, the girl too is his possession, purchased lawfully from pirates. Here we may detect the marks of the ideological premises of the play: In order that Palaestra be restored

[11]The word *scelus*, "crime" or "wickedness," and the adjectival form *scelestus*, which serves as a general term of abuse, have been prominent throughout the episode. In his introductory monologue, Daemones had used the latter term of his jealous wife (*scelesta*, 895). Trachalio insults Gripus with the term at 993 (*scelus*); Gripus returns it at 1001 (*scelus*) and again at 1015 (*sceleste*). In the arbitration scene, Trachalio applies it once more, echoed by Daemones (1058, 1059 *scelestus*), Gripus hurls it back (1093, *scelestus*), and it is picked up by Trachalio (*scelesti illius*, 1094), who varies the expression a few lines later (*scelerum caput*, 1098). In a significant twist, Gripus applies it ironically to himself (*me scelestum*, 1167) for having failed to make sure that no one was watching when he drew the chest from the sea. Then, at 1178, comes Trachalio's reference to the crimes of Gripus, cited above, and a final complaint by Gripus, who wonders whether he is a criminal for having caught the chest, or because he did not hide it safely when he brought it in (1184–85).

[12]Compare Harrison, 244–45: "Though there is no direct evidence for Athens we cannot rule out the possibility that piracy or robbery might be the origin of the legitimate ownership of a thing, but not of course if the thing had previously belonged to an Athenian citizen"; and "we can assume that this right of seizure as between citizens of different states was a general one in the Greece of the time" (245, n.4).

to her father, it is not sufficient that she be recognized. Labrax must also lose title to her, as occurs in the sequel when he is condemned in court for his attempt to defraud Plesidippus.[13] Quite parallel is the requirement that Ampelisca be purchased back from him. Furthermore, the very condition that Labrax, despite his trade, is treated as a legitimate proprietor of his wealth in gold and women sets the conditions by which he may ultimately be reincorporated into the community of citizens rather than expelled from it. Because Plautus forbore to pursue the inquisition into the sources of property to the point where Melville's vision led him, his comedy finds its resolution in the moral regeneration of Labrax and a willing exchange of goods which simultaneously symbolizes his restored status and brings about the fair and natural return for all.

After the arbitration scene, Daemones again enters with a brief monologue. Act IV concludes with three more scenes, which form a group. Each involves two characters: Daemones and Trachalio in the first, Gripus and Daemones in the second, Plesidippus and Trachalio in the third. The first and third are of a slapstick spirit, and in each the same device is employed to humorous effect, namely, repetition to the point of absurdity of a single word—*licet* seventeen times within as many verses (not counting the puns *licentia* and *infelicet* in line 1125) in the first scene, and *censeo* eighteen times in a dozen verses in the second (not counting *censionem* in line 1273).[14] By contrast, the central scene between Daemones and Gripus is

[13]Friedrich, 200, remarks "Zweifach ist . . . Palaestras Befreiung von Labrax: einmal verliert er sie durch seinen Prozess mit Pleusidippus, zum andern durch ihre Erkennung als attische Bürgerin. Dieser Prozess ist sachlich also ohne Belang, szenisch aber wichtig als das Mittel, Labrax so lange von der Bühne wegzubringen, als er dort störend oder überflüssig wäre" (The freeing of Palaestra by Labrax is double: he loses her once through his law case with Pleusidippus, and again through the recognition of her as an Attic citizen. This law case is actually without consequence, but dramatically important as the means of keeping Labrax off stage for as long as he may be in the way or superfluous). T. E. Kinsey, "Notes on the 'Rudens' of Plautus," *Latomus* 25 (1966), 272–277, argues cogently that the trial was not legally necessary; citing lines 522–26 and 864–65, he notes that "all the evidence shows that if Plesidippus got hold of Labrax, Labrax was prepared to hand over Palaestra and pretend he had always intended to keep his bargain" (276). "Why then does Plesidippus take Labrax to court?" asks Kinsey. "It looks in fact as if we have here poetic justice. Labrax deserves punishment for trying to trick Plesidippus and therefore punished he is. . . . The verdict will satisfy the audience even if not a Greek or Roman jurist" (277).

[14]Günther Jachmann, *Plautinisches und Attisches* (Berlin, 1931) [Problemata 5], 21–23, attributes the entire *licet* scene to Plautus, but his reasons, which include the premise that Plautus is always incompetent when he "proceeds on his own two feet," are not compelling.

more in earnest—even preachy—and makes explicit the moral lesson of the previous episode. The passage is nearly forty lines, too long to quote in its entirety, though it deserves careful analysis. "About that chest," says Gripus, "if you're smart, you're smart; you could have the goods the gods are giving." To which Daemones replies, "Do you think it's fair to call mine what belongs to someone else (*alienum*, 1230)?" "But if I found it in the sea?" puts in Gripus, returning to his original premise: "Whoever lost it is that much the luckier; it's no more reason why the chest should be yours." "That's why you're poor," says Gripus, "because you're too holy and good!" Hereupon Daemones, assuming a homiletic manner, intones, "O Gripus, Gripus . . ." He argues that life is full of snares, baited with morsels to tempt men's greed. But the law of prey is to be preyed upon (*mihi istaec videtur praeda praedatum irier*, 1242), and it costs more than it brings. "Should I hide what's been brought to me though I know it's someone else's (*alienum*, 1244)?" Daemones opts for a clear conscience over any amount of profit (*lucrum*, 1248). In turn, Gripus drives home his message by drawing a line between the ideal world of comedy and the real world of egotistical competition: "Long before this I've seen comic actors talk wisely that way, and get applause, when they show off the wise man's character to the people; but when they all go home to their own places, no one behaves the way they told them to" (1249–53). Daemones angrily sends him into the house and complains about the poor quality of slaves; luckily, he reflects, Gripus didn't meet another like himself, or both would have been implicated in the crime. "While he thought he had the prey, he would meanwhile have been the prey, prey leading prey" (1261–62). With this, he leaves the stage to sacrifice.

The paronomasia on the word *praeda*, "prey," points to the essential theme of Daemones' remarks. Gripus's attitude toward the chest is that of the hunter or fisherman, who captures his booty in the wild, outside the territory of the city, in which, on the contrary, wealth presents itself in the form of private possessions. With respect to wild game, the hunter and fisherman normally appropriate the bounty of nature in an allowable manner, which does not threaten the customs of the city-state.[15] The chest, however, is not

[15]Marcel Detienne and Jean-Pierre Vernant, *Cunning Intelligence in Greek Culture and Society*, trans. Janet Lloyd (Sussex, 1978), 30–31, observe that the fisherman (as

a natural product, but bears the stamp of civilization, that is, ownership. To treat such an object as booty, as prey, is to introduce the law of the wilderness into the city, in violation of urban conventions: Fishing takes the form of theft. By such a law everyone is fair game, no one is safe from arbitrary expropriation, and the man who thinks he has captured the prey falls prey himself to the next expropriator. Civilized manners and rights dissolve into their complement, the unfettered struggle for possession—the state of nature as perceived from the vantage point of the city-state. Every citizen has, Daemones affirms, a moral stake in preserving the code of property. Without it, life is but a series of traps or snares, in which the predator himself will soon be caught.

We may now take stock of the meaning of the entire act that we have been discussing. The question raised by the action is not directly the legitimacy of property, nor the immorality of stealing. It is rather a problem of boundaries, of behavior at the frontier, so to speak. Gripus may have been lawless enough to misappropriate the possessions of a fellow citizen, but that is not the position he represents in our play. He bases his claim to the chest entirely on the fact that he hauled it from the sea. Immersion in the ocean washes away, as it were, all prior titles. To leave the city, entrust oneself to the vagaries of the sea, is to enter upon the no-man's land where issues of right are settled privately, by "hard words and harder knocks—the Coke-upon-Littleton of the fist," in Melville's phrase. The city is, for Gripus, an enclave in a world of chaotic struggle and competition; outside its limits, all rules are suspended, or rather, have never been in force. Concerning the transactions that take place in that interstitial domain, there is no appeal to civil

well as the hunter) was conventionally associated with the use of tricks and traps in Greek antiquity, and was therefore sometimes characterized as thievish (cf. Trachalio's expression, *fures marutimi,* "maritime thieves," at 310). This characteristic wiliness of the fisherman corresponded, in Greek thought, to the cunning nature of fish themselves: It was necessary for the fisherman to outsmart his clever prey. In this connection one may observe that the name Labrax denotes a type of voracious fish; compare Garzya, 33, *ad v.* 492, citing D'Arcy W. Thompson, *A Glossary of Greek Fishes* (London, 1947), *s.v.* labrax. This, together with the fact that Gripus means a fishnet, sustains the thematic complex of theft, appropriation, and the realm of nature which is in the foreground in this scene. Cunning intelligence, or *mētis,* comes into its own precisely at the boundary between law and nature. The name Daemones, on the other hand, is probably invented here to suggest the piety of the man; it is derived from *daimon,* cf. Garzya, 12, *ad vv.* 42f., and Marx, 63, *ad v.* 33.

legislation. As in the old frontier novels of the American West, in the tradition established by James Fenimore Cooper, the violence of the wilderness is hidden in its secret bosom, and hunters, trappers, and adventurers may return to take up their abode in civilization, without the embarrassment of too nice an inquiry into the sources of their genteel prosperity. Daemones, on the other hand, maintains the rights of property as sacred and indelible. Once ownership has been legitimized, there can be no return to the potential and indeterminate state of natural resources. The laws of the *polis* are never abrogated, neither within nor beyond the frontier. The responsibility for upholding them resides in the personal conscience of each citizen (cf. 1246–47: *semper cavere hoc sapientis aequissumumst ne conscii sint ipsi malefici suis*); it obtains equally in the city or on the high seas, for the city exists wherever its citizens may be. Daemones's morality is independent of place, of the city walls or pomerium. What gives visible expression to this idea is the single most striking feature of the *Rudens* in the canon of new comedy, that in this play alone the scene is located, not in the heart of a city, whether Athens or some other, but on a remote and isolated strand in Africa, where everyone is far from home.[16]

The theme or argument which I have elicited from the controversy over the possession of the chest—that the moral basis of the city-state is not delimited by its physical perimeter, but extends in principle over the entire domain of nature—informs not only the fourth act but the structure and rhetoric of the entire drama. It is at once conspicuous in the opening verses of the prologue, which is spoken by an odd figure in Roman comedy, the star Arcturus: "He who guides all nations, seas and lands, I am a citizen in his city of the gods" (*civis civitate caelitum,* 2). Heaven is constituted as a republic, and man and nature alike are under its jurisdiction. Frank Copley, in his translation, obscured the significance of this introduction by altering the metaphor to that of kingship: "There is One who rules all peoples, seas, and lands; it's his subject I am: I own allegiance to Heaven."[17] A few lines later he writes: "There's a king, you know, of gods and men—Jupiter." The Latin, however, has not king but general, *imperator* (9), a civil office of republican Rome. The point is most important. Gods and men exist in a

[16]Cf. Leach (above, n.5), 915.
[17]Copley, 3.

common polity, in which Jupiter has the rank of consul. There is no hard-and-fast boundary between the two realms; the star Arcturus, which by night shines brilliantly in heaven among the gods, walks by day among mortal men (6–7). The purpose of these terrestrial perambulations is to discover the deeds and characters of men, their sense of duty and good faith (*pietatem et fidem,* 11), so that Jupiter may suitably reward the virtuous. The names of those who sue falsely, seek favorable verdicts by perjury and undeserved gain at law, are written in the book of Jove, and come up again for judgment in his court. Evil men (*scelesti,* 22; cf. 27) imagine they can placate him with sacrifices, but only those who act in good faith and piety (*cum pietate et cum fide,* 29; cf. 26) can reach him with their prayers. The message of Arcturus hardly needs explication. The moral law of the city embraces men and gods alike, and is guaranteed by Jupiter himself. His authority extends further to the entire domain of nature, which responds to his direction. No place or nation is exempt from his governance; nowhere are the laws of his polity annihilated. Justice is always rendered in the end, and the criminal pays more than he gains (20).[18] The issue between Gripus and Daemones is thus settled at the very beginning of the play, in a formula whose content Daemones will echo in his lecture to the slave. The burden of the action is to exhibit this lesson as a necessary consequence of human character and choice.

The prologue then turns to its proper task, a summary of the circumstances in which the drama opens. We are already familiar with its outlines; I should like to discuss briefly the way key terms and topics define the theme of the play. We are told that Daemones is an exile (35, 77), who lost his country not through wickedness but generosity (36–38). His daughter was stolen by a plunderer or pirate (*praedo,* 40), and sold in turn to the procurer who brought her to Cyrene, the vilest of men, who doesn't care a fig for good faith (*flocci non fecit fidem,* 47). We are introduced also to the friend of Labrax, Charmides, a Sicilian gentleman, a criminal (*scelestus,* 50), and a traitor to his city (*urbis proditor*). Arcturus then relates how

[18]See Eduard Fraenkel, "The Stars in the Prologue of the *Rudens,*" *CQ* 36 (1942) 10–14, on the sources for the prologue; Paoli, 40–42, observes that the role of Arcturus would signal to a Greek audience the onset of the stormy season when commerce was especially risky and thus prepare them for the shipwreck. See also M. Detienne, "Arcturus, démon astral," *Bollettino de l'Institut historique belge de Rome* 31 (1958), 11–14, 19–21.

Labrax had promised to deliver Palaestra into the hands of Plesidip-
pus at a temple of Venus next door to Daemones' house, before he
absconded with her for Sicily. Arcturus himself raised the storm
which sank the ship and drove the pimp, his friend, Palaestra, and
Ampelisca aground. It also tore the roof off Daemones' villa. The
action of the sea was not neutral or indifferent to human justice. On
the contrary, it was the agency of retribution in the city of gods and
men. The betrayer of the city will suffer condign punishment in
heaven's community, and the pimp will lose possession of his prey.
Daemones, who bears the civic ethos in his heart, although he is an
exile, will regain his household, and, by ties of marriage, be bound
once more to the community of his fellow citizens. Athens, that is,
the *polis,* will be reborn on the barren coast of Libya.

Act I opens with a brief exclamatory speech by Sceparnio, an-
other slave of Daemones; the role he plays in the first half of the
play answers to that of Gripus in the second, and deserves a brief
analysis. Plesidippus comes upon him working, together with
Daemones, on repairing the roof. Unlike his master, Sceparnio's
reception of the stranger is quite hostile. He accuses Plesidippus of
casing the area for a robbery (111), and of approaching a strange
household (*alienam domum,* 116) where he has no business. These
suspicions betray not only his grouchy personality, but also the
social character of the man. He is well adapted to the selfish autarky
of the homesteader, engaged in his own chores and wary of in-
terlopers. Apparently, this is not incompatible, in Plautus's mind,
with a certain empathy for strangers in distress. Sceparnio gets
quite involved in the distant spectacle of Palaestra and Ampelisca
washed ashore in a rudderless skiff (162–77), while Daemones pre-
serves a philosophical indifference.[19] "Little men, of what account
are you!" he cries at the sight of Labrax and Charmides struggling
into shore (154), and to Sceparnio's concern with the girls he re-
sponds with a cold command to follow the man who feeds him
(181–83).

In the next scene Palaestra's soliloquy, as she wanders along the
beach, encapsulates the ethical issue. She charges the gods with the
unfair tally of her woes, which she has suffered not for her own
impiety but through the wickedness of her master; once more, the

[19]On Daemones' lack of interest in the girls' fate, see the summary of the various
scholarly views in Garzya, 21, *ad vv.* 177–78 and 181–83.

terms *pietas* (190, 192, 195, 198) and *scelus* (197a, 198) represent the extremes of the moral spectrum. Palaestra's complaint deserves special attention in light of the notion, commonplace in antiquity, that the sins of a man may be visited also on his companions, especially when they are berthed together at sea.[20] Palaestra demands a finer discrimination on the part of the gods. She is, of course, unaware that the storm will be the means of her reprieve from slavery and reunion with her parents, the reward, albeit belated, of her dutiful virtue. Palaestra also emphasizes the desolation of her surroundings: unknown territory, deserted, bare rocks and sea, without a sign of cultivated fields (*cultum agrum*, 214; cf. also 188, 205–6a). She finds herself beyond the borders of civilization. Ampelisca, entering in search of her friend from the opposite side of the stage, observes the same: "There's no more isolated land than this place and territory" (227).[21] Act I ends with the girls reunited and taken in under the protection of Ptolemocratia, priestess of the temple of Venus, who is moved by pity for their plight (281).

Act II begins with the lament of some fishermen on the shore for the poverty and toil of their meager livelihood. The scene reflects the urban view of angling as a profession: poor, uncertain, subject to the whimsical largesse of a grudging sea. The men themselves are city dwellers, who hike out daily to the shoals. The proper citizen, in the ideology of ancient Greece and Rome alike, has the source of his wealth in the sure possession of land. When Trachalio comes upon the fishermen, he addresses them characteristically as "maritime thieves" (*fures maritumi*, 310).

Returning to the temple, Trachalio encounters Ampelisca, who is just emerging to borrow water from Daemones, and learns from her the treachery of Labrax and the fate of his ship. He is the first to proclaim the justice of it: "Clever fellow, Neptune! there's not a shrewder gambler than you. Very clever, that toss you threw: you wrecked a perjurer" (358–60). Ampelisca also relates the loss of

[20]The locus classicus for this notion is Antiphon's speech *On the Murder of Herodes* 82–83; cf. also Aeschylus, *Seven against Thebes* 602–8, Horace, *Odes* 3.2.26–30, Ovid, *Heroides* 7.57, and *The Book of Jonah* 1.7.8.
[21]Leach (above, n. 5), 916, n. 3, observes that the "picture of a barren Cyrene must have been extremely strange to both Greek and Roman audiences of the play, since the country was noted above all for its fertility." Also a prosperous city is within walking distance of this barren littoral; Plautus has conceived his landscape for its significance to his theme, not for its geographical precision.

Palaestra's case of birth tokens, which Labrax had kept locked in his treasure chest, and then continues on her way to Daemones' villa to fetch the water which, the priestess has assured her, will be freely given.

At the door she meets Sceparnio, whose story we may now resume. Contrary to the practice of his master, Sceparnio will not give over the water without a price. Daemones had said that "they're always asking me for water or fire or jugs, a knife, a spit, a frying pan, something—what's the use of talking? I got the pots and well for Venus, not for me" (133–36). Behind this casual allusion to neighborly impositions lies a technical point in the traditions of the Roman city-state, to which we have referred also in the chapter on the *Aulularia*. The conventional formula for banishment in Rome included the *interdictio ignis et aquae,* that is, a ban on the lending of fire and water. In the *Aulularia,* Euclio, a miser, signals his intention to cut himself off from commerce with his fellow citizens by refusing to give fire or water to his neighbors. There too the list is embellished by the addition of several other household items, which do not obliterate the allusion to the interdiction. In the case of Daemones, of course, the point is exactly the reverse: although he is, as the prologue informs us, in exile, he nevertheless continues to grant fire and water liberally to his only neighbor, the priestess of Venus. That is, he continues to respect the fundamental symbol of the bond of citizenship, maintaining in his behavior the forms of exchange which are constitutive of the city-state community. Sceparnio, on the contrary, by withholding water unless Ampelisca will reciprocate by bestowing on him her favors, gives evidence of the degree to which he has become accommodated to the isolation of his environment by ignoring the claims of civil obligation. To be sure, we can leave the social dimension out of consideration, and explain Sceparnio's attitude with reference only to his psychology: He is selfish and randy. But Ampelisca calls our attention directly to the wider significance of the gesture: "Why do you begrudge me water, which enemy provides to enemy?" (434) Sceparnio's racy retort underscores the political aspect: "Why do you begrudge me a favor which citizen provides to citizen?" (435). In her anxiety to oblige the priestess, Ampelisca promises everything, upon which Sceparnio hastens away to draw the water. The denouement of this little episode is telling. While Sceparnio is gone, Ampelisca catches sight of Labrax and Charmides on the beach and

flees at once to the temple. Sceparnio returns to find her gone, and fears she has conspired to convict him of theft, since the urn he is holding is plainly marked as temple property. In the end, he carries it himself to the priestess, grumbling that all he got for his pains was extra labor (472–84). Terror of the magistrate (477) as guardian of the institutions of property brings Sceparnio to his senses in the matter of civic responsibility.[22]

Act II draws to a close with the arrival of Labrax and Charmides, an obnoxious pair of scoundrels who greet each other with invective in just the measure in which Palaestra and Ampelisca had embraced in joy. Naturally, the thematic term *scelus* is again on their lips, as in Charmides' dig: "No wonder your boat broke, since it was carrying you, criminal, and your criminally acquired goods" (505–6; cf. 502, 508). They encounter Sceparnio, who tells them the fate of the girls. Charmides tries to borrow Sceparnio's cloak, but will not yield up his own as security. Sceparnio abandons his "barbarous guest" (*barbarum hospitem,* 583) to his own devices—the slur indicts the man's incivility in the etymological sense—and departs the stage for good.

I must give at least cursory attention to the action in the third and fifth acts, where the social interpretation of the meaning of the play, in the context of the ancient city-state ideology, will find confirmation. Daemones launches the third act with the announcement of a dream in which he protected some nestling swallows from the clutches of an ape. The meaning is immediately revealed in Trachalio's cries for help against the attack of Labrax, who is attempting to snatch Palaestra and Ampelisca from their sanctuary in the temple of Venus. The language of the scene sparkles with the technical terms of the Roman legal and moral vocabulary. Trachalio invokes first the citizen body of Cyrene (*pro Cyrenenses populares,* 615), imploring their sense of civic responsibility (*fidem*); the phrase is repeated in line 622, *vostram iterum imploro fidem.* He appeals specifically to the farmers and inhabitants of the area to uphold the rule of law over the sway of violence (616, 621). To Daemones he asserts that the seizure of Palaestra and Ampelisca is

[22]The anxiety over being caught with temple property is perhaps a characteristically Greek touch, as Paoli suggests, 42–44, whether or not there was a deliberate allusion in the original to a case involving a certain Hierocles who was apprehended with some garments labeled as the property of a temple of Artemis (Demosth., *In Aristogeitonem* I. hypoth., cit. Paoli, 44, n.1).

contrary to right and law (*advorsum ius legesque,* 643), and that Labrax is assaulting even the priestess. Daemones summons two tough slaves to intervene, and the girls flee the temple, taking refuge, upon Trachalio's suggestion, at an altar of Venus.

When Labrax is driven from the temple by Daemones and his men, he does not abandon his claim to the girls, but presses his lawful right to them (711). Trachalio urges him to select a judge from the senate of Cyrene to decide the issue of their freedom (712–14), but Labrax descends to threats and bluster, with the intention of abducting the girls from the altar. "It is not allowed," declares Daemones; "such is the law among us." "I have no business with your laws," replies the pimp (724–25), once again establishing himself outside the jurisdiction of civil authority. Trachalio further involves Daemones' sympathy by disclosing that Palaestra was born a free Athenian. "Is she one of my people?" asks the old man. "Aren't you Cyrenean?" "No, born in Athens, raised and bred in Attica." "I beg you, defend your fellow citizens," cries Trachalio (740–42). Nor does it escape Daemones that the girl is the age of his kidnapped child. The ties that bind Daemones to his city, ties which he never forsook, are roused and strengthened as he closes ranks with his people against the violence of the abductor, this time, as it will turn out, successfully defending his daughter from lawless hands. Labrax remains obstreperous, even contemplates burning the girls alive at the altar (768), but he is kept under strict guard while Trachalio seeks out Plesidippus: "Both are against me now," he mutters, "land and sea" (825). Plesidippus returns to hale Labrax, that "criminal exile" (*scelestum exsulem,* 859), as he calls him, into court for breach of contract. While the case is being adjudicated in town, the action shifts to the discovery of the chest.

In the last act, Labrax returns from town, where Plesidippus has won his suit over Palaestra and falls in with Gripus, who is grumbling about the chest. Swearing on the altar of Venus, the procurer promises to pay Gripus the large sum he demands to tell him where the chest may now be found. Of course, he intends perjury (1355), and boldly foreswears in the presence of Daemones (1372–84). Then, suddenly, the last reversal is sprung. Daemones begs Labrax to abjure the pimpish faith (*fide lenonia,* 1386) and meet with honest gratitude the decency to which he owes the recovery of his possessions. Daemones and Labrax then settle privately, to the extreme

consternation of Gripus, on an equal division of the spoils, in return for which the pimp will liberate Ampelisca, and Daemones Gripus. The play closes with an extraordinary gesture of festive reconciliation, which the learned commentator Friedrich Marx can scarcely believe was in the Greek model: Daemones invites both the slave and the procurer into dinner.[23] Only the audience is left outside the circle of general harmony, since, as Daemones says, he as actor really has nothing to offer (1419). The incorporation of the pimp characterizes the new order as universal; the exclusion of the spectators marks it as ideal. In the reconstituted world of the drama, there are no predators, and good faith reigns supreme among the class of free citizens, each holding just title to his possessions, content with his portion and fearing no encroachments. Society is grounded in the structure of relationships among equals, who are bound by rules of fair exchange and conjugal communion. The gods too are members of this commonwealth, and nature collaborates in its procedures. It is the ideal polity of petty proprietors, founded on trust, free of conflict and usurpations, secure in the confidence that the laws of property are inscribed in the heavens, and violations are never more than transient. It is the utopia of the ancient city-state.

Comparison of the *Rudens* with the *Captivi* is revealing. In both plays, a family sundered by an agency external to the community is reunited. Hegio, in the *Captivi,* takes measures that are consistent with the state of war that obtains in principle among the city-states: He purchases slaves with which to barter for the freedom of his son. It is a grim business, but it succeeds. That he is unwittingly a severe master to his own son lays bare the contingency in human affairs, and the arbitrariness of social and political divisions. Nevertheless, the structure of city-state relations is neither idealized nor conjured away. Daemones, by contrast, is civil and fair-minded toward all, respecting the proprietary rights even of a thieving pimp. While the violence and suspicion of relations among strangers penetrate Hegio's own household, Daemones extends communal protocols to the margins of the Greek world.

The theme of the *Rudens* is played out upon the contours of its plot, which may be analyzed as a version of the rival type, such as that of the *Pseudolus* or *Miles Gloriosus.* The procurer withholds the

[23]Marx, 239, *ad v.* 1417; so too P. J. Enk, "How Did Plautus Adapt His Greek Models?" in *Fontes Ambrosiani* 25 (1951) [*Miscellanea Giovanni Galbiati* vol. 1].

girl from the enamored young hero in the hopes of realizing a better profit from a rich buyer, here represented by the lucrative markets in the opulent territory of Sicily, whither Labrax and Charmides propose to deliver their women. This elementary scheme is elaborated in two ways: The girl is of citizen status, which is the cue, so to speak, for a recognition scene; the father of the girl is given a central role, casting into prominence the topic of the reunion of his household. Plesidippus, correspondingly, is not the indigent youth typical of the rival paradigm. In these respects, the *Rudens* bears a marked resemblance to Plautus' *Poenulus*.[24] And yet, as a comparison with the latter play readily reveals, the meaning of the *Rudens* is certainly not determined by the story form alone. For this, one must look also to its scene and characters, and to patterns of imagery and motif such as the benign role of the sea and the elements, or the tutelage of the gods—Jupiter and his scout, Arcturus; the hovering presence of Venus born from the sea;[25] and Neptune, so frequently invoked, who is not the unreliable power the fishermen suspect, but a purposeful gambler, as Trachalio divines, a hidden form of providence. One must take account as well of the persistent legal and moral terminology, and of such intercalated scenes as the fishermen on the beach and the contention over the chest, those "relatively unimportant" incidents so neatly placed and pointed. The pastoral quality of the setting and the final gesture of forgiveness are not a romantic whim on the part of Plautus or of Diphilus, the author of his Greek source. They are essential to the peculiar theme of the play, which is to extend boundaries, incorporating heaven and nature into the urban contract. Not that the perimeters of the city-state lose their meaning. Athenian will still

[24]The similarities in the plots of the *Rudens* and *Poenulus* are analyzed by Friedrich, 234–36 and 251. On the structure of the *Poenulus*, see also Friedrich Leo, *Plautinische Forschungen* (Berlin, 1912), 170–78; Jachmann, 195–208; Eduard Fraenkel, *Elementi Plautini in Plauto,* trans. Franco Munari (Florence, 1960), 253–67; P. J. Enk, "De Poenulo plautina," *Wissenschaftliche Zeitschrift der Universität Rostock* 12 (1963), 209–13. The whole question of contamination in the *Poenulus* is reviewed by Gregor Maurach, *Plauti Poenulus* (Heidelberg, 1975), 43–54; his conclusions are those of Fraenkel, who defended the essential unity of the plot.

[25]Compare Leach (above, n.5), 916: "The destructive capacities of the sea are balanced by the restorative powers of Venus, the goddess who emerged from the watery element; and, as the sea-storm subsides, the play moves towards a reenactment of this archetypal birth in the rescue and recognition of its heroine. In one way or another, either materially or psychologically, this pattern affects the fortunes of all of the characters"; see also 920.

wed Athenian, even if the judgment that unites them is made in the courts of Cyrene, and their embrace is on its barren littoral. The individual city-state does not perish as a form. But the void stretches in between, the wilderness, the sea, abodes of plunderers and pirates, are made to serve and guarantee the civic constitution.

Cistellaria
Noncitizen Order

In *The Portrait of a Lady* Henry James explains:

> Mrs. Touchett easily remembered that the girl had refused an English
> peer; and that a young lady with whom Lord Warburton had not
> successfully wrestled should content herself with an obscure Ameri-
> can dilettante, a middle-aged widower with an uncanny child and an
> ambiguous income, this answered to nothing in Mrs. Touchett's con-
> ception of success. She took, it will be observed, not the sentimental,
> but the political, view of matrimony—a view which has always had
> much to recommend it.[1]

In ancient comedy, parents normally took the "political view" of
marriage; what is more, they were in a position to enforce their
wishes, and a happy conclusion demanded a dramatic device or
revelation whereby the interests of the father might be made to
coincide with the desire of the son.[2] Plautus's *Cistellaria* is an exem-

[1] Henry James, *The Portrait of a Lady*, Penguin edition (Harmondsworth, 1963;
orig. 1881), 274.

[2] Of the powers of the Roman head-of-household, the jurist Gaius wrote: "Fere
nulli alii sunt homines qui talem in filios suos habent potestatem qualem nos
habemus" (There are virtually no other human beings who possess such power over
their sons as we do), *Inst.* 1.55. See John Crook, "*Patria Potestas*," *CQ* N.S. 17
(1967), 113–22; the quotation from Gaius is taken from Crook's citation on page 113
(translation my own). The father's consent to a marriage was also necessary accord-
ing to Attic law; see Antonio Martina, "Aspetti sociali e giuridici nella *Samia* di
Menandro," *Atti della Accademia delle scienze di Torino, II classe di scienze morali,
storiche e filologiche* 107 (1973), 868–75.

plary representative of the type. In the first scene we learn that a young man and woman—Alcesimarchus and Selenium—are passionately in love. They belong to different social classes, however. Alcesimarchus is a citizen, while Selenium's status is that of a courtesan (*meretrix,* in Latin, or in Greek, *hetaira*), who would be drawn from the class of free women residing in Sicyon but without citizen rights according to law.[3] Selenium has just discovered that Alcesimarchus's father has arranged a marriage for him with a woman of full citizen status from Lemnos. At the insistence of her mother, she is about to retire from the house she had shared with her lover. She does not, however, wish to impose a gratuitous pain upon Alcesimarchus, who is the first and only man she has consorted with, and so she prevails upon her friend Gymnasium, a seasoned professional of the trade, with the consent of Gymnasium's mother who acts as her procuress, to remain in the house until Alcesimarchus should arrive, and explain to him the reasons for her departure.

Selenium is clearly a noble, loyal, and sentimental sort of courtesan, and the difference between her and the practiced harlot is brought out through contrast with the character and principles of Gymnasium and her mother. The following portion of the dialogue between Selenium and Gymnasium's mother captures the spirit of the two.

> *Sel:* I'm wretchedly tormented by my own mistake and stupidity, since I chose him out as the only one with whom I would spend my life.
>
> *Procuress:* That's more profitable to a woman of standing (*matronae,* 78),[4] my Selenium, to love one man and live out one's life with the one she's married. But a courtesan is most like a prosperous city: she cannot make her fortune without many men.
>
> *Sel:* This is what I want you to do; I'll tell you the reason I've summoned you. Since I didn't want to be called a harlot, my mother

[3] I am assuming here that the status distinctions of Athens pertained as well in this period to Sicyon, or at least that an Athenian—not to say Roman—audience would have accepted them naturally. We do not know whether the Greek original by Menander was set in Sicyon.

[4] *Matrona* means "married woman," but, in opposition to *meretrix* (Lewis and Short, *s.v.* II A and B; *OLD* 5 (1978), 1084 *s.v.*), it refers more generally to the class of women who can contract a lawful marriage—women of good standing. In the context of the ancient city-state, this suggests citizen status—good women as a social order.

went along, obliged me in my entreaties, as I was obliging, and allowed me to live with the man I loved profoundly.
Pro: That was damned foolish.

　　·　·　·　·　·

Sel: What can I say? As we lived together I began to love him, and he me.
Pro: My Selenium, you're supposed to pretend to love. If you really love, you immediately think of the one you love more than your own interests.
Sel: But he swore a solemn oath to my mother that he would make me his wife! (76–86, 94–99).

The pathos of Selenium's grief, the purity of her attachment to Alcesimarchus, the contrast with the cynical maxims of the old procuress, all point to a single outcome: The rupture between the lovers is only temporary, and in the end Selenium will be reunited with Alcesimarchus. To achieve this in a way compatible with the social assumptions that inform ancient comedy, however, it is not enough that Selenium exhibit a liberal temperament; she must also be revealed as a citizen in fact, and the action of the play immediately gives way to two soliloquies, one by the old procuress herself, and a second by a god who delivers a postponed prologue, in which it is disclosed that Selenium is only the supposititious daughter of the courtesan. Actually, her father is a merchant from Lemnos, who had raped a freewoman in Sicyon years earlier. The merchant returned to Lemnos and married a relation of his, whereupon the mother exposed Selenium; the procuress retrieved the child and gave it to Melaenis, her friend, to raise. Meanwhile, however, the Lemnian wife of the merchant has died, and Demipho, as he is called, has returned to Sicyon, married the very woman he had violated, and, upon learning the fate of his child, set a slave to the task of recovering his daughter. Everything thus is set from the beginning for a happy denouement: The slave, who observed the procuress taking up the abandoned baby, will track her down, the child's identity will be established by the traditional device of tokens preserved in a small casket (whence the title, *Cistellaria,* from *cistella,* a small chest), and Selenium, now restored to her proper status as a citizen and daughter of prosperous parents, will be free to contract a legitimate marriage with Alcesimarchus.

　　Suspense did not have the same importance in ancient narrative

as it does today, but even if we judge it by the standards of its genre, the *Cistellaria* appears to have given away much of the plot before the story may be said to have commenced.[5] Lampadio, the slave of Selenium's real parents, Demipho and Phanostrata, enters toward the end of the second act, according to the conventional distribution of scenes, with the announcement that he has found the old woman after a day's search, and bribed her, with a jug of wine, to speak out (536–42). Lampadio explains to Phanostrata, who emerges from her house, how for a brief while he mistakenly imagined that the procuress had raised the child herself, and he tried to persuade Gymnasium whom he took for Selenium to quit her life as a courtesan and accept a marriage commensurate with her proper standing. Earlier in the play, Alcesimarchus's father had been a victim of this same error when he discovered Gymnasium in the house his son had appointed for Selenium. There Gymnasium had led the old man on in his illusion, and the humor had some bite because, despite his intention to break up his son's affair, he himself succumbs to the girl's charms. Lampadio's error, however, is immediately dispelled by the procuress, who identifies Melaenis by name. In the wings all the while that Lampadio is reporting to his mistress is Melaenis herself, an eavesdropper on the entire dialogue. As Lampadio departs to point out the right woman, Melaenis intercepts him to inquire more particularly into the history of her foster daughter. Lampadio runs through the complicated tale of Demipho's liaisons, and as he continues on his way to his appointment, Melaenis pronounces her intention to return Selenium, albeit reluctantly, to her legitimate parents (630).

The central portion of the *Cistellaria* is badly mutilated; beside a large number of illegible lines, several pages of the manuscript are altogether missing. If we take account of the lost verses, then the scene we have just described occurs after the play is more than four-fifths over. With the entrance of Lampadio, the comedy moves rapidly to the denouement, fulfilling, with only a few twists or surprises, the expectations aroused in the first act (lines 1–202, again approximately a fifth of the original total). We have already

[5]On the question of suspense versus dramatic preparation in ancient drama, the best introduction is still Tenney Frank's chapter "Terence and His Successors," in *Life and Literature in the Roman Republic* (Berkeley, 1965; orig. 1930), 106–23, although the extent to which Terence may be credited with advancing the techniques of suspense has been challenged by subsequent scholars.

noted one transient deflection: Lampadio's confusion over the identity of Gymnasium, which is cleared up forthwith. A second interruption follows upon Melaenis's decision to surrender Selenium: Alcesimarchus dashes onto the stage threatening suicide; Selenium, who is now apprised of her circumstances, cries out in alarm, whereupon her lover carries her off into the house they share. Melaenis reacts to this commotion with superb aplomb: She observes that the suicide threat can hardly have been sincere (646), and decides on the spot to follow Alcesimarchus indoors and calm him down by letting him too in on the news.

Lampadio now returns to the stage to report still another difficulty: The old procuress has decided to deny everything. Since the audience knows of Melaenis's plans, the delay is inconsequential. Moreover, he immediately happens upon a little chest lying in the street, which, as Phanostrata instantly perceives, contains the birth tokens of her daughter. Within moments, Halisca, a maidservant of Melaenis, comes out-of-doors searching for the box, which she had dropped during the sudden furor caused by Alcesimarchus. The matter of identity is settled with the mention of the name of Halisca's mistress: Melaenis (773). In what is now the final act, Demipho himself turns up, confirms with Lampadio the rumors he has heard that his daughter has been found and joins the others in the house of Selenium and Alcesimarchus. This exchange, together with the concluding address to the audience by the troop of actors who announce the end of the drama and solicit applause, occupies all of fourteen lines.

The last scene is so brief as to seem perfunctory, and as Walther Ludwig, for example, has argued, Plautus may have drastically condensed a more substantial finale which stood in the Greek model from which the *Cistellaria* was adapted, Menander's *Synaristosai*.[6] The hasty conclusion, however, is of a piece with the entire denouement beginning with the first entrance of Lampadio. The recognition of Selenium's true identity and her reunion with her lover and her family are managed swiftly and neatly; the few impediments—Lampadio's confusion of Gymnasium with Selenium, the procuress's unaccountable change of heart after she had

[6]Walther Ludwig, "Die plautinische *Cistellaria* und das Verhältnis von Gott und Handlung bei Menander," in Eric G. Turner, ed., *Ménandre* (Geneva, 1970) [Fondation Hardt Entretiens 16], 57–58.

seemed ready to cooperate in the discovery of Melaenis, Halisca's loss of the casket containing Selenium's infant property—are all promptly circumvented, and while they enliven the action, are not permitted to divert the direct and apparently inexorable progress toward the solution of the comedy.[7] Selenium's family history, revealed to the audience in the prologue—a history that seems excessively complicated merely to engineer a recognition scene—is disclosed to the dramatic characters in the finale, and beginning and end together thus provide a frame for the bulk of the action, the middle three-fifths of the play.

Despite the severe damage to the text in the central scenes of the *Cistellaria*, the essential action is clear enough. Alcesimarchus, whom Philip Whaley Harsh describes as "the most violent lover of New Comedy,"[8] refuses to submit to his father's injunctions. But he encounters instead an obstacle from an entirely unexpected quarter: Melaenis herself prohibits the liaison on the grounds of Alcesimarchus's bad faith, without regard for his earnest and even raving protestations and pleas for forgiveness. The first mention of Melaenis's opposition is in the opening scene, when Selenium explains to Gymnasium and her mother: "My mother is now angry at me because I have not returned home to her, now that I have found out that he is going to take a different wife" (101–3). Melaenis too had regarded the bond between Selenium and Alcesimarchus as a permanent and exclusive one, whether legitimized by marriage rites or, as is perhaps more likely given the difference in social caste between the two, continuing as an informal but nonetheless loyal cohabitation.[9] She had, as the prologue informs us, raised her foster daughter well and modestly (*bene ac pudice,* 173) and Alcesimarchus's defection, even under the orders of his father, is taken as an unendurable sign of contempt.

Alcesimarchus himself appears in the beginning of the second act with an aria on the torments of love; the song is pretty and plaintive, but the sentiment is altogether conventional. After a lacuna of

[7]Compare W. Süss, "Zur Cistellaria des Plautus," *Rh. Mus.* 84 (1935), 181–82, on the "drei Aktionen" by which the denouement is achieved.

[8]Philip Whaley Harsh, *A Handbook of Classical Drama* (Stanford, 1944), 352; cf. Süss, 169–70.

[9]Alcesimarchus plainly intends a full marriage, however, despite his father's opposition; cf. Süss, 178–79; Ludwig, 52. The law at Athens concerning marriage with alien women or metics is discussed by Hans Julius Wolff, "Marriage Law and Family Organization in Ancient Athens," *Traditio* 2 (1944), 67–70.

some hundred or more verses, Alcesimarchus reappears with a slave of his, whom he enjoins to revile him (*mala multa dici mihi volo, 233*). The slave requests assurance that he may do so with impunity, and Alcesimarchus replies with an offer of good faith (*Servus: fidem da. Alc.: do, 236*). The master then explains how he has deserted his girlfriend (*amica, 237*), who had sworn a pact with him and proved her good faith (*quae coniurasset mecum et firmasset fidem, 241*). More than this, she had been commended to his care and entrusted to his good faith (*quae mihi esset commendata et meae fide concredita, 245*), was of an age for matrimony, and loved him tenderly (243, 247). The slave castigates him roundly, and recommends he hang himself. The inversion of roles between master and slave is a familiar device of farce on the Roman stage, but it is here employed to exhibit the theme of Alcesimarchus's faithlessness, which he himself acknowledges and desires to expiate.

In the following scene, the beginning of which is missing, Gymnasium has joined Alcesimarchus and his slave. Alcesimarchus, after some sort of appeal to Gymnasium, has begun to behave as a madman, demanding weapons, a horse, and an army. This lapse in sanity is extreme even for the distraught romantics of ancient comedy.[10] I venture to suggest that it is a function of Alcesimarchus's passion, and also of his awareness that the loss of Selenium is his own fault. It is not merely failure, but guilt which deprive him of his reason. He has betrayed his responsibility toward Selenium, and thus his efforts to recover her are blocked not so much by the interdiction of his father, as by an interior doubt about his moral right to have her. Intrigue cannot rescue him from this dilemma, and so there is no room in the *Cistellaria* for the devices of a clever counselor. Alcesimarchus must either earn a reprieve from Se-

[10]The psychology of Alcesimarchus is a legitimate issue for interpretation, because the unusual figure he cuts as a lover is structurally coordinate with features of plot, setting, and characterization which distinguish this play from others in the genre, and such systematic deviation from the norm renders problematic any conventional description of motives. On this matter, see the brief but penetrating comments of Süss, 178–79, who shows that the topics of solidarity among the order of courtesans (*meretrices*) and Melaenis's resentment of Alcesimarchus correspond functionally to Alcesimarchus's unique behavior among comic inamorati. Wolf Friedrich, *Euripides und Diphilos* (Munich, 1953) [Zetemata 5], emphasizes the intimate connection between plot and character, in his superb analysis of Menander's *Perikeiromene;* for example: "Auch in dieser Beziehung stellen Handlung und Charakter eine unlösbare Einheit dar." (In this respect too plot and character form an indissociable unity, 163.)

pudiated for the Lemnian wife as soon as personal friction arose between them. Despite the inequality between rich and poor before the law, however, she determines to protect her daughter. The scene ends with Melaenis gripped by fear and anxiety, as she catches sight of Lampadio bustling onto the stage (534–35).

In his excellent essay, "Die plautinische *Cistellaria* und das Verhältnis von Gott und Handlung bei Menander," Walther Ludwig has observed that there are two strands to the plot of the *Cistellaria:* "One strand comprises the romantic action. Alcesimarchus is in love and Selenium requites his love—not in the manner of a courtesan." Ludwig then explains the insufficiency of this union: "The two lovers have met despite the conventional opposition of both the father of Alcesimarchus and of Melaenis, and thus without the benefit of legal matrimony and the consent of their relatives; therefore, their bond remains precarious and provisional. The recognition plot was developed," he continues, "separate and independent from the romantic plot, in order that their relationship could be confirmed by a legally and socially appropriate marriage between citizens."[12] Ludwig has anticipated my analysis of the play into two primary story lines, and his recognition plot and romantic plot correspond, broadly speaking, to my division between the frame and the heart or center of the drama. In accord with the common fate of pioneering studies, however, I shall pay honor to Ludwig's paper by articulating the divergence between his interpretation and my own. The essential difference is best revealed by the coupling, in Ludwig's exposition, of Alcesimarchus's father and Melaenis as blocking figures whose common opposition requires the recognition. For me, it is precisely the distinct role of each of these personalities which defines the two thematic and dramatic movements of the *Cistellaria*. The love between Alcesimarchus and Selenium is not, on this analysis, an independent development. It is rather the impulse entailed in the very idea of an obstacle. In every comedy in which parents—usually the father of the young man—are opposed to an alliance of their child, typically on the grounds of a status barrier, there exists a tension between youthful passion and the claims of convention, and within this single tension we may conceptually distinguish a romantic motif, which will be more or less elaborated in dramatic scenes and cantica, from the recognition

[12]Ludwig, 65–66.

lenium and her mother, or obliterate his guilty conscience in a spell of madness, in which he can imagine seizing the girl without regard for right or consequence. When he returns to his senses, Gymnasium advises him to petition the mercy of Melaenis. After this Alcesimarchus's father arrives for the interview with Gymnasium, mentioned above, in which she impersonates Selenium, and declares her love for Alcesimarchus. Some further action ensues involving Gymnasium's mother and very likely other characters as well, although the condition of the text renders interpretation altogether insecure. The theme of Melaenis's opposition, which dominates the central scenes of the *Cistellaria* and is framed by the recognition plot, culminates in the confrontation between Melanenis and Alcesimarchus.

The contention between Alcesimarchus and Melaenis revolves entirely about the issue of his bad faith (Selenium herself may be present at the beginning of the exchange, but there is considerable doubt about which lines, if any, are to be assigned to her).[11] He is accused of perjury, deceit, and breach of promise (*peiiuriis,* 454; *verba dare,* 459; *frangant foedera,* 460). He offers his oath (*ius iurandum,* 470), but Melaenis is chary of it (471–72); neither will his punishment win her pardon. He has been false and faithless (*falsum fallis . . .* [] *fides,* 483); if he has deceived her once, he shall not do so a second time (484). She may be poor, but no one will ever reproach her word (*hau metuo ne ius iurandum nostrum quisquam culpitet,* 495). "Will you suffer me to perjure myself?" Alcesimarchus exclaims. "Rather more readily," replies Melaenis, "than the ruin of myself and my fortune, and my daughter mocked. Go, find some extra help for your oath (*quaere ubi iuri iurando tuo sit satias supsidi,* 502); here, with us, Alcesimarchus, you have lost your credit" (500–503). When Melaenis remains obstinate, Alcesimarchus resorts to imprecations and threats—violent, confused, and disordered—which anticipate his wildness in the later scene, in which he returns with plans of suicide and finally abducts Selenium into the house he has provided for her. Melaenis muses briefly on her predicament, reflecting that even if she yielded, Selenium would continue to be at Alcesimarchus's mercy, to be re-

[11]A full discussion is in Ludwig, 59–64; Selenium's presence in the scene is ascribed to Plautus. F. H. Sandbach, one of the discussants of Ludwig's contribution to the conference, agrees (97).

plot, whereby the lovers are united in such a way as to satisfy the requirements of the elders. Such is the form of Terence's *Andria*, for example, which is also based on an original by Menander, and with which Plautus's *Cistellaria* is frequently compared.

Alcesimarchus's passion for Selenium, the objections of his father, who demands that the boy take a suitable wife, and the mistaken identity by which conflicting desires are reconciled are thus all features of a single narrative structure and pertain collectively to the frame of the *Cistellaria*. Dramatically, however, this movement of the comedy is exceptionally bland: The first act consists mostly of an exposition of Selenium's circumstances, while the conclusion represents, as we have seen, the straightforward discovery of the relevant facts by each of the concerned agents. For subtlety of plot or characterization, "the scenes of actual solution" are, as Harsh has complained, "extraordinarily ineffective."[13] All the scenes involving Alcesimarchus himself, and thus those in which his amorous intensity is exhibited, occur in the interior movement of the play, where the immediate problem is not the hostility of his father, but of Melaenis. This is why the tension between Alcesimarchus and Melaenis appears as the emotional center of the play, the essence of the drama to which the recognition motif stands as a vessel.

The shift to Melaenis as a major blocking figure, perhaps the major figure of the comedy, within the framework of a conventional recognition story is an unusual and significant move. The prejudice of Alcesimarchus's father against the liaison with Selenium is understandable. Partly it is a matter of class and politics: Marriage could be a vehicle of wealth and influence. But it is also, as we know, a social issue, whose roots reach down to the constitutive principles of the community. If the law of Sicyon, where the action is located, was like that of Athens, where the original Greek drama was undoubtedly performed, then there could be no regular conjugal ties between a citizen and a courtesan like Selenium.[14] If the world of the *Cistellaria* is like that of new comedy in general, then the father's concern is not just for a favorable but a legitimate match for his son and heirs of citizen status. As we have seen, some

[13]Harsh, 353.

[14]There seems to be no conclusive evidence on the point: Claude Vatin, *Recherches sur le mariage et la condition de la femme mariée à l'époque hellénistique* (Paris, 1970), mentions only that marriages between Athenians and Sicyonians are attested for the second century B.C. (125).

ambiguity about the matter exists in our play, since Alcesimarchus apparently intended to make Selenium his wife, and the scene may have been laid in Sicyon precisely in order to blur the sharp boundaries that divided the orders at Athens.[15] However this may be, the old man's resistance is well grounded in comic conventions of the ancient theater, and the normal solution to such a standoff between father and son was the anagnorisis or recognition. The opposition of Melaenis, however, represents an entirely different point of view, and one that questions the basis of the father's judgment. She regards the moral commitment of a citizen-lad to her foster daughter as binding despite the difference of social class. Her appeal to *fides,* good faith, invokes the fundamental concept of personal obligation among members of the ancient Roman community (the Greek was doubtless *pistis*). For Melaenis, the sin of Alcesimarchus consists in his neglect of his oath, and his guilt is not diminished by her inferior status or his father's contrary mandate. To be sure, she has no power to compel Alcesimarchus to honor his word; this is the cause of her anxiety for the future of Selenium. But she can and does decline any further association with him on the basis of so contingent a fidelity. Though she knows that she is not the social equal of Alcesimarchus, she will not allow him to use her in a way unbecoming to a citizen. Melaenis is the voice, rarely heard in ancient new comedy, of the outsider, the disfranchised, and she asserts with sober dignity her title to respect.

The discovery of Selenium's true parents, which abolishes the conflict between Alcesimarchus and his father, also solves the problem represented by Melaenis's opposition, but in a significantly different way. It becomes irrelevant whether Melaenis is reconciled to the union of her foster daughter with the impetuous Alcesimarchus, since, after the discovery, responsibility for Selenium no longer rests with her. Even in the denouement however, she is permitted to preserve her pride. After Lampadio has located the old

[15]W. Süss, "Nochmals zur Cistellaria des Plautus," *Rh. Mus.* 87 (1938), 104–5, cites the proverbially wild and ineffectual character of the Sicyonians and suggests that the location of the action is intended to correspond with the characterization of Alcesimarchus. Menander may also have exploited the Sicyonian setting to allow the legitimacy of Demipho's second marriage; a union between a Lemnian and an Athenian woman would normally have been quite impossible at this period. Once again, this is not necessarily testimony concerning the legal state of affairs at Sicyon; it may simply be that Menander could expect an Athenian audience to be relatively vague or unconcerned about such arrangements outside of Attica.

procuress, drawn from her the name of Melaenis, and arranged for the final identification, there is a sudden hitch in the plot: The procuress, it will be recalled, abruptly refuses to cooperate, and Melaenis herself, who has overheard Lampadio's report to his mistress, elects to surrender Selenium for the girl's own benefit. It is a noble act. Melaenis knows that, as a full citizen and daughter of a wealthy family, Selenium will enjoy a security which her foster mother cannot afford her. Demipho's child will be immune to the kind of arbitrary rejection that the daughter of Melaenis must fear. But even though Melaenis acknowledges the advantages of citizen status, the question posed by her stand against Alcesimarchus is not thereby answered. The interior movement of the *Cistellaria* culminates in an unreconciled opposition between Alcesimarchus's desire and Melaenis's sense of dignity. The oaths foresworn blight the faith of Alcesimarchus in the eyes of the elder courtesan. Comedy demands a happy conclusion, but the agony of Alcesimarchus and the moral superiority of Melaenis reecho across the mechanical denouement.[16]

Melaenis's stand on the rights and character of her class is pointedly different from the position of her friend, the old procuress, and her daughter Gymnasium. The two pairs, Selenium and her mother, Gymnasium and hers, are contrasted in the opening scene. The procuress observes: "Because we are freedwomen, your mother and I, we became courtesans; she raised you, and I this one here,

[16]Süss (above, n. 15), 134, observes too that the recognition scene provides only a formal conclusion rather than an inner and necessary closure to the plot. He goes on to argue ingeniously that Menander, with some help from Plautus, did everything to represent Alcesimarchus's suit for Selenium as an actual petition for marriage: He applies formally for her hand (vv. 98–99); Melaenis is treated as a *kyrios* or guardian; Selenium is the holder of the key to the house she shares with Alcesimarchus; his gift of gold and garments (487) is in the nature of a betrothal present; the pair have been carnally associated; and finally, Alcesimarchus carries Selenium over the threshold (this is Plautus's hand, for the custom is Roman, not Greek) when he seizes her and dashes into the house (136–38). These features, which surprised Süss himself (135), should not, I think, be taken to mean that Menander has stretched the legal limits on marriage for the purpose of his play; the recognition scene and its preparation, as we have observed, are no small part of the action, and their significance must not be unduly diminished. What is more, Melaenis's insecurity about the relationship between Selenium and Alcesimarchus is due precisely to a recognized marriage being out of the question. Süss's observations do, nevertheless, suggest ways in which the interior movement—as I have called it—of the *Cistellaria* is endowed with something of the weight or dignity of the marriage comedy proper, and why it is that Melaenis's opposition may seem equivalent, as Ludwig took it to be, to that of Alcesimarchus's father.

from chance fathers." She goes on to explain the reasons why she brought her daughter into her own trade: "It was not out of arrogance that I pushed her into the courtesan business, but just so I wouldn't starve." Selenium demurs: "It would have been better to give her in marriage to a man," to which the bawd replies: "Whoa! she marries a man every day, by God, married one today, will marry again this evening. I've never permitted her to sleep without a husband. Why, if she didn't marry, my family would sadly die of famine" (38–45). We have seen that the procuress considers it a mistake for Melaenis to have permitted her daughter to associate with only one man (78–86). More than this, she generalizes the contrast between her own values and those of Melaenis into a conflict between two social classes and two ways of life. She gives as her reason for coming to the assistance of Selenium the necessity for solidarity among the orders: "It is absolutely right, my Selenium, for our order to act with mutual help and loyalty, when you see women of the finest birth, the topmost women of standing (*matronas,* 25), cultivating loyalty and maintaining its tight bonds among them. If we did the same, if we imitated them, nevertheless we would hardly survive with such intense hostility" (22–28).

When the procuress speaks of her class or order (in Latin, *ordo*), in contrast to the caste of married women or matrons, there is a certain breadth or latitude to the category. Most narrowly, her reference is to the professional courtesans, *meretrices* in Latin or *hetairai* in Greek, who earned their livelihood by the commerce of their bodies. In Athenian society, where citizen-women were largely confined to the domestic quarters of the house and denied access to political life or a liberal education, the *hetairai* were drawn from the class of resident aliens or metics, who were without civic rights and could not aspire to a legitimate marriage with a citizen but led a relatively more free existence and could sometimes achieve considerable distinction in wit, skill, and grace. At its most debased, such a life was comparable to the meanest prostitution, but fortune might equip the lucky for a lifelong companionship in love and common temper with a man of high stature in the community. The range of relationships is illustrated well in Menander's *Samia,* where Demeas threatens Chrysis, the woman with whom he has shared his house for years, with a life of pain and humiliation as the price of her suspected infidelity: "In the city you will now see exactly who you are. It's not in your style, Chrysis, the courtesans

making a mere ten drachmai running to dinners and drinking hard wine until they die, or starving if they won't do it promptly and eagerly. You will learn this as well as anyone else, I'm sure, and will know just what you were when you wronged me" (390–97).[17] At one extreme, the common whore (in Greek, *pornē*); at the other, the *pallakē,* who could share all but the formal name of wife— "concubine" is the altogether inadequate term that is used to render the notion. The relationship of Selenium and Alcesimarchus comes under this description. Selenium herself is a *hetaira* less by profession than by association; her aspiration, shared by Alcesimarchus, is for a legitimate union, or, at the very least, a stable one. That such a union is foreclosed to her is less a consequence of her métier than it is of her social status: She is not a citizen. A lawful marriage, with the rights of inheritance entailed thereby, is out of the question. What may seem a matter of social prejudice against a woman of humble origins and dubious milieu is inextricably bound up with status distinctions inscribed in law. *Hetairai* are drawn solely from the noncitizen order; citizens alone may contract recognized marriages. There is a blurring of borders here, such that the tension between married women and women of pleasure overlaps with the broader problem of relations between the status groups of citizen and resident alien.[18] As the procuress says of the matrons: "They claim that we cohabit with their husbands, say that we are their concubines, move to suppress us" (36–37). The obverse of this attitude among the citizen males is represented by the father of Alcesimarchus in his lewd appraisal of Gymnasium (whom he has mistaken for Selenium): "Even though I'm an old gelding, even now, I think, I could give a whinny to this little filly, if I could have her one on one" (307–8).

Given this polarization between the images of the citizen-woman

[17]Compare Wolff, 73–74; for a general review of the status of *pallakē* or "concubine," see Hans Julius Wolff, "Die Grundlagen des griechischen Eherechts," *Tijdschrift voor Rechtsgeschiedenis* 20 (1952), 644–46, and Douglas M. MacDowell, *The Law in Classical Athens* (Ithaca, N.Y., 1978), 89. Also useful are Jean-Pierre Vernant's chapters "Le mariage" and "Entre bêtes et dieux," in *Mythe et société en Grèce ancienne* (Paris, 1974), esp. 60–61 and 150; Eugene W. Bushala, "The 'Pallake' of Philoneus," *AJP* 90 (1969), 65–72.

[18]The extent to which the strict distinction between aliens and resident aliens, or metics, was maintained in the time of Menander is uncertain. See David Whitehead, *The Ideology of the Athenian Metic* (Cambridge, 1977) [Cambridge Philological Society Supplementary Vol. 4], 163–67, for a review of the available evidence.

destined for a single lifelong bond of marriage and the alien, who at least to the extent that she entertains relations with citizen-males is regarded as improper, we may reformulate the disequilibrium or narrative tension that generates the plot of the *Cistellaria*. Consistent with the prevailing pattern of new comedy, I have so far interpreted the recognition scene as a solution to the problem of Alcesimarchus's passion for Selenium. But it may also be construed as a resolution of the anomaly between Selenium's character and her social status. She thinks and behaves as a citizen. The revelation of her proper lineage is the social correlative of her inner nature; Selenium proves in fact to be of the class for which she is fitted by feeling.[19] Her marriage to Alcesimarchus follows automatically as the appropriate fate of a citizen-woman. So understood, the outer plot of the *Cistellaria* works something like the fairy tale of the princess and the pea, in which the heroine's uncanny sensitivity to a minute bump in her mattresses corresponds to and confirms her royal blood. Distinctions of caste are represented as grounded in nature. The conclusion of the *Cistellaria* corroborates the view of the old procuress, for Selenium proves to have been only an apparent exception. If she did not confirm to the mores of her order, it was because in fact she belonged to another. The ideology of such stories is essentially conservative, in that inherited social divisions are sustained and vindicated.

The role of Melaenis in the play challenges and transcends this comfortable ideology in a way that I am moved to compare with the Book of Job, where the conventional wisdom about the rewards of virtue and piety that informs the prose frame of the story is shattered by the interior verses in which Job steadfastly denies the justice of his torments. Melaenis's liberal aspirations for her foster daughter, her defense of Selenium's dignity and security against the impulsive but unreliable love of Alcesimarchus undermine the contrast between the orders. It is not so much that the barrier to marriage between citizens and outsiders is in question here—although such an inference from the text is not insupportable—but rather that any relations between the orders must be predicated on good faith and respect for the common values of both. The profession of the procuress and her daughter is a matter of choice, not class. Melaenis has raised Selenium by a different standard, and

[19]Cf. Süss (above, n. 7), 161; Ludwig (above, n. 6), 52.

insists it be respected. That Selenium turns out to be a citizen is from this point of view a fortuitous event, which salvages her affair with Alcesimarchus but evades the issue of morality between the classes which is the key to Melaenis's actions in the play.

The contrast in theme between the recognition plot or frame of the *Cistellaria* and the panels involving Melaenis and Alcesimarchus is visible also in a remarkable formal analogy between the history of Alcesimarchus's affair with Selenium and the career of Selenium's father, Demipho. I mentioned earlier that the story used to engineer the discovery is curiously complicated. The plot alone would have been served well enough had Selenium simply been lost or abducted or exposed for reasons of which the father later repented, without the incidental episode of Demipho's Lemnian wife and daughter. This episode finds its place, however, as a counterpart to a parallel feature in Alcesimarchus's tale. We may recall that Demipho originally raped Phanostrata, a Sicyonian woman, during the festival known as the Dionysia (156); similarly, the association between Alcesimarchus and Selenium, again a Sicyonian, had its start at an encounter during the Dionysia (89). This affair is threatened when Alcesimarchus's father orders him to marry a Lemnian relative (100); to this corresponds the marriage between Demipho and the Lemnian woman, who was likewise a relation of his (174). Finally, Demipho returns to Sicyon after the death of his Lemnian wife and weds Phanostrata, just as Alcesimarchus in the end will marry Selenium. A relationship which had its source in passion is in each case vindicated against a practical and socially respectable marriage. There is one further aspect to the symmetry: The girl Alcesimarchus loves is the issue of the first passion of Demipho; the girl he is obliged to marry is the daughter of Demipho and his Lemnian wife (600–602). The very symmetry between the two, however, highlights the differences. Ludwig has observed the contrast between Demipho's abuse of a citizen and Alcesimarchus's loyalty to a courtesan.[20] Alcesimarchus's feeling for Selenium was never mere lust; he aspired to a deep and enduring liaison, and was prepared to put aside the wife his father had chosen for him for the sake of his mistress. Yet despite his callousness, Demipho can ultimately legitimize his bond with Phanostrata precisely because she is a citizen, while Selenium must always remain

[20]Ludwig, 48.

at the mercy of Alcesimarchus's pleasure. Alcesimarchus's very devotion puts the problem of relations among the orders in its sharpest form: Citizens must be scrupulously honest with outsiders, for the very reason that they have no legal redress. Alcesimarchus cannot afford to have faltered, for Melaenis is not disposed to give him a second opportunity.

When Demipho raped and then abandoned Phanostrata, he effectively precipitated her from the class of eligible citizen-women, according to the conventions of ancient comedy.[21] Thus her status became essentially like that of the resident aliens, so far as relations with members of the polity is concerned. Her daughter would be subject to the same liability, and thus her adoption by Melaenis is in a sense a symbol of the moral position of the girl. The subsequent marriage of Phanostrata and Demipho, who alone might redeem the woman's position, restores legitimacy to Selenium and is thus the condition for her achievement of full citizenship. Demipho and Alcesimarchus work in opposite directions: The one reduced the status of a citizen by treating her as an object of violent passion; the other elevated a courtesan by the promise of a legitimate or at least permanent union. Both may be construed as transgressing the protocols that define the orders. This parallel once more exhibits the offense implicit in the vows of Alcesimarchus: The victim is Selenium, and Melaenis is right to insist on absolute personal fidelity as the condition of any bond between the two.

In the above interpretation of the *Cistellaria*, I have argued that the moral center of the play is Melaenis's demand for respect and good faith. The social boundaries that divide the orders do not sanction abuse or contempt for the courtesans. Within the framework of a conventional comic story, in which the class obstacle to true love is overcome by the trick of a discovery of identity, there is introduced a second motif and a massive shift in perspective. The locus of tension moves from the conflict between young love and the sober propriety of an elder citizen to a conflict between the passion of a young citizen and the rights and needs of the socially

[21]The convention is that a man marries only a virgin, or a woman whom he himself has previously violated. This is not quite an absolute rule for the genre, as is sometimes supposed; in the *Truculentus,* the daughter of Callicles, who had borne a child to Diniarchus, was subsequently betrothed to another man (848–49); that engagement, however, is abrogated and Diniarchus assumes his responsibilities to the woman.

disadvantaged woman he has seduced. The breadth of vision or sympathy expressed in the *Cistellaria* is not surprising in Menander: the *Samia*, for example, testifies to his humane appreciation of an enduring bond between an old man and his concubine, to whom he is persuaded to grant the prerogative of a legitimate wife when he imagines that she has nursed a child of his without his permission (130ff.; note the phrase *gametēn hetairan*, 130, meaning "courtesan wife").[22]

Among the plays of Plautus, however, the *Cistellaria* is unusual both for the form of the plot—often taken as characteristic of new comedy in general, in which a recognition scene clears the way for marriage—and for the thematic concern with the courtesan class. Rome, of course, had nothing corresponding to the vast population or metics or resident aliens at Athens, and so the question of their sensibilities was not likely to preoccupy the Roman stage. The Latin allies of the Romans, however, occupied an ambiguous or halfway status which might pose problems of ideology or sentiment not entirely dissimilar to those of the Athenian metics. Moreover, during the difficult years of the second Punic war, when the *Cistellaria* was performed, the loyalty of the allies was a delicate and urgent matter. While they did not have the rights of Roman citizens, which would only be won at arms more than a century later, they had a strong moral claim to fair and honorable treatment at the hands of the Romans which the threat of Hannibal made a matter of immediate practical as well as ethical concern. In Plautus's *Cistellaria*, the name of the god who speaks the prologue is Auxilium, a common noun meaning "help" or "aid." It has been speculated that this is a translation of the Greek Boētheia, who would have played the role in the Menandrian original of our play.[23] This may be so, but nothing in the drama suggests that a deity of succour has any special relevance to the action, and external evidence is

[22]The oxymoron ("a paradoxical contradiction in terms," comments Sandbach, in A. W. Gomme and F. H. Sandbach, *Menander: A Commentary* [Oxford, 1973]), indicates clearly that the boundary between courtesan and wife, between *meretrix* and *matrona*, is not merely one of mores but of status. For a full discussion of this and related questions of Attic law, see Martina, 853–58, 876–78.

[23]Ludwig, 53–54, 68–70; compare also Karlhans Abel, *Die Plautusprologe* (Frankfurt am Main, 1955) [Diss. Goethe-Universität], 63. Süss (above, n. 7), 164, argues that the connection between Auxilium and *auxilia* can scarcely be coincidental; he cites the role of Fides in the *Casina* to show that Plautus will employ allegorical figures which in the Greek original had no particular connection with the plot (165).

altogether wanting. In Plautus's version, however, there is a pun that motivates or at least exploits the particular personification. The prologue concludes with a direct address to the audience exhorting them to success in the current war: "Be well and conquer with true courage, as you have before. Preserve your allies, old and new, and augment your auxiliaries with your just laws. Destroy your enemies, win praise and victory, so that the conquered Phoenicians may suffer punishment at your hands" (197–202). The Latin word for auxiliaries is *auxilia*, the troops drawn from allied populations who fought alongside the citizen legions. Plautus several times encouraged his fellow citizens in the struggle against the Carthaginians, as in the prologues to the *Asinaria* (14–15), the *Captivi* (67–68), the *Rudens* (82), and the *Casina* (87–88), which shares a line with the prologue delivered by Auxilium (*Cas.* 88 = *Cist.* 198). Only in the *Cistellaria,* however, is there any mention of the auxiliaries.

At the climax of Melaenis's confrontation with Alcesimarchus is, I believe, still another allusion to the allied soldiers. Melaenis dismisses Alcesimarchus's appeal for mercy with the words: *"abi, quaere ubi iuri iurando tuo sit satias supsidi"* (502). I have translated the verse as follows: "Go, find some extra help for your oath." The word for "help"—*supsidium,* or in the classical orthography, *subsidium*—again is a standard term for reserves or auxiliaries among the legions, and the somewhat strange locution, "sufficiency of help" (*satias supsidi*), betrays, I think, a still living military metaphor. Having lost his credibility, Alcesimarchus must go in search of other allies.

One cannot convincingly point to a specific crisis between Rome and her allies which might have motivated Plautus's reference in the prologue, and hence one cannot say that Plautus chose the name Auxilium or Menander's *Synaristosai* as his model for the sake of a didactic message. What we may more safely infer is that Plautus perceived the moral significance of Melaenis's role in the Greek play he elected to adapt, and that in the prologue he took the opportunity to exhibit the relevance of its theme to an abiding issue of Roman social relations.

Phormio

Citizen Disorder

Terence particularly favored such plots as the frame story in *Cistellaria,* based on the elementary triangle of stubborn father, enamored son, and maiden apparently ineligible for marriage. Thus R. H. Martin remarks, in the introduction to his excellent school edition of the *Phormio:*

> The following elements of plot are found in all Terence's plays except the *Hecyra*. Two young men, often brothers, are engaged in love affairs. One of them loves a courtesan, the other wishes to marry a young woman, who is either poor but freeborn, or ostensibly a courtesan. The father opposes his son's marriage or even wants him instead to marry the daughter of a friend or relation. The young woman turns out to be freeborn or the daughter in question, and all ends well.[1]

In a general way, the *Phormio* may be seen to fit this pattern. Antipho is in love with and, in his father's absence, has actually married a poor young woman called Phanium; his father, Demipho, is opposed to the match, because he intends the boy to marry his niece, the daughter of his brother Chremes; by means of a recognition scene, it is discovered that the niece is none other than Phanium, Antipho's bride, thereby bringing about the congruence of the father's wishes with the son's.

A closer look at the structure of the *Phormio,* however, questions

[1] *Terence: Phormio* (London, 1959), 3.

the simplicity of this analysis. For the play falls into two distinct parts or movements, each of which appears to have its own theme and resolution. The two parts are joined by an elegant turn of the plot, and in their synthesis the proper significance of the *Phormio* emerges.

From a conversation between two slaves, Geta and Davus, we learn at the beginning of the play that the girl with whom Antipho has become infatuated is an Athenian citizen (114). As a result, he is unable to arrange the kind of irregular liaison that might have been formed with a woman of inferior status. He is obliged, if he will have her, to take her as his wife, but recognizes in her poverty a social barrier his father will not ignore. As Geta says: "Would he give him a maiden dowerless and common? Never!" (*ille indotatam virginem atque ignobilem daret illi? numquam faceret*, 120–21). Since it was scarcely possible for an Athenian youth to marry against the wishes of his father—while at Rome, it was entirely out of the question, since the boy would be *in patria potestate*, in the power of his father, and therefore without the status of a person before the law—it was necessary to devise a stratagem that would prevent Demipho from anulling the arrangement upon his return. This purpose is accomplished according to the advice of Phormio, who plays a role technically known as a parasite, that is, a free man of no property who lives by his wits at the expense of others.[2] Phormio's scheme is to pass himself off as a friend of the girl's father, who had been, he will allege, a relative of Demipho's; according to Attic law, the nearest kin is obliged to marry an orphaned maiden, or provide five hundred drachmae for her dowry.[3]

The action begins when Geta announces to the fainthearted Antipho and his cousin, Phaedria, the imminent arrival of Demipho.

[2]For a summary description of the parasite, and his status in Greek society, see J. O. Lofberg, "The Sycophant-Parasite," *CP* 15 (1920), 61–72, esp. 68–72 on the *Phormio*, and the same author's "Phormio and 'Art for Art's Sake,'" *CW* 22 (1929), 183–84. With Phormio's description of the nature and advantages of his position at 330–45, one may compare the encyclopedic collection of passages in Athenaeus's *Deipnosophistae* 6.235e–248c.

[3]On the law, see A. R. W. Harrison, *The Law of Athens*, vol. 1: *Family and Property* (Oxford, 1968), 9–12, 132–38. The sum of five minae (= 500 drachmae) was set for the wealthiest class of citizens (Demosthenes 43.54), to which Demipho obviously belongs. Eckard Lefèvre, *Der Phormio des Terenz und der Epidikazomenos des Apollodor von Karystos* (Munich, 1978 [Zetemata 74]), 9–15, argues plausibly that in the Greek original Antipho does not marry Phanium at this point, but merely obtains (or seeks to obtain, pp. 23–24) a judgment from the archon that he must do so.

Antipho flees in panic, and Geta and Phaedria are left to handle his defense. Their argument is well rehearsed: Antipho's natural modesty tied his tongue in court; Geta, as a slave, was unable to testify; neither had the resources to raise or borrow the money necessary to provide a dowry and wed the girl to some other suitor. Finally, Demipho demands an interview with Phormio himself. Phormio is in no way daunted by Demipho and the three elders he brings with him as witnesses and counselors; he refuses to discuss the case, reminding Demipho that the law does not allow double jeopardy (403–6).[4] The ruse thus proves entirely successful, and with it the plot is brought to a stalemate. Demipho is trapped, so long as Phormio refuses to negotiate. The action is set in motion again through a subplot involving an affair of Phaedria's with a lute girl called Pamphila. Before examining this transition, we may review the basic elements in the first movement of the comedy.

The issue that divides father and son is one of social class or caste. When Demipho denies any connection or acquaintance with Phanium's father, Phormio rejoins: "Really? Aren't you ashamed? But if he had left an estate of ten talents, you'd promptly summon up your lineage mindfully all the way back to your grandfather and greatgrandfather" (392–95). The theme is familiar in new comedy, and central to such plays as Menander's *Samia* and Terence's *Adelphoe*.

The prejudice of the father and the passion of the son are essentially correlative motives. Demipho endorses a customary exclusiveness; Antipho's desire, like that of young men generally in the comic tradition, is heedless of status and defies the respect for

[4]The sources for this rule are collected in A. R. W. Harrison, *The Law of Athens,* vol. 2: *Procedure* (Oxford, 1971), 119 n.3. Among the texts cited is a speech by Demosthenes in behalf of Phormio, a former slave of the banker Pasio who, upon the instructions of the latter, married his widow and assumed the guardianship of his younger son. We know from Donatus that the parasite in Apollodorus's original also bore the name Phormio. Had Apollodorus, who appears to have been exceptionally careful with legal and other details of plot construction, checked Demosthenes' oration for the point of law when he was composing his *Epidikazomenos?* For other interpretations of the possible significance of the name Phormio, see James Curtiss Austin, *The Significant Name in Terence,* University of Illinois Studies in Language and Literature 7.4 (1921), 34–37. Lefèvre, 15–17, attributes this entire scene to Terence, since the procedure of *restitutio in integrum* was Roman rather than Greek, and may have been introduced by a praetor's edict shortly before the original performance of Terence's *Phormio.* I am inclined to believe that some version of this confrontation between Phormio and Demipho occurred in the Greek original.

conventional boundaries characteristic of the older generation. The dramatic function of passion is thus determined in relation to the particular norms that contain it, here the restrictions pertaining to class, represented by Demipho. This relationship between the father and son is captured in their names: Demipho suggests something like "voice of the people," Antipho, "voice of the opposition." In general, names with the root *dēm,* meaning "the people" or "the community," are reserved for figures of authority.[5] Put another way, we may say that while love is a personal emotion, it acts in tension with a social code, and this polarity of rule and passion constitutes the theme of the play.

Phormio's cunning abuse of the law relating to orphaned women succeeds, as we have seen, in baffling Demipho. In effect, Antipho has triumphed over his father, achieving the union he desires in spite of his father's opposition. But this victory does not furnish a comic closure. Ordinarily, in new comedy, the point is not the mere discomfiture of the paterfamilias and his conservative ideals. Rather, the denouement reestablishes the harmony of the group, reconciling the interests of father and son. Without this harmony, Antipho's success appears not as a resolution of the tension but as a standoff, demanding some further action or revelation to complete the story. Let us consider, moreover, the ways in which the complication might be satisfactorily resolved. We usually think of the recognition scene as the favored device in situations of this sort: Unexpected tokens or testimony reveal the eligibility of the girl. But in fact this means is normal only in questions of citizenship or civic status. Where the obstacle is simply a matter of wealth, the reconciliation was conventionally achieved through a change of heart or a revelation of true feelings in the blocking character. In Menander's *Samia,* for example, where a young man has had a child by the daughter of a humble neighbor, it turns out that the two fathers had independently decided to arrange the match between them. In Terence's *Adelphoe,* based on a play by Menander, Micio insists that his son meet his responsibilities by marrying the

[5]"The name was common in Greece, and in comedy used exclusively of old men," Austin, 33. The element *-pho* in the names Demipho and Antipho is not related etymologically to the word *phōnē,* but "it is not impossible that by a folk-etymology the *-phōn* was associated with *phōnē* by similarity of sound, at least, if the root meaning was lost, and the name Antipho might have suggested 'Contradicens' to those of the audience who knew some Greek," Austin, 31.

impoverished young woman who has borne his child.[6] The difference in the treatment of themes of class and citizenship reflects the ideology of the classical city-state. The discriminations that separate members of the community from outsiders—whether strangers, slaves, resident aliens, or otherwise illegitimate or disfranchised individuals—were sanctified by law and custom, and their abrogation was a serious matter.[7] Divisions based on wealth, on the other hand, were felt to strike at the solidarity of the community and were therefore regarded as the baleful effects of prejudice and greed. Their proper resolution is thus alteration of character or opinion. To reveal a poor citizen as an heiress or heir would imply that boundaries of class are in principle absolute and unbridgeable, like the boundaries that delimit the community, and this would be incompatible with the spirit of civic unity that reigns in comedy. In the *Phormio,* as we shall see, the problem assumes an entirely different form because of the supervention of the second movement of the play.

The argument we have been analyzing occupies the first two acts into which the *Phormio* is conventionally divided. Geta had indicated, in his conversation with Davus, that Phaedria had conceived a passion for a lute girl while his father, Chremes, the brother of Demipho, was abroad. In the third act we learn that Pamphila's master, Dorio, has sold her to a foreign soldier, but if Phaedria can raise the sum of thirty minae within a day, he can preempt the contract (531–33; 557). In the fourth act, Phormio rises once more to the occasion by pretending that he will marry Phanium himself if Demipho will provide a dowry of thirty minae. This sum he will lend to Phaedria, until the lad can collect the like amount from his friends (703). Then he will return both the money and the girl to Demipho on the pretext that the omens are against the marriage, thereby saving at a single stroke Antipho his bride and Phaedria his concubine. The transfer of the money to Phormio is accomplished by the beginning of Act V.

The second stage of the intrigue occupies a considerable part of the action in the *Phormio* (all of Act III; Act IV except for the first

[6]The status barrier in Terence's *Andria,* which is resolved by an *anagnorisis* (908), was converted into a class barrier by Richard Steele, in his adaptation of Terence's play entitled *The Conscious Lovers.* The communal spirit of ancient new comedy was no longer vital in the drama of eighteenth-century England.

[7]See Harrison, vol. 1, 24–29.

scene; and four scenes—two through five, omitting an intercalary scene following number three—in the final act). Nevertheless, Phaedria's affair remains a subplot rather than a second plot for two reasons. First, it never achieves the confrontation and resolution that occur between Antipho and Demipho. Indeed, after the third act, Phaedria disappears from the play. To be sure, he gets his money and his girl, but the machinations in his behalf on the part of Geta and Phormio occur in the new context that arises with the second movement of the play, in which Phaedria's problem is overshadowed by quite different concerns. The subordination of Phaedria's complication is a good illustration of the essentially correlative nature of passion in new comedy: Without an articulated opposition from Chremes, it recedes to an ancillary status in the drama. The second reason is that the exchange of the thirty minae and the right to wed Phanium serve formally to facilitate the second movement, which requires that Demipho and Chremes work to recover the girl for Antipho. We may now examine this unusual conversion of the plot in detail.

In the first scene of the fourth act, it is disclosed, through a dialogue between Chremes, who has just arrived home, and Demipho, that Chremes has been maintaining on the island of Lemnos the daughter of a bigamous marriage.[8] The purpose of his trip was to fetch the girl, since he and his brother have conspired to marry her to Antipho in order to conceal his conduct from his legitimate wife, Nausistrata, whose dowry is the sole source of his wealth (586–87). With this brief conversation, the entire structure of the plot is transformed. Demipho's objection to Phanium is now revealed as unrelated to her poverty; he was not motivated by avarice or class feeling, but by his desire to protect his brother's domestic peace and security. The issue of class was only virtual, based on Antipho's natural assumption that this would be the basis of his father's anger. When it emerges that Demipho's opposition stems not from conventional prejudices but from private contingencies,

[8]Whether this information was disclosed in a prologue in Apollodorus's original must remain moot. Tenney Frank, "Terence's Contribution to Plot-Construction," *AJP* 49 (1928), 321, argued that it was. He has won the assent of most scholars, for example, W. Geoffrey Arnott, "Phormio Parasitus," *Greece and Rome* ser. 2, no. 17 (1970) 39, n. 2; Eckard Lefèvre, *Die Expositionstechnik in den Komödien des Terenz* (Darmstadt, 1969), 82–83; Orazio Bianco, *Terenzio* (Rome, 1962), 170. Contra: Karl Büchner, *Das Theater des Terenz* (Heidelberg, 1974), 356; Martin, 10–11, is doubtful.

the meaning of Antipho's passion is correspondingly reduced from a challenge, albeit personal and accidental, to public norms to a matter of individual disobedience. Thus the issue shifts from social boundaries, which had been represented by parental authority, to authority itself, without that embeddedness in communal values by which it is legitimized. With the disclosure of Demipho's true motives, the play begins anew, because the obstacle has been altered, and the obstacle is the essence of the comic tension. To be sure, Demipho remains the blocking figure, and this sustains the continuity of the narrative, but here we may see once again and most clearly how the conflict in comedy is located not simply in the struggle between the characters but in the complex of values and impulses which they enact.

For the rest of Act IV, Demipho and Chremes continue their efforts to end the marriage between Antipho and Phanium, and finally accede to Phormio's demand for thirty minae as her dowry. However, the change in focus from class division to domestic imbroglio opens the way to a recognition scene, which comes at the beginning of Act V: Chremes encounters Sophrona, the nurse of his Lemnian daughter, and learns that she is the very girl whom Antipho has taken as his wife. Naturally, the brothers make haste to recover the thirty minae, which have already been transferred to Phormio, but the parasite, informed of the circumstances by Geta, sees a way to press his advantage: He will give up his claim to Phanium only on condition that the dowry remain with him, as compensation for the one he lost when he broke off—he pretends— a previous engagement in their behalf (927–29). Phormio's real purpose, as he reveals in an earlier soliloquy, is to relieve Phaedria once and for all of his financial anxieties and to enjoy the utter duping of the two old men (885–86). When the brothers hesitate to concede, Phormio informs them that he is apprised of their secret, and is prepared to reveal it to Chremes' wife. Chremes is inclined to submit, Demipho to resist the extortion, now that the truth is out in any case and must soon reach the ears of Nausistrata. The plot has here arrived at an ambiguous juncture, at which it might develop in either of two ways, depending on whether Chremes and Demipho can come to terms with Phormio. Here, we may evaluate the significance of both the second movement, and the shift in content from the first part to the second, for in this transformation resides the theme of the play as a whole.

The action following the revelation of Phanium's relationship to Chremes has an unusual twist: Father and uncle striving to recover for the son the object of his enamorment. This situation is contrived by the placement of the recognition scene in the subplot: Had it occurred earlier, Chremes and Demipho would still have been in possession of the girl and their money; later, and Phormio's intention to renounce Phanium would have been realized. This inversion of dramatic vectors, in which the two old men suddenly are made to swing round and contend for the girl they have just contrived to be rid of, may be taken as an image of a deeper reversal of roles on the thematic level. Because Demipho and Chremes are abetting a marriage for private rather than social reasons—reasons which they must conceal, for they have their source in a violation of the conjugal code—they are more in the position customarily occupied by the wayward young lover than that of the stern, old-fashioned paterfamilias. This reversal stands out most clearly when we see the play as a whole, projecting the argument of the second movement upon that of the first.

Let us look once more at the characteristic paradigm of ancient new comedy; we have observed that, in the formal pattern of separation and union of lovers structuring virtually every play in the genre, the differentiating principle essentially lies in the nature of the obstacle, and further that this obstacle is best understood as a code of values or motives represented in the blocking character. The opposition of the father, then, is normally predicated on the status rules of the city-state, and the recognition is designed to remove an apparent violation by bringing the woman into the community. In the *Phormio,* however, the discovery of Phanium's identity appears to have the reverse effect. In the first part of the play, where the central issue is class, the citizenship of the girl is not in doubt. But in the second part, when she is revealed as the illegitimate daughter of Chremes' Lemnian mistress, Phanium's civic status would seem most precarious. In real life, of course, her citizenship would be crucial, since she would, at Athens or at Rome, be ineligible for connubial rights as a foreigner. Commentators have therefore been concerned to explain away the contradiction. Thus, Bond and Walpole, in their note to line 114, where Phanium's nurse asserts her citizenship, remark: "The Lemnian mother must have been of genuine Athenian extraction: otherwise Phanium could only have been made legitimate by a vote of the citizens or by

proclamation at the meeting of the *phratries*. The penalty for a false claim of citizenship was very heavy."[9] This kind of solution, I believe, is beside the point. The character Phanium serves different functions in the two parts of the play. In the first, she must be a citizen, since her status is critical to Phormio's scheme of forcing her marriage to Antipho. In the second, where the focus is on Chremes' domestic difficulties, the technical point of citizenship can remain moot. The decision of the court in favor of Phormio's suit may of course be construed as internal evidence in support of Phanium's claims, but her foreign birth, the bigamous marriage of her parents, and the need to preserve secrecy concerning her identity all create an aura of illegitimacy which is both the dominant and relevant aspect for the later developments in the plot.[10] Rather than attend too nicely, therefore, to the legal status of Phanium, we might better consider the implications of the shift in story paradigms from one in which her status is secure and significant to a second in which it is dubious and peripheral.

[9]John Bond and Arthur Sumner Walpole, eds., *The Phormio of Terence,* 3d ed. (London and New York, 1964; orig. 1889), 93.

[10]On the question of bigamy, Douglas M. MacDowell, *The Law in Classical Athens* (Ithaca, N.Y., 1978), 89, writes: "A man could not legally be married to more than one wife at a time." He notes further: "in fourth-century speeches it is clear that only the children of a duly married wife were legitimate" (90). Harrison doubts "that there was a rule of law enforcing monogamy" (vol. 1, 15). The more important question is whether there was any legal obstacle to the marriage Chremes intends between his daughter and Antipho. That Chremes' daughter was illegitimate as the child of a bigamous union may not, in itself, have rendered her ineligible for a recognized marriage, however much it may have been a personal embarrassment to Chremes himself. Compare Harrison, 68; Antonio Martina, "Aspetti sociali e giuridici nella *Samia* di Menandro," *Atti della Accademia delle scienze di Torino, II classe di scienze morali, storiche e filologiche* 107 (1973), 876–79; and especially Hans Julius Wolff, "Marriage Law and Family Organization in Ancient Athens," *Traditio* 2 (1944), 82. There remains the question of the nationality of Chremes' second wife. If she was Lemnian, the daughter cannot have entered into a marriage with an Athenian citizen. How troublesome the point might have been to the audience of the Greek original is difficult to say. See Clinton W. Keyes, "Half-Sister Marriage in New Comedy and the *Epidicus,*" *TAPA* 71 (1940), 217–29, and the chapter on the *Cistellaria* in this volume, n. 15. Lefèvre (above, n. 3), 39–44 maintains that in Apollodorus's original play Chremes did not marry the Lemnian woman, nor did he continue to visit her after the night on which his daughter was conceived. He argues further (41) that Phanium, though illegitimate, was certainly a citizen, on the grounds that Lemnos was host to an Athenian cleruchy, a form of settlement in which members retained their original citizenship and did not form an independent community. Phanium's mother, on this reasoning, will have belonged to a cleruch family. Lefèvre's argument is ingenious but inconclusive, and assumes a radical recasting by Terence of the structure of his Greek model. See below, n.13.

The plot of the *Phormio* advances from the conventional world of comedy, where order and authority are respected, even if in the breach, to a topsy-turvy situation in which everyone is involved in a transgression of the rules. The fathers had been perceived as defenders of the boundaries, but with the revelation of their true motives, the tension between impulse and custom which had informed the first movement gives way to a morally ambiguous opposition, where fathers and sons alike evade the social code and undermine its distinctions. Thus the recognition scene seems perverse: Instead of resolving the issue of class with which the *Phormio* began, it merely provides for the convergence of Antipho's and Demipho's private intentions. Since Demipho's reasons for desiring the marriage are if anything more scandalous than Antipho's, Phanium comes off the worse for the revelation of her identity.

That the play displaces rather than mends the violation of convention is thematically significant. In the archetypal story forms of ancient new comedy, the denouement normally accommodated apparent dislocations in the social structure by revealing that the actual state of affairs was as it should be. The principle was not unlike the Persian belief concerning parricide, according to the report of Herodotus: "They say that no one has ever killed his own father or mother, but that every time such things have happened, it is absolutely necessary that upon close examination they would be discovered to involve either supposititious or adulterous children. For they say that it is against reason that a true parent should die at the hands of his own child" (1.137). John K. Davies, in his article "Athenian Citizenship," analyzes this pattern in the plays of Menander:

> If one stands back from the wild complexities of Menandros' plots, they can be seen to share one primary characteristic—an intense, even obsessive awareness of the status boundaries separating citizen from foreigner, citizen from slave, well-born from low-born, legitimate from illegitimate, wife from concubine, wealthy man from poor man from beggar. Plot after plot is exploring this sensitive area and mediating a transition from one status to another—always, of course, in the fantasy, in an upwards direction. For example, the cardinal fact of *Heros* and *Epitrepontes* is that young man rapes girl, and they subsequently marry without knowing that the other was the person involved, while the children born of the rape are exposed. However, they then turn up, to cause embarrassments and suspicions till the

heavy use of the *gnorismata* [i.e., recognitions] motif makes every-
thing straightforward again between virtuous wife, mortified and
repentant husband, and (after all) legitimate children. Or again the
Sikyonios, where Stratophanes is in love with Philoumene but (a) he
though rich is a Sikyonian and therefore a foreigner, and (b) she,
though upperclass Athenian by origin, had been kidnapped and sold
as a slave, and though Stratophanes knows her real status it will be
hard to get it publicly recognized. Difficulty (a) disappears when it
emerges that Stratophanes was 'really' an Athenian all the time: diffi-
culty (b) vanishes when Stratophanes' parasite Theron tries to find
someone to impersonate her father and just happens, as it were, to
stumble upon the one man, Kichesias, who can perform that role
without pretense. Since so much depends on citizenship, while for
fifteen years of Menandros' adult lifetime Athens was powerless to
determine her own citizenship criteria, his obsession with the theme is
understandable: he was dealing with something of crucial contempo-
rary importance. Of course, in his fantasies things come right in the
end without the need for action and change, since the plots consist of
discovering what is the case, which is what the participants want. In
that sense Menandros is deeply escapist, since for the facts once dis-
covered *not* to be as the participants want them to be would constitute
a recipe for neurosis, tragedy, or revolution.[11]

Clearly, the *Phormio* is a different kind of play. The transition of
status is not upward but sideways at best. The characters get what
they want, but not because they discover what is the case, for what
is the case at the end is as incompatible with public norms as it was
at the beginning. When Demipho and Chremes learn the identity of
Phanium, they are as much at pains as before to keep her real
position concealed.

The facts, however, do not remain a secret, since Phormio de-
nounces the whole affair to Nausistrata, just when it seemed that
the last loose end of the plot had been tied. Herbert Charles Elmer,
in the introduction to his commentary on the play, wonders about
the reasons for this coda:

> To one feature of the play, critics may, perhaps, take exception. Why
> does not Phormio, after having sufficiently bantered the old men and
> compelled them, by threatening to tell Nausistrata of the secret mar-
> riage, to give up all claim to the money already paid him,—why does

not Phormio content himself with this result? Why does he, by carrying out his threat, again set at stake what he has won? He must indeed have foreseen that he would not be able to carry out his plan without exposing the secret of Phaedria. The play might well have come to a rapid close after vs. 947, when all the complications had come to a happy termination.[12]

To this question, which is plainly an important one for the theme since it touches on the action just where it exceeds the plot, Elmer offers the following series of responses:

> Still, it is quite in harmony with the bold, determined character of Phormio, that he improves the opportunity for the spirited scene which follows; and again the demands of justice, as it were, required that Chremes should be made to pay the penalty of his faithlessness and ill-becoming conduct. For Phaedria there was the prospect of winning his mother as an ally in his love-affair, and for Phormio that of becoming a permanent guest in the house of Chremes.[13]

Elmer does not, however, seem altogether satisfied with his own explanation, for he adds: "Whatever may be said regarding this

[12]Herbert Charles Elmer, *P. Terenti Phormio* (Boston, 1901), xlviii–xlix.

[13]Elmer, xlix; compare also Karl Dziatzko and Edmund Hauler, eds., *Ausgewählte Komödien des P. Terentius Afer*, vol. 1: *Phormio* (Leipzig, 1913), 81. Arnott suggests that without the final scene "the dramatist's portrait of Phormio would have been unsatisfactory and incomplete. This portrait was designed . . . with careful chiastic symmetry, and at 947 the final touches—Phormio's second display of vividly pictorial language—are still missing" (51). The suggestion of Büchner, 356, that the final scene is Terence's own contribution to the plot, is not convincing, although it has been seconded with great vigor and subtlety by Lefèvre (above, n. 3), 46–56, 76–78, who indeed holds that Terence is entirely on his own from v. 936 (99). Lefèvre eliminates the role of Nausistrata altogether from the Greek original (46), and believes that in Apollodorus's version Chremes was a noble and dignified figure (102–3). Just why he should have been at such great pains to marry his daughter to Antipho, when he had nothing to fear from his wife and the girl herself was perfectly eligible, albeit illegitimate, to marry elsewhere, Lefèvre does not satisfactorily explain. His detailed reconstruction of the original calls for a precise symmetry in the arrangement of scenes which has no parallel in the Greek plays of Menander whose structure we can make out with any confidence, while the conclusion to the *Dyscolus* reveals that Menander, at least, was quite prepared to end a comedy on a note of exuberant farce not unlike the finale of the *Phormio*. Lefèvre's comment on the last scene in Terence's version, that "diese Wendung ist ungewöhnlich, denn in diesem Fall ist die typische Situation der Komödienschlüsse auf den Kopf gestellt" (this development is unusual, for in this instance the typical situation of the comic ending is turned on its head, 56), has a measure of truth in it, but it does not follow that a Greek dramatist could not have been responsible for the experiment.

addition from an artistic point of view, it may at any rate be said that the play is thereby enriched by a very effective scene."

The exposure of Chremes and Demipho forecloses a hypocritical accommodation to public sentiment and obliges the characters to confront openly the improprieties related to Phanium's situation. Chremes and Demipho in other ways have betrayed a concern with appearances. Chremes, for example, was at pains earlier to make the repudiation of Phanium as seemly as possible, both by providing her a dowry and by assuaging her distress through the offices of Nausistrata. When Demipho protests against this officiousness, Chremes replies: "It is not enough to have done your duty if public opinion does not approve it; I want this to happen in accord with her own wishes too, so that she doesn't spread the word that she has been kicked out" (724–25). Later, when the brothers are trying to recover their money from Phormio, Demipho explains his change of heart about Phanium as a scruple for his reputation: "He [i.e. Chremes] convinced me not to give her to you. 'For what will people say,' he said, 'if you do it? Before, when it could have been done honorably, she wasn't given; to drive her out now is foul.' Pretty much the same things which you were accusing me of a while back to my face" (910–14). Demipho is being dishonest here of course, but the excuse reveals what he and his brother think of as a persuasive consideration. In the end, however, the strong-willed Demipho decides to face disclosure rather than endure the mockery of Phormio (955–56), and Chremes reluctantly follows suit.[14]

For all her distress, Nausistrata will finally forgive her husband, in accord with the requirements of the genre. But before she grants her pardon, Phormio slips in a word about Phaedria's affair, and his need for thirty minae (1038–39). Chremes is taken aback, but Nausistrata turns on him at once: "Does it seem so wrong to you that your son, a young man, has one girlfriend, when you have two wives? Shameless! With what countenance will you rebuke him? Answer me!" (1040–42). Chremes meekly submits, but Nausistrata goes further, putting the whole matter before the judgment of her son (1045–46); a moment later, it is Phormio she elects as arbiter: "Phormio, from now on to the best of my ability I shall do

[14]For the characterization of Chremes and Demipho, cf. Arnott, 45–46, and Victor A. Esteves, S. J., "*Senex* as Spouse in Plautus and Terence," *Classical Bulletin* 42 (1966), 73–76.

and say whatever you want" (1050–51), and then, at his suggestion, she invites him in to dinner as a final insult to her husband. The play closes with the matron, the youth, and the parasite in command, while the two old men are humbled and obedient.

The *Phormio* began with a son in dread of his father; it ends with a father at the mercy of his son. This reversal mirrors the progression from the first movement of the play to the second, in which the fathers have lost their role as guarantors of social exclusiveness and restraints and are shown themselves to be transgressors. In the ancient city-state, adult propertied males constituted the citizen body. Normally, they are the repository of those values by which distinctions of status are maintained. The lapse in the moral authority of Demipho and Chremes produces a certain blurring of the boundaries, a relaxation in the conventional structures. The old men are obliged to be more tolerant once their own motives are publicly known to be compromised, while Nausistrata, Phaedria, and Phormio—all of them disfranchised in varying degrees—have less of a stake in preserving the traditional social codes. When Nausistrata learns that Chremes has changed his mind about evicting Phanium, though she does not yet know the reasons why, she remarks: "It's much better this way for everybody, I think, than what you started to do—that the girl should stay. For when I saw her, she seemed a thoroughly fine girl (*perliberalis*)" (814–15). Nausistrata judges by her sense of the person and is indifferent to considerations of class. Radical divisions of status are tempered by a spirit of humanity.

This spirit of humanity presides over the opening scenes of the play, where the slaves Geta and Davus are portrayed seriously and sensitively, and endowed with a generosity and good faith, despite their straitened circumstances, which put to shame the greed and casuistry of their masters. But the figure who best incarnates the challenge to the narrow exclusivism of the conservative city-state ideology is the parasite, Phormio himself. Many have acclaimed the subtlety and artistry of the characterization in the *Phormio,* and certainly the personality for whom Terence named the play is done with special brilliance and verve.[15] Phormio is clever, bold, gener-

[15]See, for example, Gilbert Norwood, *The Art of Terence* (Oxford, 1923), 75–77, and especially the excellent study by Arnott, cited above. Donatus, *ad v.* 315, seems to indicate that Terence elaborated the more rascally features of the parasite in

ous, loyal, independent, and ironic. He is, like many another of his métier in comedy, proud of his style of life (see especially lines 326–45). It is not that of a respectable citizen, and Phormio's social status is most dubious. Yet without question he is the hero of the comedy, in whose hands Antipho and Phaedria rest their fate. He manipulates each stage of the action successfully and in the end triumphs personally over Demipho and Chremes. His encouragement of love and disdain for conventional barriers suit perfectly his ambiguous station in society. Phormio's victory is also a victory for his point of view, that of a marginal person who is prepared to improvise with laws and customs in order to facilitate passionate, if not quite socially acceptable, unions. He is a fixer, who bends the rules and softens the lines that define the social structure. Each time his work is vindicated: The fathers turn out to desire the marriage he has brought about, although for personal reasons of their own; Phaedria is indulged in his affair by a broad-minded mother and a crestfallen father. Phormio's invitation to dinner and elevation to arbiter of the household's destiny are the confirmation of his wisdom. With the inner dislocation of the old structure, the old men cede place to a new type: Phormio, rootless and humane, is at the moral center of gravity of his play and the society it represents.

comparison to the Greek original. The emphasis on the personality of the parasite is also evident in Terence's choice of title for the play; in this comedy alone did he alter the title of his model, although his primary reason for doing so was doubtless the unfamiliarity at home of the Greek legal procedure alluded to in Apollodorus's *Epidikazomenos,* a procedure which, if Lefèvre is right (above, n. 3), Terence in any case eliminated in his version of the play.

Hecyra
Ironic Comedy

The tension between father and son in new comedy was available, as we have seen, as a vehicle for representing issues of caste and class in ancient society. At a certain level, to be sure, these issues manifest themselves as moral conflicts, which we may interpret according to the traditional Roman disjunction of virtue and passion: Modesty and obedience contend with amorous impulses which conventional wisdom regarded as selfish or antisocial. For this reason, moral or psychological interpretations of the plays inevitably come to mind. The plays we have considered so far, however, point beyond such abstract values to the matrix of social relations which endows them with content, and the social interest is, accordingly, essential to an adequate exegesis. In certain plays, however, the traditional moral psychology may itself be problematized in ways involving special permutations of the usual narrative formulas. Such works seem to exploit the conventions of new comedy so as to challenge the ideological premises of the genre. In this chapter, I shall take up an ingenious play of this sort by Terence.

Sidney G. Ashmore, in his school edition of Terence's comedies, pronounced that the *Hecyra,* or "Mother-in-Law," was "the one of least merit."[1] He has not been alone in this verdict. At the first two performances of the play, the Roman audience deserted the theater before the show was over. The first time they abandoned it to see a

[1]Sidney G. Ashmore, ed., *The Comedies of Terence* (repr. New York, 1967), 33.

tightrope walker or some boxers, as the prologue indicates, while, at the second performance, they were seduced, soon after the first act, by the report of a sideshow featuring gladiators. Only at the third performance, it appears, the Romans saw it through.

There are exceptions to this general repudiation, of course. The most outstanding, certainly, is Gilbert Norwood, who described the *Hecyra* as "possibly the finest masterpiece of high comedy in the world."[2] The problem, as Norwood saw it, was to discover why the glories of the play lay unperceived. The reaction of the Romans was easy to explain: "Barbarians," Norwood calls them, who "did not appreciate good art" (2–3). What then of all those succeeding generations who have failed to appreciate the play? "Tempting as it is," writes Norwood, "to refer these extraordinary criticisms to the Victorian blight which brought both drama and popular taste to the lowest point compatible with civilization, we must remember that all other opinion, tacitly or not, has pointed the same way."[3] Our error, he explains, is to have confused comedy with farce, "to follow Roman tradition, and look upon a markedly unfarcical comedy as no comedy at all" (90). I take it, on the other hand, that this near unanimous sentiment which has persisted over two millennia responds to a reality in the *Hecyra,* which distinguishes this play from others of the genre.

The first scene of Terence's *Hecyra* consists of a very brief exchange between a young courtesan and an old madam or adviser. The old lady counsels the girl to be merciless with her lovers, to make them, take them, and break them, one and all (*spolies, mutiles, laceres quemque nacta sis,* 65), for they seek nothing but their own pleasure at the cheapest price. "But it's wrong," replies the girl, "to treat them all the same." "Wrong to punish the enemy?" the old lady asks; "if only I had your looks or you had my brains," she sighs. This rather cynical piece of dialogue is motivated by the news that Pamphilus, the hero of the play, has reneged on his promise to his mistress Bacchis and taken a wife. Otherwise, it contributes nothing to the plot of the *Hecyra.* The girl and the old woman will remain through the next scene so that they may learn, and the audience with them, something of the background, but

[2]Gilbert Norwood, *The Art of Terence* (Oxford, 1923), 3.

[3]Norwood, 8. Since Norwood wrote, several defenses of Terence have appeared, of which E. Reitzenstein, *Terenz als Dichter* (Leipzig, 1940), may be cited as the most influential in initiating a revaluation of Terence's art.

after that they will disappear for good, for they are what the ancients called protatic characters, a dramatic device which Terence favored in place of the narrative prologue.[4] I have described the scene rather fully because the egotistical idea of *amor* or love expressed so wittily sets a tone for the play which is out of keeping with the more romantic or passionate moods prevailing in Terence's other comedies. In the *Andria,* the hero, also called Pamphilus, swears to endure anything rather than abandon his beloved, whom he maintains in his heart as his true wife (270ff.). Alternatively, in less pensive, more melodramatic comedies such as the *Eunuch,* love appears as an elemental force that cannot be contained or controlled.[5] The opening scene of the *Hecyra* presents the passion of love as a base and selfish desire and thereby anticipates an important theme in the play.

In the second scene, Parmeno, the slave of Pamphilus, arrives with news of his master's situation. Terence's commentator Donatus (p. 335W) exhorts us to "notice the fact that from the beginning of the comedy to the end Parmeno is sent about running and kept in the dark despite his passionate curiosity." Gilbert Norwood observed quite rightly that Parmeno was anything but the usual comic slave:

> Parmeno understands what is expected of him, but he is never given his chance. Never was there a role more desperately devoid of what professional slang calls "fat." Every time this unhappy satellite enters manfully to perform his duty as a *veterator,* a *versutus servus,* and the rest, he is mercilessly ordered off the stage to make room for the play.

It is true: Parmeno, like the two protatic prostitutes, has only a limited part in the play, which will get on without the entertaining wiles of the clever slave. In this reduction of the role of the comic slave, to be sure, Norwood did not find fault. Terence sacrificed the stereotype here, according to Norwood, and in the case of other

[4]The opening scene, with protatic characters, in the *Hecyra* is derived from Apollodorus's original: Donatus quotes the first line of the scene, P. Wessner, *Aeli Donati quod fertur commentum Terenti,* vol. 2 (Leipzig, 1905), 204.

[5]On the nature of love in the comedies of Terence, see Peter Flury, *Liebe und Liebessprache bei Menander, Plautus und Terenz* (Heidelberg, 1968); also Archibald W. Allen, "Elegy and the Classical Attitude toward Love: Propertius I, 1," *YCS* 11 (1950), 255–77. Plautus too has scenes such as this but again they are thematically significant; see the chapters on the *Asinaria, Cistellaria,* and *Truculentus.*

characters in the play as well, for the sake of truth. In fact, it was just this originality, this realism, which offended the Roman "barbarians." "Terence has failed ignominiously," Norwood wryly complains, "through giving us real people and natural conduct." Parmeno reports that Pamphilus had been in love with the courtesan (*meretrix*) Bacchis, when his father began to urge him to take a wife of his own station. Pamphilus was torn between the *pudor* or modest respect he owed to his father, and the *amor* which he felt for Bacchis. In the end, his father's insistence won out, and Pamphilus married a neighbor's daughter called Philumena. So vexed did he remain, however, that for months he refused to touch his wife, visiting instead with Bacchis. But Bacchis understandably grew cold toward him under the circumstances, and the noble patience of Philumena gradually overcame his disdain, arousing first his pity, and, at last, his love.

Now, a most interesting feature of this play is that it begins where many other ancient comedies leave off—with a legitimate and acknowledged marriage.[6] Here the young hero does not swear loyalty to his beloved in the teeth of his father's opposition, so that the standoff can only be resolved through a recognition scene, revealing that the beloved, after all, is that very daughter of the rich neighbor to whom he had long since been betrothed. The conflict between *amor* and *pietas*, the warring claims of personal passion and obligations to parent and class, all this, it appears, is long since ended, not through comic coincidence, where the tensions of real life find a fictive reconciliation, but through the pragmatic victory of responsibility over passion. This is as it should be, says Donatus (p. 214W). But such a story is not the stuff of comedy. Impulse has yielded to necessity; we are in the ordinary world. The cynicism of the opening scene seems confirmed: Love is selfish, inconstant, unreliable; authority conquers all. The *Hecyra* reveals at once that the ideal reconciliation between all claims and all parties, between passion and duty, cannot be achieved.

In the meantime, Pamphilus has been obliged to leave Athens on business for several months, and in his absence things have gone badly. ("Good," says the *meretrix*, "if it will help Bacchis!") Philumena appears to have quarreled with Pamphilus's mother,

[6]Compare Norwood, 93. In the *Phormio* too the young couple are married from the beginning, but without the knowledge or consent of the father.

Sostrata, with whom she had been living; in any case, she has returned to her own mother's house. This is the situation to which Pamphilus returns. The audience of the original Greek *Hecyra,* written by Apollodorus of Carystus, was perhaps not so perplexed as readers of Terence are at this point about the reasons for the separation, for Apollodorus may have provided his play with an expository prologue, in which one would have learned that the unlucky Philumena was in fact expecting a baby, and that the child was conceived shortly before her marriage, when she was raped one night by a drunken brawler.[7] Terence abandoned such prologues for his own prefatory monologue, which touches upon literary debates of his own age rather than the plot of the drama. But the effect, in Terence's version, of the drastic delay in exposition is to focus all attention on the background narrative, which no longer appears as a prelude to the chief problem of the play, but is recorded, so far as the audience can tell, for its own interest. What is more, the absence of the prologue gives special emphasis to the first scene, and its cynical view of passion. We are not prepared for a conventional comedy of intrigue and recognition. What we expect is an investigation of a marriage in which passion has been sacrificed to social conformity. There is a morning-after feeling here which may be Terence's own contribution.

The second act of the play dramatizes the suspicions and the growing certainty of Pamphilus's father, Laches, that Sostrata was the cause of the quarrel. Only in the third act does Pamphilus himself appear, with a soulful lament on his ill-starred life in love. Parmeno quite sensibly reminds him that the problem between his wife and his mother will doubtless be easily resolved, now that he is back, but Pamphilus significantly interprets his present situation in terms of his earlier misfortune in his love for Bacchis. This reminder of Bacchis is important for the plot of the play; for Bacchis will later be summoned by Laches on the suspicion that she is still involved with Pamphilus, and, as it will turn out, she bears the clue or token which will undo the comic knot. But however much the audience may have known of these developments in Apollodorus's original, readers of Terence are in the dark about them.

[7]See Eckard Lefèvre, *Die Expositionstechnik in den Komödien des Terenz* (Darmstadt, 1969), 60–67, and 60, n.1, for bibliography; Orazio Bianco, *Terenzio: Problemi et aspetti dell'originalità* (Rome, 1962), 104; Karl Büchner, *Das Theater des Terenz* (Heidelberg, 1974), 124–25, n.6.

What stands out in Pamphilus's speech is that he sees himself involved once more in the conflict between love, which he now bears toward his wife, and the filial piety due his mother. The tension described in the first act seems to be replicated. Pamphilus's lament is interrupted by Philumena's cry—she is suffering the pains of childbirth, but Pamphilus guesses only that she must be severely ill—and the scene draws to a close with Pamphilus's passionate apostrophe to his wife, "whatever danger you face, it is certain that I shall perish together with you" (326).

Pamphilus rushes into Philumena's house. When he reemerges, he relates his discovery of Philumena's real situation in a long soliloquy, which was very likely adapted from a dramatic dialogue in Apollodorus's original.[8] Pamphilus deduces that the child is not his own, because he had not lain with his wife during the first months of his marriage.[9] No one but Philumena and her mother share with Pamphilus full knowledge of all the damaging facts. Pamphilus is disconsolate. He relates the prayer of Philumena's mother, Myrrhina, that he keep secret the circumstance of her daughter's dishonor, even if he cannot bring himself to take his wife back again. It is this exchange that was enacted dramatically by Apollodorus, but which Terence has presented, in his preferred way, as a struggle in the soul of Pamphilus. Passion, conjugal affection, even pity bind him to his wife, but taking her back, he declares (403–4), is out of the question. So much for that selfless participation in her trials which he had so recently proclaimed. He concludes his speech with the recollection once more of his former experience in love, which, as he says, makes him a practiced hand at quenching his feelings.

Pamphilus must now justify his decision not to take back his wife to his father and to hers, without revealing, if possible, the matter of the child. For pity inclines him to respect his wife's desire. And so he will, but in such a way as to preserve his filial piety, his *pietas*.

[8]Compare Wolfgang Schadewaldt, "Bemerkungen zur 'Hecyra' des Terenz," *Hermes* 66 (1931), 10ff. = *Hellas und Hesperien* (Zurich and Stuttgart, 1970) vol. 1, 2d ed., 730ff.; Bruno Denzler, *Der Monolog bei Terenz* (Zurich, 1968), 69ff. Lefèvre, 67–71, argues that Pamphilus's monologue uses material originally in Apollodorus's expository prologue.

[9]On whether Pamphilus would have had reason to suspect the legitimacy of a (supposedly) seven-month infant, see Schadewaldt, 723–25, who argues that the birth must have occurred seven months after the wedding, and only five months after the consummation of the marriage.

For he must obey his parent rather than the claims of love (448–49). We have once again a reminiscence of his earlier experience with Bacchis, but it is not altogether appropriate here. Donatus explains simply that Pamphilus "has recalled the fact that his mother was hurt by his wife" (p. 269W). But Ashmore aptly remarks that "Terence would appear to be woolgathering just at this point. Pamphilus," he continues, "is no longer ignorant of the reason why his wife left her mother-in-law's house" (231). We can account for the apparent lapse, however: Pamphilus is speaking *ironically*. The thought has only just struck him, and its source is surely the analogy which Pamphilus has long since perceived between his present situation and his former love for Bacchis. He will yet hesitate for a couple of lines, wondering just what to say, before he announces firmly: "Now I am resolved to follow the path I have decided upon" (454). He will keep up the pretense of a quarrel between his mother and his wife, so that he may extricate himself from the again unwanted marriage by pleading his filial duty. This he does to a father who affirms that he is pleased to have so loyal a son—no Roman father could quarrel with *pietas*—but he at once urges his son to come to his senses, for his conduct is mad.

I like to think that it was at this point that the Roman audience deserted the first performance of the play. Certainly they might well have found themselves uncomfortable at the turn of events here. For Pamphilus has invoked the traditional tension between passion and responsibility, but twisted it in an extraordinary and hypocritical way to serve his own interest in what is now, as Ashmore puts it, "a personal matter only" (loc. cit.). Take first his love. It is compromised in advance: Pamphilus gave up Bacchis when pressed by his father, a fact which echoed the cynical dialogue on love with which the play began; and here he will give up love again.[10] His protestations that piety obliges him are false, of

[10]It is tempting to suggest that Pamphilus's comparisons between his present plight and his former relationship to Bacchis are due largely to Terence rather than to Apollodorus. Lines 407–8, for example, are easily detachable from their context 409 follows quite as well on 406—and they anticipate too early the course Pamphilus will take in Act 3, Scene 5. Much of lines 293–303, moreover, could well be a Terentian interpolation into Apollodorus's original. Donatus remarks that Parmeno's reply to Pamphilus in 306ff. is "slavish and base and does not answer to all Pamphilus has said, but only to the very last part" (p. 246W). We may add that Parmeno's remarks in 306ff. maintain the line of argument he had begun in 288–92. Such arguments for Terentian originality are difficult to control, however, and do not command confidence. See Walther Ludwig, "The Originality of Terence and His Greek Models," *Greek, Roman and Byzantine Studies* 9 (1968), 169–82.

course. The inhibition is his own. Its source is in conventional values, but of these Pamphilus is now the vehicle, and he is obliged, accordingly, to contain his own passion. His passion is clearly a domitable one—a subtle variation in the comic phenomenology of *amor.* Indeed, when he speaks his mind openly, he speaks of pity (446), not of love, as the bond between himself and Philumena. As for his piety, moreover, it is doubly counterfeit, for it is the pretense of a diminished and hollow version of the virtue. For *pietas* does not mean that one obliges the whims of parents, their inconsequential and personal likes and dislikes. That view involves a contradiction in the idea of piety, reminiscent of the problem in Plato's *Euthyphro,* where obedience toward one of the gods may entail contempt for another. Worse, Pamphilus's mother, Sostrata, will urge him herself, naturally enough, to overlook the alleged quarrel and take back his wife. So Pamphilus must then disobey both his parents, adducing as his reason—filial piety. No, the object of filial piety is not a parent's whim or convenience, what Pamphilus calls *commoda* (481,495); it is rather a social code which is understood to be objective, to be represented by the parents, chiefly the father. Pamphilus, we might say, exploits the fact that the subjective and objective content of *pietas* are not clearly distinguished, that they dwell undifferentiated under the cover of a single term. Terence has re-created the conventional conflict between *amor* and *pietas,* which he probes in other plays with remarkable psychological insight—an insight, as Peter Flury has shown,[11] distinctly his own—and which he suggests in this play in the background story of Pamphilus and Bacchis; but he has re-created it in a way that appears perverse. *Pietas* is distorted from the idea of obligation to traditional authority to an indulgence of an elder's tastes; *amor* is neither an unquenchable force nor a deep and reasoned affection engaging one's loyalties (*fides*) on the deepest level, but a negotiable feeling which retreats, now all too readily, before more interested concerns. Finally, the entire conflict is a mock-up, pretended by Pamphilus so that he can escape a threat, not to conscience or to passion, but to ego. And escape he does, running off before his father or father-in-law can pursue him with their angry questions.

The appeal to a ternary conception of the psyche, which we today associate, broadly speaking, with the doctrines of Freud, should be explained. Romans did not interpret their own psychol-

[11]Flury, esp. chaps. 1 and 2.

ogy in these terms. We have seen that their own language points rather to a binary division, between *pietas* and associated virtues on the one hand, and *cupidines* or passionate desires such as love (or ambition or avarice) on the other. This dichotomous structure can in general give an account of the kind of situation in which Pamphilus finds himself in this play. Love for Philumena inclines Pamphilus in one direction, while his concern for his status or *dignitas*, which would be compromised if he accepted his violated wife, inclines him in another. Concern for *dignitas* is part of the complex of tradition-regarding virtues which the Romans subsumed under the notion of *boni mores*. In Menander's *Epitrepontes*, which many scholars believe to have been the model for Apollodorus's *Hecyra*, the situation of Charisios is practically the same as that of Pamphilus here, yet his behavior does not appear to challenge the concepts of conventional psychology. The character of Pamphilus seems exceptional, perhaps, because the domain of *pietas* and its cognate virtues is, as it were, preempted by his pretended obligations toward his mother, while his true motives are kept concealed. Thus Pamphilus appears to bear a private responsibility for his behavior, which accordingly seems willful or egotistical. The action of the play so divides the psychological field that neither duty nor passion but selfishness alone is left to account for Pamphilus's choice.[12]

In the fourth act, Philumena's father reasons that his own wife must be the cause of his daughter's estrangement, harboring, he supposes, a resentment about Pamphilus having maintained relations with Bacchis for some time after he was married. His wife does not disabuse him of this suspicion, for otherwise he may press her too closely concerning Philumena's child, whose existence he has just discovered. He, for his part, broadcasts the news of the child, which delights Laches, though both men are perplexed why its birth was concealed. Pamphilus, finding that his argument from *pietas* is beginning to totter, now that his mother is planning to

[12]For the notion of "semantic field" or *Sinnbezirk*, see Jost Trier, *Der deutsche Wortschatz im Sinnbezirk des Verstandes: Die Geschichte eines sprachlichen Feldes* (Heidelberg, 1931); Bruno Snell, *Die Ausdrücke für den Begriff des Wissens in der vorplatonischen Philosophie* (Berlin, 1924) [Philologische Untersuchungen 29]; John Lyons, *Structural Semantics* (Oxford, 1963) [Philological Society Publications 20]. A developed vocabulary in Latin to express the three functions of the psyche appears first, I believe, in the amatory poems of Ovid, with the term *ratio* expressing the mediating operations of the ego.

retire to the country with his father, quickly changes strategy, claiming that the concealment of the child shows plainly that Philumena is loath to be his wife (655–60). From here to the end of the play, the developments are rapid, tight, and masterful. Laches perceives his son's tergiversations and accuses him of still harboring a love for Bacchis—untrue, but a natural supposition, resurrecting the original conflict of *amor* and *pietas* in a way that reverses Pamphilus's argument: *Pietas* should induce him to keep his wife, not reject her, while it is *amor* which tears him from her. Laches thus reverts to the standard paradigm of this moral tension. Both old men decide to summon Bacchis for a showdown. She appears, denies any connection now with Pamphilus, and agrees to go in to Philumena to lay to rest any unease which she and her mother may have on that score. This she does because she wishes, contrary to the rule of her profession, to see Pamphilus prosper in marriage. When she emerges, she, like Pamphilus earlier, speaks in a long monologue which we know, from Donatus, was originally a dramatic dialogue at least in part.[13] She tells us how a ring she was wearing, which Pamphilus had given her, was recognized as Philumena's, the very one which had been stolen from her on the night she was raped. Thus, the rapist was none other than Pamphilus himself, and the play ends happily for all, though not in what Northrop Frye calls a scene of "festive ritual."[14] Bacchis and Pamphilus agree to keep the unsavory details of the affair confidential. There is no general participation in the comic revelation, "as happens in comedies" (the phrase is Pamphilus's, lines 866–67). Dante Nardo has observed that "the expression, *ut in comoediis,* represents the repudiation, conscious and deliberate, of a drama where everything always goes one way, and that not the way of human truth."[15]

Several scholars have suggested that this conclusion, with its humble resignation to the plain demands of common experience,

[13]Cf. Denzler, 13ff.

[14]Northrop Frye, *Anatomy of Criticism* (repr. New York, 1967), 163.

[15]Dante Nardo, "Il significato della Hecyra terenziana," *Memorie della Accademia Patavina di scienze, lettere, ed arti* 79 (1966–67), 36–37; quoted from Nardo's notes to his translation of Heinz Haffter's monograph under the title, *Terenzio e la sua personalità artistica* (Rome, 1969), 129. For exceptions to the rule of full disclosure at the end of a comedy, one may compare the conclusion to Oscar Wilde's *Lady Windemere's Fan,* and also, for an ancient play in a different but related genre, Euripides' *Ion.*

reveals an essentially Terentian humanism at its best.[16] Here is realism rather than stock comic types and scenes, a universalism that derives from fidelity to human truth rather than hackneyed formulas. Certainly the *Hecyra* shows a deep sensitivity to human differences, and portrays especially well a certain nobility of mind in both mothers-in-law, in Bacchis, even in the two fathers, types who are ordinarily imprisoned in their rather rigid and sterile roles. The character of Pamphilus is exceptionally complex.

Much of this was doubtless in the Greek original.[17] Terence's own contribution, perhaps, lies in the emphasis—for, in the end, it is no more than an emphasis—on the formal or conventional opposition between love and filial duty. We should be hard pressed to find a real Greek equivalent for the Latin *pietas:* It is a concept peculiarly Roman, and Terence has, in the *Hecyra,* laid out and drawn taut the structure of this traditional Roman psychology on the rack of Apollodorus's drama. In so doing, he revealed stresses within the concept of *pietas* and the nature of *amor* which put in question the fundamental ideological presuppositions of new comedy as a genre. These tensions are factitiously resolved, of course, through the brilliant recognition scene with which the play concludes. But the resolution fails to dispel the conflict between personal feeling and public forms. Instead of comic relief there is a peculiar sense that familiar moral categories have become opaque or ambivalent, and the hero of the play does not seem to be a comic scoundrel or a mad lover, but a subtle and dubious manipulator of the moral tradition.

The air of secrecy, of conspiracy, at the resolution of the play is an emblem of its dubious propriety. It is also coordinate with the interiorization of social inhibitions within the person of Pamphilus. Indeed, a remarkable feature of the *Hecyra* is that the blocking character is identical with the lover himself—a feature which strangely anticipates some comedies of Shakespeare. Pamphilus for this reason seems a more fully realized individual than is the rule for

[16]See Haffter, 100–104; Bianco, 226–33; W. Beare, "The Secret of Terence," *Hermathena* 56 (1940), 38–39; E. Paratore, "Il teatro latino nei suoi rapporti col pubblico antico e nei suoi riflessi sulla spiritualità moderna," *Dioniso* 39 (1965), 65–66; Benedetto Croce, "Intorne alle commedie di Terenzio," *La critica* 34 (1936), 412ff.

[17]Maria Rosa Posani provides a sensitive appreciation of Terence as a continuator of Menander in "Aspetti del comico in Terenzio," *Atene e Roma* N.S. 7 (1962), 75–76. Contrast Haffter, 86, 95f.

new comedy, and he has won the praise and sympathy of several critics and commentators, beginning with Donatus.[18] For all that, the interest in Terence is not finally in issues of personal identity and development, but in the operations and tensions of the traditional moral code. The inversions and reversals in the story come near to stripping this code of all normal sense. Remaining within the formal conventions of its genre, the *Hecyra* challenges and confounds their customary meanings. In this respect, it represents the ironic moment in new comedy.

[18]See Denzler, 134ff: Bianco, 115–16; James Curtiss Austin, *The Significant Name in Terence,* University of Illinois Studies in Language and Literature 7.4 (1921), 85; Betty Radice, trans., *Terence: The Brothers and Other Plays* (Harmondsworth, 1965), 85; Donatus, preface to the commentary on *Hecyra* (1.9, p. 190W): "for we have on stage kindly mothers-in-law, a modest daughter-in-law, a husband at once tender to his wife and devoted to his mother, and a virtuous prostitute."

Truculentus
Satiric Comedy

The *Truculentus* has been singled out as an exceptional play in the domains of form and of content. With regard to form, the plot—or rather, its deficiencies—has drawn the attention of critics. I cite a few representative comments: "The play has almost no plot. It is merely the spectacle of a very real Circe turning men into swine." "There is very little plot." "The *Truculentus* is so loosely put together that it is hardly a fair example of normal procedures." "Well-constructed in spite of its disappointing plot."[1]

As to content, it is more difficult to specify the quality that distinguishes the *Truculentus* from the other members of its genre. Some have found it simply obscene.[2] Others have seen it as an

[1]Philip Whaley Harsh, *A Handbook of Classical Drama* (Stanford, 1944), 373; George E. Duckworth, *The Nature of Roman Comedy* (Princeton, 1952), 145; Henry W. Prescott, "Inorganic Roles in Roman Comedy," *CP* 15 (1920), 277; John Newbold Hough, "The Development of Plautus' Art," *CP* 30 (1935), 56. Compare Cynthia Dessen, "Plautus' Satiric Comedy: The *Truculentus*," *Philological Quarterly* 56 (1977), 145: "The plot and structure of the *Truculentus* are admittedly weaker than those of Plautus' more popular plays." Not every critic has shared the view that the *Truculentus* is exceptional; Kenneth McLeish, in his primer, *Roman Comedy* (London, 1976), has a section entitled "A typical Plautus play: *Truculentus*" (38), and observes: "This is a perfectly satisfactory—if rather unlikely—story, and very typical of the plots of most New Comedies" (39).

[2]C. R. Post, "The Dramatic Art of Menander," *HSCP* 24 (1913), speaking of new comedy in general, writes: "Profligacy and prostitution are taken as matters of course and encounter no real reprobation. Truth and honor fall prey to artful slaves or courtesans for the diversion of the spectators. The scapegrace son is victorious over his honest father. Many examples may be noted . . . ; one of the worst of all is the *Truculentus*. . . . The closest analogy is the polite but festering Restoration Comedy ensuing upon the rough but wholesome drama of the Elizabethan era" (125–26).

extraordinary example of realism. Duckworth, for example, calls it "lifelike" and cites with approval Harsh's opinion that it is "one of the most remarkable pieces of stark realism in classical drama." Another remarks: "It is as realistic as Hogarth, as immoral as Restoration Drama, and is completely devoid of sentiment."[3] Lately, the consensus appears to be that it is satirical. Thus Duckworth observes: "The depressing nature of *Truculentus* and its low moral tone have led to much adverse criticism. More modern writers consider it a masterpiece, one of Plautus' cleverest plays, a satiric comedy in which Plautus portrays with bitter cynicism an unpleasant aspect of society." P. Lejay put it most emphatically: "The *Truculentus* is an exception in the corpus of Plautus in that it is a satiric comedy. It is the only one. It anticipates Lucilius and above all Horace. . . . From other plays, the spectators could only derive distraction. In watching the *Truculentus,* they were obliged to add reflection." P. J. Enk, the great editor of the *Truculentus,* follows Lejay's characterization of the play as a "satiric comedy," by reason of which it occupies, as he says, a unique place among the dramas of Plautus, and he quotes an Italian history of Roman literature by Curcio for the view that "it was not an allurement to vice, but a lesson to drive young and old from it."[4] What seems generally agreed is that the *Truculentus* shows the domination of base im-

P. J. Enk, *Plauti Truculentus,* vol. 1 (Leyden, 1952), 25, cites the Rev. W. Lucas Collins, *Plautus and Terence* (Edinburgh, 1873), 94, who, following the mention of the *Casina, Curculio, Asinaria, Truculentus, Mercator,* and *Persa,* remarks: "The morality of all these is of the very lowest, and the three last are stupid besides."

[3]Duckworth, 145; Alan McN. G. Little, "Plautus and Popular Drama," *HSCP* 49 (1938), 222. Compare also W. Beare, *The Roman Stage,* 3d ed. (London, 1968; orig. 1950), 61: "the cynical studies in debauchery afforded by the *Bacchides* and the *Truculentus*"; and George E. Duckworth, *The Complete Roman Drama,* vol. 2 (New York, 1942) 94: "The *Truculentus* stands alone among Roman comedies for its bitter treatment and sardonic humour and for its life-like portrayal of one unpleasant aspect of ancient society."

[4]Duckworth, *Nature,* 145; P. Lejay, *Plaute* (Paris, 1925), 110–11 (cit. Enk, 26); Enk, vol. 1, 27; Gaetano Curcio, *Storia della letteratura latina,* vol. 1 (Naples, 1920), 195; and see Hazel Toliver, "The Fabulae Palliatae and the Spread of Hellenism," *CJ* 49 (1954), 305; Joseph T. Shipley, *Guide to Great Plays* (Washington, D.C., 1956) 531–32; and Dessen for the most comprehensive analysis of the satirical elements in the play. Enk elaborated his own view in his article, "Plautus' *Truculentus,*" in Charles Henderson, Jr., ed., *Classical Mediaeval and Renaissance Studies in Honor of Berthold Louis Ullman,* vol. 1 (Rome, 1964), 49–65, esp. 60–63; he remarks (61): "If the Roman spectators, in seeing a comedy like the *Truculentus,* did not learn that the Greek world with which they were coming more and more into touch was radically depraved, if they did not realize that traffic with women like Phronesium meant a leap into the abyss, nothing would teach them this."

pulses, the course of unchecked greed and lust. The critics differ in their estimation of the moral attitude implicit in this portrait. Is the play an invitation to indulge in such licentiousness? A disinterested imitation of life as it is? Or, finally, a mordant diatribe on the morals of the age, a demonstration, as Enk sees it, of "how unfaithful, how greedy of gain, how inhuman, how dangerous are those harlots who reduce young men to extreme poverty by means of their flattery and lies."[5] I should like to suspend the ethical question—whether the play is wicked, true to life, or sardonic—and attend rather to the common denominator of all three views, that the world as represented in the *Truculentus* reveals the uninhibited operation and ultimate triumph of sordid and materialistic passions.

These, then, are the special characteristics of the *Truculentus:* the apparent tenuousness of the plot and the ascendancy of the lowest motives. Now, plot may be regarded as the sum of the actions in a narrative; action, in turn, may be construed as the exhibition of character, and character as the potential for action. Aristotle had intimated this connection in the *Poetics,* when he said that *ethos* necessarily entailed choice, and so was practical and active.[6] Henry James, in *The Art of Fiction,* put it clearly and categorically: "What is character but the determination of incident? What is incident but the illustration of character? What is either a picture or a novel that is *not* of character? What else do we seek in it and find in it?"[7] If character and narrative are so closely connected, if indeed they may be regarded as two aspects of a single phenomenon, the faculty and its activity, potency and its actualization, may it not be that the two singular qualities of Plautus's *Truculentus*—its seemingly exiguous plot and its realism or cynicism, at any rate the kinds of motives it represents or exposes—are not separate and accidentally related, but rather mutually implicated, each a natural function of the other?

We must be clear: There is no want of incident in the *Truculentus,* which offers numerous conflicts and reversals, even a recognition

[5]Enk (above, n.2), 27. I am indebted to my former student, Diana Adams, for several of the above citations.

[6]Aristotle, *Poetics* 1450b8-9: "Character [*ēthos*] is the sort of thing that reveals choice [*proairesin*], what kinds of things one chooses or avoids." See also 1449b36–1450a4.

[7]Henry James, "The Art of Fiction," in *The House of Fiction: Essays on the Novel by Henry James,* ed. Leon Edel (London, 1957), 34.

scene, and a healthy dose of intrigue. It is rather the sequence of events—their arrangement and the nature of the resolution—that seems faulty or queer. If the characterization in the play is "satiric," then the plot may be strained to accommodate and express an unusual complex of motives. In the *Truculentus*, precisely where the conventions of new comedy are under stress, we may best apprehend how they are bound up with patterned values and meanings which are acknowledged even in the breach.

After a brief prologue, in which Plautus ironically contrasts the venerable virtues of his audience—who would not part with a penny—with the loose ethics of his times, where whores strip their infatuated lovers of their last dime (6–8; 13–17),[8] the *Truculentus* opens with a monologue, by the character Diniarchus, who has recently returned to Athens with the intention of resuming his ruinous affair with the courtesan Phronesium. He complains that lovers are tricked and mocked in every way to separate them from their wealth. The original enticements of cunning women are merely bait: Once the hook is swallowed, the man is quickly ruined (31–42; 43–56). What is more, pimps and whores are thicker than flies in summer (64–65). After these moralizing generalities, Diniarchus gets down to present circumstances: He himself has squandered his estates for Phronesium, who has now turned him out for another who can give more. This rival, a Babylonian soldier, is about to arrive from abroad. In the meantime, Diniarchus knows that Phronesium has pretended to give birth to a child, which she intends to pass off as the son of the soldier (77–88a).[9] At this moment, Astaphium, the maid of Phronesium, emerges from her mistress's house.

In one way, this initial state of affairs is quite familiar: A young man is in love with a courtesan or brothel slave, but his attachment is jeopardized by a rich and powerful rival, often, as here, a soldier

[8]P. J. Enk in *Plauti Truculentus*, vol 2 (Leyden, 1953), 10–11, states that the prologue originally contained some expository material which was lost in the transmission of the text; indeed, it is remarkably bare of anything relating to the plot. On the *mores pristini* (7), and the contrast with *huius saecli mores* (13)—equated ironically with the *mos mulierum* (16)—compare also lines 98–99, 639, 677.

[9]This material possibly was originally part of the expository prologue; it is not clear how Diniarchus would know that the pregnancy was simulated, and later (194–99) he appears to have forgotten it. If Plautus was in fact responsible for the alteration, his purpose may have been to make even clearer Diniarchus's willful and conscious pursuit of his own ruin, in full knowledge of Phronesium's duplicity.

from foreign parts. In situations of this sort, the young lover may be expected to conspire, with the aid of a clever slave, perhaps, or a parasite, friend, or elderly adviser, to obtain the money he requires, often at the expense of his rival, whose very confidence will be his undoing. Our sympathies are with the youth because he is the underdog—still under the absolute control of his father, without access to money, callow, and given to despair. Adulthood, wealth, and independence give the soldier easy access to the object of desire. In the discomfiture of the rival, power is made to bow before luck and cunning, the weapons of the weak. The *Miles Gloriosus* and the *Pseudolus* are paradigmatic for this type, but this situation is used in the composition of many plays. We have seen it in the *Asinaria*, and have observed that the *Casina* and *Mercator*, where the father acts as rival, may be construed as a version. It serves as a subplot in Terence's *Phormio, Eunuch,* and *Adelphoe,* as well as in Plautus's *Bacchides,* to name only a few. We have remarked that the *Rudens* and *Poenulus* are built upon a variant of the formula. But in the *Truculentus* alone, the rivalry between the lover Diniarchus and the Babylonian mercenary is in the service of an entirely different idea.

To begin with, Diniarchus is not under the authority of an elder, nor is he poor. Like Pleusicles in the *Miles Gloriosus* (102)—also an independent *adulescens*—he has served as an official legate, in this case on a mission to Lemnos (91–92), and even after wasting his substantial estates, he will still have enough left to make handsome presents to Phronesium, and later to take a wife with a diminished dowry. Second, and this is crucial, the obstacle to Diniarchus's hopes is not the purchase price demanded by a pimp, or the prior claim of the rival, but rather the insatiable avarice of the woman herself. Phronesium is owned by no one, she is at once procuress and prostitute, and Astaphium can speak of her profession indifferently as *lena* or *meretrix*.[10] If there is little intrigue in the *Truculentus,* it is because there is no one to be outwitted, at least not by Diniarchus. Phronesium provides her services only on payment. There is no set sum of money to be earned or stolen, no conditions to be met by which she may be won. All that Diniarchus can do is spend, to the ruin of his property. The pompous soldier is in fact no

[10]See lines 224, *lenam,* and 227, *meretricem;* Phronesium herself uses *meretrix,* 854 and 889.

rival at all; he is just another victim of the courtesan, who holds all the strings.

Given the autonomy of both Phronesium and Diniarchus, there clearly is no room in this play for the theme of thwarted mutual love. Phronesium may have her preferences among her suitors, but her overriding preoccupation is with cash. Diniarchus, in turn, has no expectation of purchasing her affections; he is content if he can buy her favors. Lust and greed nourish one another. In a way, it is the character of Phronesium that determines all the rest. Her single-minded avarice elicits as a reflex Diniarchus's prodigal sensuality and interferes with the usual competition between the rival lovers. We may observe, then, how the transformation of the narrative paradigm—the shift in the role of blocking character, the want of intrigue against the rival—is a function of the altered status and motives of the principal agents. The comic story of rival lovers is evoked and leaves its mark upon the action in several important respects. But it is metamorphosed into quite another tale, in which the characters have different values and their actions compose a different narrative structure.

Phronesium's intended deception of the Babylonian soldier, about which Diniarchus is surprisingly well informed, does, of course, furnish the otherwise missing element of intrigue, albeit translated into the idiom of the *Truculentus*. We shall return to this feature later, when the action will have unfolded. For the present, Diniarchus's knowledge of a conspiracy aimed at his rival intimates his potential complicity in the scheme of his mistress, and thus opens up the possibility of an alliance between them, a bond that will unite them in a felicitous resolution of the plot. There is such a move, as we shall see, but it proves to be congruent once again with the peculiar mood of the *Truculentus*, rather than with the spirit of comic reconciliation.

The next phase of the action is punctuated by two arias or cantica sung by Phronesium's maid, Astaphium. They frame a dialogue—in the beginning, a duet—between Astaphium and Diniarchus. Astaphium begins with a complaint about the morals of young men, who visit brothels in gangs, so that some may steal while others distract the household. The ensuing encounter between Diniarchus and Astaphium essentially dramatizes and embroiders upon the relationship between lover and courtesan which Diniarchus had outlined in his opening soliloquy, much the way Euripides will

often stage a scene immediately after the prologue which exhibits the situation just described. Diniarchus whimpers plaintively about his former benefactions, but Astaphium reminds him sharply that, with the collapse of his fortune, he is as good as dead (162–67). A lover, she reasons, is like an enemy fortress: The best thing for the girl is to sack it at once (170–71). Diniarchus concedes the point, but draws a distinction between a lover (*amator*) and a friend (*amicus*): Oldest friends, he says, are best (172–73). This hint that Diniarchus may have with Phronesium a different relationship from that of her other lovers again raises the possibility, however muted, that he may ultimately draw Phronesium to his side, and that the two together will profit from the plot against the soldier. As we shall see, this idea is carefully cultivated at several crucial points in the drama. But Diniarchus here drops it at once to reveal that he is not utterly destitute, but retains some land and buildings (*fundi et aedes,* 174; the phrase becomes a leitmotiv, cf. 177, 186–214). Astaphium immediately ingratiates herself with him, declaring finally that Phronesium loves him alone among the lot; Diniarchus shrewdly exclaims at the timely intervention of his land and buildings (186–87). The scene closes with something of a regression in the plot. When Astaphium first appeared on stage, Diniarchus had overheard her say that she was sent to fetch a man (114); though she denies it, he is not deceived, and assumes it must be a new lover (135). Toward the end of the dialogue, Astaphium insists that Phronesium really was pregnant, but concealed the fact from Diniarchus because she feared he would compel her to abort the child (200–201). Diniarchus this time is persuaded, and concludes both that the father in fact is the Babylonian soldier, and that it is he whom Phronesium is expecting. Astaphium leaves him to wait upon Phronesium's ablutions (197, 208), while she herself pursues her errand.

Astaphium's second song is a spritely extravaganza on the courtesan's duty to put profit before passion and wring her clients of their last cent, then turn them from her door. Only once, for a brief two verses, does she drop the cynical banter to concede that Phronesium is in the habit of freely sharing her most important plans with Diniarchus, and that as a friend he is more a counselor than benefactor (215–16). When she arrives at her destination, it emerges that she had been sent to fetch yet another admirer of Phronesium's, this one a rustic youth who, behind the back of his

father, has been paying court to the lady. Astaphium must first, however, deal with a surly slave who violently disapproves of the licentiousness of his young master: This slave is the man called Truculentus, from whom the play derives its name (246–53; 265).

The role of Truculentus and his master, Strabax, is worked into the action with great elegance. Inasmuch, however, as it impinges directly on the plot only much later, when the play is two-thirds over, we shall postpone discussion of it for the time being and pursue the dominant theme of Diniarchus's rivalry with the *miles gloriosus* for the graces of Phronesium.

When Astaphium returns to her mistress's house, she finds Diniarchus still waiting and petulant about the delay. Plautus takes advantage of the situation to make a few jokes: Fish do less washing than Phronesium; lovers will have to become bath-house attendants; Diniarchus is so tired he himself needs a shower (322–28); when Phronesium appears, he asks if she is finally clean, and she inquires in return whether she looks dirty—time was, says Diniarchus, when the two of them did some pretty dirty things together (378–81). I mention all this to show the care with which the interruption caused by the scene with Truculentus is covered by direct comic exploitation of the pause. In a brief monologue, Diniarchus laments the loss of his fortune; if he had it to do over again, he would, he says, squander it once more in no time flat (347–48). In the following scene with Phronesium, after some amiable chatter, Diniarchus opens the question of her motherhood. Phronesium immediately takes him into her confidence: "You are the only one left for me to talk to; I have always confided my most important plans to you" (387–88). She tells him that her pregnancy was a hoax (as he had surmised earlier), designed to trap the soldier; her hairdresser, Syra, had discovered, at her orders, an unwanted baby in the neighborhood. As she says here and later, everyone must be sharp at his own trade (416, 932). As for Diniarchus, she will give herself to him unstintingly when she has what she wants from the other, whom she will then dismiss on some ready pretext (418–22). At this point, the plot appears to take a turn, or to exhibit a facet of itself, which is in conformity with the standard comic paradigm; the hints of a special connection between Diniarchus and Phronesium are here realized, and we may imagine a conventional solution to the story, according to which the lover and his girl humiliate the rich and mighty rival, in order to enjoy each other's

company in the bliss of a romantic union. Phronesium seems not to be the calculating profiteer that Astaphium had painted. Her motive is true love and loyalty to Diniarchus. To be sure, it is unusual for the girl herself, rather than a clever slave, for example, to play so large a role in conceiving and carrying out the deception, leaving her lover both mystified and without a part of his own to play in the intrigue. But this could be construed as an adaptation to the special circumstances of the drama, in which both principals have, as we have seen, complete autonomy. Given that alteration in what we may call the initial conditions, the plot, as it now presents itself, seems well suited to bring about a denouement entirely consistent with the comic paradigm of the rival type.

The entire set of expectations conditioned by the evocation of the *miles gloriosus* archetype is suddenly exploded when Phronesium requests of Diniarchus a little gift (425). Though he leaps at the opportunity to demonstrate his goodwill, even to the point of saying that he chalks it up to profit when she asks something of him (426–27)—to which Phronesium replies, she too, when she receives it—nevertheless, he is at once reduced to just another of her paying customers. As the mercenary impulse surfaces in the courtesan, there can no longer be any question of a genuine bond between her and Diniarchus. Her materialism fractures the potential community of interest, and with this change in characterization, the plot must undergo a corresponding alteration. Whatever the resolution, it will not involve a festive union of hero and heroine. Thus, while I am not suggesting that there is a relationship as strong as entailment between plot and characterization, which would compromise the autonomy of one or the other, nevertheless within a broad literary or cultural tradition certain narrative forms are associated significantly, and not altogether accidentally, with sets of motivations. This simultaneous variation of mythos and ethos, superimposed upon the lineaments—so subtly yet unmistakably evoked—of the comic archetype, is responsible, I shall argue, for the pervasive feeling that the *Truculentus* is realistic or satirical.

When Phronesium reenters her house, Diniarchus, still exulting at the token of her trust in him, utters a brief profession of his ecstasy: "O immortal gods! that's no lover-woman, but a soul-deep, faithful comrade, to do the service which she just did for me, confiding in me the substitution of the baby, which a girl wouldn't tell her closest sister. She revealed herself to me from the heart, that

she will never be unfaithful to me so long as she lives. Should I not love her? not respect her? I'd sooner stop loving myself than lose my love for her" (434–42). The language here is conspicuously political: *socia, fidens, officium facere*. It is the most powerful metaphor for an enduring bond of love in the Roman vocabulary, and, I believe, is distinctly a Plautine touch.[11] This is the acme of the narrative tension: Diniarchus fancies he has won the day, having discovered the real quality of Phronesium and thereby switching the story to a more pleasing track. In an exuberant expression of joy and gratitude, he continues: "Shall I not send her a present? Why, I shall order five minae brought to her at once, and another mina on top of that for the festivities" (443–45). This is a fatal confusion; the sum is enough to waste him, and money is his only lure. At the same time, however, Diniarchus's munificence will put the soldier at a disadvantage, exciting Phronesium's scorn for his more modest contributions. Thus, Diniarchus's mistaken perception of Phronesium and the course of events to come will survive a while longer. So long as he can play to the greed of the courtesan, he is free to imagine that his story is a comic romance.

Phronesium's soliloquy in the next scene proclaims her philosophic pride in treachery and wrong-doing (cf. the forms of *dolus* in 456, 458, 461, and of *malus, malitia* in 452, 465, 468, 470, 471 *ter*, 473). She simulates a recent parturition as Stratophanes, the Babylonian soldier, stalks onto the stage. Stratophanes' opening pronouncements compose an elegant praeteritio: His virtues are proclaimed in deeds, says he, not words (483); one eyewitness is worth ten who know by hearsay (489), and so forth. The tone is bombastic, and Stratophanes achieves the customary absurdity of the comic soldier when he inquires whether his son has yet joined the legions and brought home the spoils (508), or announces himself as Mars returning to his Nereid (515). Nevertheless, he is dis-

[11]Compare David O. Ross, Jr., *Style and Tradition in Catullus* (Cambridge, Mass. 1969), the section entitled "Lesbia and the Vocabulary of Political Alliance," 80–95. Friedrich Zucker, "Socia unanimans," *Rh. Mus.* 92 (1944), 193–217, furnishes an extensive survey of the ethical language and spirit of Greek new comedy in the context of fourth-century philosophical and moral literature; his title is borrowed from line 435 of the *Truculentus* where, as Zucker observes (193), it is employed in a context that is not entirely respectable. Its effect will have been to evoke a vigorous ethical tradition, which is represented in Plautus's *Stichus* (adapted from Menander's *Adelphoe*, though not the same play that inspired Terence's like-named comedy); Zucker analyzes the *Stichus* in detail (195–207).

tinctly a modest example of the type, unattended by the usual entourage of flatterers—cooks, parasites, ingratiating slaves who mockingly magnify his exploits. This reduction fits his status in the play, for his only power over Phronesium is in the gifts he bears, and of these she is openly contemptuous. Stratophanes is shocked by her ingratitude (535); his presents, as he says, were worth twenty minae, and he received not a single kind word in return (543–44). Given his tender feeling for the child, he cuts a pathetic figure—not at all the sort of alazon in whose discomfiture the spectator readily rejoices. He is a poor, though not impossible, specimen for the comedy of rivals.

Stratophanes' reflections are interrupted by the arrival of Diniarchus' slave, Cyamus, who brings on the provisions ordered by his master. His canticum is particularly cynical: Inasmuch as the courtesan is like a sea which consumes all but never flows over, and is one who has stripped his master of goods, life, reputation, and friends, he has had no compunctions about diverting a part of the mina entrusted to him by Diniarchus into his own purse (561–74). Phronesium accepts the offerings, together with the five minae in silver, with a great display of satisfaction: "Tell him," she says, "that on account of these gifts he has sent me I love him most of all, that he of all men has my greatest esteem, and beg him to come to me" (589–92). Now, even though Cyamus has just called her a veritable stable of vice (stabulum flagiti, 587), Phronesium might still appear to be moved by feeling for Diniarchus in preferring his six minae to the soldier's twenty, save that our attention is immediately drawn to Stratophanes by Cyamus's inquiry concerning the identity of the wretched bystander (593–95). With this, Phronesium's protestations take on the appearance of a charade, designed to humiliate the soldier and extract some further donations. Stratophanes is outraged at Phronesium's fickleness (607–11, 616–18) and, after an exchange of threats, drives Cyamus from the stage, upon which Phronesium retires, complaining of a headache. Stratophanes utters a brief but bitter soliloquy which is dignified and menacing; then he too departs.

The drama of Diniarchus and Stratophanes is interrupted at this point—two-thirds of the way through the play—by the first appearance of Strabax, the country boy and third contender for the attentions of Phronesium. The rival paradigm does not, of course,

require a third, and while the situation of three suitors for a single girl finds a parallel, for example, in the *Asinaria,* it signals, there as here, a substantial departure from the conventional form, with important consequences for the meaning and structure of the work. Strabax's function in the story of Diniarchus and the soldier is to effect the final sublation of their competition. He is no fit obstacle to either of them: not to Diniarchus, because he has no prior claim over Phronesium; not to Stratophanes, because there can be no question of a personal attraction between Strabax and the courtesan. The potential antithesis of causes or motives congruent with a pair of lovers—passion versus power, or, in its most reduced form, predilection versus the charm of wealth—collapses with the introduction of a third suitor into a single motive, indefinitely iterable: Pure greed, unopposed and therefore not limited by love or attraction. Material desires in tension with romantic love may take on the appearance of needs, as the antithesis to the free expression of the feelings. Thus Phronesium seems caught, so long as the competition is binary, between passion (for Diniarchus) and compulsion (exercised by the superior resources of Stratophanes), however attenuated this opposition may be, for this conflict of motives is coordinate with the roles of lover and rival. Add Strabax, and the polarity is immediately collapsed into a single drive, at once free and calculating, which defines in turn a single role for all Phronesium's admirers: They become customers.

The characterization of Strabax, however, has its own features, which do more than serve the bare requirement of deflecting the rival plot. As Erich Segal has observed, Strabax defines himself against the authority of his parents.[12] Eight times in eighteen lines he underscores his disobedience to his mother and father (645–62). He has cheated the old man out of twenty minae to spend on the prostitute, then blithely decides to wipe him out altogether, and after that his mother too (660–61). The figure of the prodigal son is a familiar one in ancient comedy. The most straightforward exposition of his story is perhaps Plautus's *Mostellaria,* and it may be regarded as a variation on what we have called the basic plot form. With the help of a wily slave or other intriguer, he dissipates the family fortune on a woman he fancies. When the deception is at

[12]Erich Segal, *Roman Laughter: The Comedy of Plautus* (New York, 1971), 67–69.

last exposed, a recognition scene may be engineered to give him his beloved as a lawful spouse, or, alternatively, the father may relent in his moral rage and accept his son's repentance for the youthful lapse. The tension between Strabax's reckless infatuation and his father's practical parsimony, together with the misappropriation of the twenty minae, thus has all the earmarks of this paradigm. What is more, the earlier interview between his slave, Truculentus, and Astaphium intimates the kind of confrontation between father and son which demands a conventional resolution. For there, after some preliminary and vehement abuse of the girl, Truculentus declares his intention of revealing Strabax's liaison with Phronesium to the senior master (308; contrast *erilis noster filius,* 297)—that is, the father—and sets off for the forum to find the old man (313). When he is gone, Astaphium mutters that though he is severe, he is nevertheless loyal to his master. She then suggests that, despite his violent nature, she has hopes of seducing him with a courtesan's blandishments (315–19).

It is a well-known problem in the analysis of the play that Truculentus, when he returns to the stage for his second and final appearance, immediately after Strabax's entering soliloquy, seems to have undergone a complete change of heart on his own, without having encountered Astaphium in the interval or, so far as we know, having fulfilled his purpose of informing Strabax's father of the son's behavior. To Astaphium he says: "I am waiting for your kiss. Tell me, order me whatever you like, any way at all. I have a completely new character, and have lost the old. I can fall in love and even take a whore now" (675–78). The last we see of him, he suppresses a momentary recrudescence of indignation, then follows the maid indoors, having learned that Strabax is within (693–98).

This transformation of Truculentus's nature certainly is both abrupt and unmotivated. Indeed, Plautus seems to have planted an anticipatory clue in Astaphium's earlier boast that she can win him over, and then unaccountably ignored it just when some such explanation was required. Interpretations of the episode are of three kinds. The first is that it is satisfactory as it stands, according to the practice of the ancient comic dramatists. The critic at his leisure may be punctilious about details; the audience will have responded to the broad humor in the humbling of a puritanical grouch, while, on the level of the theme, the about-face, unexpected as it is, reconfirms the uncanny power which the prostitutes in this play exercise

on all the males who chance within their orbit.[13] A second line of criticism is that something of the Greek original of this play has been omitted in Plautus's adaptation, perhaps little more than the report that Truculentus failed to find Strabax's father in the forum, or, on the other hand, some lines or even a scene to give greater plausibility to Truculentus's new image. The strongest statement of this position is that of Ernout, in his edition of Plautus's comedies, although Ernout does not blame Plautus, but some later redactor of the play: "It is obvious that the play itself, in the state in which we have it, has been reworked and abridged so thoroughly that the original composition has become unrecognizable; and the intrigue, mistreated so, furnishes obscurities, incoherences, defects of every sort for which one should not hold Plautus entirely responsible."[14] A third strategy is to hypothesize two entirely distinct models for the *Truculentus,* one centered about Diniarchus and Stratophanes, the other involving Strabax and his slave, which Plautus conflated to produce the version we possess.[15]

The relevant point for our analysis is that the story of Diniarchus and the soldier, and that of Strabax, are paradigmatically distinct, irrespective of the nature of the Greek source. It is of less consequence, from this point of view, whether Plautus found the Strabax material in his model substantially as we have it, or in an expanded form which he condensed without too nice a regard for consistency; whether he extracted it from a wholly different Greek comedy, or, finally, invented it entirely on his own. For behind this interesting question is the prior or more general issue of archetypal synthesis, whether this was managed by Plautus himself, in accord with the two latter procedures, or by the author of the Greek original, as the first two procedures imply. The identification of compatible source texts and the capacity to weld them into a co-

[13]Enk is among those who are untroubled by Truculentus's conversion; see *Plauti Truculentus,* vol. 1, 19, and vol. 2, 153–54, *ad v.* 673, where he cites Ussing's comment *ad loc.,* that Plautus was not so much concerned to discover the reasons for Truculentus's change of heart, as he was to portray the depravity of mankind and offer it for the amusement of his spectators.

[14]A. Ernout, ed., *Plaute: Comédies,* vol. 7 (Paris, 1940) 92. Cf. also Otto Ribbeck, "Marginalien zum Truculentus," *Rh. Mus.* N.S. 37 (1882) 417–24.

[15]On this kind of conflation, see Lothar Schaaf, *Der Miles Gloriosus des Plautus und sein griechisches Original: Ein Beitrag zur Kontaminationsfrage* (Munich, 1977), 11–18, and passim; also useful is P. J. Enk, "How Did Plautus Adapt His Greek Models?," in *Miscellanea Giovanni Galbiati,* vol. 1 (Milan, 1951), 105–20.

herent unity presuppose an intuition of the kinds of elements out of which stories are constructed and the way they are put together. These elements are precisely the forms which we have posited as paradigmatic for the genre, and therefore those with which the original poet must work, that is, the author of the Greek model, if it was unitary, or Plautus himself, if free invention on this scale was an admissible part of his craft.

Whatever the textual source, if any, for the roles of Strabax and Truculentus, they represent the insertion into the rival paradigm of characters whose normal place is in the story of the prodigal son, or more generally, of the conflict between youthful passion and paternal authority. However, the same forces that were at work in subverting or rendering satirical the competition between Diniarchus and Stratophanes—that is, the operation of pure greed untempered by love, unchecked by power—leave their mark on the picture of Strabax as well. Like Diniarchus and Phronesium, Strabax is autonomous, since the father who might be the obstacle to his dissipation is conjured out of the action, and Truculentus, his would-be surrogate, is himself metamorphosed into a lusty wastrel. The potential blocking figures, having been powerfully evoked, evanesce, and with them the tension between conventional values and private impulse which is the heart and soul of the plot they serve. What remains is unobstructed commerce with the courtesans, so long as money lasts. The ordinary father and son paradigm, with its mainspring of opposed motivations, is projected as a subtext or countertext, against which Strabax's and Truculentus's unhindered submission to their desires appears as a reduced or collapsed narrative. Thus, the complex and apparently inconsistent characterization of Truculentus is coordinate with a transformation of the conventional plot in a manner exactly parallel to the inversion of the usual rivals paradigm and the concomitant changes in the natures of Diniarchus and Stratophanes. In the *Truculentus,* where the only motives are lust and greed, the only obstacle to the consummation of desire is the wealth of a competitor. Thus Strabax, the prodigal son, is made to enter the action solely in the capacity of a rich rival, a transformation that simultaneously dissolves the opposition between Diniarchus and Stratophanes and reduplicates the satiric inversion of their story.

The balance of the play exhibits the effects of Strabax's position upon the fortunes of Diniarchus and Stratophanes, except for one

extraordinary episode, in which the rival paradigm achieves a brilliantly ironic denouement. This phase of the action begins with the return of Diniarchus, who is exultant over Phronesium's reception of his gifts and her contempt for the soldier's offerings (703–5). "It's my ball," he says. "If the soldier is rejected, the woman will be mine" (706). At this point Astaphium emerges from the house, and reveals that Strabax is within. "What's this? Some new lover?" asks Diniarchus. "She's found a treasure-chest, full and intact," replies Astaphium. "He has sole authority with us, he is now our new estate" (724–27). And when Diniarchus complains, "Won't you now let me in?" Astaphium answers, "Why you more than the soldier" (732), evoking the former rivalry only to reveal its irrelevance. Diniarchus and Stratophanes have the same status now. After some witty repartee and abuse, Astaphium reenters the house, and Diniarchus toys with the idea of denouncing Phronesium's entire operation to the magistrates (759–65). Of course, it is not to be; there is always the chance, he reflects, that she may yet allow him inside (766).

With Diniarchus thoroughly humbled, the action suddenly takes a surprising turn with the arrival of three new characters: an old man named Callicles, his maidservant, and Syra, the hairdresser who had assisted Phronesium in finding the decoy baby. As Diniarchus hides in the wings, the following circumstances are exposed: The baby is in fact the bastard son of Callicles' daughter and Diniarchus, to whom she had been betrothed. When he is explicitly identified, Diniarchus confesses his guilt and requests the girl's hand in marriage, agreeing to a substantial reduction of the dowry. Callicles departs to break off the engagement he had subsequently arranged with a neighbor's son, and Diniarchus primes himself to demand back his son from Phronesium, who now appears with Astaphium, apprised by Syra of the new state of affairs. Her manner is conciliatory and seductive, coaxing Diniarchus into lending her the baby for a few more days, so that she can complete her plot against the soldier. After some perfunctory resistance, Diniarchus submits, in return for which she guarantees him access to her establishment in case of trouble at home; "at least," she says, "be a partner in plunder" (*amicus manubiarius,* 880). With a nod to the offer, Diniarchus leaves the stage. Alone, Phronesium is free to speak her mind and returns to character: "Friends are wealth" (*ubi amici, ibidem opes,* 885).

This episode has no effect on the next and final scene of the play. The soldier returns, equipped with a mina of gold, but Phronesium, alleging the costs of raising his child, frowns at his parsimony. Strabax comes out of Phronesium's place to look for her, and Stratophanes, like Diniarchus before him, learns for the first time of the new challenger. Her conspicuous attentions to Strabax are more than the soldier can endure, and he exclaims, in a formula reminiscent of Diniarchus's earlier exasperation, that he would rather be dead (Diniarchus: *mortuom hercle me quam ut id patiar mauelim*, 742; Stratophanes: *ego illam patiar alios amplexarier? mortuom hercle me satiust*, 925–26). At Phronesium's prompting, Stratophanes and Strabax vie with one another to win the courtesan with bribes—it is a contest of gold, not steel, she warns the volatile soldier (929), and Strabax observes that it is preferable to fight it out with minae rather than menaces (*meliust te minis certare mecum quam minaciis*, 948). Astaphium's cynical aside sums up the competition: "A fool and a madman are contending in their losses; we are saved" (950). In a final burst of expansiveness, Phronesium invites them both inside and, satisfied with a good day's work, extends her offer to the audience as well, bidding them applaud the play for Venus's sake.

The final scene between Stratophanes, Strabax, and Phronesium thus corresponds to the previous dialogue between Diniarchus and Astaphium. In each, one of the rivals discovers with some surprise that Strabax has preempted the prostitute. The tension between Diniarchus and Stratophanes is dissolved, and their initial sense of indignation at the rude interloper each time gives way before the inevitable allure of the whore. The ruse of the baby helps to snare the soldier, but this is in no way affected by the revelation of its true paternity. So far as that goes, the scene with Callicles is canceled by the deal between Phronesium and Diniarchus: Once she borrows the baby back, it might as well have remained an orphan, for all the difference it will make to Phronesium's plans—save for the complications that may arise unless the soldier departs before the three days are up for which she has it (there is no earlier indication that Stratophanes' sojourn in Athens will be a brief one). If we are to understand the significance of Callicles' role, we shall have to look to its meaning for the relationship between Diniarchus and Phronesium.

Diniarchus's paternity has two consequences: His marriage to

Callicles' daughter, and the special bond between him and Phronesium which results from his complicity in the fraud involving the child. The same turn of events which might have given Diniarchus the decisive advantage in his struggle with the soldier for Phronesium's favors threatens to remove him from the scene of battle. He is no longer merely a friendly counselor, more even than a friendly ally (*amicus consiliarius; amicus auxiliarius,* 216); he is a friendly looter (*amicus manubiarius,* 880), a full partisan of Phronesium's conspiracy against Stratophanes. This connection might have served as a superb solution to the rivalry theme: Given all the distortions of the conventional plot produced by the atypical status and characterization of the three protagonists in this paradigm, the story could have been brought to something like the normal denouement, that is, an effective liaison between Diniarchus and Phronesium. Two circumstances, of course, interrupt this conclusion. The first is the role of Strabax, which, as we have seen, annihilates the rivals plot and renders the stratagem with the baby irrelevant to Diniarchus's ultimate success. The second is Diniarchus's anticipated marriage. By this, Diniarchus is obliged to rejoin respectable society, as it is represented by the elderly Callicles. In itself, such a reintegration of the lover into the traditional community is a very common occurrence at the end of a comedy. But nowhere in ancient comedy is the bride so extraneous to the theme and action of the play as here. The marriage is normally germane to the resolution of the social and psychological tensions of the drama. Georg Lukács describes its function: "When all the major characters with the exception of the unmasked hypocrites and villains marry one another at the end of the great comedies, this is just as much a symbolic ceremony as the hero's death at the end of tragedy; both are no more than symbols indicating the drawing of a boundary, the drawing of the sharp outline required by the sculptural essentiality of the drama."[16] Symbols, yes—but not arbitrary or purely formal. Marriage is the symbol of the presupposed harmony between public values and private passions which informs the genre of comedy and gives to its story patterns their characteristic lineaments, their closure. In the *Truculentus,* however, the betrothal of Diniarchus and Callicles's daughter is

[16]Georg Lukács, *The Theory of the Novel,* trans. Anna Bostock (Cambridge, Mass., 1975), 108.

irrelevant to the main comic tension, save as a device that permits Diniarchus to ingratiate himself further with Phronesium through his authority over the supposititious baby. Its function in the larger story is to serve the cause of Diniarchus's affair with the courtesan, a benefit of which he is fully cognizant. In such a context, the role of marriage as a symbol of comic closure is simply inverted.

The history of Diniarchus's relations with Callicles's daughter, however, summons up its own archetype, one of the most familiar in the comic repertoire. His seduction of the girl represents a breach in the social code, which must be mended by their lawful union. Passionate impulse is thus brought under the sway of civic morality. Menander's *Samia* and *Epitrepontes,* Terence's *Hecyra* and *Adelphoe,* Plautus's own *Aulularia* and *Cistellaria* are predicated on a rape or seduction which in the end is translated into a bond both erotic and conjugal, the happy intersection of desire and social constraint. But the episode of Callicles' daughter conforms to this pattern only in its extrinsic features. There is no hint that Diniarchus is in love with the girl; quite the contrary, he is still hopelessly infatuated with Phronesium (853). He accepts her simply because he has been shamed into it (826–28, 835). This is a victory for the public ethic all right, but comedy demands not the repression of private passion but rather its coincidence with the claims of duty. The continued dissonance between the two is signaled by Diniarchus's expressed intention of revisiting Phronesium on the sly (882). Nowhere else in what survives of ancient comedy, so far as I know, is the tension between love and obligation permitted to survive the pact that culminates the drama. In this connection, one further detail deserves mention. The seduction of Callicles' daughter, and the birth of a child, did not compromise her eligibility for marriage. The facts were kept well hidden, and she had already been betrothed, as we have seen, to the son of a neighbor or relative.[17] The marriage with Diniarchus, then, is not absolutely enjoined by the social code. Apart from a possible sentimental attachment to his grandson, Callicles' motives for uniting his daughter with Diniarchus are obscure. Neither love nor necessity requires such an arrangement.

[17]True, the marriage is forestalled; nevertheless, this is an important exception to the rule that a woman in comedy, if she is not a virgin, may marry only the man she has known carnally.

The episode of Callicles' daughter thus betrays an inversion or disruption of content within the scaffolding of a conventional form, analogous to the dislocations in the stories of Diniarchus and Stratophanes on the one hand, and of Strabax on the other. There is one important difference: In the rest of the play, the dominant social institutions, such as marriage among citizens, preservation of one's estate, trade along acceptable and productive channels, do not in any way define the motives of the characters. Diniarchus, Strabax, and Phronesium simply scorn the moral categories of conventional society. Only Callicles is guided by them, and Diniarchus briefly submits to his authority, until he comes back again into the presence of Phronesium. But Callicles' role does nothing to alter Diniarchus's nature, nor does it bring about any turn in the plot by which his desires and duties may be made fortuitously to coincide. The distance between the communal order and personal impulses remains as great as ever, both in the moral awareness of the characters (which is normal for comedy) and in the final situation engendered by the plot.[18] Once again, the comic paradigm fails to achieve its proper resolution.

The absence or inconsequentiality of socially approved motives and the hegemony of private impulse in the personality are characteristic of the world of satire, and these features, as they affect both the ethos and the plot of the *Truculentus,* endow it with its satirical spirit. Cynthia Dessen has investigated in considerable detail those aspects of the play which resemble the conventions of classical satire.[19] She points to the large number of monologues, many of which have the moralizing pungency of satiric diatribes (2–3); to the hostile epithets which, she says, "betray a genuine tension between the characters" (12); the subtly exaggerated, ironic, and bitter portraits of the protagonists, Diniarchus and Phronesium; the inversion of values, by which *aequus* and *probus* define the rapaciousness of the courtesan; the satiric imagery, which "emphasizes the bestial, aggressive side of man and his insensitivity to his

[18]Cf. Leo Bersani, *A Future for Astyanax: Character and Desire in Literature* (Boston, 1976), 54–55, who alludes to the observation by Georg Lukács cited above, and then expands upon it as follows: "In Molière, the obstacles to the good lovers' marriages are simply pushed aside by happy strokes of fate. The young people's union is not the result of any growth of moral consciousness: *they* have generally been in love from the very start."

[19]Dessen (above, n. 1).

fellow men" (28). None of these features is uncommon in the corpus of ancient comedy, but in the case of the *Truculentus,* Dessen observes, "instead of having occasional satiric moments, the entire play satirizes the courtesan's excessive power over her lovers" (2). But this satiric quality is not the mere sum or frequency of satiric elements; it pertains rather to the essence of the drama, the combination of plot and characterization which creates a universe of satiric personalities, dominated by such private obsessions as lust or greed, unconstrained by social etiquette, impeded only as they collide with one another in the pursuit of their compulsive goals, or drop out of the fray for having annihilated their resources. This world of satire is an underworld, existing in essential opposition to the dominant, structured values of the community. Horace introduces the reader to this restless, driven, atomized population, more a congeries than a social organism, in his first and programmatic satire. In the *Truculentus,* however, this world is made to emerge out of the stock types and narrative paradigms of new comedy, which is a wholly different mode—integrative, reconciling, affirming in the main the compatibility of the individual and society. The *Truculentus* is not merely ironic, the way Terence can be, casting the pall of doubt upon the conventional happy denouement, implicitly negating the moral content of the archetypes. Here, rather, they are utterly evacuated of their ordinary function and remain as mere forms, which the spirit of satire has appropriated to another use. To understand the plot of the *Truculentus,* we must see it as a comedy *sous rature,* a kind of canceled presence, metamorphosed by the pressure of a different genre.[20]

[20]I borrow the term *sous rature* from Jacques Derrida, *Of Grammatology,* trans. Gayatri Chakravorty Spivak (Baltimore, 1976), 19–26, see especially the "Translator's Preface," xv–xviii. See also George E. Rowe, Jr., *Thomas Middleton and the New Comedy Tradition* (Lincoln, Neb., 1979), 5–6: "The more thoroughly conventional (and thus uniform) a given genre is, the more strongly it controls our expectations and responses. . . . Such is the case with New Comedy, a genre which is highly conventional and thus remarkably consistent in the kinds of characters and events it describes. . . . At the end of the play we applaud a state of affairs which we have recognized since the beginning of the drama to be both beneficial and *inevitable.* Because New Comedy is so stylized and therefore creates strong and specific patterns of expectations, a comic play's failure to fulfill those expectations is usually disturbing. This failure and disturbance are precisely what happen with many of Middleton's dramas. Having assumed that we have entered a New Comedy world and established a certain perspective as a result, we are confronted suddenly by characters and incidents which violate the rules of the generic category we have assigned to the play. . . . We are left confused, unsatisfied, and perhaps slightly uneasy."

Satire is, in principle, independent of the moral intention or attitude of the writer. It is not essential to decide whether Plautus deprecated in a didactic manner the vices he portrayed, or took a wicked pleasure in them, or was content to represent them mimetically in the interest of dramatic realism. In each case, there hangs about the objects of satire an air of negation, the destructured underside of the prevailing code, defiant of self-control and the claims of social cohesiveness.

Those steeped in the classical theory of genres, however, may question whether it is legitimate to interpret ancient literature according to such general notions. Ulrich Knoche, for example, who has written an authoritative handbook on the Roman satirists, begins with the following observations: "Anyone attempting a historical treatment of Roman satire has to free himself right at the start from the contemporary concept of satire and the satiric. Nowadays we understand the 'satiric' as a specific attitude which can be expressed in a number of ways. . . . So conceived, satire feeds on the tension between what is ideal and what is real, and its purpose is to portray reality as a situation causing aversion or even disgust." Knoche contrasts this modern approach with the ancient: "To the Roman way of thinking this kind of thing would be inconceivable. The Latin word *satiricus* is not attested until relatively late times. . . . The ancients used it almost without exception to designate the poet who writes satires. . . . Even in antiquity the word *satura/satira,* from which the adjective is derived, did not simply denote a specific attitude of mind involving the contemporary scene, but was the term used for an independent literary genre of a particular kind with well-defined limits and a unique profile."[21] Now, I do not wish to dispute that for the Romans the word satire denoted a particular department of literature, defined by certain formal properties; but this department was understood to serve a proper, that is to say, satiric content. When Juvenal exclaimed, "it is hard not to write satire!" he was not expressing a compulsion to write hexameter verses, but rather to portray an imaginative world for which hexameter verses had become the appropriate literary vehicle. Horace is explicit about the continuity of the satiric impulse. He begins his fourth satire of the first book: "Eupolis and Cratinus and Aristophanes, and the other poets who were the masters of old comedy, used to brand with complete license anyone who deserved

[21]Ulrich Knoche, *Roman Satire,* trans. Edwin S. Ramage (Bloomington, 1975), 3.

to be stigmatized because he was wicked and a thief, or an adulterer or an assassin or notorious in some way or other. From this derives the whole of Lucilius, who followed them, changing only the meter and rhythm."

Horace's designation of old comedy as the progenitor of satire is especially suggestive in connection with the *Truculentus,* for Phronesium resembles the heroes or heroines in many of Aristophanes' plays, who are driven by some mighty impulse and succeed in refashioning the world around their own private desires.[22] Satire here is more than the disposition to expose and criticize vice, a kind of prissy wagging of the finger at human foibles. These contrary, energetic, passionate rascals are drawn bigger than life, boisterous, earthy, even grotesque—in a word, gargantuan. In a world governed by selfish, coarse desires they emerge joyously triumphant. There is, after all, something Rabelaisian about Phronesium, who draws her lovers about her with calculating guile and exuberant abandon, ultimately uniting them all in a communion of sensuality, bringing them under a single roof and into a single family, the underworld society of the whorehouse. As satire, the *Truculentus* bites; as comedy, it exults. The spirit of the marketplace, the abuse, the coarse imagery—even the absurd charade of postpartum spite on the part of Phronesium—have the vitality and optimism not so much of the saturnalian carnival as of everyday life as it is lived beneath and alongside the official seriousness of the imperial city-state.[23] The *Truculentus* is not merely satiric comedy; it is comic satire as well and takes its place in that antic tradition which extends from Aristophanes to Rabelais, from Ben Jonson's *Volpone* to the Marx brothers.

[22]For this view of Aristophanic comedy, see Cedric H. Whitman, *Aristophanes and the Comic Hero* (Cambridge, Mass., 1964).

[23]For this conception of comedy, see above all Mikhail Bakhtin, *Rabelais and His World,* trans. Helene Iswolsky (Cambridge, Mass., 1968). Dessen reflects: "The cruelty of these women, their cynicism and utter heartlessness, particularly Astaphium's, may cause one to wonder why they attract us at all. Perhaps it is their aggressive vitality and candid self-interest that fascinates us" (160). Dessen too makes the connection between Plautus and Ben Jonson (164–65).

Conclusion

Each of the eight interpretations I have offered in this book iden-
tifies a tension in values as the mainspring of the drama, which,
through plot, characterization, and such features of style as the
deployment of imagery and verbal associations, operates upon the
values so as to bring them into a new relationship to each other.
This operation I have taken as the locus of meaning in the plays;
because the motives that inspire the action are grounded in social
interests in the comedies under consideration, the meaning is in
each case a version of the ideology of the city-state. Accordingly,
the plays have much to tell us about the institutions of the ancient
Greek and Roman communities, and about the ways in which these
institutions were perceived. But my purpose has not been to call
the works of Plautus and Terence to witness for these institutions
and usages. My endeavor has been different from those investiga-
tions—very useful in themselves—of slaves or cooks or soldiers in
ancient comedy, or those which mine comedy for evidence of civil
statutes or religious practices.[1] My concern has been with the
meaning of each play, and that meaning reciprocally conditions and
is conditioned by the representation of character and motive.

[1]See, for example, P. P. Spranger, *Historische Untersuchungen zu den Sklavenfiguren des Plautus und Terenz* (Wiesbaden, 1961); Hans Dohm, *Mageiros: Die Rolle des Kochs in der griechisch-römischen Komödie* (Munich, 1964) [Zetemata 32]; John Arthur Han-son, "The Glorious Military," in T. A. Dorey and Donald R. Dudley, eds., *Roman Drama* (London, 1965); John A. Hanson, "Plautus as a Source Book for Roman Religion," *TAPA* 90 (1959), 48–101; Ugo Enrico Paoli, *Comici latini e diritto attico* (Milan, 1962).

Roman Comedy

I have identified a variety of narrative paradigms, together with their characteristic personae, as the basic components of comic structure. These paradigms are the conventional forms by which tensions in values are manifested and brought to a resolution. They are themselves subject to complex combinations, ironic inversions, or radical transformations which are the grounds of new and varied meanings. The ancient comic poets were consummate masters of this art. Working from the plays, one may, in this case or that, abstract an idealized image of the codes or value structures of the ancient city-state. But this image does not necessarily reflect or reveal the lineaments of actual social life. Undoubtedly, it sheds a certain light upon that life, and particularly upon the structure of popular conceptions, in which the complexities of social interactions are often reduced or regularized. Even so, the angle of vision in the several plays varies greatly, and their composite picture will not necessarily yield a single image. The comedies create worlds as much as they reflect a world, and the relationship between the world found and the worlds made is a function of theory, of literary and historical interpretation. Even when the plays appear to project a norm against which the drama takes place, it is unsafe to assume that this represents society as it is given, for ground and figure, norm and variation are always codetermined. The plays are not enacted within a matrix of values, but in each case precipitate the matrix, or a form of it.

It would be wrong, then, to see the several comedies as fragments of an ideology, still worse to recover that ideology by reducing their differences to a lowest common denominator. Perhaps one may best describe the plays, like all literature, as inventions in ideology; and in this they are like creative experiments in the institutions themselves, innovations in law or in custom, except that literary meaning—and that of comedy in particular—is mediated through the exploitation of the forms and materials available to the genre.[2] The historical organization of social relations in the form of the city-state is the ground of the common problematic which endows the genre with its unity as the product of a single culture.

From the foregoing considerations, we can see that the social

[2]Fredric Jameson, *The Prison-House of Language* (Princeton, 1972), 95, commenting on the theory of the Russian formalist Yury Tynyanov, writes of "the insistence . . . on the enabling role of the appropriate content or raw material, as well as on the ex post facto and non-predictive nature of literary analysis."

content of a comedy is indisseverable from its meaning and thus necessarily resides in the interpretation of the individual work. The entire corpus, moreover, stands to the ideology in a generative relation rather than as a reflection: The ideology is not manifested in its pure state in any one source, but exists as a deep structure. This structure organizes values and motives, however, and therefore presupposes the division of society into classes, strata, status groups, genders, as the condition for conformity with or violation of the social protocols. Thus, the social structure is always reproduced, albeit in distinct variants, in each literary product of an age. Some features of this structure may be more abiding than others, or even pertain to the nature of societies in general, while others, such as those we have investigated in the chapters of this book, may be specific to one or another social form. I have examined the structures implicit in the values and choices of the characters in the several plays, and determined the narrative forms in which they are typically expressed. I have explored how these forms are variously deployed to register different versions of the classical ideology, some of which may present themselves as conservative, others as critical, some as reflecting, others as challenging the prevailing codes—though the image of these codes too is a product of the narrative. In each case, moreover, I have interpreted the significance of the narrative structure through an examination of the verbal and metaphorical texture of the work, as in the operation of legal or ethical terminology, the occurrence of doublets among scenes or personae, imagery drawn from the spheres of nature or religion, and—most important of all—the formal, explicit statements and arguments of the characters themselves. No matter how embroidered with comic extravagance they are, I have always given them close and serious attention. The virtues of my categories and approach may be judged by the power of the individual interpretations, and by the extent to which, taken together, they exhibit the resources of the ancient comic dramatists to realize the meanings of the ancient city-state ideology.

Bibliography

Abel, Karlhans. *Die Plautusprologe.* Frankfurt am Main, 1955 [Diss. Goethe-Universität].

Adams, Diana. "The Truculentus of Plautus: A Play of Contrasts." Middletown, Conn., 1978 [Wesleyan University Master's Essay].

Allen, Archibald W. "Elegy and the Classical Attitude toward Love: Propertius I, 1," *YCS* 11 (1950), 255–77.

Arnott, W. Geoffrey. "Phormio Parasitus," *Greece and Rome,* ser. 2, no. 17 (1970), 32–57.

Ashmore, Sidney G., ed. *The Comedies of Terence.* Oxford, 1908.

Austin, James Curtiss. *The Significant Name in Terence,* University of Illinois Studies in Language and Literature 7.4 (1921).

Bakhtin, Mikhail. *Rabelais and His World.* Trans. Helene Iswolsky. Cambridge, Mass., 1968.

Baldry, H. C. *The Unity of Mankind in Greek Thought.* Cambridge, 1965.

Barber, C. L. *Shakespeare's Festive Comedy.* Princeton, 1959.

Beare, W. "The Secret of Terence," *Hermathena* 56 (1940), 21–39.

——. *The Roman Stage.* 3d ed. London, 1968; orig. 1950.

Bersani, Leo. *A Future for Astyanax: Character and Desire in Literature.* Boston, 1976.

Bertini, F. *Plauti Asinaria.* Genova, 1968.

Besnier, Maurice. "pomerium," in C. Daremberg and E. Saglio, *Dictionnaire des antiquités grecques et romaines.* Vol. 4.1. (Paris, 1892), 543–47.

Bianco, Orazio. *Terenzio: Problemi e aspetti dell' originalità.* Rome, 1962.

Blumenthal, von. "pomerium," *RE* 21.2 (1952), 1867–76.

Bond, John, and Walpole, Arthur Sumner, eds. *The Phormio of Terence.* 3d ed. London and New York, 1964; orig. 1889.

169

Bibliography

Brunt, Peter A. *Italian Manpower 225 B.C.–A.D. 14*. Oxford, 1971.

——. *Social Conflicts in the Roman Republic*. New York, 1971.

Büchner, Karl. *Das Theater des Terenz*. Heidelberg, 1974.

Buck, Charles Henry, Jr. *A Chronology of the Plays of Plautus*. Baltimore, 1940.

Bushala, Eugene W. "The 'Pallake' of Philoneus," *AJP* 90 (1969), 65–72.

Campbell, Joseph. *The Hero with a Thousand Faces*. 2d ed. Princeton, 1968.

Caputi, Anthony. *Buffo*. Detroit, 1978.

Cawelti, John G. *Adventure, Mystery and Romance: Formula Stories as Art and Popular Culture*. Chicago, 1976.

Collins, Rev. W. Lucas. *Plautus and Terence*. Edinburgh, 1873.

Copley, Frank O., ed. *Plautus, The Rope*. New York, 1956.

Corte, Francesco della. "La commedia dell' Asinaio," *RFIC* 79 (1951), 289–306.

——. "Contaminatio e retractatio nell' Asinaria," *Dioniso* 35 (1961), 30–52.

——. *Da Sarsina a Roma*. Florence, 1967.

Croce, Benedetto. "Intorne alle commedie di Terenzio," *La critica* 34 (1936), 401–423; repr. in *Poesia antica e moderna*, 2d ed. (Bari, 1943).

Crook, John. "Patria Potestas." *CQ* N.S. 17 (1967), 113–22.

Curcio, Gaetano. *Storia della letteratura latina*. Vol. 1. Naples, 1920.

Davies, John K. "Athenian Citizenship," *CJ* 73 (1977–78), 105–21.

Denzler, Bruno. *Der Monolog bei Terenz*. Zurich, 1968.

Derrida, Jacques. *Of Grammatology*. Trans. Gayatri Chakravorty Spivak. Baltimore, 1976.

Dessen, Cynthia. "Plautus' Satiric Comedy: The *Truculentus*," *Philological Quarterly* 56 (1977), 145–68.

Detienne, Marcel. "Arcturus, démon astral," *Bollettino de l'Institut historique belge de Rome* 31 (1958), 5–21.

——, and Vernant, Jean-Pierre. *Cunning Intelligence in Greek Culture and Society*. Trans. Janet Lloyd. Sussex, 1976.

Dohm, Hans. *Mageiros: Die Rolle des Kochs in der griechisch-römischen Komödie*. Munich, 1964 [Zetemata 32].

Dover, K. J. *Greek Popular Morality in the Time of Plato and Aristotle*. Oxford, 1974.

Drexler, Hans. "Die moralische Geschichtsauffassung der Römer," *Gymnasium* 61 (1954), 168–90, repr. in Richard Klein, ed., *Das Staatsdenken der Römer*. Darmstadt, 1966.

Duckworth, George E., ed. *The Complete Roman Drama*. Vol. 2. New York, 1942.

——. *The Nature of Roman Comedy*. Princeton, 1952.

Dziatzko, Karl, and Hauler, Edmund, eds. *Ausgewählte Komödien des P. Terentius Afer*. Vol. 1. *Phormio*. Leipzig, 1913.

Bibliography

Eagleton, Terry. *Criticism and Ideology*. London, 1976.

Earl, D. C. "Political Terminology in Plautus," *Historia* 9 (1960), 234–43.

——. "Terence and Roman Politics," *Historia* 11 (1962), 469–85.

——. *The Political Thought of Sallust*. London, 1966.

——. *The Moral and Political Tradition of Rome*. Ithaca, N.Y., 1967.

Elmer, Herbert Charles, ed. *P. Terenti Phormio*. Boston, 1901.

Enk, P. J. "How Did Plautus Adapt His Greek Models?" in *Fontes Ambrosiani* 25 (1951) [*Miscellanea Giovanni Galbiati* vol. 1 Milan, 1951], 105–20.

——. *Plauti Truculentus*. Vol. 1, Leyden, 1952; vol. 2, Leyden, 1953.

——. "De Poenulo plautina," *Wissenschaftliche Zeitschrift der Universität Rostock* 12 (1963), 209–13.

——. "Plautus' *Truculentus*," in Charles Henderson, Jr., ed., *Classical Medieval and Renaissance Studies in Honor of Berthold Louis Ullman*. Vol. 1 (Rome, 1964), 49–65.

Ernout, A., ed. *Plaute: Comédies*, vol. 7. Paris, 1940.

Esteves, Victor A., S. J. "*Senex* as Spouse in Plautus and Terence," *Classical Bulletin* 42 (1966), 73–76.

Flores, Enrico. *Letteratura latina e ideologia de III-II a.c.* Naples, 1974.

Flury, Peter. *Liebe und Liebessprache bei Menander, Plautus und Terenz*. Heidelberg, 1968.

Forehand, Walter E. "Plautus' *Casina:* An Explication," *Arethusa* 6 (1973), 233–56.

Forster, E. M. *Aspects of the Novel*. New York, 1927.

Fraenkel, Eduard. "Zur Geschichte des Wortes *fides*," *Rh. Mus.* 71 (1916), 187–99.

——. *Plautinisches im Plautus*. Berlin, 1922. Trans. Franco Munari as *Elementi Plautini in Plauto*. Florence, 1960.

——. "The Stars in the Prologue of the *Rudens*," *CQ* 36 (1942), 10–14.

Frank, Tenney. "Terence's Contribution to Plot-Construction," *AJP* 49 (1928), 309–22.

——. *Life and Literature in the Roman Republic*. Berkeley, 1965; orig. 1930.

Freud, Sigmund. *Totem and Taboo*. Vol. 13 of James Strachey et al., eds., *The Complete Psychological Works of Sigmund Freud*. London, 1953– .

Friedrich, Wolf H. *Euripides und Diphilos: Zur Dramaturgie der Spätformen*. Munich, 1953 [Zetemata 5].

Frye, Northrop. "The Argument of Comedy," in *English Institute Essays* 1948–1949. New York, 1949.

——. *Anatomy of Criticism*. Princeton, 1957; repr. New York, 1967.

Fustel de Coulanges, N. D. *The Ancient City*. Trans. Willard Small. New York, n.d.

Gagliardi, Donato. "Aspetti del teatro comico latino: La 'politica' di Plauto," *Le parole e l' idée* 5 (1963), 167–74.

Bibliography

Garzya, Antonio. *Note al Rudens di Plauto*. Naples, 1967.

Geertz, Clifford. *The Interpretation of Cultures*. New York, 1973.

Genovese, Eugene E. *Roll Jordan Roll: The World the Slaves Made*. New York, 1972; repr. 1976.

Gomme, A. W., and Sandbach, F. H. *Menander: A Commentary*. Oxford, 1973.

Green, William M. "Greek and Roman Law in the 'Trinummus,'" *CP* 24 (1929), 183–92.

Griffith, G. T. *The Mercenaries of the Hellenistic World*. Cambridge, 1935.

Grimal, Pierre. "Le modèle et la date des *Captivi* de Plaute," *Latomus* 101 (1969), 394–414.

Haffter, Heinz. "Terenz und seine künstlerische Eigenart," *Museum Helveticum* 10 (1953), 1–20, 73–102. Trans. Dante Nardo as *Terenzio e la sua personalità artistica*. Rome, 1969.

Hansen, William F. "An Oral Source for the *Menaechmi*," *CW* 70 (1977), 385–90.

Hanson, John A. "Plautus as a Source Book for Roman Religion," *TAPA* 90 (1959), 48–101.

——. "The Glorious Military," in T. A. Dorey and Donald R. Dudley, eds., *Roman Drama*. London, 1965.

Harrison, A. R. W. *The Law of Athens*. Vol. 1. *The Family and Property*, Oxford, 1968; vol. 2. *Procedure*, Oxford, 1971.

Harsh, Philip Whaley. *A Handbook of Classical Drama*. Stanford, 1944.

Havet, L. "Etudes sur Plaute, *Asinaria* I: La seconde et la troisième scènes et la composition générale," *Révue de philologie* 29 (1905), 94–103.

——, and Freté, A. *Pseudo-Plaute, le prix des ânes*. Paris, 1925.

Hayford, Harrison, and Parker, Hershel, eds. *Herman Melville: Moby-Dick*. New York, 1967.

Heinze, Richard. "*fides*," *Hermes* 64 (1929), 140–66.

Herington, John. "Rudens," *Greece and Rome* 12 (1943), 78–79.

Hopkins, Keith. "Economic Growth and Towns in Classical Antiquity," in Philip Abrams and E. A. Wrigley, eds. *Towns in Societies: Essays in Economic History and Historical Sociology*. Cambridge, 1978.

Hough, John Newbold. "The Development of Plautus' Art," *CP* 30 (1935), 43–57.

——. "The Structure of the *Asinaria*." *AJP* 58 (1937), 19–37.

Humbert, C. "exsilium," in C. Daremberg and E. Saglio, *Dictionnaire des antiquités grecques et romaines*. Vol. 2.1 (Paris, 1892), 940–45.

Immerwahr, Henry R. *Form and Thought in Herodotus*. Cleveland, 1966.

Jachmann, Günther. *Plautinisches und Attisches*. Berlin, 1931 [Problemata 5].

James, Henry. "The Art of Fiction," in Leon Edel, ed., *The House of Fiction: Essays on the Novel by Henry James*. London, 1957.

——. *Portrait of a Lady*. Harmondsworth, 1963; orig. 1881.

Bibliography

Jameson, Fredric. *The Prison-House of Language.* Princeton, 1972.

Karabelias, Evanghelos. "L'épiclérat dans la comédie nouvelle et dans les sources latines," in Hans Julius Wolff, ed., *Symposion 1971* (Cologne, 1975), 215–54.

Kauer, Robert, and Lindsay, Wallace M., eds. *P. Terenti Afri Comoediae.* Oxford, 1958.

Kavanagh, James H. "'Marks of Weakness': Ideology, Science, and Textual Criticism," *Praxis* 5 (1981), 23–38.

Kermode, Frank. *The Sense of an Ending.* Oxford, 1966.

Keyes, Clinton W. "Half-Sister Marriage in New Comedy and the *Epidicus*," *TAPA* 71 (1940), 217–29.

Kinsey, T. E. "Notes on the 'Rudens' of Plautus," *Latomus* 25 (1966), 272–77.

Kleinfeller. "exilium," *RE* 6 (1909), 1683–85.

Knoche, Ulrich. *Roman Satire.* Trans. Edwin S. Ramage. Bloomington, 1975.

Knox, Bernard. "Euripidean Comedy," in Alan Cheuse and Richard Koffler, eds. *The Rarer Action.* New Brunswick, N.J., 1970; repr. in Bernard Knox, *Word and Action.* Baltimore, 1979.

Kock, T. *Comicorum Atticorum Fragmenta.* Leipzig, 1880.

Konstan, David. "Terence's *Hecyra*," *Far-Western Forum* 1 (1974), 23–34.

——. "Plautus' *Captivi* and the Ideology of the Ancient City-State," *Ramus* 5 (1976), 76–91.

——. "Plot and Theme in Plautus' *Asinaria*," *Classical Journal* 73 (1976), 215–21.

——. "The Social Themes in Plautus' *Aulularia*," *Arethusa* 10 (1977), 307–20.

——. *Catullus' Indictment of Rome: The Meaning of Catullus 64.* Amsterdam, 1977.

——. "A Comment on Class and Labor in Ancient Society," *Marxist Perspectives* 7 (1979), 124–31.

Kornhardt, Hildegard. "Regulus und die Cannaegefangenen," *Hermes* 82 (1954), 85–123.

Kunkel, Wolfgang. "Fides als schöpferisches Element in römischen Schuldrecht," in *Festschrift Paul Koschaker.* Vol. 2. Weimar, 1939, 1–15.

Lattimore, Richmond. *The Poetry of Greek Tragedy.* New York, 1958.

Leach, Edmund. *Claude Lévi-Strauss.* 2d ed. New York, 1974.

Leach, Eleanor Winsor. "*Meam quom formam noscito*: Language and Characterization in the *Menaechmi*," *Arethusa* 2 (1969), 30–45.

——. "Ergasilus and the Ironies of the Captivi," *Class. et Med.* 30 (1969), 263–96.

——. "Plautus' *Rudens*: Venus Born from a Shell," *Texas Studies in Literature and Language* 15 (1974), 915–31.

Bibliography

——. "The Soldier and Society: Plautus' *Miles Gloriosus* as Popular Drama," *Rivista di Studi Classici* 28 (1980), 185–209.

Lefèvre, Eckard. *Die Expositionstechnik in den Komödien des Terenz.* Darmstadt, 1969.

——. *Der Phormio des Terenz und der Epidikazomenos des Apollodor von Karystos.* Munich, 1978. [Zetemata 74].

Lehmann, Ernst R. "Der Verschwender und der Geizige: Zur Typologie der griechisch-römischen Komödie," *Gymnasium* 67 (1960), 73–90.

Lejay, P. *Plaute.* Paris, 1925.

Leo, Friedrich. *Plautinische Forschungen.* Berlin, 1912.

Lévi-Strauss, Claude. *The Elementary Structures of Kinship.* Trans. James Harle Bell, John Richard von Sturmer, and Rodney Needham. Boston, 1969.

Lindsay, W. M., ed. *T. Macci Plauti Comoediae.* 2 vols. Oxford, repr. 1959.

Little, Alan McN. G. "Plautus and Popular Drama," *HSCP* 49 (1938), 205–28.

Lofberg, J. O. "The Sycophant-Parasite," *CP* 15 (1920), 61–72.

——. "Phormio and 'Art for Art's Sake,'" *CW* 22 (1929), 183–84.

Ludwig, Walther. "*Aulularia*-Probleme," *Philologus* 105 (1961), 44–71.

——. "The Originality of Terence and His Greek Models," *Greek, Roman and Byzantine Studies* 9 (1968), 169–82.

——. "Die plautinische *Cistellaria* und das Verhältnis von Gott und Handlung bei Menander," in Eric Turner, ed., *Ménandre.* Geneva, 1970 [Fondation Hardt Entretiens 16].

Lukács, Georg. *The Theory of the Novel.* Trans. Anna Bostock. Cambridge, Mass., 1975.

Lyons, John. *Structural Semantics.* Oxford, 1963 [Philological Society Publications 20].

MacCary, W. Thomas. "The Comic Tradition and Comic Structure in Diphilos' Kleroumenoi," *Hermes* 101 (1973), 194–208.

——. "Patterns of Myth, Ritual, and Comedy in Plautus' *Casina*," *Texas Studies in Literature and Language* 15 (1974), 881–89.

MacDowell, Douglas M. *The Law in Classical Athens.* Ithaca, N.Y., 1978.

Macherey, Pierre. "The Problem of Reflection," trans. S. S. Lanser, *SUBSTANCE* 15 (1976), 6–19.

——. *A Theory of Literary Production.* Trans. Geoffrey Wall. London, 1978.

McLeish, Kenneth. *Roman Comedy.* London, 1976.

Martin, R. H., ed. *Terence: Phormio.* London, 1959.

Martina, Antonio. "Aspetti sociali et giuridici nella *Samia* di Menandro," *Atti della Accademia delle scienze di Torino, II classe di scienze morali, storiche e filologiche* 107 (1973), 853–940.

Marx, Friedrich. *Plautus Rudens.* Amsterdam, 1959; orig. 1928.

Mast, Gerald. *The Comic Mind: Comedy and the Movies.* 2d ed. Chicago, 1979.

Bibliography

Maurach, Gregor. *Plauti Poenulus*. Heidelberg. 1975.

Merry, Bruce. *Anatomy of the Spy Thriller*. Montreal, 1977.

Meyer, Maximilianus. *De Plauti Persa*. Leipzig, 1907.

Mossé, Claude. *La fin de la démocratie athénienne*. Paris, 1962.

———. "Métèques et étrangers à Athènes aux IV^c-III^c siècles avant notre ère," in Hans Julius Wolff, ed. *Symposion 1971* (Cologne, 1975), 205–13.

Munari, Franco. "La composizione dell' *Asinaria*," *SIFC* N.S. 22 (1947), 5–32.

Nardo, Dante. "Il significato della Hecyra terenziana," *Memorie della Accademia Patavina di scienze, lettere, ed arti* 79 (1966–67), 33–37.

Needham, Rodney. "Remarks on the Analysis of Kinship and Marriage," in Rodney Needham, ed., *Rethinking Kinship and Marriage*. London, 1971.

Norwood, Gilbert. *The Art of Terence*. Oxford, 1923.

Padgug, Robert A. "Classes and Society in Classical Greece," *Arethusa* 8 (1975), 85–117.

Paoli, Ugo Enrico. *Comici latini e diritto attico*. Milan, 1962.

Paratore, E. "Il teatro latino nei suoi rapporti col pubblico antico e nei suoi riflessi sulla spiritualità moderna," *Dioniso* 39 (1965), 57–81.

Peek, W. *Griechische Versinschriften*. Berlin, 1955.

Posani, Maria Rosa. "Aspetti del comico in Terenzio," *Atene e Roma* N.S. 7 (1962), 65–76.

Pöschl, Viktor. *Grundwerte römischer Staatsgesinnung in den Geschichtswerken des Sallust*. Berlin, 1940.

Post, C. R. "The Dramatic Art of Menander," *HSCP* 24 (1913), 111–45.

Prescott, Henry W. "Inorganic Roles in Roman Comedy," *CP* 15 (1920), 245–81.

Radice, Batty, trans. *Terence: The Brothers and Other Plays*. Harmondsworth, 1965.

Ramage, Edwin S. *Urbanitas: Ancient Sophistication and Refinement*. Norman, Okla., 1973 [University of Cincinnati Classical Studies].

Rambelli, Giuseppe. "Studi Plautini, I: *Asinaria*," *Dioniso* 19 (1956), 45–81.

Reitzenstein, E. *Terenz als Dichter*. Leipzig, 1940.

Ribbeck, Otto. "Marginalien zum Truculentus," *Rh. Mus.* N.S. 37 (1882), 417–24.

Ross, David O., Jr. *Style and Tradition in Catullus*. Cambridge, Mass., 1969.

Rowe, George E., Jr. *Thomas Middleton and the New Comedy Tradition*. Lincoln, Nebr., 1979.

Ruyt, Franz de. "Le thème fondamental de l'*Aululaire* de Plaute," *Les études classiques* 29 (1961), 375–82.

Salingar, Leo. *Shakespeare and the Traditions of Comedy*. Cambridge, 1974.

Sandbach, F. H. *The Comic Theatre of Greece and Rome*. New York, 1977.

Bibliography

Schaaf, Lothar. *Der Miles Gloriosus des Plautus und sein griechisches Original: Ein Beitrag zur Kontaminationsfrage.* Munich, 1977.

Schadewaldt, Wolfgang. "Bemerkungen zur 'Hecyra' des Terenz," *Hermes* 66 (1931), 1–29; repr. in Wolfgang Schadewaldt, *Hellas und Hesperien.* 2d ed. Zurich und Stuttgart, 1970.

Schuhmann, Elisabeth. "Der Typ der *uxor dotata* in den Komödien des Plautus," *Philologus* 121 (1977), 45–65.

Segal, Erich. *Roman Laughter: The Comedy of Plautus.* Cambridge, Mass., 1968; repr. New York, 1971.

Sherwin-White, A. N. *The Roman Citizenship.* 2d ed. Oxford, 1973.

Shipley, Joseph T. *Guide to Great Plays.* Washington, D.C., 1956.

Slotkin, Richard. *Regeneration through Violence: The Mythology of the American Frontier 1600–1860.* Middletown, Conn., 1973.

Small, Jocelyn Penny. "Plautus and the Three Princes of Serendip," *Renaissance Quarterly* 29 (1976), 183–94.

Snell, Bruno. *Die Ausdrücke für den Begriff des Wissens in der vorplatonischen Philosophie.* Berlin, 1924 [Philologische Untersuchungen 29].

Spranger, P. P. *Historische Untersuchungen zu den Sklavenfiguren des Plautus und Terenz.* Wiesbaden, 1961.

Süss, W. "Zur Cistellaria des Plautus," *Rh. Mus.* 84 (1935), 161–87.

——. "Nochmals zur Cistellaria des Plautus," *Rh. Mus.* 87 (1938), 97–141.

Thomas, E. J., ed. *T. Macci Plauti Aulularia.* Oxford, 1913.

Thompson, D'Arcy W. *A Glossary of Greek Fishes.* London, 1947.

Toliver, Hazel. "The Fabulae Palliatae and the Spread of Hellenism," *CJ* 49 (1954), 303–6.

Toynbee, Arnold. *Hannibal's Legacy.* 2 vols. London, 1965.

Trier, Jost. *Der deutsche Wortschatz im Sinnbezirk des Verstandes: Die Geschichte eines sprachlichen Feldes.* Heidelberg, 1931.

Vatin, Claude. *Recherches sur le mariage et la condition de la femme mariée à l'époque hellénistique.* Paris, 1970.

Vernant, Jean-Pierre. "Tensions et ambiguïtés dans la tragédie grecque," in Jean-Pierre Vernant and Pierre Vidal-Naquet, *Mythe et tragédie en Grèce ancienne.* Paris, 1973; English version under the title "Tensions and Ambiguities in Greek Tragedy," in Charles Singleton, ed., *Interpretation: Theory and Practice.* Baltimore, 1969, 105–22.

——. *Mythe et société en Grèce ancienne.* Paris, 1974.

Viljoen, G. van N. "The Plot of the *Captivi* of Plautus," *Acta classica* 6 (1963), 38–63.

Volkmann, Hans. *Die Massenversklavungen der Einwohner eroberter Städte in der hellenistisch-römischen Zeit.* Mainz, 1961.

Wagner, Wilhelm, ed. *T. Macci Plauti Aulularia.* Cambridge, 1892.

Waldock, A. J. A. *Sophocles the Dramatist.* Cambridge, 1966.

Watson, Alan. *Rome of the XII Tables: Persons and Property.* Princeton, 1975.

Bibliography

Webster, T. B. L. *Studies in Menander*. Manchester, 1950.

——. *An Introduction to Menander*. New York, 1974.

Wessner, P. *Aeli Donati quod fertur commentum Terenti*. Vol. 2. Leipzig, 1905.

White, Leslie A. *The Concept of Cultural Systems*. New York, 1975.

Whitehead, David. *The Ideology of the Athenian Metic*. Cambridge, 1977 [Cambridge Philological Society Supplementary Vol. 4].

Whitman, Cedric H. *Aristophanes and the Comic Hero*. Cambridge, Mass., 1964.

Wolff, Hans Julius. "Marriage Law and Family Organization in Ancient Athens," *Traditio* 2 (1944), 43–95.

——. "Die Grundlagen des griechischen Eherechts," *Tijdschrift voor Rechtsgeschiedenis* 20 (1952), 620–54.

Zucker, Friedrich. "Socia unanimans," *Rh. Mus.* 92 (1944), 193–217.

Index

Index

Index

Library of Congress Cataloging in Publication Data

Konstan, David.
 Roman comedy.

 Bibliography: p.
 Includes index.
 1. Latin drama (Comedy)—History and criticism. I. Title.
PA6069.K66 1983 872'.01'09 82-22112
ISBN 0-8014-1531-4

The Ernst & Young Almanac and Guide to U.S. Business Cities

65 Leading Places to Do Business

Also from Ernst & Young

The Ernst & Young Business Plan Guide, Second Edition
The Ernst & Young Guide to Total Cost Management
The Complete Guide to Special Events Management
Managing Information Strategically
*Understanding and Using Financial Data: An Ernst & Young
 Guide For Attorneys*

Forthcoming from Ernst & Young

The Ernst & Young Guide to Financing for Growth
Mergers and Acquisitions, Second Edition
The Name of the Game: The Business of Sports
*Development Effectiveness: Strategies for IS Organizational
 Transition*
Privatization: Investing in Infrastructures Around the World

The Ernst & Young Almanac and Guide to U.S. Business Cities

65 Leading Places to Do Business

Michael L. Evans
Barry M. Barovick

John Wiley & Sons, Inc.
NEW YORK • CHICHESTER • BRISBANE • TORONTO • SINGAPORE

Copyright 1994 by Ernst & Young
Published by John Wiley & Sons, Inc.

This publication is designed to provide accurate and
authoritative information in regard to the subject
matter covered. It is sold with the understanding that
the publisher is not engaged in rendering legal, accounting,
or other professional services. If legal advice or other
expert assistance is required, the services of a competent
professional person should be sought.

Library of Congress Cataloging in Publication Data:
The Ernst & Young almanac and guide to US business Cities: 65
leading places to do business/Ernst & Young.
 p. cm.
 Includes bibliographical references.
 ISBN 0-471-58964-0. — ISBN 0-471-58965-9 (pbk.)
1. United States—Industries—Location—Handbooks, manuals, etc.
2. Cities and towns—United States—Handbooks, manuals, etc.
3. Quality of life—United States—Handbooks, manuals, etc.
I. Ernst & Young. II. Title: Ernst and Young almanac and guide to US business
cities.
HC110.D5E76 1994
338.6′ 042′ 0973—dc20 93-28022

Printed in the United States of America
10 9 8 7 6 5 4 3 2 1

Contents

PART II

Acknowledgments

In compiling a work of more than 10,000 statistics and data, the efforts of a great many people, who are too numerous to mention here, were required. A number of notable contributions, however, were made by the following:

Michael Buckley, National Director of Real Estate Consulting, who authored "The Strategic Planning Process for American Site Selection."

Nancy Ashken, as associate director in the International Services Organization, who helped organize and manage the project.

Larry Forman, market research manager, who served as technical adviser on research and helped us formulate the surveys.

Andrew Heisey, a senior consultant in the real estate group, who helped locate much hard-to-find data.

Ellen Rand, who helped with the writing and editing of the narrative sections.

Sebastian Von Bulow, an international marketing consultant, who made especially strong and constructive contributions on a steady day-to-day basis.

In addition, our partner, Bob Snyder, of the International Services Organization, helped ensure the inclusion of important data for international investors.

We'd also like to thank Mort Meyerson, our national director of Public Communications, who first conceptualized the work and coordinated it.

The Ernst & Young Almanac and Guide to U.S. Business Cities is a collaborative effort by many staff members, as well as consultants and outside sources.

Much of the historical information has been amassed in Ernst & Young's 20 years of experience in the field. To ensure the information's timeliness, a comprehensive questionnaire was sent to economic development officials at each of the 65 metro areas reviewed, and we appreciate the time and effort they took to respond to it.

The questionnaire covered the key issues reviewed in this guide: population; transportation and access; labor force size and unemployment statistics; key businesses attracted; foreign-owned companies active in each area; education and training; and quality of life including housing, recreation, culture, sports, and special events and attractions. (Because certain areas relied on federal statistics for certain categories, some information may reflect data released a year or more before the questionnaire was answered. In such instances, further investigation by the reader is called for.)

To supplement information received from each area's economic development officials, additional research was conducted. Specifically, the following sources were utilized:

Salary Data: Occupational Compensation Survey: U.S. Department of Labor, Bureau of Labor Statistics, 1991–1992. Metropolitan Statistical Profiles, Real Estate Consulting Group, Ernst & Young, 1993.

Average Unemployment Rate: State and Area Employment, Bureau of Labor Statistics, February 1993.

Employment by Sector: State and Area Employment, Bureau of Labor Statistics, April 1993.

Number of Persons Employed by Business: Dun & Bradstreet, August 1993.

Unemployment Insurance Rate: Highlights of State Unemployment Compensation Laws. ICESA, January 1993. Metropolitan Statistical Profiles, Real Estate Consulting Group, Ernst & Young, 1993.

Civilian Labor Force: State and Area Employment, Bureau of Labor Statistics, April 1993.

Population: Metropolitan Statistical Profiles, Real Estate Consulting Group, Ernst & Young, 1993.

Number of Foreign-Owned Businesses: Dun & Bradstreet, July 1993.

Number of Persons Employed by Foreign-Owned Businesses: Dun & Bradstreet, July 1993.

Number of Foreign-Owned Banks: Polk Bank Directory, North American Edition (Fall 1992), Nashville, TN: R.L. Polk, 1992.

Number of International Flight Departures: (Custom-ordered) Official Airlines Guide, Oak Brook, IL: Official Airlines Guides, June 1993.

Housing Data: Metropolitan Statistical Profiles, Real Estate Consulting Group, Ernst & Young, 1993.

County Tax, City Tax, Other Taxes: Advisory Commission on Intergovernmental Relations, February 1993 M-185 Reports.

Construction Cost: Marshall Valuation Service, Marshall & Swift, April 1993.

Occupancy Cost: National Real Estate Index (Customized research), June 1993.

Education Statistics: The Wadley-Donovan Group, Inc., May 1993.

Crime Data: U.S. Department of Justice, Federal Bureau of Investigation, 1991.

Media Profile: Broadcasting and Cable Yearbook, 1992. Providence, NJ: RR Bowker, A Reed Reference Publishing Company, 1993. Editor and Publisher Market Guide, 1993. New York, NY: Editor & Publisher, 1993.

Climate and Rainfall: Official Airlines Guide Business Travel Planner, Fall 1992, Oak Brook, IL: Official Airlines Guides, 1992.

Cultural and Leisure Highlights: Official Airlines Guide Business Travel Planner, Fall 1992.

Introduction

There is no question that corporate America faces intense pressure to become more competitive, more flexible, and swifter in its response to changing market demands. In this environment, site section and relocation decision making have become more complex, and the issues of labor force quality and occupancy cost have never been more critical. This decision making, moreover, relates not just to relocation, but to expansion, the opening of new branches, and acquisitions.

With so much at stake, making the right decisions on location can be both a challenge and an opportunity. We believe that before embarking upon the decision-making process, one must first ask the right questions.

Ernst & Young has prepared this book as a first step in helping you to frame those questions. The guide, which will be updated periodically, reviews 65 metropolitan areas in seven regions in the United States. It provides the most extensive business-oriented overview available in such a format.

It is important to understand, however, that this guide is an introductory overview. Using the information here as a starting point, one can begin to analyze and, with "qualitative objectivity," focus on the factors essential to location decision making.

We selected these particular metro areas because they represent a cross-section of small, midsize, and large business centers in the United States, with widely diverse economic histories and futures. We also selected them for the variety of businesses and industries they would appeal to.

We did not attempt to cover every city in each of the seven regions. This guide will be revised regularly, in part to provide an opportunity to spotlight cities not covered in this first edition, and to chronical the inevitable changing economic environment of many of the areas already reviewed.

We felt that it was important to publish this guide to help dispel some of the preconceived notions about various metro areas. A danger in making location decisions lies in falling prey to misconceptions and generalities. In seeking the "top five" business locations in vogue at any given time, decision makers may overlook areas with positive attributes but less-than-positive marketing ability.

This guide does not rank metro areas on any "best–worst" scale, because such rankings are inherently superficial and misleading. Moreover:

- Ranking cities based on a current "snapshot" of economic

conditions is misleading, because a given area's *future* is more critical to a business facing a location decision.

- Companies have become increasingly diversified, which means that different operations within those companies have different types of personnel needs. Thus, a community that might serve a data processing division very well may be seriously inappropriate for a marketing and customer-support division.
- The range of location choices has become more diverse as well. Business has truly become global, and the current state of telecommunications allows a business the potential to function just as well in Antwerp, Dublin, or Glasgow as it might in Louisville, Phoenix, or Seattle.
- It is virtually impossible to provide an "apples-to-apples" comparison of metro areas so diverse in size, scope, and ambiance; for example, one cannot compare Albuquerque or Oklahoma City with New York or Dallas.

We define each of the areas as a Metropolitan Statistical Area (MSA), based on the U.S. government's definition. We have used MSAs because they allow more uniform and comparable statistics. There is great diversity within these areas. An MSA may encompass an area of literally several hundred square miles, comprising a central business district (CBD) as well as adjoining rural communities. Moreover, several of the MSAs reviewed in this book straddle two states, a circumstance that has tax, business, and incentive implications.

For specific business purposes, use the book's information as a starting point for more in-depth analysis. If one area's crime statistics, housing costs, taxes, or prevailing wages are higher than those of another comparably sized area, the reader must ask why.

Is crime limited to one particular section of the city? Do families spend a higher or lower proportion of their income on housing? Are infrastructure, public services, and municipal management more effective? Are wage statistics skewed by the presence of a few national companies, while local and regional companies' track records present a different picture if you exclude them?

In studying locations, it is important to be aware that communities are constantly evolving. Past performance should be examined, but an area's future is more important. Many cities reviewed in this book have experienced a period of retooling, and their more positive attributes may still be relatively unknown. Examples include Cleveland, which has rebuilt its downtown area and prospered, and Louisville, which has significantly diversified its economic base.

Currently, the so-called second-tier cities are becoming more popular as they reinvent themselves. Even in strong communities, however, downtown areas are less robust than the suburbs.

Most of the country's job growth in the 1980s took place in the suburbs. In the future, we expect to see more suburban-to-suburban relocations. Yet many suburbs have also begun to experience the same challenges—high housing costs, traffic congestion, social problems—that have plagued the cities.

Future growth will focus on mid-sized metro areas with diverse economies, well-educated labor, a well-maintained infrastructure, and a less stressful quality of life. Contrary to popular opinion, growth will by no means be limited to the Southeast, Mountain, and Southwest regions of the United States. The dynamics of growth will vary from region to region. For example, some areas, such as Connecticut and California, have been particularly hard hit by military cutbacks and face a greater challenge to their economic lives than others.

Each of the regions reviewed in this book has its own unique strengths, and each is poised to benefit from the inevitable economic impact of NAFTA and the new European Community. The Northwest's and Northeast's positions as gateways to the Pacific Rim, Canada, and Europe, for example, are as significant as the Southwest's relationship to Mexico and Latin America.

As the regional overviews illustrate, the U.S. economy's shift from manufacturing to service-driven industries is readily apparent and continuing. The areas experiencing the greatest growth are those that can tap and retain talented workers in growing industrial sectors. Those areas that offer a synergy between university-sponsored research centers, private corporations, and proactive public economic development policies are perhaps best positioned to capture the lion's share of future job growth.

Well positioned, too, are those areas that have been successful in attracting a diverse mix of businesses and industries rather than becoming dependent on any one industry in particular. Pittsburgh has overcome the impact of the steel industry's departure, and Houston and Denver's reliance on the energy industry has lessened considerably in the 1990s.

As issues of air quality, traffic congestion, and energy conservation become more important, areas that offer access via efficient and modern mass transit will reap the benefits in attracting new business.

Each of the seven regions is reviewed in Part I of this guide. Discussion begins with an overall introduction, followed by specific metro area reviews, which combine a brief narrative overview and detailed statistical information presented in a graphically, user-friendly manner. Part II addresses issues in location analysis and recent trends occurring across the United States.

PART I

Regional Overviews and City Profiles:

An Examination of Demographics and Economic Strengths

NORTHEAST

Overview

To paraphrase Mark Twain, reports of the Northeastern economy's death are greatly exaggerated. Although the recession has been less kind to this region than it has to some others, the areas reviewed in this section have shown significant strength in disparate categories. Some have clearly been more successful than others in diversifying their economy and marketing their strengths to U.S.-based and foreign-owned businesses, however.

Several of these areas, such as Buffalo and Rochester, benefit from their access to Canada. These areas are major exporters of products as diverse as precision instruments, transportation equipment, and printing, publishing, and telecommunications equipment. Moreover, because occupancy and labor costs are lower in western New York than they are in Toronto, hundreds of Canadian companies have established operations there. Connecticut ranks high among the U.S. states involved in exporting; an estimated 20% of its manufacturing firms shipping products across U.S. borders. Canada is Connecticut's biggest trading partner.

High technology businesses—including what civic leaders in Massachusetts call the "knowledge creation business"—have clustered in several Northeast areas largely because of the concentration of talented and skilled people trained there. The region is rich in technically oriented universities, colleges, and research laboratories, ranging from the Massachusetts Institute of Technology in Boston to the General Electric Research and Development headquarters in Albany.

In addition to a skilled and educated labor force and access to major markets, the areas reviewed in this section have key quality-of-life advantages in their favor. Several offer relatively short commuting times to and from a variety of affordable residential communities. Generally, housing costs are higher in this region than in others around the country, but costs must be viewed in relation to family incomes, which are also higher.

Housing stock is generally older in many of these areas than in other regions of the country, which suits many preservation-minded residents. Rich in history, the Northeast offers an unending array of historical sites to explore. It is also rich in recreational attractions, ranging from beaches and lakes to mountains and heavily forested parks. The handiwork of Hartford native Frederick Law Olmsted can be found in the parks of several of

the areas reviewed in this section, of which New York City's Central Park is the most notable.

It is true that border skirmishes have erupted between some metro areas in the Northeast. The competition between New York City, New Jersey, and Connecticut is particularly fierce, with business retention or new business location "victories" announced on a regular basis. Emblematic of this rivalry is New York's promoting itself as being served by two airports, even though a third airport (in New Jersey) allows for quicker access than Kennedy Airport.

Yet it is equally true that several of the areas reviewed in this section have banded together to promote themselves regionally and to act as catalysts in public/private economic development partnerships. The Metro Buffalo Alliance for Economic Development, for example, promotes western New York, chiefly to Canadian companies. Locally, Buffalo economic development officials have gone several steps further, by building a new industrial flex-space facility targeted to the Canadian market and by arranging for additional services, such as immigration processing and incorporation services, to current and prospective tenants.

Public/private partnerships have been used by many of these areas to revivify their downtown sections. In Rochester, for example, improvements have included a new convention center and a new cultural district. In New York City, civic leaders have been focusing in recent years on promoting economic development activity outside Manhattan, and significant commercial, retail, and cultural projects have been undertaken in each of those four boroughs.

The urban/suburban dilemma facing many metro areas of the country are ever-present in the Northeast as well. Hartford's current struggle to develop an equitable urban/suburban education strategy is perhaps most representative of this dilemma.

In the past, much of the Northeast's growth was predicated on manufacturing and the jobs it provided. Many of those jobs have migrated, and the region has become more service and trade oriented. Future population growth is expected to be modest in most of these areas. The Northeast's future as a business center will depend on its ability to continue "reinventing" itself to capture the nimble, globally oriented companies that will shape the twenty-first century.

Albany

NEW YORK

The state capital of New York, Albany, is growing as a finan-
cial center, with Norstar Bancorp and KeyCorp headquar-
tered here. Between 1980 and 1992, employment in Finance,
Insurance, and Real Estate (FIRE) businesses increased by 68%,
followed closely by services, which increased by 66.5%.
Combined, these jobs more than made up for the 26% drop in
manufacturing jobs the area sustained during the same period.

The area has also drawn high-tech facilities, such as General
Electric's Research and Development Headquarters and
Intermagnetics General. Not coincidentally, the State University
of New York's Applied Research Laboratory and Rensselaer
Polytechnic Institute, a leading engineering school, are also
located here. There are more than a dozen other colleges and
universities in the region. An alumni data bank has been estab-
lished to help match graduates with potential employers.

This six-county metro area in the east-central part of New
York State is home to approximately 900,000 people. Albany's
location is a case of geographic serendipity. Situated at the cross-
roads of the Hudson and Mohawk rivers, it has a deep water
inland port. The area also has an extensive transportation net-
work, including a half-dozen state highways, four U.S. high-
ways, and a beltway surrounding the center city. Served by
Amtrak, Conrail, and CP Rail, Albany is within an 850-mile
radius of half the population of the United States and Canada.

The highway system also eases access to residential communi-
ties. Average price for a three bedroom home in the metro area is
about $152,000, in such prime middle-management areas as
Colonie (north), Guilderland, Bethlehem, southern Saratoga
County, and Niskayuna.

Cultural attractions include several professional theater
groups as well as ballet, two orchestras and two opera compa-
nies. During the summer, the Saratoga Performing Arts Center is
host to visiting orchestra, ballet, and opera companies from
Philadelphia and New York City.

Famous for the Saratoga Race Track and Saratoga Harness
Track, the area is also the site of the National Museum of Racing
and Hall of Fame, as well as the New York State Museum and
State Capital Museum. Nearby, in Cooperstown, is Mecca for
baseball fans: the Baseball Hall of Fame. Outdoor recreation
areas are plentiful, including the Lake George resort area, Lake
Champlain, Saratoga Spa State Park, and Adirondack State Park,
a six-million-acre forest preserve an hour away from Albany's
CBD.

CITY PROFILE

Population in Thousands

1980	835.9
1990	874.3
1992	899.5
1995 Estimate	901.1

Socioeconomic Factors

Average Household Income
1980	$16,224
1991 Estimate	$41,794
% Change	157.6
1996 Projection	$52,952

Median Household Income
1980	$12,711
1991 Estimate	$28,854
% Change	127.0
1996 Projection	$36,343

Labor Force & Employment

	1993
Total Number of Persons in the Labor Force (in 1000's)	469.7
Total Number of Persons Employed (in 1000's)	442.5
Average Unemployment Rate	5.8%

Total Employment in Thousands by Sector

	1980	1992
Construction	11.5	15.7
Manufacturing	60.5	44.8
Transportation/Utilities	16.8	16.4
Trade	70.6	85.6
F.I.R.E.	16.0	26.9
Services	73.4	122.2
Government	101.2	111.9

Education

1992 Enrollment:
Two Year College	12,834
Four Year Undergraduate	33,677
Four Year Graduate	12,337
Average SAT Score	950
Total Possible Score: 1600	
Average ACT Score	N/A
Total Possible Score: 36	

Business Environment

Selected Major Employers
New York State
General Electric
Golub Corporation
Albany Medical Center
The Grand Union Co.
New York Telephone
Niagara Mohawk
Key Corp
Empire Blue Cross & Blue Shield
St. Peter's Hospital

Media Profile
1 newspaper
17 radio stations
4 network television stations
1 cable television operator

State Taxes[1]

Corporate Income/Franchise Tax	10.35%
Sales/Use Tax	8.0%
Individual Income Tax	7.875%
Unemployment Insurance Rate	2.90%

[1]See the State Tax Notes on page 308.

City Taxes[2]

County Tax	4.00%
City Tax	None
Other Taxes	None

Property Tax Rates [3,4]

$110.35 in $ per $1000

International Profile

Number of Foreign Banks	0
Number of Foreign-owned Businesses	25
Number of Persons Employed by Foreign-owned Businesses	104
Number of Daily International Flights	6

Real Estate

Occupancy Cost per Square Foot (Annual)

	Sq. Foot	Sq. Meters
Average Rental-Class A Office (Central Business District)	$17.00	$182.92
Average Rental-Class A Apartment	$9.60	$103.30
Average Rental-Warehouse	$3.75	$40.35

Construction Cost per Square Foot

	Sq. Foot	Sq. Meters
Excellent Class A Office	$133.52	$1,436.67
Class A Industrial/ Manufacturing	$81.46	$876.51

	Sq. Foot	Sq. Meters
Class A Distribution Warehouse	$57.39	$617.30
Excellent Class C Single Family Residential	$104.60	$1,125.49

Average Electric Cost (Cents per KwH)

	1992
Residential	$0.1061
Commercial	$0.1001
Industrial	$0.555
Average Price for a 3-bedroom Family House (in 1000's)	$151.8

Quality of Life

Climate

	Fahrenheit		Celsius	
	High	Low	High	Low
Winter	30	12	-1	-11
Spring	58	36	14	2
Summer	83	60	28	16
Autumn	62	40	17	4

Rainfall

	Inches	Millimeters
January	2.4	61
February	2.3	58
March	3.0	76
April	2.9	74
May	3.3	84
June	3.3	84
July	3.0	76
August	3.3	84
September	3.2	81
October	2.9	74
November	3.0	76
December	3.0	76

Cultural Highlights
Albany Institute of History & Art
Capitol Repertory Company
Empire State Plaza
New York State Capitol

[2]See the State-Local General Sales Taxes Notes on page 310.
[3]See the Property Tax Rate Notes on page 314.
[4]See the Classification of Real Property and Tangible Personal Property table on page 316.

Cultural Highlights (Continued)
 Knickerbocker Arena

Leisure Highlights
 Palace Theatre
 Starlite Music Theatre
 Saratoga Springs Race Track
 OTB Tele-Theater
 Empire State Historical Park

Crime

Rate per 100,000 Inhabitants	1991
Number of violent crimes	729.7
Number of property crimes	4,823.0

Average Wages for Selected Occupations

	Average Hiring Salary
Secretary (LR-3)	$16,016
Computer Systems Analyst III	$26,416
Computer Programmer III	$30,004
Engineer II	$26,520
Maintenance Machinist	$21,424

Boston

MASSACHUSETTS

Like other Northeastern cities, Boston lost a significant number of manufacturing jobs during the 1980s—approximately one-third of its 1980 total of 313,200. The high-tech corridor that had blossomed along I-128 has also lost some of its lustre. However, the services sector gained about 150,000 jobs during the 1980s and now represents the largest business group in the area, followed by wholesale/retail trade.

During the 1980s, Boston's population grew modestly, from 3.66 million to 3.78 million, and is expected to decrease to 3.74 million by 1995. Boston's current unemployment rate is 7%.

One of Boston's greatest strengths is that it is home to some of the best-known universities and colleges in the United States, one of the reasons that high-skill-dependent high-tech research and design companies, such as Digital Equipment Corporation and Prime Computer, have found the environment supportive. There are enough students enrolled in undergraduate and graduate programs in the larger institutions here to populate a small city. Education is also big business—Harvard University and the Massachusetts Institute of Technology are among the area's largest employers.

Navigating some of downtown Boston's famed narrow streets may be confusing, but the area has worked to upgrade traffic circulation through such infrastructure improvements as a crosstown freeway renovation and a third harbor tunnel, as well as improvements at Logan Airport and at the seaport.

Boston is rich in historical, cultural, and recreational attractions. Two orchestras, the Boston Symphony and the well-known Boston Pops, are based here, and they jointly present free, openair concerts in July in the Hatch Memorial Shell on the Charles River. Opera, ballet, and chamber music are also part of the city's cultural life. Theatrical performances are presented by groups in the city, as well as by universities and colleges in the area.

The metro area offers professional football, baseball, basketball, hockey, and horse racing. Within a few hours' drive are lush recreation areas such as the Berkshire Mountains and the coastal communities of Cape Cod, Nantucket, and Edgartown.

CITY PROFILE

Population in Thousands

1980	3,662.8
1990	3,783.8
1992	3,787.8
1995 Estimate	3,739.4

Socioeconomic Factors

Average Household Income

1980	$22,285
1991 Estimate	$56,872
% Change	155.2
1996 Projection	$71,019

Median Household Income

1980	$18,875
1991 Estimate	$43,227
% Change	129.0
1996 Projection	$54,843

Labor Force & Employment

	1993
Total Number of Persons in the Labor Force (in 1000's)	1,538.9
Total Number of Persons Employed	1,430.9
Average Unemployment Rate	7.0%

Total Employment in Thousands by Sector

	1980	1992
Construction	43.0	36.8
Manufacturing	294.9	207.7
Transportation/Utilities	73.1	71.6
Trade	320.0	332.7
F.I.R.E	109.4	135.2
Services	420.1	580.3
Government	213.6	186.7

Education

1992 Enrollment:

Two Year College	31,855
Four Year Undergraduate	139,512
Four Year Graduate	55,890
Average SAT Score	760
Total Possible Score: 1600	
Average ACT Score	N/A
Total Possible Score: 36	

Business Environment

Selected Major Employers

John Hancock Mutual LIfe
Bank of Boston Corp.
Mass Mutual Life
State Street Boston Corp.
New England Mutual Life
Baybanks
Gillette
Cabot
Amoskeag

Media Profile

3 newspapers
31 radio stations
9 network television stations
1 cable television operator

State Taxes[1]

Corporate Income/Franchise Tax	9.5%
Sales/Use Tax	5.0%
Individual Income Tax	5.95%
Unemployment Insurance Rate	N/A

[1]See the State Tax Notes on page 308.

City Tax

County Tax	None
City Tax	None
Other Taxes	None

Property Tax Rates[2,3]

$8.93 in $ per $1000

International Profile

Number of Foreign Banks	8
Number of Foreign-owned Businesses	340
Number of Persons Employed by Foreign-owned Businesses	10,955
Number of Daily International Flights	184

Real Estate

Occupancy Cost per Square Foot (Annual)

	Sq. Foot	Sq. Meters
Average Rental-Class A Office (Central Business District)	$24.00	$258.24
Average Rental-Class A Apartment	$11.08	$119.22
Average Rental-Warehouse	$5.17	$55.63

Construction Cost per Square Foot

	Sq. Foot	Sq. Meters
Excellent Class A Office	$149.59	$1,609.59
Class A Industrial/ Manufacturing	$91.27	$982.06

[2]See the Property Tax Rate Notes on page 314.
[3]See the Classification of Real Property and Tangible Personal Property table on page 316.

	Sq. Foot	Sq. Meters
Class A Distribution Warehouse	$64.30	$691.87
Excellent Class C Single Family Residential	$118.99	$1,280.33

Avg. Electric Cost (Cents per KwH)

	1992
Residential	$0.1078
Commercial	$0.906
Industrial	$0.811
Average Price for a 3-bedroom Family House (in 1000's)	$149.0

Quality of Life

Climate

	Fahrenheit		Celsius	
	High	Low	High	Low
Winter	45	22	2	-5
Spring	57	41	14	5
Summer	82	65	28	18
Autumn	63	47	17	8

Rainfall

	Inches	Millimeters
January	4.0	102
February	3.7	94
March	4.1	104
April	3.7	94
May	3.5	89
June	2.9	74
July	2.7	69
August	3.7	94
September	3.4	86
October	3.4	86
November	4.2	107
December	4.5	114

Cultural Highlights

Boston Tea Party Ship & Museum
Museum of Afro-American History
Museum of Fine Arts

Cultural Highlights (Continued)
 The Computer Museum
 Faneuil Hall Marketplace

Leisure Highlights
 Cheers/Hampshire House
 Hancock Observatory
 The Boston Commons
 New England Aquarium
 Fenway Park

Crime

Rate per 100,000 Inhabitants	1991
Number of violent crimes	832.3
Number of property crimes	4,642.7

Average Wages for Selected Occupations

	Average Hiring Salary
Secretary (LR-3)	$21,168
Computer Systems Analyst III	$41,664
Computer Programmer III	$29,568
Engineer II	$26,250
Maintenance Machinist	$24,528

Buffalo

NEW YORK

Located on the eastern end of Lake Erie and on the Niagara River, the five-county Buffalo metro area's biggest current drawing card is its proximity to Canada. Linked to Ontario by four vehicular and three rail bridges, Buffalo offers lower business occupancy and labor costs than Toronto, one reason that more than 500 Canadian companies have established operations here. More than half of the populations of both Canada and the United States are within 500 miles of Buffalo.

Once heavily reliant on the steel industry, whose departure left the area reeling in the early 1980s, Buffalo's manufacturing base has since diversified into such industries as food processing, color printing, medical instruments, fabricated metals, and computer equipment and software. Automotive components are a significant factor here: General Motors and Ford Motor Company among the city's largest employers. Diversification has also encompassed financial services, with three major banks headquartered here.

Considerable public/private investments have been made to revitalize the downtown area. Buffalo Place, for example, is an 18-block pedestrian mall, and new townhouses and condominiums have sprouted along the Waterfront area. Buffalo boasts the largest arts district outside of New York City. Its heart also belongs to sports, most notably to the Buffalo Bills football team.

Some 1 million people live in this metro area, predominantly in the suburbs, where growth continues to be modest. Average selling price for a typical middle-management home is $143,725. Among the residential communities surrounding the city is Grand Island, which features waterfront homes with boat launches and open wooded areas. An attraction here is Beaver Island State Park, featuring golf courses, a beach, and a boardwalk.

Snow is a fact of life for area residents: there is an average of 90 inches annually, with an expected 20 days per year of snowfalls of more than one inch. This makes for abundant skiing opportunities within an hour's drive of the CBD. In warmer weather, the area's parks offers extensive bicycling, hiking, golfing, and boating opportunities. Its largest tourist attraction is Niagara Falls, followed by the Buffalo Zoological Gardens.

CITY PROFILE

 ## Population in Thousands

1980	1,015.5
1990	968.5
1992	960.3
1995 Estimate	956.9

 ## Socioeconomic Factors

Average Household Income

1980	$19,549
1991 Estimate	$34,972
% Change	78.9
1996 Projection	$42,139

Median Household Income

1980	$17,309
1991 Estimate	$28,244
% Change	63.2
1996 Projection	$33,372

 ## Labor Force & Employment

	1993
Total Number of Persons in the Labor Force (in 1000's)	462.6
Total Number of Persons Employed (in 1000's)	429.7
Average Unemployment Rate	7.1%

Total Employment in Thousands by Sector

	1980	1992
Construction	13.8	16.0
Manufacturing	101.0	70.7
Transportation/Utilities	24.1	21.1
Trade	97.0	112.5
F.I.R.E	20.3	26.9
Services	86.8	126.5
Government	75.1	74.8

 ## Education

1992 Enrollment:

Two Year College	13,916
Four Year Undergraduate	36,012
Four Year Graduate	10,884
Average SAT Score	838
Total Possible Score: 1600	
Average ACT Score:	N/A
Total Possible Score: 36	

 ## Business Environment

Selected Major Employers

General Motors Corp.
U.S. Postal Service
Erie County
Buffalo Public Schools
Marine Midland Bank N.A.
Tops Markets, Inc.
City of Buffalo
University at Buffalo
The Buffalo General Hospital
Ford Motor Co.

Media Profile

1 newspaper
23 radio stations
7 network television stations
1 cable television operator

 ## State Taxes[1]

Corporate Income/Franchise Tax	10.35%
Sales/Use Tax	8.5%
Individual Income Tax	7.875%
Unemployment Insurance Rate	5.40%

[1]See the State Tax Notes on page 308.

City Taxes[2]

County Tax	4.00%
City Tax	None
Other Taxes	None

Property Tax Rates

$9.100204 in $ per $1000

International Profile

Number of Foreign Banks	4
Number of Foreign-owned Businesses	251
Number of Persons Employed by Foreign-owned Businesses	7,178
Number of Daily International Flights	1

Real Estate

Occupancy Cost per Square Foot (Annual)

	Sq. Foot	Sq. Meters
Average Rental-Class A Office (Central Business District)	$18.00	$193.68
Average Rental-Class A Apartment	$6.30	$67.79
Average Rental-Warehouse	$2.50	$26.90

Construction Cost per Square Foot

	Sq. Foot	Sq. Meters
Excellent Class A Office	$140.94	$1,516.51
Class A Industrial/ Manufacturing	$85.99	$925.25

	Sq. Foot	Sq. Meters
Class A Distribution Warehouse	$60.58	$651.84
Excellent Class C Single Family Residential	$109.40	$1,137.76

Avg. Electric Cost (Cents per KwH)

	1992
Residential	$0.1061
Commercial	$0.1001
Industrial	$0.555
Average price for a 3-bedroom Family House (in 1000's)	$88.0

Quality of Life

Climate

	Fahrenheit		Celsius	
	High	Low	High	Low
Winter	32	19	-1	-8
Spring	54	36	12	2
Summer	78	59	27	16
Autumn	60	43	16	6

Rainfall

	Inches	Millimeters
January	3.0	76
February	2.4	61
March	3.0	76
April	3.1	79
May	2.9	74
June	2.7	69
July	3.0	76
August	4.2	107
September	3.4	86
October	2.9	74
November	3.6	91
December	3.4	86

[2]See the State-Local General Sales Tax Notes on page 310.
[3]See the Property Tax Rate Notes on page 314.
[4]See the Classification of Real Property and Tangible Personal Property table on page 316.

Cultural Highlights

Albright-Knox Art Gallery
Buffalo & Erie Co. Naval & Serviceman's Park
Buffalo & Erie County Botanical Gardens
Darwin D. Martin House
Buffalo & Erie County Historical Society

Leisure Highlights

Broadway Market
Fantasy Island Theme Park
Miss Buffalo Cruise Boats
Niagara Falls Convention & Civic Center
Buffalo Museum of Science

Crime

Rate per 100,000 Inhabitants	1991
Number of violent crimes	850.0
Number of property crimes	4,842.5

Average Wages for Selected Occupations

	Average Hiring Salary
Secretary (LR-3)	$21,710
Computer Systems Analyst III	$34,606
Computer Programmer III	$31,668
Engineer II	$20,576
Maintenance Machinist	$29,910

Hartford

CONNECTICUT

Known as the insurance capital of the United States, because it serves as headquarters of such giants as Aetna Life and Casualty and The Travelers Companies, the Hartford metro area also has a strong presence of aircraft manufacturing companies and banks/financial services. Located halfway between Boston and New York City, it is the 850-square-mile hub of the north-central portion of the state and has a population of more than 700,000.

Between now and the year 2000, civic leaders expect only modest gains in employment (2% or less) in services, trade, FIRE, and construction. Currently its unemployment rate is 7.5%, but they are confident that the export business (especially for such products as transportation equipment, machinery, chemicals and allied products, and electronic equipment and supplies) will continue to play a key role in the area's economy.

The contrast between city and suburbs is pronounced in this metro area; the suburbs are literally a 5-minute drive from the CBD, one reason that the CBD has not grown as a residential center. The metro area is one of the wealthiest in the United States, in terms of median income, but there are vast differences between the city, where more than one-third of the population lives below the poverty line, and suburban areas such as Avon and Simsbury, where the average home sells for about $265,000 and $211,000, respectively.

The city/suburban contrast is seen most particularly in education, and Hartford is one of the few cities in the United States to have begun to address such issues as broadening cultural diversity in the suburbs and boosting academic instruction and achievement in the city.

Among the city's greatest strengths are its cultural attractions, including the Hartford Stage (which has served as incubator to a number of Broadway-bound shows and talents), ballet, opera, and a symphony orchestra. Hartford is the state capital, and its Capitol building and Old State House are among the area's historical attractions. This city is also the home of the American Clock and Watch Museum, the New England Carousel Museum, the New England Air Museum, and the Old Tolland Jail Museum.

Hartford native Frederick Law Olmsted, who designed Central Park in New York City, is well represented throughout the parks in greater Hartford. The area has an extensive system of state-operated parks and forests, freshwater and salt water beaches, hiking, and cross-country skiing.

CITY PROFILE

Population in Thousands

1980	668.0
1990	709.0
1992	717.2
1995 Estimate	731.0

$ Socioeconomic Factors

Average Household Income

1980	$23,639
1991 Estimate	$59,517
% Change	151.8
1996 Projection	$74,663

Median Household Income

1980	$20,728
1991 Estimate	$45,947
% Change	121.7
1996 Projection	$58,981

Labor Force & Employment

	1993
Total Number of Persons in the Labor Force (in 1000's)	414.7
Total Number of Persons Employed (in 1000's)	383.5
Average Unemployment Rate	7.5%

Total Employment in Thousands by Sector

	1980	1992
Construction	12.4	11.9
Manufacturing	100.4	71.5
Transportation/Utilities	13.8	17.8
Trade	80.9	92.0
F.I.R.E	60.3	70.7
Services	74.6	107.4
Government	53.8	62.4

Education

1992 Enrollment

Two Year College	15,396
Four Year Undergraduate	7,933
Four Year Graduate	6,442
Average SAT Score	730
Total Possible Score: 1600	
Average ACT Score	N/A
Total Possible Score: 36	

Business Environment

Selected Major Employers

Pratt & Whitney
State of Connecticut
Aetna Life & Casualty
The Travelers Companies
Hamilton Standard
First National Supermarkets
USAir
Connecticut National Bank
Asea Brown Boveri
Saint Francis Hospital

Media Profile

1 newspaper
19 radio stations
11 network television stations
1 cable television operator

% State Taxes[1]

Corporate Income/Franchise Tax	11.5%
Sales/Use Tax	6.0%
Individual Income Tax	4.5%
Unemployment Insurance Rate	3.10%

[1]See the State Tax Notes on page 308.

 City Taxes

County Tax	None
City Tax	None
Other Taxes	None

 Property Tax Rates[2]

$34.40 in $ per $1000

International Profile

Number of Foreign Banks	0
Number of Foreign-owned Businesses	51
Number of Persons Employed by Foreign-owned Businesses	1,816
Number of Daily International Flights	15

Real Estate

Occupancy Cost per Square Foot (Annual)

	Sq. Foot	Sq. Meters
Average Rental-Class A Office (Central Business District)	$26.19	$281.80
Average Rental-Class A Apartment	$11.24	$120.94
Average Rental-Warehouse	$5.00	$53.80

Construction Cost per Square Foot

	Sq. Foot	Sq. Meters
Excellent Class A Office	$142.18	$1,529.86
Class A Industrial/Manufacturing	$86.74	$933.32

	Sq. Foot	Sq. Meters
Class A Distribution Warehouse	$61.11	$657.54
Excellent Class C Single Family Residential	$109.40	$1,177.14

Avg. Electric Cost (Cents per KwH)

	1992
Residential	$0.1088
Commercial	$0.959
Industrial	$0.817
Average Price for a 3-bedroom Family House (in 1000's)	$164.0

 Quality of Life

Climate

	Fahrenheit		Celsius	
	High	Low	High	Low
Winter	34	17	1	-8
Spring	60	38	16	3
Summer	85	62	29	17
Autumn	64	41	18	5

Rainfall

	Inches	Millimeters
January	3.5	89
February	3.2	81
March	4.2	107
April	4.0	102
May	3.4	86
June	3.4	86
July	3.1	79
August	4.0	102
September	3.9	99
October	3.5	89
November	4.1	104
December	4.2	107

Cultural Highlights

Connecticut Historical Society
Harriet Beecher Stowe House
Mark Twain House
Hill-Stead Museum
Old State House Museum

[2]See the Classification of Real Property and Tangible Personal Property table on page 316.

Leisure Highlights
Wadsworth Atheneum
Webb-Deane-Stevens Museum
Science Museum of Connecticut
Trinity College
Museum of American Political Life

Crime

Rate per 100,000 Inhabitants	1991
Number of violent crimes	648.4
Number of property crimes	5,049.6

Average Wages for Selected Occupations

	Average Hiring Salary
Secretary (LR-3)	$23,296
Computer Systems Analyst III	$40,638
Computer Programmer III	$30,550
Engineer II	N/A
Maintenance Machinist	$28,704

New York City

New York City is an area of seemingly endless, inherent contradictions. It is a magnet for highly skilled, educated, and motivated people from all over the world, determined to make their mark, as it is for the globally oriented corporations seeking this talent. It continues to be a world capital in the realms of finance, fashion, media, the arts, and advertising.

At the same time, New York suffers from a beleaguered and underachieving educational system, high unemployment among its youth, and perennially high occupancy costs, which run counter to civic leaders' determination to continue to retain and attract business, and a social fabric that often seems to be unraveling at the seams.

Still, in an era when companies can literally choose to do business anywhere, New York's prestige value still counts for a lot. After a brief period of absence, foreign-owned companies and investors have returned to New York City, too. The German-based media/entertainment company Bertelsmann, for example, has given the Times Square area a major boost by selecting a new building there as its U.S. headquarters and home to 1,700 employees.

Civic leaders are actively encouraging business opportunities beyond the confines of Manhattan. For example, the 100-acre Teleport development in Staten Island is a major telecommunications center, and the Brooklyn Army Terminal and MetroTech Center in downtown Brooklyn have created new industrial office uses for old industrial and government facilities and "back office" financial services.

If cultural attractions are a key component in the "quality of life" decision-making process, New York is at a distinct advantage. Home to more than 1,300 music, theater, dance, and other arts organizations, New York City is an undisputed world cultural capital, and its museums and galleries form an epicenter for visual art. The city's extensive parks play host to innumerable outdoor concerts and special events and, notwithstanding the sporadic grisly crime stories, are well used for picnicking, bicycling, hiking, and jogging.

CITY PROFILE

Population in Thousands

1980	8,274.9
1990	8,546.8
1992	8,576.1
1995 Estimate	8,693.2

Socioeconomic Factors

Average Household Income

1980	$19,622
1991 Estimate	$42,513
% Change	116.7
1996 Projection	$52,227

Median Household Income

1980	$14,931
1991 Estimate	$29,556
% Change	98.0
1996 Projection	$36,153

Labor Force & Employment

	1993
Total Number of Persons in the Labor Force (in 1000's)	4,002.9
Total Number of Persons Employed (in 1000's)	3,587.4
Average Unemployment Rate	10.4%

Total Employment in Thousands by Sector

	1980	1992
Construction	95.4	106.6
Manufacturing	586.6	358.6
Transportation/Utilities	280.3	231.1
Trade	719.0	655.1
F.I.R.E	469.7	512.0
Services	1,002.0	1,247.4
Government	596.0	666.0

Education

1992 Enrollment

Two Year College	71,358
Four Year Undergraduate	241,226
Four Year Graduate	102,625
Average SAT Score	834
Total Possible Score: 1600	
Average ACT Score	N/A
Total Possible Score: 36	

Business Environment

Selected Major Employers

Citicorp
American Express
Solomon Brothers
Chemical Banking Corp.
Metropolitan Life
Philip Morris
RJR Nabisco Holdings
Bristol-Myers Squibb
Unilever U.S.
American Home Products

Media Profile

6 newspapers
45 radio stations
22 network television stations
1 cable television operator

State Taxes[1]

Corporate Income/Franchise Tax	10.35%
Sales/Use Tax	8.5%
Individual Income Tax	7.87%
Unemployment Insurance Rate	5.40%

[1]See the State Tax Notes on page 308.

City Tax

County Tax	None
City Tax	4.25%
Other Taxes	None

Property Tax Rates[3,4]

$129.03 in $ per $1000

International Profile

Number of Foreign Banks	299
Number of Foreign-owned Businesses	3,184
Number of Persons Employed by Foreign-owned Businesses	96,570
Number of Daily International Flights	487

Real Estate

Occupancy Cost per Square Foot (Annual)

	Sq. Foot	Sq. Meters
Average Rental-Class A Office (Central Business District)	$26.69	$287.18
Average Rental-Class A Apartment	$13.05	$140.42
Average Rental-Warehouse	$4.95	$52.94

Construction Cost per Square Foot

	Sq. Foot	Sq. Meters
Excellent Class A Office	$180.50	$1,942.18
Class A Industrial/ Manufacturing	$110.13	$1,184.99

	Sq. Foot	Sq. Meters
Class A Distribution Warehouse	$77.59	$834.86
Excellent Class C Single Family Residential	$141.06	$1,517.80

Avg. Electric Cost (Cents per KwH)

	1992
Residential	$0.1499
Commercial	$0.1196
Industrial	$0.1207
Average Price for a 3-bedroom Family House (in 1000's)	$167.0

Quality of Life

Climate

	Fahrenheit		Celsius	
	High	Low	High	Low
Winter	38	26	3	-3
Spring	61	44	16	7
Summer	85	68	29	20
Autumn	66	50	19	10

Rainfall

	Inches	Millimeters
January	3.0	76
February	3.0	76
March	4.0	102
April	4.0	102
May	4.0	102
June	3.0	76
July	4.0	102
August	4.0	102
September	4.0	102
October	3.0	76
November	4.0	102
December	4.0	102

Cultural Highlights

Rockefeller Center
Greenwich Village
United Nations
World Trade and World Financial Centers
Ellis Island Immigration Museum

[2]See the State-Local General Sales Tax Notes on page 310.
[3]See the Property Tax Rate Notes on page 314.
[4]See the Classification of Real Property and Tangible Personal Property table on page 316.

Leisure Highlights
Central Park
Yankee Stadium
Bronx Zoo
Brooklyn Botanical Gardens
Strawberry Fields in Central Park

Crime

Rate per 100,000 Inhabitants	1991
Number of violent crimes	2,044.4
Number of property crimes	6,440.2

Average Wages for Selected Occupations

	Average Hiring Salary
Secretary (LR-3)	$29,536
Computer Systems Analyst III	$52,364
Computer Programmer III	$39,156
Engineer II	$40,300
Maintenance Machinist	$39,540

Rochester

NEW YORK

Eastman Kodak is a dominant presence in the Rochester area, providing a large manufacturing base that employs almost 30% of the work force. Imaging, lasers, and optics have a supportive environment here, through the University of Rochester, the Rochester Institute of Technology, and the Eastman Kodak, Bausch & Lomb, and Xerox research labs.

There has also been growth in the service sector, which now accounts for approximately one-quarter of the area's jobs. As an exporter of goods, Rochester ranks slightly higher than the state of Virginia and almost as high as Illinois.

The third largest metropolis in New York State, the Rochester metro area lies halfway between Buffalo and Syracuse along Lake Ontario and has a population of 1 million. The area is expected to grow to more than one million in population by the year 2000.

Beginning in the early 1980s, many public and private improvements have been undertaken, including a Main Street improvement project, the Riverside Convention Center, and Eastman Place in the new cultural district. Private investment has included the Rochester Telephone headquarters and Clinton Square office building.

Housing is a diverse mix of urban/suburban, Victorian/modern, and other styles. In the city, for example, Olde Rochesterville, a group of restored nineteenth-century office buildings has become a residential/commercial center with loft apartments, restaurants, and offices. Corn Hill has also witnessed restoration of nineteenth-century homes. Since the typical commute from the suburbs is 20 minutes, the suburbs are home to most residents. Generally, the bulk of existing homes in the area are valued between $60,000 and $100,000.

Not surprisingly, cultural attractions include museums devoted to photography and science. However, Rochester also has its own Philharmonic Orchestra, a theater group, and a dance company. Access to the Finger Lakes and Lake Ontario provides a variety of water-oriented recreation, and 25 of the area's 120 parks are larger than 100 acres.

CITY PROFILE

 Population
in Thousands

1980	971.2
1990	1,002.4
1992	1,013.6
1995 Estimate	1,016.0

 Socioeconomic
Factors

Average Household Income

1980	$21,956
1991 Estimate	$45,979
% Change	109.4
1996 Projection	$56,355

Median Household Income

1980	$19,569
1991 Estimate	$37,294
% Change	90.6
1996 Projection	$45,753

 Labor Force &
Employment

	1993
Total Number of Persons in the Labor Force (in 1000's)	515.6
Total Number of Persons Employed (in 1000's)	488.6
Average Unemployment Rate	5.3%

Total Employment in Thousands by Sector

	1980	1992
Construction	11.4	15.6
Manufacturing	126.4	128.3
Transportation/Utilities	12.8	15.8
Trade	76.7	101.5
F.I.R.E	15.9	22.6
Services	79.1	130.3
Government	61.7	69.3

 Education

1992 Enrollment:

Two Year College	15,106
Four Year Undergraduate	32,354
Four Year Graduate	10,533
Average SAT Score	922
Total Possible Score: 1600	
Average ACT Score	N/A
Total Possible Score: 36	

 Business
Environment

Selected Major Employers

Rochester Community Savings
Eastman Kodak
Bausch & Lomb
University of Rochester
Rochester Gas & Electric
Rochester Telefon
General Motors
Wegman's
Mobil

Media Profile

2 newspapers
21 radio stations
6 network television stations
1 cable television operator

 State Taxes[1]

Corporate Income/Franchise Tax	10.35%
Sales/Use Tax	8.5%
Individual Income Tax	7.87%
Unemployment Insurance Rate	5.40%

[1]See the State Tax Notes on page 308.

 City Tax

County Tax	3.50%
City Tax	None
Other Taxes	None

 Property Tax Rates[3,4]

$22.26 in $ per $1000

 International Profile

Number of Foreign Banks	2
Number of Foreign-owned Businesses	34
Number of Persons Employed by Foreign-owned Businesses	3,424
Number of Daily International Flights	4

 Real Estate

Occupancy Cost per Square Foot (Annual)

	Sq. Foot	Sq. Meters
Average Rental-Class A Office (Central Business District)	$30.50	$328.18
Average Rental-Class A Apartment	$7.30	$78.55
Average Rental-Warehouse	$3.80	$40.89

Construction Cost per Square Foot

	Sq. Foot	Sq. Meters
Excellent Class A Office	$142.18	$1,529.86
Class A Industrial/ Manufacturing	$86.74	$933.32

[2]See the State-Local General Sales Tax Notes on page 310.
[3]See the Property Tax Rate Notes on page 314.
[4]See the Classification of Real Property and Tangible Personal Property table on page 316

	Sq. Foot	Sq. Meters
Class A Distribution Warehouse	$61.11	$657.54
Excellent Class C Single Family Residential	$109.40	$1,177.14

Avg. Electric Cost (Cents per KwH)

	1992
Residential	$0.1062
Commercial	$0.955
Industrial	$0.737
Average Price for a 3-bedroom Family House (in 1000's)	$86.0

 Quality of Life

Climate

	Fahrenheit		Celsius	
	High	Low	High	Low
Winter	31	16-	-1	-9
Spring	56	36	13	2
Summer	82	60	28	16
Autumn	62	42	17	6

Rainfall

	Inches	Millimeters
January	2.3	58
February	2.3	58
March	2.5	64
April	2.6	66
May	2.6	66
June	2.8	71
July	2.5	64
August	3.2	81
September	2.7	69
October	2.5	64
November	2.7	69
December	2.6	66

Cultural Highlights

Genesee Country Village
International Museum of Photography at George Eastman House
Memorial Art Gallery

Cultural Highlights (Continued)
 Rochester Museum & Science Center
 Susan B. Anthony House
 The Strong Museum

Leisure Highlights
 Curbstone Craft Festival
 Oktoberfest
 Cornhill Art Festival

Crime

Rates per 100,000 Inhabitants	1991
Number of violent crimes	342.2
Number of property crimes	4,909.2

Average Wages for Selected Occupations

	Average Hiring Salary
Secretary (LR-3)	$24,700
Computer Systems Analyst III	$33,684
Computer Programmer III	$39,520
Engineer II	$45,396
Maintenance Machinist	$28,870

MID-ATLANTIC

Overview

Economic necessity has required that several of the Mid-Atlantic areas reviewed in this section reinvent themselves. Perhaps the most striking example is Pittsburgh, which had been devastated by the loss of the steel industry's overwhelming presence in the early 1980s and has emerged as a diverse center for electronics, biotechnology, and financial services. This city has used public funding and public/private partnerships to help revive its CBD and has experienced significant growth as a convention center.

The confluence of research centers and well-educated students continues to be a strength of several of the Mid-Atlantic areas. Philadelphia's growth as a health care center, for example, depends on a clustering of teaching and research hospitals, medical and dental schools, as well as pharmaceutical firms and medical equipment manufacturers. Similarly, the presence of Carnegie Mellon University and the University of Pittsburgh is a key factor in Pittsburgh's growth as a technology center.

All of the metro areas in this region are within a short distance of the most densely populated areas of the United States, and although the quality and efficiency of their transportation networks vary, they have, nonetheless, advantageous access to large markets. These areas are also steeped in colonial history, as evidenced by an ample array of historical towns, buildings, sites, and monuments; Independence Hall and the Liberty Bell in Philadelphia are among the best known.

Foreign-owned companies—primarily from the United Kingdom, Germany, and Japan—have established a strong foothold in several Mid-Atlantic areas, most notably in Philadelphia, Baltimore, and Pittsburgh.

Because most of these metro areas are located along rivers (or on the Chesapeake Bay), water sports are a major attraction. Only Dade County, Florida, has more pleasure boats registered than Allegheny County (Pittsburgh), Pennsylvania, for example. The waterfront also plays a major role in the cultural life of several of these areas. Baltimore and Philadelphia have taken pains to develop a mixture of retail, restaurant, cultural, and commercial uses on their waterfronts, and tourism has grown as a result.

Each of these areas is also rich in traditional cultural attractions, including outstanding museums (such as the Franklin Institute in Philadelphia), theater (the John F. Kennedy Center for the Performing Arts in Washington, D.C.), and art (the Carnegie Museum of Art in Pittsburgh). Avid football, baseball, and basketball fans will also find a broad array of teams to root for.

Although the Mid-Atlantic region suffers from constant stereotyping in regard to high housing costs, high taxes, and congestion, the reality of several of the areas reviewed here counters that image. The average home price in the New Castle County, part of Wilmington's metro area, for example, is $123,110, and Pittsburgh's is $84,800. Washington, D.C., is a notable exception, with home prices averaging more than $220,000, but civic leaders point out that such prices are proportionate to the salary levels common in the area.

One of the Mid-Atlantic region's real, persistent problems, however, is the gap between the well educated and the poorly educated. According to the Washington, D.C., Chamber of Commerce, for example, although its metro area has one of the highest concentrations of residents with advanced degrees in the United States, nearly one-third of the population in the District has failed to complete high school. This metro area also recognizes that it seems to be behind the curve in terms of tailoring vocational and technical curricula to the technical needs of the area's employers.

At the other end of the spectrum is Wilmington, Delaware, where more than two-thirds of high school students participate in some form of vocational/technical education and the curriculum is flexible enough to meet the needs of the area's employers. This, too, is a matter of economic necessity. One of the smallest states in the country, Delaware has a high concentration of chemical industry jobs—many of which are in research and development—and an unemployment rate considerably below the national average.

Baltimore

MARYLAND

Located within an hour's drive of the nation's capital, Baltimore has a reputation as an urban revitalization success story, derived in large part from its embrace of its waterfront. This metro area, which now numbers approximately 2.4 million residents, covers Baltimore City, Baltimore County, and Carroll, Harford, Howard, and Anne Arundel Counties. The most dramatic population growth has occurred in Carroll County, to the west of Baltimore County. The area's overall unemployment rate is 7.5%.

That Baltimore's tourism business has grown significantly since the 1980s is fairly well known. Perhaps less well known is the repositioning of Baltimore's economic base to a diverse mix of financial and insurance businesses, high technology (particularly biotechnology), health care, services, and wholesale/retail trade.

Among the area's largest employers are Johns Hopkins University and Hospital, Westinghouse Electric, MNC Financial, Baltimore Gas & Electricity, Chesapeake & Potomac Telephone Company, Blue Cross & Blue Shield, and First Maryland Bancorp. Of the recent relocations into the area, three have been from Europe: FILA (from Italy), AEGON USA (from the Netherlands), and Maryland Casualty (from Switzerland). Approximately 116 foreign-owned companies have operations here.

Baltimore's extensive transportation network includes eight interstate highways, Conrail and CSX Transportation freight trains, a subway system, Baltimore-Washington International Airport (located 15 minutes from the CBD), and the Port of Baltimore, the second largest U.S. port in automobile imports/exports. In addition to its Metro subway system, a new light rail system is planned to link the city with its outlying counties.

Housing choices are extensive, too, ranging from in-town restored row houses to country estates, rural cottages, and contemporary subdivisions. The average price for a three-bedroom home is approximately $127,100. Prime middle-management areas include Federal Hill, Ellicott City, Columbia, Towson, Annapolis, Woodlawn, and Owings Mills.

Baltimore offers such unique recreational attractions as sailing on the Chesapeake Bay, horseback riding in rural hunt country, and quietly enjoying the more than 100,000 acres of parklands in this metro area. Its Inner Harbor attractions include the National Aquarium, the Harborplace mixed-use complex, the Maryland Science Center, and the Pier Six Concert Pavilion.

City Profile

Population in Thousands

1980	2,199.5
1990	2,382.2
1992	2,426.2
1995 Estimate	2,480.2

Socioeconomic Factors

Average Household Income

1980	$21,785
1991 Estimate	$45,777
% Change	110.1
1996 Projection	$56,735

Median Household Income

1980	$19,075
1991 Estimate	$36,548
% Change	91.6
1996 Projection	$45,399

Labor Force & Employment

	1993
Total Number of Persons in the Labor Force (in 1000's)	1,219.9
Total Number of Persons Employed (in 1000's)	1,128.4
Average Unemployment Rate	7.5%

Total Employment in Thousands by Sector

	1980	1992
Construction	51.4	55.6
Manufacturing	160.8	112.2
Transportation/Utilities	57.6	54.3
Trade	218.4	253.9
F.I.R.E.	57.0	74.6
Services	191.7	332.2
Government	228.7	207.9

Education

1992 Enrollment:

Two Year College	45,349
Four Year Undergraduate	47,634
Four Year Graduate	23,120
Average SAT Score	793
Total Possible Score: 1600	
Average ACT Score	N/A
Total Possible Score: 36	

Business Environment

Selected Major Employers

Johns Hopkins
Westinghouse Electric
MNC Financial
Baltimore G&E
Bethlehem Steel Corp. Sparrow Point Plant
Chesapeake & Potomac Telephone Co. of MD
Blue Cross & Blue Shield
First Maryland Bancorp
General Motors
Martin Marietta Aero & Naval Systems

Media Profile

1 newspaper
31 radio stations
7 network television stations
1 cable television operator

State Taxes

Corporate Income/Franchise Tax	7.0%
Sales/Use Tax	5.0%
Individual Income Tax	6.0%
Unemployment Insurance Rate	2.30%

 City Taxes

County Tax	None
City Tax	None
Other Taxes	None

Property Tax Rates [1,2]

$90.55 in $ per $1000

International Profile

Number of Foreign Banks	2
Number of Foreign-owned Businesses	116
Number of Persons Employed by Foreign-owned Businesses	4,288
Number of Daily International Flights	70

Real Estate

Occupancy Cost per Square Foot (Annual)

	Sq. Foot	Sq. Meters
Average Rental-Class A Office (Central Business District)	$18.22	$196.05
Average Rental-Class A Apartment	$8.86	$95.33
Average Rental-Warehouse	$3.71	$39.92

Construction Cost per Square Foot

	Sq. Foot	Sq. Meters
Excellent Class A Office	$127.34	$1,370.18
Class A Industrial/ Manufacturing	$77.69	$835.94

	Sq. Foot	Sq. Meters
Class A Distribution Warehouse	$54.74	$589.00
Excellent Class C Single Family Residential	$97.88	$1,053.19

Average Electric Cost (Cents per KwH)

	1992
Residential	$0.865
Commercial	$0.799
Industrial	$0.546
Average Price for a 3-bedroom Family House (in 1000's)	$127.1

 Quality of Life

Climate

	Fahrenheit		Celsius	
	High	Low	High	Low
Winter	41	24	5	-4
Spring	65	43	18	6
Summer	87	67	31	19
Autumn	68	46	20	8

Rainfall

	Inches	Millimeters
January	3.0	76
February	3.0	76
March	3.7	94
April	3.4	86
May	3.4	86
June	3.8	96
July	3.9	99
August	4.6	117
September	3.5	89
October	3.1	79
November	3.1	79
December	3.4	86

Cultural Highlights

B & O Railroad Museum
Baltimore Maritime Museum
The Baltimore Museum of Art

[1]See the Property Tax Rate Notes on page 314.
[2]See the Classification of Real Property and Tangible Personal Property table on page 316.

Cultural Highlights (Continued)
 Walters Art Gallery
 U.S. Frigate Constellation

Leisure Highlights

 The Baltimore Zoo
 Fort McHenry National Monument &
 Historic Shrine
 Maryland Science Center
 National Aquarium in Baltimore

Crime

Rate per 100,000 Inhabitants **1991**

Number of violent crimes 1,255.0
Number of property crimes 6,011.7

Average Wages for Selected Occupations

	Average Hiring Salary
Secretary (LR-3)	$21,996
Computer Systems Analyst III	$42,640
Computer Programmer III	$30,160
Engineer II	$43,524
Maintenance Machinist	$26,000

Philadelphia

PENNSYLVANIA

The Philadelphia story is that although such firms as Cigna Corporation, Bell Atlantic, Sun Company, Unisys, Campbell Soup, Scott Paper, and Alco Standard constitute this 4.9-million-population metro area's largest employers, job growth lies beyond financial services and manufacturing; chiefly in retail trade and health services. High tech has made important strides as well.

Several elements form the basis of the area's appeal as a health care center: a number of teaching and research hospitals, six medical schools, two dental schools, nearly four dozen pharmaceutical firms, and approximately 80 manufacturers of medical equipment and supplies call greater Philadelphia home.

The metro area's population had declined between 1970 and 1980, but increased slightly, by approximately 3%, between 1980 and 1990. More than 320 foreign-owned companies have operations in the area employing approximately 16,068 people, with the lion's share coming from the United Kingdom, Japan, and Germany. Overall, the area's unemployment rate is 7.8%.

The median home price here is $108,200, but housing prices vary dramatically throughout the metro area. A Center City home might sell for approximately $140,000, wheras a comparable home in Upper Makefield (Bucks County) might sell for more than $380,000, or $92,000 in Upper Darby (Delaware County), or more than $410,000 in Gladwyne (Philadelphia's Main Line). Area communities where more than 90% of high school graduates go on to college include Haddonfield and Cherry Hill (New Jersey) and Jenkintown, Radnor Township, New Hope-Solebury, and Lower Moreland (Pennsylvania).

Civic leaders take pride in the ongoing renewal of the Delaware River waterfront, whose mixed-use centerpiece, Penn's Landing, plays host to cultural festivals, concerts, and fireworks. The city is also getting a boost from a new convention center, located at a mass transit hub and within walking distance of more than half of the area's hotel rooms.

Among Philadelphia's cultural attractions are the historical square-mile Center City district, site of Independence Hall and the Liberty Bell, and the Franklin Institute, a leading science museum and planetarium. In addition to a symphony orchestra and Mozart Orchestra, ballet, opera, and several theater companies, Philadelphia currently has a $250 million "Avenue of the Arts" in the planning stages.

The city also offers a full complement of spectator sports, including professional baseball, basketball, football, and hockey, as well as indoor box lacrosse and the largest collegiate crew race in the United States, held on the Schuylkill River. Active recreational opportunities are widely available within the metro area, as well as along the New Jersey and Delaware shores, the Pocono Mountains, and the Chesapeake Bay.

City Profile

Population in Thousands

1980	4,716.6
1990	4,856.9
1992	3,729.0
1995 Estimate	5,027.5

Socioeconomic Factors

Average Household Income

1980	$21,192
1991 Estimate	$47,765
% Change	125.4
1996 Projection	$59,223

Median Household Income

1980	$18,215
1991 Estimate	$36,234
% Change	98.9
1996 Projection	$45,479

Labor Force & Employment

	1993
Total Number of Persons in the Labor Force (in 1000's)	2,417.2
Total Number of Persons Employed (in 1000's)	2,229.7
Average Unemployment Rate	7.8%

Total Employment in Thousands by Sector

	1980	1992
Construction	76.9	73.7
Manufacturing	440.1	313.0
Transportation/Utilities	98.4	97.8
Trade	416.0	468.8
F.I.R.E.	125.9	157.4
Services	460.9	685.0
Government	304.6	299.7

Education

1992 Enrollment:

Two Year College	59,859
Four Year Undergraduate	121,447
Four Year Graduate	43,8907
Average SAT Score	771
Total Possible Score: 1600	
Average ACT Score	N/A
Total Possible Score: 36	

Business Environment

Selected Major Employers

Cigna Corp.
Bell Atlantic Corp.
Sun Co. Inc.
Unisys Corp.
Campbell Soup Co.
Scott Paper Co.
Alco Standard Corp.
Philadelphia Electric Co.
Rhone-Poulenc Rorer Inc.
Crown Cork & Seal Co. Inc.

Media Profile

1 newspaper
34 radio stations
21 network television stations
1 cable television operator

% State Taxes[1]

Corporate Income/Franchise Tax	12.25%
Sales/Use Tax	7.0%
Individual Income Tax	2.8%
Unemployment Insurance Rate	3.50%

[1]See the State Tax Notes on page 308.

 City Taxes

County Tax	None
City Tax	1.00%
Other Taxes	None

 Property Tax Rates [2,3]

$78.65 in $ per $1000

 International Profile

Number of Foreign Banks	4
Number of Foreign-owned Businesses	326
Number of Persons Employed by Foreign-owned Businesses	16,068
Number of Daily International Flights	78

Real Estate

Occupancy Cost per Square Foot (Annual)

	Sq. Foot	Sq. Meters
Average Rental-Class A Office (Central Business District)	$21.27	$228.87
Average Rental-Class A Apartment	$10.13	$109.00
Average Rental- Warehouse	$4.58	$49.28

Construction Cost per Square Foot

	Sq. Foot	Sq. Meters
Excellent Class A Office	$144.65	$1,556.43
Class A Industrial/ Manufacturing	$88.25	$949.57

[2]See the Property Tax Rate Notes on page 314.
[3]See the Classification of Real Property and Tangible Personal Property table on page 316.

	Sq. Foot	Sq. Meters
Class A Distribution Warehouse	$62.18	$669.06
Excellent Class C Single Family Residential	$113.23	$1,218.35

Average Electric Cost (Cents per KwH)

	1992
Residential	$0.1324
Commercial	$0.1250
Industrial	$0.774
Average Price for a 3-bedroom Family House (in 1000's)	$113.0

 Quality of Life

Climate

	Fahrenheit		Celsius	
	High	Low	High	Low
Winter	39	24	4	-4
Spring	63	43	17	6
Summer	86	67	30	19
Autumn	67	47	19	8

Rainfall

	Inches	Millimeters
January	3.0	76
February	3.0	76
March	4.0	102
April	3.0	76
May	3.0	76
June	4.0	102
July	4.0	102
August	4.0	102
September	3.0	76
October	3.0	76
November	3.0	76
December	3.0	76

Cultural Highlights

Afro-American Historical & Cultural Museum
Betsy Ross House
Independence Hall

Cultural Highlights (Continued)
Philadelphia Museum of Art
The Franklin Institute Science Museum

Leisure Highlights
Zoological Society of Philadelphia
Franklin Court
Liberty Bell Pavilion
New Jersey State Aquarium at Camden
Second Bank of the United States

Crime

Rate per 100,000 Inhabitants	1991
Number of violent crimes	759.0
Number of property crimes	4,095.6

Average Wages for Selected Occupations

	Average Hiring Salary
Secretary (LR-3)	$24,050
Computer Systems Analyst III	$41,444
Computer Programmer III	$32,968
Engineer II	$39,832
Maintenance Machinist	$36,046

Pittsburgh

PENNSYLVANIA

Emblematic of Pittsburgh's shift from a smoky steel city to economic diversity is the Pittsburgh Technology Center, rising on a former steel mill site on the banks of the Monongahela River. Technology—including research and development, robotics, computer software and hardware, and biotechnology—has become one of Pittsburgh's strengths, along with health care, education, and services. Yet industry has not vanished completely from the 2.3-million-population metro area; among the larger employers here are USX, Westinghouse, Alcoa, PPG Industries, Allegheny Ludlum, Aristech Chemical, and H.J. Heinz.

Located in southwestern Pennsylvania at the juncture of the Allegheny, Monongahela, and Ohio Rivers, Pittsburgh has a busy inland port and is within 500 miles of half the population of both the United States and Canada. More than 135 foreign-owned companies have operations here, and access to and from the city has been eased with the recent opening of a new airport.

A regional financial center, Pittsburgh is home to PNC Financial, Mellon Bank, Integra Financial, Equimark, and Dollar Bank. Although it poses no threat to Hollywood, Pittsburgh has also attracted a number of production companies involved in films, television programs, and commercials. *Silence of the Lambs* and *Robocop* are among the films that have been made here.

The area's topography of rolling hills, lakes, and rivers provides an amenable setting for housing and recreation. Median housing cost is $84,800, although homes in middle-management suburban communities might range up to $110,000. A typical one-way commute takes some 25 minutes.

Golfing, spelunking, river rafting, hiking, hunting, and camping are among the recreational opportunities here. Ten ski centers are located near Pittsburgh, three of which are within 45 minutes of the CBD. Some 26,000 pleasure boats are registered in Allegheny County, second only to the number in Dade County, Florida.

Cultural attractions include the Carnegie Museum of Art (featuring works by Pittsburgh native Andy Warhol), ballet, theater, opera and a symphony orchestra. The sports-oriented have baseball's Pirates, football's Steelers, and hockey's Penguins to root for.

City Profile

Population in Thousands

1980	2,218.9
1990	2,056.7
1992	2,019.1
1995 Estimate	2,002.4

Socioeconomic Factors

Average Household Income

1980	$20,560
1991 Estimate	$38,123
% Change	85.4
1996 Projection	$45,993

Median Household Income

1980	$17,780
1991 Estimate	$29,405
% Change	65.4
1996 Projection	$34,862

Labor Force & Employment

	1993
Total Number of Persons in the Labor Force (in 1000's)	1,036.0
Total Number of Persons Employed (in 1000's)	955.4
Average Unemployment Rate	7.8%

Total Employment in Thousands by Sector

	1980	1992
Construction	44.0	42.4
Manufacturing	213.5	111.1
Transportation/Utilities	54.4	55.3
Trade	206.8	224.0
F.I.R.E.	45.7	55.1
Services	211.1	319.0
Government	121.1	102.7

Education

1992 Enrollment:

Two Year College	21,792
Four Year Undergraduate	51,458
Four Year Graduate	16,430
Average SAT Score	903
Total Possible Score: 1600	
Average ACT Score	N/A
Total Possible Score: 36	

Business Environment

Selected Major Employers
PNC Bank Corp.
Mellon Bank Corp.
Integra Financial
Consol. Natural Gas
USX
Westinghouse Electric
Aluminum Co. of America
H.J. Heinz
Miles
Allegheny Ludlum

Media Profile
2 newspapers
31 radio stations
10 network television stations
1 cable television operator

State Taxes[1]

Corporate Income/Franchise Tax	12.25%
Sales/Use Tax	7.0%
Individual Income Tax	2.8%
Unemployment Insurance Rate	3.50%

[1]See the State Tax Notes on page 308.

 City Taxes

County Tax	None
City Tax	None
Other Taxes	None

 Property Tax Rates [3,4]

$32.00 in $ per $1000

International Profile

Number of Foreign Banks	2
Number of Foreign-owned Businesses	135
Number of Persons Employed by Foreign-owned Businesses	3,324
Number of Daily International Flights	20

Real Estate

Occupancy Cost per Square Foot (Annual)

	Sq. Foot	Sq. Meters
Average Rental-Class A Office (Central Business District)	$21.15	$227.57
Average Rental-Class A Apartment	$9.43	$101.47
Average Rental-Warehouse	$5.05	$54.34

Construction Cost per Square Foot:

	Sq. Foot	Sq. Meters
Excellent Class A Office	$129.81	$1,396.76
Class A Industrial/ Manufacturing	$79.20	$852.19

	Sq. Foot	Sq. Meters
Class A Distribution Warehouse	$55.80	$600.41
Excellent Class C Single Family Residential	$99.80	$1,073.85

Average Electric Cost (Cents per KwH)

	1992
Residential	$0.1399
Commercial	$0.969
Industrial	$0.695
Average Price for a 3-bedroom Family House (in 1000's)	$68.0

 Quality of Life

Climate

	Fahrenheit		Celsius	
	High	Low	High	Low
Winter	34	19	1	-7
Spring	61	39	16	4
Summer	83	61	28	16
Autumn	63	42	17	6

Rainfall

	Inches	Millimeters
January	3.0	76
February	2.0	51
March	4.0	102
April	3.0	76
May	4.0	102
June	3.0	76
July	4.0	102
August	3.0	76
September	3.0	76
October	2.0	51
November	2.0	51
December	3.0	76

Cultural Highlights

Carnegie Museum of Art
Associated Artists of Pittsburgh
Buhl Science Center

[2]See the Property Tax Rate Notes on page 314.
[3]See the Classification of Real Property and Tangible Personal Property table on page 316.

Cultural Highlights (Continued)
 Fisher Collection
 Fort Pitt Museum
 Pittsburgh Zoo

Leisure Highlights
 Three Rivers Art Festival
 Pittsburgh Folk Festival

Crime

Rate per 100,000 Inhabitants	1991
Number of violent crimes	429.1
Number of property crimes	3,073.4

Average Wages for Selected Occupations

	Average Hiring Salary
Secretary (LR-3)	$23,296
Computer Systems Analyst III	$46,228
Computer Programmer III	$34,008
Engineer II	$32,500
Maintenance Machinist	$32,260

Washington

DISTRICT OF COLUMBIA

Government is big business in Washington, D.C., the capital of the United States, but it is not the only business here. Tourism is a significant industry, as is education. Among the major nongovernment employers, for example, are George Washington University, Georgetown University, and the George Washington University Hospital. Medical, biotechnical, electronics, and telecommunications firms have established a strong foothold in this metro area.

However, the federal government's presence is the key reason that the metro area has also been a magnet for government contractors (particularly aerospace and defense) and for industry associations, nonprofit organizations, and lobbying groups who require proximity to the nation's legislators. Growth is projected to continue in the services sector, at a greater pace in the suburbs than in the CBD. In fact, if there is any cloud on the area's horizon, it is that if the federal functions now located in Washington, disperse to the suburbs or to other regions, nongovernment activities will follow them.

Bounded by northern Virginia to the south and Maryland to the north and east, Washington, D.C., is located at the juncture of the Potomac and Anacostia Rivers. It is home to approximately 3.9 million residents, and much of the area's population growth comes from the in-migration of younger, well-educated professionals. Not surprisingly, opportunities for well-paying and challenging work are balanced by relatively high housing costs: The average price of a three-bedroom home in the immediate metro area is approximately $220,000.

Watching politics and government at work is not the only form of recreation in Washington. The metro area offers a myriad of cultural activities, sports, and special events in addition to its famed memorials and museums. The John F. Kennedy Center for the Performing Arts, for example, is a complex of five theaters (housing the Washington Opera and the American Film Institute, and others), and the National Theatre and Ford's Theater and Lincoln Museum offer additional theatrical presentations. RFK Stadium is home to the Washington Redskins, to whom area residents are fiercely devoted.

Washington, D.C., itself still reflects the grace with which French surveyor Pierre L'Enfant designed the city; greenery and extensive parklands are an integral element of the city's ambiance. Most widely known is Rock Creek Park, offering 1,800 acres of trails for hiking, biking, and horseback riding, as well as tennis, picnic areas, and playgrounds. The park is also the site of an amphitheater that presents jazz, classical, Latin, and rock music during the summer.

City Profile

Population in Thousands

1980	3,250.9
1990	3,923.6
1992	4,186.8
1995 Estimate	4,241.3

Socioeconomic Factors

Average Household Income

1980	$27,589
1991 Estimate	$58,606
% Change	112.4
1996 Projection	$71,324

Median Household Income

1980	$23,522
1991 Estimate	$47,849
% Change	103.4
1996 Projection	$60,412

Labor Force & Employment

	1993
Total Number of Persons in the Labor Force (in 1000's)	2,252.9
Total Number of Persons Employed (in 1000's)	2,146.7
Average Unemployment Rate	4.7%

Total Employment in Thousands by Sector

	1980	1992
Construction	85.9	96.3
Manufacturing	64.7	79.2
Transportation/Utilities	73.3	103.1
Trade	312.5	408.1
F.I.R.E.	91.6	127.7
Services	437.2	764.2
Government	571.9	607.6

Education

1992 Enrollment:

Two Year College	73,360
Four Year Undergraduate	96,832
Four Year Graduate	60,261
Average SAT Score	904
Total Possible Score: 1600	
Average ACT Score	N/A
Total Possible Score: 36	

Business Environment

Selected Major Employers

Fed. Natl. Mtg. Assn.
Student Loan Mkt. Assn.
MCI Communications
Potomac Elec. Power
First Amer. Bankshare
Riggs National Corp.
GEICO
Washington Post
Danaher
Harman Intl. Industries

Media Profile

3 newspapers
47 radio stations
14 network television stations
1 cable television operator

State Taxes

Corporate Income/Franchise Tax	10.25%
Sales/Use Tax	6.0%
Individual Income Tax	9.5%
Unemployment Insurance Rate	2.70%

City Taxes

County Tax	None
City Tax	6.00%
Other Taxes	None

Property Tax Rates

$32.90 in $ per $1000

International Profile

Number of Foreign Banks	18
Number of Foreign-owned Businesses	461
Number of Persons Employed by Foreign-owned Businesses	11,755
Number of Daily International Flights	137

Real Estate

Occupancy Cost per Square Foot (Annual)

	Sq. Foot	Sq. Meters
Average Rental-Class A Office (Central Business District)	$27.36	$294.39
Average Rental-Class A Apartment	$11.74	$126.32
Average Rental-Warehouse	$4.95	$53.26

Construction Cost per Square Foot

	Sq. Foot	Sq. Meters
Excellent Class A Office	$124.87	$1,343.60
Class A Industrial/ Manufacturing	$76.18	$819.70
Class A Distribution Warehouse	$53.67	$577.49
Excellent Class C Single Family Residential	$96.92	$1,042.86

Average Electric Cost (Cents per KwH)

	1992
Residential	$0.661
Commercial	$0.691
Industrial	$0.568
Average Price for a 3-bedroom Family House (in 1000's)	$144.0

Quality of Life

Climate

	Fahrenheit		Celsius	
	High	Low	High	Low
Winter	43	28	6	-2
Spring	67	46	19	8
Summer	88	70	31	21
Autumn	69	50	21	10

Rainfall

	Inches	Millimeters
January	2.8	71
February	2.6	66
March	3.5	89
April	2.9	74
May	3.5	89
June	3.4	86
July	3.9	99
August	4.4	112
September	3.2	81
October	2.9	74
November	2.8	71
December	3.2	81

Cultural Highlights

National Gallery of Art
National Museum of Natural History
Smithsonian Institution
National Air and Space Museum
Vietnam Veterans Memorial

Leisure Highlights

The Pavilion at the Old Post Office
John F. Kennedy Center for the
Performing Arts
National Zoological Park
Library of Congress
Lincoln Memorial

Crime

Rate per 100,000 Inhabitants	1991
Number of violent crimes	785.1
Number of property crimes	5,113.5

Average Wages for Selected Occupations

	Average Hiring Salary
Secretary (LR-3)	$27,404
Computer Systems Analyst III	$50,804
Computer Programmer III	$35,256
Engineer II	$36,816
Maintenance Machinist	$31,220

Wilmington

DELAWARE

Rich in colonial history and lower in occupancy and living costs than some areas in neighboring states, Wilmington is known as a center of research and development activity. Prominent among the area's R&D corporate citizens are the DuPont Company, Hercules, ICI Americas, and HIMONT. The metro area is also home to W.L. Gore and Associates, a manufacturing firm involved in electronics, fiber, filtration, fabric, and medical products, perhaps best known as the producer of Gore-Tex materials.

More than one-fifth of the state's jobs, in fact, are in manufacturing, but nearly half of those jobs are in chemical companies and half of those chemical manufacturing jobs are in home office and research operations.

Located in the northern part of Delaware, this metro area covers two states: New Castle County in Delaware and Cecil County in Maryland. Population in New Castle County has grown modestly from 398,115 in 1980 to nearly 450,000 and is projected to grow to 461,350 by 1995. Of significance is that the labor force has grown close to 23% since 1982, and that the 20-year-old-and-over population is expected to increase by 4.3% between 1990 and 1995. The unemployment is 6.1%.

Supporting the area's R&D base, more than two-thirds of Delaware's secondary students participate in some form of vocational/technical education. Vocational/technical students must satisfy minimum competency requirements before graduating. The vocational/technical curriculum is flexible enough to meet employer needs. At the higher education level, the University of Delaware has partnered with industry in such areas as composite materials, information science, biotechnology, and energy.

Part of one of the smallest states in the United States, this metro area nevertheless lies within 350 miles of major population centers from Boston to Raleigh and west to Cleveland. Its closest hub airport is Philadelphia, a half-hour's drive away. The Port of Wilmington is located within a quarter-mile of I-495, providing access to East Coast markets.

The average price of a three-bedroom home in New Castle County is $123,110. Prime middle management areas include Brandywine, Greenville, Hockessin, and Newark. Among the cultural attractions in the area is Brandywine Valley, with its eight museums and elegant country estates. The performing arts are also well represented here. Wilmington's Grand Opera House, a restored 1871 building, for example, is home to the Delaware Symphony Orchestra and OperaDelaware. Ballet and theater companies are also based here.

City Profile

Population in Thousands

1980	398.1
1990	441.9
1992	456.2
1995 Estimate	461.4

Socioeconomic Factors

Average Household Income

1980	$22,199
1991 Estimate	$44,138
% Change	98.8
1996 Projection	$53,796

Median Household Income

1980	$19,305
1991 Estimate	$35,467
% Change	83.7
1996 Projection	$43,462

Labor Force & Employment

	1993
Total Number of Persons in the Labor Force (in 1000's)	319.4
Total Number of Persons Employed (in 1000's)	299.8
Average Unemployment Rate	6.1%

Total Employment in Thousands by Sector

	1980	1992
Construction	14.9	15.4
Manufacturing	64.5	57.6
Transportation/Utilities	11.7	16.3
Trade	47.2	57.9
F.I.R.E.	11.4	29.4
Services	48.7	72.8
Government	36.0	38.0

Education

1992 Enrollment:

Two Year College	6,909
Four Year Undergraduate	17,023
Four Year Graduate	5,025
Average SAT Score	921
Total Possible Score: 1600	
Average ACT Score	N/A
Total Possible Score: 36	

Business Environment

Selected Major Employers

The DuPont Company
State of Delaware
Dover Air Force Base
U.S. Government
Medical Center of Delaware
MBNA America Bank
ICI Americas Inc.
University of Delaware
Chrysler Corporation

Media Profile

1 newspaper
8 radio stations
21 network television stations
1 cable television operator

% State Taxes

Corporate Income/Franchise Tax	8.7%
Sales/Use Tax	0.0%
Individual Income Tax	7.7%
Unemployment Insurance Rate	1.00%

 City Taxes

County Tax	2.00%
City Tax	None
Other Taxes	None

 Property Tax Rates [1,2]

$11.01 in $ per $1000

 International Profile

Number of Foreign Banks	0
Number of Foreign-owned Businesses	78
Number of Persons Employed by Foreign-owned Businesses	4,385
Number of Daily International Flights	0

Real Estate

Occupancy Cost per Square Foot (Annual)

	Sq. Foot	Sq. Meters
Average Rental-Class A Office (Central Business District)	$18.59	$200.03
Average Rental-Class A Apartment	$8.05	$86.62
Average Rental-Warehouse	$3.25	$34.97

Construction Cost per Square Foot

	Sq. Foot	Sq. Meters
Excellent Class A Office	$134.76	$1,450.02
Class A Industrial/ Manufacturing	$82.22	$884.69

[1]See the Property Tax Rate Notes on page 314.
[2]See the Classification of Real Property and Tangible Personal Property table on page 316.

	Sq. Foot	Sq. Meters
Class A Distribution Warehouse	$57.92	$623.22
Excellent Class C Single Family Residential	$101.72	$1,094.51

Average Electric Cost (Cents per KwH)

	1992
Residential	$0.859
Commercial	$0.643
Industrial	$0.448
Average Price for a 3-bedroom Family House (in 1000's)	$123.1

Quality of Life

Climate

	Fahrenheit		Celsius	
	High	Low	High	Low
Winter	39	23	4	-5
Spring	63	42	17	6
Summer	86	66	30	19
Autumn	67	46	19	8

Rainfall

	Inches	Millimeters
January	3.1	79
February	3.0	76
March	3.6	99
April	3.4	86
May	3.2	81
June	3.5	89
July	3.9	99
August	4.0	102
September	3.6	91
October	2.9	74
November	3.3	84
December	3.5	89

Cultural Highlights
Brandywine River Museum
Delaware Art Museum
Delaware Museum of Natural History

Cultural Highlights (Continued)
 Hagley Museum & Library
 Rockwood Museum

Leisure Highlights
 Brandywine Zoo
 Longwood Gardens
 Nemours Mansion & Gardens
 The Read House & Garden
 Winterthur Museum, Garden & Library

Crime

Rate per 100,000 Inhabitants	1991
Number of violent crimes	642.2
Number of property crimes	4,975.4

Average Wages for Selected Occupations

	Average Hiring Salary
Secretary (LR-3)	$24,180
Computer Systems Analyst III	$50,492
Computer Programmer III	$33,228
Engineer II	$41,600
Maintenance Machinist	$34,736

SOUTHEAST

Overview

Population growth and business migration to the Southeast—notably by manufacturing, high-tech, biomedical, health care, and warehousing/distribution businesses—have been dramatic. Once dominated by textiles, tobacco, and furniture manufacturing, the region has become economically diverse, with a growing international presence.

Availability and cost of labor explain part of the region's appeal, but they don't tell the whole story. Geography and climate are key factors as well. Most of the metro areas reviewed in this section offer excellent access—by air, rail, highway and often by sea—to a multiplicity of markets. Airports are generally located within an easy commute to an area's central business district.

Climate in these areas ranges from moderate to subtropical, and this has a number of implications. First, transportation of people and goods is usually unhampered by foul weather. Second, construction costs are more moderate because of fewer interruptions and a longer building season. Third, and certainly not least, people enjoy living in a climate that affords them an opportunity to spend much of their free time pursuing outdoor recreational activities.

Beaches, boating, swimming, fishing, and a myriad of other water-oriented activities are available in most of the metro areas covered in this section, particularly those in south Florida. North Carolina, Georgia, and Virginia offer the additional advantage of being a few hours' drive from spectacular mountain scenery. In addition to the usual spectator sporting events, the region is rich in special attractions, such as dog racing, jai alai, polo, stock car racing, Disney World, Busch Gardens, Kings Dominion theme park, and Mt. Trashmore, a recreational complex built on landfill.

Among the surprises to be found in the metro areas reviewed in this section are population trends. Although one often thinks of many of these areas (particularly in south Florida) as retirement meccas, the fact is that the under-44 age groups constitute the largest percentage of their total population. Whether they are drawn by excellence in higher education (as is the case in North Carolina) or by the climate itself, migrants to many of these areas tend to put down roots in their adopted communities.

However, growth in the Southeast has been neither uniform nor recession-proof. Some areas, such as Atlanta and Raleigh-Durham, have fared better than others, such as Miami. Moreover, most of these metro areas are grappling with the issue of promoting economic and cultural revitalization of their downtown areas. Vacancies in older buildings in downtown areas are still high, partly as a result of the recession and partly as a result of overbuilding.

Several areas have been proactive in their approach to their downtowns, developing public/private partnerships to promote evening activities, safety, and security, and to sponsor large-scale rehabilitation and new development. Jacksonville, for example, has extensive plans to invigorate its downtown, and Orlando has instituted a business-oriented crime prevention program. Durham, too, is addressing the issue of crime head-on.

From a different perspective, unchecked growth is not necessarily perceived as desirable by all metro areas. The state of Florida, for example, enacted a Growth Management Plan that requires municipalities to establish levels of service for public infrastructure and to adopt land development regulations to implement the policies in the plan.

In short, this means that no new development may be approved unless the necessary infrastructure is available to handle its impact, and that any development *not* consistent with the comprehensive plan is precluded. Most of the comprehensive plans in the state restrict the conversion of agricultural lands to suburban development.

Regardless of ambivalence about growth, however, these metro areas are striving for greater recognition as international business centers, often with remarkable success. Atlanta and Charlotte are in the forefront of these efforts, and south Florida is key to international trade with Latin America, the Caribbean, and South America. Limited direct airline service to destinations overseas hampers some areas; others make up for such drawbacks with alternative services, such as busy seaports.

Atlanta

GEORGIA

When Atlanta was named as host for the 1996 Summer Olympics, the city's long-sought prominence as an international business center was capped. Approximately 350 international companies have facilities here, ranging from corporate headquarters to manufacturing plants. In addition to banking, finance, and other business services, cultural support is available too. For example, the bilingual Atlanta International School caters to K-12 students, and special Japanese, Korean, and German schools provide cultural enrichment for children.

Atlanta's business style is a unique blend of cosmopolitan sophistication and high energy with traditional hospitality. Although labor cost, operating costs, and the cost of living may be somewhat higher in comparison with smaller markets in the Southeast, civic leaders prefer to point out more favorable comparisons with the markets in New York, Los Angeles, Chicago, and Dallas.

Access to labor and markets is also part of Atlanta's appeal. The Atlanta metro area, comprising more than 5,000 square miles in 18 counties, is home to approximately three million people. Its airport, the second busiest in the world, offers flights to 28 international destinations. Closer to home, Atlanta is within a 2-hour flight to 80% of the U.S. population.

With neither direct access to a major port, a tradition of heavy industry, nor a single, dominant category of manufacturing, Atlanta has emerged as a diversified center for services, information, and high-technology businesses. The presence of the Georgia Institute of Technology, whose research institute is among the country's leaders in engineering research, enhances the area's ability to attract high-tech businesses. Health sciences research is prominent at Emory University in DeKalb County.

Cultural and recreational attractions are as diverse as the economy: the baseball Braves and the football Falcons are significant community rallying points, and the notable Richard Meier designed High Museum, the Atlanta Symphony, and the Atlanta Ballet contribute to midtown Atlanta's cultural cache.

City Profile

 Population in Thousands

1980	2,138.1
1990	2,833.5
1992	3,174.1
1995 Estimate	3,337.2

 Socioeconomic Factors

Average Household Income

1980	$21,608
1991 Estimate	$48,690
% Change	125.3
1996 Projection	$60,563

Median Household Income

1980	$18,425
1991 Estimate	$37,246
% Change	102.1
1996 Projection	$46,760

 Labor Force & Employment

	1993
Total Number of Persons in the Labor Force (in 1000's)	1,518.8
Total Number of Persons Employed (in 1000's)	1,421.9
Average Unemployment Rate	6.4%

Total Employment in Thousands by Sector

	1980	1992
Construction	47.6	61.5
Manufacturing	160.0	170.6
Transportation/Utilities	87.3	132.4
Trade	272.0	409.3
F.I.R.E.	68.6	105.2
Services	201.6	396.2
Government	166.7	222.8

 Education

1992 Enrollment

Two Year College	32,388
Four Year Undergraduate	53,965
Four Year Graduate	16,070
Average SAT Score	762
Total Possible Score: 1600	
Average ACT Score	N/A
Total Possible Score: 36	

 Business Environment

Selected Major Employers
Suntrust Banks
Bellsouth
Southern
Delta Air Lines
United Parcel Service
Bank South Corp.
Home Depot
Turner Broadcasting
Genuine Parts
First Financial Mgmt.

Media Profile
2 newspapers
34 radio stations
10 network television stations
1 cable television operator

% State Taxes

Corporate Income/Franchise Tax	6.0%
Sales/Use Tax	6.0%
Individual Income Tax	6.0%
Unemployment Insurance Rate	2.70%

 City Taxes[1]

County Tax	1.00%
City Tax	None
Other Taxes	1.00%

Property Tax Rates [2,3]

$74.58 in $ per $1000

International Profile

Number of Foreign Banks	18
Number of Foreign-owned Businesses	514
Number of Persons Employed by Foreign-owned Businesses	13,574
Number of Daily International Flights	119

Real Estate

Occupancy Cost per Square Foot (Annual)

	Sq. Foot	Sq. Meters
Average Rental-Class A Office (Central Business District)	$19.08	$205.30
Average Rental-Class A Apartment	$7.92	$85.22
Average Rental-Warehouse	$3.13	$33.68

Construction Cost per Square Foot

	Sq. Foot	Sq. Meters
Excellent Class A Office	$114.98	$1,237.18
Class A Industrial/ Manufacturing	$70.15	$754.18

	Sq. Foot	Sq. Meters
Class A Distribution Warehouse	$49.42	$531.56
Excellent Class C Single Family Residential	$89.24	$960.22

Average Electric Cost (Cents per KwH)

	1992
Residential	$0.755
Commercial	$0.745
Industrial	$0.472
Average Price for a 3-bedroom Family House (in 1000's)	$105.0

 Quality of Life

Climate

	Fahrenheit		Celsius	
	High	Low	High	Low
Winter	51	33	11	1
Spring	73	50	23	10
Summer	88	69	31	21
Autumn	73	51	23	11

Rainfall

	Inches	Millimeters
January	4.9	124
February	4.4	112
March	5.9	150
April	4.4	112
May	4.0	102
June	3.4	86
July	4.7	119
August	3.4	86
September	3.2	81
October	2.5	64
November	3.4	86
December	4.2	107

Cultural Highlights

Atlanta History Center
CNN Studio Tours
Georgia State Capitol

[1] See the State-Local General Sales Tax Notes on page 310.
[2] See the Property Tax Rate Notes on page 314.
[3] See the Classification of Real Property and Tangible Personal Property table on page 316.

Cultural Highlights (Continued)
 Martin Luther King Jr. National
 Historic Site
 SciTrek, the Science & Technology
 Museum of Atlanta

Leisure Highlights
 Georgia's Stone Mountain Park
 Six Flags Over Georgia
 Zoo Atlanta
 New Georgia Railrload
 Underground Atlanta

Crime

Rate per 100,000 Inhabitants	1991
Number of violent crimes	987.9
Number of property crimes	7,329.1

Average Wages for Selected Occupations

	Average Hiring Salary
Secretary (LR-3)	$25,688
Computer Systems Analyst III	$50,960
Computer Programmer III	$33,228
Engineer II	$35,568
Maintenance Machinist	$36,025

Charlotte

NORTH CAROLINA

Charlotte's paradox is this: a mid-sized city of less than 500,000 in population, it is at the heart of the fifth largest urban region in the United States—with more than 5.4 million people living within a 100-mile radius. The MSA itself, spanning seven counties in two states, grew in population to 1.2 million from approximately 970,000 between 1980 and 1992.

Charlotte has become the third largest financial center in the United States, after New York and San Francisco, and is the sixth largest U.S. wholesale center as well as the nation's seventh largest trading center. Although textile and fiber mills are still among the area's largest employers, electronics, printing and publishing, and medical and financial service companies are becoming prominent corporate citizens as well. The area has drawn relocating companies from the East and West coasts as well as the midwest and southwest.

Some 20,000 people work for more than 300 foreign-owned companies, from 21 countries, located in the region. So committed is the area to its growth as an international center that its literature is printed with sections written in German and Japanese, as well as in English. Charlotte-Douglas International Airport has direct flights to London and Frankfurt, and the city has a Foreign Trade Zone and an inland port facility.

There is a variety of housing in the area: large Victorian and historical properties, traditional and contemporary styles, and country farmhouses. Residential growth for the middle-management market has taken place in Olde Providence, Quail Hollow, Myers Park, and Carmel Providence; an average three-bedroom house sells for $115,800.

Lakes Wylie and Norman and the Catawba River also offer housing communities with built-in recreation such as boating, fishing, water skiing, and tennis. Arts and entertainment are varied, ranging from the Coca Cola 600 (a major NASCAR race), to the North Carolina Performing Arts Center at Charlotte, the Mint Museum, and Discovery Place Museum, to Carowinds Theme Park. The region ranks ninth in the United States in contributions to the arts and sciences.

City Profile

 ## Population in Thousands

1980	971.4
1990	1,162.1
1992	1,206.7
1995 Estimate	1,276.8

 ## Socioeconomic Factors

Average Household Income

1980	$19,583
1991 Estimate	$40,733
% Change	108.0
1996 Projection	$50,407

Median Household Income

1980	$17,049
1991 Estimate	$32,103
% Change	88.3
1996 Projection	$39,810

 ## Labor Force & Employment

	1993
Total Number of Persons in the Labor Force (in 1000's)	656.0
Total Number of Persons Employed (in 1000's)	622.5
Average Unemployment Rate	5.1%

Total Employment in Thousands by Sector

	1980	1992
Construction	18.6	31.3
Manufacturing	94.2	143.5
Transportation/Utilities	31.2	50.1
Trade	83.4	151.3
F.I.R.E.	21.2	38.8
Services	52.2	132.3
Government	36.8	73.4

 ## Education

1992 Enrollment

Two Year College	25,728
Four Year Undergraduate	20,192
Four Year Graduate	5,867
Average SAT Score	877
Total Possible Score: 1600	
Average ACT Score	N/A
Total Possible Score: 36	

 ## Business Environment

Selected Major Employers

Duke Power
Fieldcrest Cannon
Carolinas Medical
USAir Group
Springs Industries
IBM
Ruddick Corp.
First Union
Hoechst Celanese
Stowe Pharr Mills

Media Profile

1 newspaper
17 radio stations
11 network television stations
1 cable television operator

 ## State Taxes[1]

Corporate Income/Franchise Tax	7.905%
Sales/Use Tax	6.0%
Individual Income Tax	7.75%
Unemployment Insurance Rate	1.00%

[1]See the State Tax Notes on page 308.

 City Taxes

County Tax	2.00%
City Tax	None
Other Taxes	None

 Property Tax Rates [2,3]

$6.275 in $ per $1000

International Profile

Number of Foreign Banks	2
Number of Foreign-owned Businesses	151
Number of Persons Employed by Foreign-owned Businesses	4,754
Number of Daily International Flights	6

Real Estate

Occupancy Cost per Square Foot (Annual)

	Sq. Foot	Sq. Meters
Average Rental-Class A Office (Central Business District)	$16.16	$173.88
Average Rental-Class A Apartment	$7.02	$75.53
Average Rental- Warehouse	$3.93	$42.29

Construction Cost per Square Foot

	Sq. Foot	Sq. Meters
Excellent Class A Office	$103.85	$1,117.43
Class A Industrial/ Manufacturing	$63.36	$681.75

	Sq. Foot	Sq. Meters
Class A Distribution Warehouse	$44.64	$480.33
Excellent Class C Single Family Residential	$80.61	$867.36

Average Electric Cost (Cents per KwH)

	1992
Residential	$0.740
Commercial	$0.598
Industrial	$0.450
Average Price for a 3-bedroom Family House (in 1000's)	$115.8

 Quality of Life

Climate

	Fahrenheit		Celsius	
	High	Low	High	Low
Winter	50	31	10	-1
Spring	72	48	22	9
Summer	88	69	31	21
Autumn	72	50	22	10

Rainfall

	Inches	Millimeters
January	4.0	102
February	4.0	102
March	5.0	127
April	3.0	76
May	4.0	102
June	4.0	102
July	4.0	102
August	4.0	102
September	4.0	102
October	3.0	76
November	3.0	76
December	3.0	76

Cultural Highlights

Afro-American Cultural Center
Charlotte Museum/Alexander Homesite
James K. Polk Memorial North Carolina
State Historic Site

[2]See the Property Tax Rate Notes on page 314.
[3]See the Classification of Real Property and Tangible Personal Property table on page 316.

Cultural Highlights (Continued)
 Mint Museum of Art
 Carowinds Theme Park

Leisure Highlights
 Charlotte Motor Speedway
 Discovery Place
 Energy Explorium
 Spirit Square Center for the Arts
 Metrolina Expo Center

Crime

Rate per 100,000 Inhabitants	1991
Number of violent crimes	1,159.2
Number of property crimes	6,876.7

Average Wages for Selected Occupations

	Average Hiring Salary
Secretary (LR-3)	$26,460
Computer Systems Analyst III	$36,996
Computer Programmer III	$29,736
Engineer II	$35,376
Maintenance Machinist	$20,883

Fort Lauderdale

FLORIDA

Although tourism and retailing have been important to the Broward County economy, the service industry sector is prominent too, underscored by the establishment of numerous regional data processing operations in recent years. Broward's location also allows for convenient transportation of goods to Latin America, the Caribbean, Europe, Canada, and the Pacific Rim countries. The western section of the county, with new arterial roads, is growing as a distribution center.

Central to Fort Lauderdale's strength as a transportation hub is Port Everglades, a 2,100-acre seaport that transports more than 17 million tons of commerce and generates some $30 million in maritime business annually. Florida's deepest port, it is also said to be the world's fastest-growing cruise port.

Broward County has a strong nucleus of high-tech development and manufacturing companies, supported in part by the area's vocational/technical training. Approximately 27,000 students are enrolled full-time at three vocational/technical schools in Hollywood, Davie, and Coconut Creek. More than 50 foreign-owned companies are located in the area; newcomers include Gribetz International, from Japan; Racal DataCom, from England; and Selkirk Communications, from Canada.

Climate and proximity to area beaches are among Fort Lauderdale's greatest residential drawing cards. Prime middle-management residential areas include Plantation, Weston/Sunrise, and Coral Springs. The average three-bedroom house sells for more than $150,000.

In addition to its beaches, the area boasts numerous land- and water-oriented recreational attractions, including boating, fishing, airboat rides through the Everglades, golf, tennis, camping, and more. The newly completed Broward County Center for the Performing Arts houses a 2,700-seat theater for drama, opera, concerts, and Broadway shows. This facility anchors the downtown Riverwalk project.

City Profile

Population in Thousands

1980	1,018.2
1990	1,255.5
1992	1,294.1
1995 Estimate	1,378.0

Socioeconomic Factors

Average Household Income

1980	$20,870
1991 Estimate	$40,125
% Change	92.3
1996 Projection	$49,085

Median Household Income

1980	$16,942
1991 Estimate	$30,744
% Change	81.5
1996 Projection	$37,608

Labor Force & Employment

	1993
Total Number of Persons In the Labor Force (in 1000's)	704.4
Total Number of Persons Employed (in 1000's)	656.9
Average Unemployment Rate	6.8%

Total Employment in Thousands by Sector

	1980	1992
Construction	32.2	26.1
Manufacturing	41.3	39.2
Transportation/Utilities	16.8	24.8
Trade	103.5	147.9
F.I.R.E.	29.6	39.5
Services	82.0	160.1
Government	43.9	73.4

Education

1992 Enrollment

Two Year College	18,373
Four Year Undergraduate	3,562
Four Year Graduate	3,618
Average SAT Score	884
Total Possible Score: 1600	
Average ACT Score	N/A
Total Possible Score: 36	

Business Environment

Selected Major Employers

School Board of Broward County
Publix Supermarkets
Broward County
Winn Dixie Supermarkets
North Broward Hospital District
Eckerd Drug Co.
Southern Bell Telephone
American Express
Memorial Hospital
Waste Management

Media Profile

2 newspapers
12 radio stations
17 network television stations
1 cable television operator

State Taxes

Corporate Income/Franchise Tax	5.5%
Sales/Use Tax	7.0%
Individual Income Tax	0.0%
Unemployment Insurance Rate	2.60%

 City Taxes[2]

County Tax	None
City Tax	None
Other Taxes	None

 Property Tax Rates [3,4]

$21.5470 in $ per $1000

 International Profile

Number of Foreign Banks	1
Number of Foreign-owned Businesses	172
Number of Persons Employed by Foreign-owned Businesses	4,502
Number of Daily International Flights	12

Real Estate

Occupancy Cost per Square Foot (Annual)

	Sq. Foot	Sq. Meters
Average Rental-Class A Office (Central Business District)	$20.12	$216.49
Average Rental-Class A Apartment	$8.78	$94.47
Average Rental-Warehouse	$3.98	$42.82

Construction Cost per Square Foot

	Sq. Foot	Sq. Meters
Excellent Class A Office	$116.21	$1,250.42
Class A Industrial/Manufacturing	$70.90	$762.88

	Sq. Foot	Sq. Meters
Class A Distribution Warehouse	$49.95	$537.46
Excellent Class C Single Family Residential	$92.12	$991.21

Average Electric Cost (Cents per KwH)

	1992
Residential	$0.800
Commercial	$0.664
Industrial	$0.500
Average Price for a 3-bedroom Family House (in 1000's)	$153.8

Quality of Life

Climate

	Fahrenheit		Celsius	
	High	Low	High	Low
Winter	75	59	24	15
Spring	82	68	28	20
Summer	89	76	32	24
Autumn	84	72	29	22

Rainfall

	Inches	Millimeters
January	2.1	53
February	2.0	51
March	1.9	49
April	3.1	79
May	6.5	165
June	9.2	234
July	6.0	152
August	7.0	178
September	8.1	206
October	7.1	180
November	2.7	69
December	1.9	48

Cultural Highlights
Bonnet House
Museum of Art
War Memorial Auditorium

[2]See the State-Local General Sales Tax Notes on page 310.
[3]See the Property Tax Rate Notes on page 314.
[4]See the Classification of Real Property and Tangible Personal Property table on page 316.

Cultural Highlights (Continued)
 Butterfly World
 Ocean World

Leisure Highlights
 Dania Jai Alai
 Flamingo Gardens
 Pompano Harness Track
 Bonaventure Resort & Spa
 Fort Lauderdale Swap Shop

Crime

Rate per 100,000 Inhabitants	1991
Number of violent crimes	908.4
Number of property crimes	7,605.9

Average Wages for Selected Occupations

	Average Hiring Salary
Secretary (LR-3)	$22,090
Computer Systems Analyst III	$38,896
Computer Programmer III	$32,718
Engineer II	$45,885
Maintenance Machinist	$21,861

Greensboro

NORTH CAROLINA

The Greensboro/Winston-Salem/High Point MSA, also known as the Piedmont Triad, is located halfway between Washington, D.C., and Atlanta—one of the reasons that it is growing as a manufacturing and warehousing/distribution center.

Textiles, furniture, and tobacco still rank among the largest employers in the area, but added to these traditional categories have been food (Sara Lee Corporation), biomedical (Roche Biomedical), financial services (NationsBank and First Wachovia), and health care (Carolina Medicorp).

To support its industrial base, the area has an extensive system of vocational/technical schools offering programs in business, computer science and other technical occupations. Largest is Guilford Technical Community College, with campuses in Jamestown, Greensboro, and High Point. More than 30,000 people enroll in GTCC courses annually.

The area's population has grown steadily to more than 1 million in 1992, and is estimated to exceed 1.1 million by 1995. Unemployment is 4.6%. The population is relatively young, with the largest percentage in the 25-to-44 age group; median age is 31.6. More than 75% of graduating seniors in Guilford and Forsyth Counties attend college. The average three-bedroom home price is $115,000, with middle-management residents drawn to the northwest sections of Greensboro, Winston-Salem, and High Point.

Like Raleigh-Durham, the Piedmont Triad's lush terrain and access to both Atlantic coastline and mountain areas add up to a profusion of recreational opportunities. For example, Greensboro itself has 18 golf courses, more than 3,000 acres of public parks, and a large zoological park.

The area's cultural life is enhanced by the North Carolina Shakespeare Festival, the Piedmont Opera Company, and the Greensboro Symphony/Winston-Salem Symphony. Special recreational events include the Kmart Greater Greensboro Open, an annual stop on the PGA tour.

City Profile

Population in Thousands

1980	926.6
1990	1,050.3
1992	1,071.1
1995 Estimate	1,107.4

Socioeconomic Factors

Average Household Income

1980	$19,205
1991 Estimate	$39,134
% Change	103.8
1996 Projection	$48,189

Median Household Income

1980	$16,245
1991 Estimate	$30,351
% Change	86.8
1996 Projection	$37,151

Labor Force & Employment

	1993
Total Number of Persons in the Labor Force (in 1000's)	536.2
Total Number of Persons Employed (in 1000's)	511.5
Average Unemployment Rate	4.6%

Total Employment in Thousands by Sector

	1980	1992
Construction	16.9	21.4
Manufacturing	148.5	143.6
Transportation/Utilities	21.3	26.9
Trade	77.7	112.1
F.I.R.E.	18.2	25.5
Services	56.9	112.2
Government	46.4	56.7

Education

1992 Enrollment

Two Year College	13,389
Four Year Undergraduate	24,141
Four Year Graduate	5,861
Average SAT Score	
Total Possible Score: 1600	854
Average ACT Score	
Total Possible Score: 36	N/A

Business Environment

Selected Major Employers

R. J. Reynolds
Bowman Gray/Baptist Hospital
Sara Lee Corp.
Sears Roebuck
Burlington Ind.
AT&T
LADD Furniture
UNIFI
Cone Mills
USAir

Media Profile

1 newspaper
15 radio stations
9 network television stations
2 cable television operators

% State Taxes[1]

Corporate Income/Franchise Tax	7.905%
Sales/Use Tax	6.0%
Individual Income Tax	7.75%
Unemployment Insurance Rate	2.25%

[1]See the State Tax Notes on page 308.

 City Taxes

County Tax	2.00%
City Tax	None
Other Taxes	None

 Property Tax Rates [2,3]

$11.955 in $ per $1000

 International Profile

Number of Foreign Banks	0
Number of Foreign-owned Businesses	69
Number of Persons Employed by Foreign-owned Businesses	3,141
Number of Daily International Flights	2

 Real Estate

Occupancy Cost per Square Foot (Annual)

	Sq. Foot	Sq. Meters
Average Rental-Class A Office (Central Business District)	$16.25	$174.85
Average Rental-Class A Apartment	$7.13	$76.72
Average Rental-Warehouse	$3.65	$39.27

Construction Cost per Square Foot

	Sq. Foot	Sq. Meters
Excellent Class A Office	$103.85	$1,117.43
Class A Industrial/ Manufacturing	$63.36	$681.75

	Sq. Foot	Sq. Meters
Class A Distribution Warehouse	$44.64	$480.33
Excellent Class C Single Family Residential	$78.69	$846.70

Average Electric Cost (Cents per KwH)

	1992
Residential	$0.740
Commercial	$0.598
Industrial	$0.450
Average Price for a 3-bedroom Family House (in 1000's)	$115.0

★ Quality of Life

Climate

	Fahrenheit		Celsius	
	High	Low	High	Low
Winter	48	27	9	-3
Spring	71	46	22	8
Summer	87	67	31	19
Autumn	70	47	21	8

Rainfall

	Inches	Millimeters
January	3.5	89
February	3.4	86
March	3.9	99
April	3.4	81
May	3.4	86
June	3.9	99
July	4.3	109
August	4.2	107
September	3.6	91
October	3.2	81
November	2.6	66
December	3.4	86

Cultural Highlights
Bicentennial Gardens
Blandwood Mansion
Green Hill Center for North Carolina Art

[2]See the Property Tax Rate Notes on page 314
[3]See the Classification of Real Property and Tangible Personal Property table on page 316.

City Profile

Cultural Highlights (Continued)
 Greensboro Historical Museum
 Weatherspoon Art Gallery

Leisure Highlights
 Natural Science Center
 Old Mill of Guilford
 Tannenbaum Park
 Greensboro Coliseum Complex
 Guilford Courthouse National Military Park

Crime

Rate per 100,000 Inhabitants	1991
Number of violent crimes	732.9
Number of property crimes	5,706.4

Average Wages for Selected Occupations

	Average Hiring Salary
Secretary (LR-3)	$26,884
Computer Systems Analyst III	$56,524
Computer Programmer III	$33,228
Engineer II	N/A
Maintenance Machinist	$29,390

Jacksonville

FLORIDA

A four-county MSA in the uppermost northeast corner of Florida, Jacksonville is expected to pass the one-million population mark by 1995, up from some 720,000 in 1980. Both Jacksonville's economic and recreational life are dependent on the St. Johns River and the Atlantic Ocean. Its deep-water port is located 9 miles from the Atlantic and 30 international shipping lines connect Jacksonville with 75 foreign countries.

At the crossroads of three major rail lines and three interstate highways, the area is also serviced by more than 100 trucking lines. Jacksonville International Airport has been renovated and expanded and handles approximately three million passenger arrivals and departures a year.

Wholesale/retail trade and services are the area's biggest employers; companies with a major presence in the area include AT&T, CSX Transportation, Blue Cross/Blue Shield, Winn Dixie, Barnett Banks, and Southern Bell.

The area has the third-largest military presence in the United States, with three naval air stations within Jacksonville's city limits. The local work force includes 20,000 former Navy members; approximately 2,000 leave the service annually.

Downtown Jacksonville is the cultural and special events heart of the city; the Civic Auditorium, a convention center, a science and history museum, and the Gator Bowl are prominent features. The Downtown Development Authority's goal is to enhance downtown's strength as a lively, "people-oriented" center. Older buildings and riverfront amenities are being revitalized, as are downtown parks.

Jacksonville's beaches offer some unique features. Fernandina Beach, for example, includes a 30-block district listed in the National Register of Historic Places, and Amelia Island is an environmentally sensitive, planned resort that also features a Ritz-Carlton hotel. Other widely available recreational activities include golf, tennis, boating, and fishing.

City Profile

Population in Thousands

1980	722.3
1990	906.7
1992	943.7
1995 Estimate	1,001.4

Socioeconomic Factors

Average Household Income
1980	$18,598
1991 Estimate	$36,559
% Change	96.6
1996 Projection	$45,185

Median Household Income
1980	$15,298
1991 Estimate	$28,699
% Change	87.6
1996 Projection	$35,031

Labor Force & Employment

	1993
Total Number of Persons in the Labor Force (in 1000's)	466.0
Total Number of Persons Employed (in 1000's)	437.8
Average Unemployment Rate	6.1%

Total Employment in Thousands by Sector

	1980	1992
Construction	16.3	22.3
Manufacturing	33.7	33.5
Transportation/Utilities	24.4	31.0
Trade	75.2	109.2
F.I.R.E.	27.7	44.2
Services	N/A	116.0
Government	51.6	61.8

Education

1992 Enrollment
Two Year College	15,072
Four Year Undergraduate	8,708
Four Year Graduate	3,288
Average SAT Score	885
Total Possible Score: 1600	
Average ACT Score	N/A
Total Possible Score: 36	

Business Environment

Selected Major Employers
- U.S. Navy
- Duval Co. Board
- State of Florida
- AT&T
- City of Jacksonville
- Blue Cross/Blue Shield
- Winn Dixie
- CSX Transportation
- Barnett Banks
- U.S. Postal Service

Media Profile
- 1 newspaper
- 28 radio stations
- 7 network television stations
- 1 cable television operator

State Taxes

Corporate Income/Franchise Tax	5.5%
Sales/Use Tax	7.0%
Individual Income Tax	0.0%
Unemployment Insurance Rate	2.70%

City Taxes[1]

County Tax	.50%
City Tax	None
Other Taxes	None

Property Tax Rates [2,3]

$20.5 in $ per $1000

International Profile

Number of Foreign Banks	1
Number of Foreign-owned Businesses	33
Number of Persons Employed by Foreign-owned Businesses	822
Number of Daily International Flights	6

Real Estate

Occupancy Cost per Square Foot (Annual)

	Sq. Foot	Sq. Meters
Average Rental-Class A Office (Central Business District)	$16.79	$180.66
Average Rental-Class A Apartment	$7.14	$76.83
Average Rental-Warehouse	$3.33	$35.83

Construction Cost per Square Foot

	Sq. Foot	Sq. Meters
Excellent Class A Office	$108.80	$1,170.69
Class A Industrial/Manufacturing	$66.38	$714.25

[1]See the State-Local General Sales Tax Notes on page 310.
[2]See the Property Tax Rate Notes on page 314.
[3]See the Classification of Real Property and Tangible Personal Property table on page 316.

	Sq. Foot	Sq. Meters
Class A Distribution Warehouse	$46.76	$503.14
Excellent Class C Single Family Residential	$85.41	$919.01

Average Electric Cost (Cents per KwH)

	1992
Residential	$0.703
Commercial	$0.668
Industrial	$0.580
Average Price for a 3-bedroom Family House (in 1000's)	$79.0

Quality of Life

Climate

	Fahrenheit		Celsius	
	High	Low	High	Low
Winter	65	42	18	6
Spring	80	56	27	13
Summer	91	72	33	22
Autumn	80	59	27	15

Rainfall

	Inches	Millimeters
January	3.1	79
February	3.5	89
March	3.7	94
April	3.3	84
May	4.9	124
June	5.4	137
July	6.5	165
August	7.2	183
September	7.3	185
October	3.4	86
November	1.9	48
December	2.6	66

Cultural Highlights

Cummer Gallery of Art
Jacksonville Art Museum
Museum of Science & History
Anheuser-Busch Brewery

Cultural Highlights (Continued)
 The Riverwalk

Leisure Highlights
 The Jacksonville Landing
 Jacksonville Zoological Park
 Greater Jacksonville Fairgrounds
 Prime F. Osborn III Convention Center
 Ponte-Vedra Golf Resorts

Crime

Rate per 100,000 Inhabitants	1991
Number of violent crimes	404.5
Number of property crimes	4,523.8

Average Wages for Selected Occupations

	Average Hiring Salary
Secretary (LR-3)	$21,778
Computer Systems Analyst III	$39,707
Computer Programmer III	$27,997
Engineer II	$46,550
Maintenance Machinist	$24,253

Miami

FLORIDA

Miami is a city with salsa, of both the literal and figurative varieties. Though hard-hit by the recession (bank and airline failures have contributed to a current unemployment rate of 8%), this metro area projects an unmistakable exuberance, from its dynamic architecture, to its distinctive ethnic neighborhoods, to the newly chic areas that appeal to cognoscenti in the fashion and entertainment fields.

Economically, the area's strength lies largely in its status as a center for international trade, with excellent access to Latin American, Caribbean, and South American markets. The Port of Miami generates more than $4 billion annually for greater Miami's economy, and Miami International Airport provides direct service to more than 150 U.S. and international cities. In all, there are close to 820 foreign-owned companies located in the area.

Civic leaders, who like to stress the area's tropical life-style in a metropolitan setting, expect that through the 1990s close to 19 out of every 20 new jobs created will be in the service sector. Tourism, finance, health care, bio-tech businesses, and wholesale/retail trade provide the bulk of employment in the area, which covers all of Dade County. Among the largest nongovernment employers are Publix Supermarkets, Jackson Memorial Hospital, Florida Power and Light, Southern Bell, and Burger King, whose corporate headquarters is located here.

Miami's work force is relatively young and multicultural. Nearly half the population is Latino, and one-fifth is black. Almost one-third of the population is in the 25-to-44 age group.

Business leaders have expressed reservations about greater Miami's schools, but Dade County is in the midst of long-term building and renovation programs, designed to upgrade existing facilities, relieve overcrowded classrooms, and add art, music, science labs, and media centers in many schools. Partnerships with businesses have been established, as have magnet schools and satellite learning centers. In addition, some 49,000 students are enrolled full-time in vocational/technical schools.

City Profile

 Population in Thousands

1980	1,626.0
1990	1,937.0
1992	1,983.0
1995 Estimate	2,083.0

 Socioeconomic Factors

Average Household Income

1980	$20,402
1991 Estimate	$36,035
% Change	76.6
1996 Projection	$43,650

Median Household Income

1980	$15,689
1991 Estimate	$27,028
% Change	72.3
1996 Projection	$32,473

 Labor Force & Employment

	1993
Total Number of Persons in the Labor Force (in 1000's)	982.6
Total Number of Persons Employed (in 1000's)	904.1
Average Unemployment Rate	8.0%

Total Employment in Thousands by Sector

	1980	1992
Construction	39.6	30.7
Manufacturing	99.7	83.4
Transportation/Utilities	72.1	66.3
Trade	192.4	227.6
F.I.R.E.	53.6	62.9
Services	176.9	261.2
Government	96.2	125.4

 Education

1992 Enrollment

Two Year College	39,980
Four Year Undergraduate	24,638
Four Year Graduate	14,318
Average SAT Score	822
Total Possible Score: 1600	
Average ACT Score	N/A
Total Possible Score: 36	

 Business Environment

Selected Major Employers

Dade County Public Schools
Metro Dade County
Federal Government
State of Florida
Jackson Memorial Hospital
University of Miami
American Airlines
Florida Power & Light
Southern Bell

Media Profile

2 newspapers
35 radio stations
17 network television stations
4 cable television operators

 State Taxes

Corporate Income/Franchise Tax	5.5%
Sales/Use Tax	7.0%
Individual Income Tax	0.0%
Unemployment Insurance Rate	2.70%

City Taxes[1]

County Tax	.50%
City Tax	None
Other Taxes	None

Property Tax Rates [2,3]

$25.6335 in $ per $1000

International Profile

Number of Foreign Banks	52
Number of Foreign-owned Businesses	820
Number of Persons Employed by Foreign-owned Businesses	8,793
Number of Daily International Flights	397

Real Estate

Occupancy Cost per Square Foot (Annual)

	Sq. Foot	Sq. Meters
Average Rental-Class A Office (Central Business District)	$20.19	$217.24
Average Rental-Class A Apartment	$9.50	$102.22
Average Rental-Warehouse	$4.01	$43.15

Construction Cost per Square Foot

	Sq. Foot	Sq. Meters
Excellent Class A Office	$114.98	$1,237.18
Class A Industrial/ Manufacturing	$70.15	$754.81

	Sq. Foot	Sq. Meters
Class A Distribution Warehouse	$49.42	$531.76
Excellent Class C Single Family Residential	$91.16	$980.88

Average Electric Cost (Cents per KwH)

	1992
Residential	$0.800
Commercial	$0.664
Industrial	$0.500
Average Price for a 3-bedroom Family House (in 1000's)	$104.0

Quality of Life

Climate

	Fahrenheit		Celsius	
	High	Low	High	Low
Winter	75	59	24	15
Spring	82	68	28	20
Summer	89	76	32	24
Autumn	84	72	29	22

Rainfall

	Inches	Millimeters
January	2.1	53
February	2.1	53
March	1.9	48
April	3.1	79
May	6.5	165
June	9.2	234
July	6.0	152
August	7.0	178
September	8.1	206
October	7.1	180
November	2.7	69
December	1.9	48

Cultural Highlights
Vizcaya Museum & Gardens
Bayside Marketplace
SeaEscape

[1]See the State-Local General Sales Tax Notes on page 310.
[2]See the Property Tax Rate Notes on page 314.
[3]See the Classification of Real Property and Tangible Personal Property table on page 316.

Cultural Highlights (Continued)
 Fairchild Tropical Garden
 Coconut Grove Convention Center

Leisure Highlights
 Gulfstream Park Race Track
 Miami Metrozoo
 Miami Seaquarium
 Monkey Jungle
 Parrot Jungle & Gardens

Crime

Rate per 100,000 Inhabitants	1991
Number of violent crimes	2,194.9
Number of property crimes	10,591.0

Average Wages for Selected Occupations

	Average Hiring Salary
Secretary (LR-3)	$24,284
Computer Systems Analyst III	$52,208
Computer Programmer III	$36,868
Engineer II	$37,232
Maintenance Machinist	$27,227

Norfolk

VIRGINIA

Encompassing Norfolk, Virginia Beach, and Newport News, this MSA's defining characteristic is its port location, which leads the United States in seagoing exports. Now home to more than 1.4 million people, this area, also known as Hampton Roads, is expected to grow modestly to nearly 1.5 million by 1995. The Norfolk Naval Base, the largest in the world, contributes to a strong military presence in the area. There is one drawback: although the MSA is well served by highway, seaport, and rail transport and has its own airport, the closest hub airport is Dulles International, some three and one half hours away.

Close to 900 manufacturing companies are active here, producing a variety of goods, from chain saws to computer diskettes. Retailing is also a major employer in the area. Norfolk's one-square-mile downtown area is the financial and legal center of southeastern Virginia.

Companies relocating to the area recently have come from California, Pennsylvania, and New Jersey, varying from financial services to printing, steel fabrication, telecommunications, and manufacturing. Forty-three foreign-owned companies, from 20 countries, are located in the area, employing more than 1,600 people. Foreign-owned newcomers to the area include Lucas Industries, Volvo Penta (for its U.S. headquarters), and Alfa Laval.

Not surprisingly, much of the area's recreational life centers on the waterfront and beaches. However, there are other attractions, including Colonial Williamsburg and other historical sites, Busch Gardens, state and national wildlife parks, 26 golf courses, and Harborfest. Theater, ballet, opera, and a symphony orchestra round out Norfolk's cultural attractions.

Myriad waterfront locales also provide a broad choice in housing; beach cottages, midrise condominiums, townhouses, and riverside mansions are several possibilities. The average price for a three-bedroom home (not necessarily with a waterfront location) is $105,000.

City Profile

 Population in Thousands

1980	1,160.3
1990	1,396.1
1992	1,432.4
1995 Estimate	1,486.9

 Socioeconomic Factors

Average Household Income

1980	$19,355
1991 Estimate	$43,542
% Change	124.9
1996 Projection	$54,543

Median Household Income

1980	$16,657
1991 Estimate	$33,701
% Change	102.3
1996 Projection	$42,570

Labor Force & Employment

	1993
Total Number of Persons in the Labor Force (in 1000's)	656.8
Total Number of Persons Employed (in 1000's)	617.3
Average Unemployment Rate	6.0%

Total Employment in Thousands by Sector

	1980	1992
Construction	24.7	30.3
Manufacturing	63.4	63.1
Transportation/Utilities	24.0	28.0
Trade	96.9	138.4
F.I.R.E.	20.0	25.7
Services	85.8	159.5
Government	120.5	139.2

Education

1992 Enrollment

Two Year College	21,927
Four Year Undergraduate	32,390
Four Year Graduate	8,337
Average SAT Score	798
Total Possible Score: 1600	
Average ACT Score	N/A
Total Possible Score: 36	

Business Environment

Selected Major Employers
Norfolk Naval Shipyard
Sentara Health System
National Aviation Depot
Farm Fresh
NORSHIPCO
NationsBank
Tidewater Health Care
Southland Corporation
Food Lion
Landmark Communications

Media Profile
2 newspapers
26 radio staions
7 network television stations
1 cable televison operator

 State Taxes

Corporate Income/Franchise Tax	6.0%
Sales/Use Tax	4.5%
Individual Income Tax	5.75%
Unemployment Insurance Rate	2.50%

 City Taxes[1]

County Tax	None
City Tax	1.00%
Other Taxes	None

Property Tax Rates [2,3]

$13.50 in $ per $1000

International Profile

Number of Foreign Banks	0
Number of Foreign-owned Businesses	43
Number of Persons Employed by Foreign-owned Businesses	1,600
Number of Daily International Flights	10

Real Estate

Occupancy Cost per Square Foot (Annual)

	Sq. Foot	Sq. Meters
Average Rental-Class A Office (Central Business District)	$15.31	$164.74
Average Rental-Class A Apartment	$7.68	$82.64
Average Rental-Warehouse	$4.28	$4605

Construction Cost per Square Foot

	Sq. Foot	Sq. Meters
Excellent Class A Office	$113.74	$1,223.84
Class A Industrial/ Manufacturing	$69.39	$746.64

[1] See the State-Local General Sales Tax Notes on page 310.
[2] See the Property Tax Rate Notes on page 314.
[3] See the Classification of Real Property and Tangible Personal Property table on page 316

	Sq. Foot	Sq. Meters
Class A Distribution Warehouse	$48.89	$526.06
Excellent Class C Single Family Residential	$87.32	$932.56

Average Electric Cost (Cents per KwH)

	1992
Residential	$0.816
Commercial	$0.634
Industrial	$0.448
Average Price for a 3-bedroom Family House (in 1000's)	$105.0

Quality of Life

Climate

	Fahrenheit		Celsius	
	High	Low	High	Low
Winter	48	32	9	0
Spring	68	48	20	9
Summer	87	70	31	21
Autumn	70	53	21	12

Rainfall

	Inches	Millimeters
January	3.7	94
February	3.3	84
March	3.9	99
April	2.9	74
May	3.8	96
June	3.5	89
July	5.2	132
August	5.3	135
September	4.4	112
October	3.4	86
November	2.9	74
December	3.2	81

Cultural Highlights

Adam Thoroughgood House
Douglas MacArthur Memorial Museum
The Chrysler Museum

Cultural Highlights (Continued)
 Willoughby-Baylor House
 Moses Myers House

Leisure Highlights
 Norfolk Botanical Garden
 Waterside Festival Marketplace
 Norfolk Naval Base Tour Office
 Virginia Zoological Park
 Waterside Convention Center

Crime

Rate per 100,000 Inhabitants	1991
Number of violent crimes	635.9
Number of property crimes	6,051.4

Average Wages for Selected Occupations

	Average Hiring Salary
Secretary (LR-3)	$20,946
Computer Systems Analyst III	$40,373
Computer Programmer III	$29,681
Engineer II	$31,657
Maintenance Machinist	$28,288

Orlando

FLORIDA

In a recent issue, *Orlando* magazine posed the question: "What's the best reason for living here?" A whopping 77 % of voters cited the weather as number one. In fact, the climate is balmy, with an average annual temperature of 72 degrees, making outdoor living and recreation appealing. Though not a coastal community, this four-county MSA in central Florida has more than 2,000 lakes for a variety of water sports, not to mention such attractions as Disney World, Universal Studios, and Sea World.

Orlando's attractive business climate is due to more than the weather. The area has one of the state's largest and youngest labor pools and has grown dramatically to a current population of more than 1.3 million. Services (especially hospitality) and wholesale/retail trade are the dominant categories, and high-tech businesses have made strides as well. During the 1980s, employment in high-tech business increased by more than 100%, and more than three-quarters of the manufacturing growth has been in this sector.

Partly because of the presence of Disney/MGM Studios, Universal Studios, and ancillary facilities, as well as encouragement from the state, the area has become an attractive center for movie and television production.

Among the companies that have relocated to the area recently have been distribution operations, corporate headquarters, printers, and manufacturers. These businesses have come from the East Coast as well as from the Midwest and California. Approximately 118 foreign-owned companies are located here, including Alfa Romeo, Graseby Infrared, and Wurth.

Supporting this growth is a network of five vocational/technical schools that at last count had a combined full-time enrollment of more than 10,000. The state's Industry Services Training Program coordinates with these and other vocational schools in Florida to provide help in recruiting, testing, and upgrading employees.

City Profile

 ## Population in Thousands

1980	805.0
1990	1,224.9
1992	1,300.8
1995 Estimate	1,426.9

$ Socioeconomic Factors

Average Household Income

1980	$19,311
1991 Estimate	$43,573
% Change	125.6
1996 Projection	$54,484

Median Household Income

1980	$15,970
1991 Estimate	$33,643
% Change	110.7
1996 Projection	$42,258

Labor Force & Employment

	1993
Total Number of Persons in the Labor Force (in 1000's)	673.9
Total Number of Persons Employed (in 1000's)	632.4
Average Unemployment Rate	6.2%

Total Employment in Thousands by Sector

	1980	1992
Construction	19.9	28.6
Manufacturing	36.7	46.6
Transportation/Utilities	15.0	32.5
Trade	75.1	143.8
F.I.R.E.	20.5	34.2
Services	79.4	216.7
Government	41.4	69.2

Education

1992 Enrollment

Two Year College	18,497
Four Year Undergraduate	16,405
Four Year Graduate	4,941
Average SAT Score	891
Total Possible Score: 1600	
Average ACT Score	N/A
Total Possible Score: 36	

 ## Business Environment

Selected Major Employers

Walt Disney World
Orange Co. Public Schools
Naval Training Center
Martin Marietta
Florida Hospital
U.S. Postal Service
Seminole Co. Public Schools
AT&T Information Systems
Orange County Government

Media Profile

1 newspaper
23 radio stations
13 network television stations
2 cable television operators

% State Taxes

Corporate Income/Franchise Tax	5.5%
Sales/Use Tax	7.0%
Individual Income Tax	0.0%
Unemployment Insurance Rate	2.70%

City Taxes[1]

County Tax	None
City Tax	None
Other Taxes	None

Property Tax Rates [2,3]

$19.6265 in $ per $1000

International Profile

Number of Foreign Banks	0
Number of Foreign-owned Businesses	118
Number of Persons Employed by Foreign-owned Businesses	1,311
Number of Daily International Flights	90

Real Estate

Occupancy Cost per Square Foot (Annual)

	Sq. Foot	Sq. Meters
Average Rental-Class A Office (Central Business District)	$17.03	$183.24
Average Rental-Class A Apartment	$7.74	$83.28
Average Rental- Warehouse	$3.12	$33.57

Construction Cost per Square Foot

	Sq. Foot	Sq. Meters
Excellent Class A Office	$116.21	$1,250.42
Class A Industrial/ Manufacturing	$70.90	$762.88

[1]See the State-Local General Sales Tax Notes on page 310.
[2]See the Property Tax Rate Notes on page 314.
[3]See the Classification of Real Property and Tangible Personal Property table on page 316.

	Sq. Foot	Sq. Meters
Class A Distribution Warehouse	$49.95	$537.46
Excellent Class C Single Family Residential	$90.20	$970.55

Average Electric Cost (Cents per KwH)

	1992
Residential	$0.724
Commercial	$0.528
Industrial	$0.420
Average Price for a 3-bedroom Family House (in 1000's)	$87.6

Quality of Life

Climate

	Fahrenheit		Celsius	
	High	Low	High	Low
Winter	72	49	22	9
Spring	84	60	29	16
Summer	92	73	33	23
Autumn	84	65	29	18

Rainfall

	Inches	Millimeters
January	2.0	51
February	3.0	76
March	3.0	76
April	2.0	51
May	4.0	102
June	7.0	178
July	8.0	203
August	6.0	152
September	6.0	152
October	3.0	76
November	2.0	51
December	2.0	61

Cultural Highlights
Cartoon Museum
Elvis Presley Museum
Orlando Museum of Art
Church Street Station

Leisure Highlights

Central Florida Zoological Society
Central Florida Railroad Museum
Gatorland Alligator Capital of the World
Sea World of Florida
Disney World

Crime

Rate per 100,000 Inhabitants	1991
Number of violent crimes	943.1
Number of property crimes	7,239.1

Average Wages for Selected Occupations

	Average Hiring Salary
Secretary (LR-3)	$22,672
Computer Systems Analyst III	$41,652
Computer Programmer III	$37,336
Engineer II	$41,652
Maintenance Machinist	$29,224

Raleigh-Durham

NORTH CAROLINA

The seeds of Raleigh-Durham's current economic landscape were planted in 1959 with the establishment of Research Triangle Park, the largest of its type in the United States. Located on 6,800 acres 4 miles south of Durham, its appeal as a center for research, development and scientifically related production stems from the proximity of three major universities: Duke in Durham, the University of North Carolina in Chapel Hill, and North Carolina State University in Raleigh.

As a result, although it has not been completely immune to the effects of the recession, the Raleigh-Durham area, covering Durham, Franklin, Orange, and Wake Counties in central North Carolina, has remained relatively unscathed. In fact, its population has grown steadily and dramatically since 1980 (at a growth rate of more than 31%, it was the second fastest growing MSA in North Carolina in the 1980s). Although health care, telecommunications, and high-tech companies dominate the economic landscape, the economy of the area is notably diverse. More than 58% of the population is under the age of 35, because many students settle in the area to work and raise families, and unemployment is at a low rate of 3.8%.

Manufacturing and warehousing/distribution have grown steadily since 1980, aided by the area's location within 600 miles of half the U.S. population. Raleigh-Durham also continues to grow from within; more than 80% of the area's companies have fewer than 100 employees. The presence of foreign-owned companies is notable for a mid-sized city; nearly 6,739 people work in the area for such companies as The Body Shop, Inc., Reichhold Chemicals, and Ericsson GE Mobile Communications.

The concept of promoting economic development regionally has helped to establish a high profile for the area. Yet individual differences abound; Durham, for example, takes pains to project itself not only as "the city of medicine" (Duke University Medical Center is located here) but also as an eclectic, diverse mix of urban charm and small-town ambience.

With its relatively moderate climate and accessibility to coastline beaches and mountains (both are several hours' drive away), the Raleigh-Durham area offers variety in recreational attractions: camping, golf, fishing, hunting, skiing, and windsurfing, among others.

City Profile

 Population in Thousands

1980	561.2
1990	735.5
1992	775.5
1995 Estimate	829.2

Socioeconomic Factors

Average Household Income

1980	$19,938
1991 Estimate	$43,408
% Change	117.7
1996 Projection	$54,047

Median Household Income

1980	$17,060
1991 Estimate	$34,417
% Change	101.7
1996 Projection	$43,216

Labor Force & Employment

	1993
Total Number of Persons in the Labor Force (in 1000's)	456.3
Total Number of Persons Employed (in 1000's)	438.8
Average Unemployment Rate	3.8%

Total Employment in Thousands by Sector

	1980	1992
Construction	14.3	19.7
Manufacturing	45.0	65.1
Transportation/Utilities	13.4	22.3
Trade	53.2	92.5
F.I.R.E.	15.6	23.3
Services	59.0	129.0
Government	73.9	101.4

 Education

1992 Enrollment

Two Year College	10,884
Four Year Undergraduate	52,320
Four Year Graduate	16,925
Average SAT Score	924
Total Possible Score: 1600	
Average ACT Score	N/A
Total Possible Score: 36	

 Business Environment

Selected Major Employers
- State of North Carolina
- Duke University and Medical Center
- IBM
- Wake County Schools
- North Carolina State Univ.
- Northern Telecom
- University of North Carolina
- Glaxo
- American Airlines
- Winn-Dixie

Media Profile
- 1 newspaper
- 19 radio stations
- 10 network television stations
- 1 cable television operator

 State Taxes[1]

Corporate Income/Franchise Tax	7.905%
Sales/Use Tax	6.0%
Individual Income Tax	7.75%
Unemployment Insurance Rate	2.25%

[1]*See the State Tax Notes on page 308.*

City Taxes

County Tax	2.00%
City Tax	None
Other Taxes	None

Property Tax Rates [2,3]

$16.55 in $ per $1000

International Profile

Number of Foreign Banks	0
Number of Foreign-owned Businesses	55
Number of Persons Employed by Foreign-owned Businesses	6,739
Number of Daily International Flights	0

Real Estate

Occupancy Cost per Square Foot (Annual)

	Sq. Foot	Sq. Meters
Average Rental-Class A Office (Central Business District)	$17.00	$182.92
Average Rental-Class A Apartment	$7.41	$79.73
Average Rental-Warehouse	$3.75	$40.35

Construction Cost per Square Foot

	Sq. Foot	Sq. Meters
Excellent Class A Office	$110.03	$1,183.92
Class A Industrial/ Manufacturing	$67.13	$722.32
Class A Distribution Warehouse	$47.30	$508.95

[2]See the Property Tax Rate Notes on page 314.
[3]See the Classification of Real Property and Tangible Personal Property table on page 316.

	Sq. Foot	Sq. Meters
Excellent Class C Single Family Residential	$84.45	$908.68

Average Electric Cost (Cents per KwH)

	1992
Residential	$0.834
Commercial	$0.692
Industrial	$0.560
Average Price for a 3-bedroom Family House (in 1000's)	$115.0

Quality of Life

Climate

	Fahrenheit		Celsius	
	High	Low	High	Low
Winter	50	29	10	-2
Spring	72	47	22	8
Summer	88	67	31	19
Autumn	72	48	22	9

Rainfall

	Inches	Millimeters
January	3.6	91
February	3.4	86
March	3.7	94
April	2.9	74
May	3.7	94
June	3.7	94
July	4.4	112
August	4.4	112
September	3.3	84
October	2.7	69
November	2.9	74
December	3.1	79

Cultural Highlights

North Carolina Museum of Art
North Carolina Museum of History
North Carolina Museum of Natural Sciences
Oakwood Historic District
North Carolina State Capitol

Leisure Highlights
State Farmers Market
Walnut Creek Amphitheater
The City Market
Mordecai Historic Park
Executive Mansion

Crime

Rate per 100,000 Inhabitants	1991
Number of violent crimes	639.2
Number of property crimes	5,956.7

Average Wages for Selected Occupations

	Average Hiring Salary
Secretary (LR-3)	$21,112
Computer Systems Analyst III	$49,764
Computer Programmer III	$36,192
Engineer II	$32,344
Maintenance Machinist	$24,918

Richmond

VIRGINIA

Steeped in history dating back before the American Revolution, contemporary Richmond seems to have multiple business personalities. Because of its location (within a day's drive to half the country's population) and access to labor at reasonable wages, the Richmond area has long been a manufacturing and distribution center. As state capital and home to the Fifth District Federal Reserve Bank, however, it is also growing as a financial center and data center.

The area enjoys diversity not only in categories of employers, but within each of these categories as well. Tobacco, aluminum, food, and fibers are among the larger manufacturing categories, but this group is joined by paper and printing, chemicals and pharmaceuticals, commercial machinery, electronics, and computer equipment. At the same time, more than a dozen Fortune 500 companies have corporate headquarters here including CSX, Signet Bank, and James River Corporation.

Called a "mini-Atlanta" by some, Richmond has also benefited from upgraded and expanded roadways and airport expansion. The MSA covers nine counties and four cities in central Virginia, whose population is projected to pass the 900,000 mark by 1995. Commuting to the central business district from the suburbs has been clocked at less than a half hour.

Revitalization has turned some of the downtown's old plants into shops and restaurants. Plans for 1996 completion of Valentine Riverside, a $26 million history park and museum complex—including an amphitheater, auditorium, cafe, and more—on the site of the historic Tredegar Iron Works along the James River, should bring more life to the downtown area.

Home to numerous theater groups as a well as a ballet company, an opera and a symphony orchestra, Richmond also offers numerous recreational attractions and special events, including Kings Dominion theme park, an annual state fair, NASCAR stock racing, hot air ballooning, white water rafting, and tours to many Revolutionary and Civil War sites.

City Profile

 Population in Thousands

1980	761.3
1990	865.6
1992	887.4
1995 Estimate	934.0

 Socioeconomic Factors

Average Household Income

1980	$21,037
1991 Estimate	$48,717
% Change	131.6
1996 Projection	$61,339

Median Household Income

1980	$18,293
1991 Estimate	$39,165
% Change	114.1
1996 Projection	$49,279

 Labor Force & Employment

	1993
Total Number of Persons in the Labor Force (in 1000's)	476.2
Total Number of Persons Employed (in 1000's)	451.4
Average Unemployment Rate	5.2%

Total Employment in Thousands by Sector

	1980	1992
Construction	22.2	27.0
Manufacturing	67.2	62.6
Transportation/Utilities	21.0	22.9
Trade	84.4	106.7
F.I.R.E.	27.7	38.4
Services	64.4	108.4
Government	86.6	95.8

 Education

1992 Enrollment

Two Year College	15,870
Four Year Undergraduate	23,006
Four Year Graduate	7,283
Average SAT Score	853
Total Possible Score: 1600	
Average ACT Score	N/A
Total Possible Score: 36	

 Business Environment

Selected Major Employers
- Philip Morris USA
- Virginia Power
- Reynolds Metals Company
- Allied-Signal, Inc.
- E.I. duPont de Nemours
- NationsBank
- Signet Banking Corp.
- Blue Cross/Blue Shield
- Ukrops Supermarket
- C & P Telephone

Media Profile
- 2 newspapers
- 25 radio stations
- 8 network television stations
- 1 cable television operator

 State Taxes

Corporate Income/Franchise Tax	6.0%
Sales/Use Tax	4.5%
Individual Income Tax	5.75%
Unemployment Insurance Rate	2.50%

 City Taxes[1]

County Tax	None
City Tax	1.00%
Other Taxes	None

 Property Tax Rates [2,3]

$14.60 in $ per $1000

 International Profile

Number of Foreign Banks	0
Number of Foreign-owned Businesses	41
Number of Persons Employed by Foreign-owned Businesses	1,244
Number of Daily International Flights	10

Real Estate

Occupancy Cost per Square Foot (Annual)

	Sq. Foot	Sq. Meters
Average Rental-Class A Office (Central Business District)	$17.00	$182.92
Average Rental-Class A Apartment	$8.29	$89.20
Average Rental-Warehouse	$3.37	$36.26

Construction Cost per Square Foot

	Sq. Foot	Sq. Meters
Excellent Class A Office	$113.74	$1,221.57
Class A Industrial/ Manufacturing	$69.39	$746.64

	Sq. Foot	Sq. Meters
Class A Distribution Warehouse	$48.89	$526.06
Excellent Class C Single Family Residential	$86.36	$929.23

Average Electric Cost (Cents per KwH)

	1992
Residential	$0.816
Commercial	$0.634
Industrial	$0.448
Average Price for a 3-bedroom Family House (in 1000's)	$93.2

Quality of Life

Climate

	Fahrenheit		Celsius	
	High	Low	High	Low
Winter	47	27	8	-3
Spring	71	45	22	7
Summer	88	67	31	19
Autumn	71	47	22	8

Rainfall

	Inches	Millimeters
January	3.2	81
February	3.1	79
March	3.6	91
April	2.9	74
May	3.6	91
June	3.6	91
July	5.1	129
August	5.0	127
September	3.5	89
October	3.7	94
November	3.3	84
December	3.4	86

Cultural Highlights

Agecroft Hall
Maggie L. Walker National Historic Site
Maymont Victorian Estate

[1]See the State-Local General Sales Tax Notes on page 310.
[2]See the Property Tax Rate Notes on page 314.
[3]See the Classification of Real Property and Tangible Personal Property table on page 316.

Cultural Highlights (Continued)
 Museum & White House of the Confederacy
 Virginia Museum of Fine Arts

Leisure Highlights
 Richmond National Battlefield Park
 Scotchtown
 Shockoe Slip
 Virginia State Capitol

Crime

Rate per 100,000 Inhabitants	1991
Number of violent crimes	597.6
Number of property crimes	5,643.0

Average Wages for Selected Occupations

	Average Hiring Salary
Secretary (LR-3)	$20,696
Computer Systems Analyst III	$34,070
Computer Programmer III	$27,352
Engineer II	$36,795
Maintenance Machinist	$28,329

Tampa/St. Petersburg

FLORIDA

Tampa Bay, which covers four counties in west central Florida, grew dramatically to a population of 2.1 million from approximately 1.6 million in 1980 and is projected to lead the state in job creation through 1999. The Port of Tampa, located on the northeast edge of downtown, is the state's largest, handling more than 50 million tons of goods annually.

One of the area's attractions is a relatively young labor force; more than one-third of the population is between the ages of 25 and 44. Among the major nongovernment and nonmilitary employers are GTE Florida, Publix Supermarkets, Florida Progress Corporation, Kash N' Karry Food Stores, Home Shopping Network, Tampa General Hospital, and Tampa Electric Company.

At the opposite end of the spectrum, the area is working to attract small high-tech and biomedical companies. Joining these efforts is the Enterprise Corporation of Tampa Bay, which established an "incubator" space in the University Technology Center at the University of South Florida.

Accessibility to downtown is provided by a beltway road, as well as three other local and state highways, allowing for a short commute from the suburbs. Downtown Tampa is one of the few CBDs that offer a monorail system (which links the CBD to Harbour Island) as well as a buses-only thoroughfare.

Accessibility to water also defines some of the area's residential neighborhoods, as well as its recreational opportunities. Downtown Tampa has a flourishing residential community—Historic Hyde Park—many of whose 1920s and 1930s homes have been restored. In the metro area, the average three-bedroom house sells for $75,000.

In addition to Busch Gardens, the Florida State Fair, and Tampa Jai Alai, the area offers numerous cultural attractions, including the Tampa Bay Performing Arts Center, the Museum of Art, the Museum of Science and Industry, and the African-American Museum of Art. A new aquarium is being built downtown. Local "must attend" events include Hyde Park Village's summer jazz series and fall arts festival, as well as Guavaween, the annual Halloween event in heavily Cuban-influenced Ybor City.

City Profile

 ## Population in Thousands

1980	1,569.0
1990	2,067.0
1992	2,113.0
1995 Estimate	2,233.0

 ## Socioeconomic Factors

Average Household Income
1980	$17,125
1991 Estimate	$35,957
% Change	110.0
1996 Projection	$44,722

Median Household Income
1980	$13,693
1991 Estimate	$27,097
% Change	97.9
1996 Projection	$33,532

 ## Labor Force & Employment

	1993
Total Number of Persons in the Labor Force (in 1000's)	1,052.8
Total Number of Persons Employed (in 1000's)	983.9
Average Unemployment Rate	6.5%

Total Employment in Thousands by Sector

	1980	1992
Construction	41.5	41.0
Manufacturing	77.3	84.9
Transportation/Utilities	30.9	39.9
Trade	154.4	229.3
F.I.R.E.	39.5	62.5
Services	130.1	288.3
Government	82.1	117.7

 ## Education

1992 Enrollment
Two Year College	34,799
Four Year Undergraduate	30,670
Four Year Graduate	9,648
Average SAT Score	909
Total Possible Score: 1600	
Average ACT Score	N/A
Total Possible Score: 36	

 ## Business Environment

Selected Major Employers
GTE Florida Inc.
U.S. Department of Defense, Data Automation
County of Pasco School Board
University of South Florida
Tampa General Hospital
U.S. Postal Service
Home Shopping Network, Inc.
CSX Transportation Inc.
St. Joseph's Hospital Inc.
James A. Haley Veterans Hospital

Media Profile
1 newspaper
23 radio stations
13 network television stations
2 cable television operators

 ## State Taxes

Corporate Income/Franchise Tax	5.5%
Sales/Use Tax	7.0%
Individual Income Tax	0.0%
Unemployment Insurance Rate	2.70%

City Taxes[1]

County Tax	.50%
City Tax	None
Other Taxes	None

Property Tax Rates [2,3]

$24.6257 in $ per $1000

International Profile

Number of Foreign Banks	0
Number of Foreign-owned Businesses	136
Number of Persons Employed by Foreign-owned Businesses	2,497
Number of Daily International Flights	58

Real Estate

Occupancy Cost per Square Foot (Annual)

	Sq. Foot	Sq. Meters
Average Rental-Class A Office (Central Business District)	$15.84	$170.43
Average Rental-Class A Apartment	$7.40	$83.28
Average Rental-Warehouse	$3.88	$41.75

Construction Cost per Square Foot

	Sq. Foot	Sq. Meters
Excellent Class A Office	$112.50	$1,210.50
Class A Industrial/Manufacturing	$68.64	$738.57

	Sq. Foot	Sq. Meters
Class A Distribution Warehouse	$48.36	$520.35
Excellent Class C Single Family Residential	$87.32	$939.56

Average Electric Cost (Cents per KwH)

	1992
Residential	$0.800
Commercial	$0.663
Industrial	$0.444
Average Price for a 3-bedroom Family House (in 1000's)	$75.0

Quality of Life

Climate

	Fahrenheit		Celsius	
	High	Low	High	Low
Winter	70	50	21	10
Spring	82	61	28	16
Summer	90	74	32	23
Autumn	84	65	29	18

Rainfall

	Inches	Millimeters
January	2.0	51
February	3.0	76
March	3.0	76
April	3.0	76
May	4.0	102
June	7.0	178
July	6.0	152
August	5.0	127
September	8.0	203
October	6.0	152
November	3.0	76
December	2.0	51

Cultural Highlights

Children's Museum of Tampa
Henry B. Plant Museum
Museum of African-American Art

[1]See the State-Local General Sales Tax Notes on page 310.
[2]See the Property Tax Rate Notes on page 314.
[3]See the Classification of Real Property and Tangible Personal Property table on page 316.

Cultural Highlights (Continued)
 Museum of Science & Indsutry
 Tampa Museum of Art
 Ybor City State Museum

Leisure Highlights
 Busch Gardens
 Lowry Park Zoo
 The Shops on Harbour Island Ybor Square

Crime

Rate per 100,000 Inhabitants	1991
Number of violent crimes	1,264.5
Number of property crimes	7,003.3

Average Wages for Selected Occupations

	Average Hiring Salary
Secretary (LR-3)	$24,388
Computer Systems Analyst III	$52,104
Computer Programmer III	$33,696
Engineer II	$36,192
Maintenance Machinist	N/A

West Palm Beach

FLORIDA

The West Palm Beach metro area entered the 1990s with a big boost to its status as a business center, thanks in part to W.R. Grace & Co.'s headquarters relocation from New York to Boca Raton. Long known more as a resort/residential community for the elite, West Palm Beach area has become the business home for many in the high-tech, research and development, telecommunications, and health care fields.

Agriculture is a billion-dollar business in the region providing more than one-fifth of the sugar produced in the United States—close to 14 million tons.

The county has a modern air, sea, and rail transportation system. To accommodate business and tourism growth in the county, for example, Palm Beach International Airport has been expanded, and planners expect to add another 25 gates in the next 10 years. The Port of Palm Beach ranks second among Florida's deep-water ports. The Tri-Rail Commuter service, in operation since 1989, is a single-line system running from West Palm Beach to Miami, with 15 stops in between.

Like Dade and Broward Counties, this region offers a variety of water-oriented residential neighborhoods, including high-rise condominiums and private country club communities. Palm Beach County residents can easily avail themselves of cultural and recreational opportunities in nearby Dade and Broward Counties, but Palm Beach has its own attractions. The PGA Seniors' Championship is held here, as is a South Florida Fair, "Fourth on Flagler" and "Fiesta on Flagler" events, an Oktoberfest, and the Florida Heritage Festival.

Palm Beach also has its own opera, ballet, theater groups, and orchestra. The new Raymond F. Kravis Center for the Performing Arts is the hub of the area's cultural activities. Notable among Palm Beach's shopping attractions is Worth Avenue, possibly as well known as Rodeo Drive in Beverly Hills.

City Profile

 Population in Thousands

1980	576.8
1990	863.5
1992	896.9
1995 Estimate	967.0

Socioeconomic Factors

Average Household Income

1980	$21,755
1991 Estimate	$43,821
% Change	101.4
1996 Projection	$54,152

Median Household Income

1980	$17,019
1991 Estimate	$33,294
% Change	95.6
1996 Projection	$41,574

Labor Force & Employment

	1993
Total Number of Persons in the Labor Force (in 1000's)	446.8
Total Number of Persons Employed (in 1000's)	410.7
Average Unemployment Rate	8.1%

Total Employment in Thousands by Sector

	1980	1992
Construction	20.6	18.7
Manufacturing	28.6	32.0
Transportation/Utilities	8.4	14.1
Trade	53.7	95.6
F.I.R.E.	17.5	25.6
Services	49.2	120.5
Government	30.3	47.4

Education

1992 Enrollment

Two Year College	12,742
Four Year Undergraduate	8,792
Four Year Graduate	3,982
Average SAT Score	894
Total Possible Score: 1600	
Average ACT Score	N/A
Total Possible Score: 36	

Business Environment

Selected Major Employers

Pratt & Whitney
IBM
Motorola
St. Mary's Hospital
Siemans
Florida Power & Light
Southern Bell
Boca Raton Hospital
Boca Raton Hotel
JFK Memorial Hospital

Media Profile

1 newspaper
12 radio stations
11 network television stations
2 cable television operators

 State Taxes

Corporate Income/Franchise Tax	5.5%
Sales/Use Tax	7.0%
Individual Income Tax	0.0%
Unemployment Insurance Rate	2.60%

City Taxes

County Tax	None
City Tax	None
Other Taxes	None

Property Tax Rates

$22.619 in $ per $1000

International Profile

Number of Foreign Banks	0
Number of Foreign-owned Businesses	88
Number of Persons Employed by Foreign-owned Businesses	905
Number of Daily International Flights	3

Real Estate

Occupancy Cost per Square Foot (Annual)

	Sq. Foot	Sq. Meters
Average Rental-Class A Office (Central Business District)	$17.05	$183.46
Average Rental-Class A Apartment	$8.47	$91.14
Average Rental-Warehouse	$4.11	$44.22

Construction Cost per Square Foot

	Sq. Foot	Sq. Meters
Excellent Class A Office	$117.45	$1,263.76
Class A Industrial/ Manufacturing	$71.66	$771.06
Class A Distribution Warehouse	$50.48	$543.16
Excellent Class C Single Family Residential	$92.12	$991.21

Average Electric Cost (Cents per KwH)

	1992
Residential	$0.800
Commercial	$0.664
Industrial	$0.500
Average Price for a 3-bedroom Family House (in 1000's)	$97.5

Quality of Life

Climate

	Fahrenheit		Celsius	
	High	Low	High	Low
Winter	75	56	24	13
Spring	83	65	28	18
Summer	90	74	32	23
Autumn	84	70	29	21

Rainfall

	Inches	Millimeters
January	2.7	69
February	2.6	66
March	2.7	69
April	3.2	81
May	6.0	152
June	7.9	21
July	6.1	155
August	5.8	147
September	9.3	236
October	7.8	198
November	3.4	86
December	2.3	58

Cultural Highlights

Henry Morrison Flagler Museum
Morikami Museum & Japanese Gardens
Norton Gallery of Art

Leisure Highlights

Dreher Park Zoo
Lion Country Safari
Palm Beach Jai Alai
Palm Beach Kennel Club
Palm Beach Polo & Country Club

Crime

Rate per 100,000 Inhabitants	1991
Number of violent crimes	966
Number of property crimes	7,608

Average Wages for Selected Occupations

	Average Hiring Salary
Secretary (LR-3)	N/A
Computer Systems Analyst III	$42,993
Computer Programmer III	$34,673
Engineer II	N/A
Maintenance Machinist	$22,859

SOUTH-CENTRAL

Overview

At first blush, the dozen metro areas in the South-Central Region might not seem to have a lot in common. Their appeal, however, is similar: these are "livable" cities with a hometown feel, but with big-city amenities and sophistication. The mammoth cities, Dallas/Fort Worth and Houston, express it the other way around, but the message is essentially the same.

If you hunger for four-star or ethnic dining, in short, you can find it. If you want a 20-minute commute to a house in a quiet neighborhood where you can involve your kids in community and recreational activities, you can find it. If you want employees who can respond cheerfully to a customer's request on a toll-free line at 4 A.M., you can find that too.

Since 1980 the growth of some of the region's cities has been spectacular, whereas others have grown slowly and dependably. If there is an overriding theme throughout the economies of these cities, it is *diversification*. Once reliant on single industries, such as oil and gas, many of these cities have emerged from recessionary times and worse by attracting businesses from a variety of sectors.

Health care, telecommunications, and technology are the big winners in these areas. The nation's well-documented shift from a manufacturing- to a service-based economy has also been amply demonstrated in this region over the past several years. For the most part, its unemployment rate is lower than the national average.

Because most of the South-Central cities benefit from strategic access to air, rail, highway, and sea transportation, they are well positioned to deliver and receive goods to and from a sizable portion of the U.S. population. Ports in two of the cities in this region are among the largest and most active in the world. Several have grown in stature as distribution centers.

The strategic location of several of these cities—notably Dallas, Fort Worth, Houston, and San Antonio—also positions them to expand their international business opportunities in Mexico, because of North American Free Trade Agreement (NAFTA).

A few of the cities in this region are hampered by the lack of a hub airport (the closest hub to Little Rock is in Memphis, for example), but some are addressing the problem. Louisville, for

instance, is among those that are investing in major airport improvements, and Austin will be relocating its airport to accommodate more activity.

These cities also share in a concerted effort to overcome past problems arising from racial conflicts and a reputation for poor education. Public and private groups unite to promote harmony and to encourage minority growth both within corporations and as entrepreneurs. The development of corporate adopt-a-school programs is just one of the ways that the importance of education is recognized as the engine of economic growth.

Located along rivers or close to lakes and rolling hillsides, these cities' lush natural beauty and their abundant parklands offer an unending array of recreational opportunities. To this geographic serendipity are added countless special events: arts festivals, music festivals, state fairs, rodeos, aeronautic exhibitions, and much more.

These cities offer an abundance of cultural opportunities through large theater companies, ballet, and symphony orchestras, as well as smaller repertory companies. All of this region's cities share a fierce pride in their individual histories and cultural heritage, which give rise to their unique attractions.

Some consider retailing an art, too, and these cities provide myriad opportunities for those who would rather shop than exercise or see a show. The exuberance of RiverWalk in San Antonio and the elegance of Houston's Galleria are but two notable examples.

Home prices in these cities are lower than on the East and West Coasts, as are the costs of maintaining them. Diversification, which is characteristic of the economy of the region, is also a watchword in housing, which ranges from stately mansions to funky, rehabilitated lofts with river views.

Austin

The robust Austin MSA that covers three counties in central Texas has a population of 816,300, a dramatic increase from 536,700 in 1980. (The pace is expected to slow somewhat through 1995.) The Texas capital enjoys a growing economy and a relatively low unemployment rate of 5.1%.

Austin's economy is primarily service oriented. Its largest employers are IBM, Motorola, Seton Medical Center, Texas Instruments, and Southwestern Bell. Of the more than 800 manufacturing companies based here, more than half are related to high technology, including electronics, semiconductor manufacturers and suppliers, and computer and software development companies. Approximately 23 foreign-owned companies employ 481 people in the Austin area.

The metro area is home to the University of Texas, the third largest public university in the United States and one with a strong emphasis on research and development and a commitment to working with industry, particularly in microelectronics and engineering research. At the elementary and secondary levels, the Austin Independent School District has ranked as the number one urban school district in the state for the past several years. Nearly one-third of the adults in Austin have a college degree, and more than two-thirds of the work force use a computer at work or at home.

Housing costs are low; the average price for a three-bedroom, 2,000-square-foot house in a middle-management area is $125,000, comparable with those of Albuquerque, Salt Lake City, and Charlotte. Taxation is low because of the absence of corporate or personal income taxes, and utility costs are relatively low. The area's natural beauty—particularly its scenic Hill Country—provides a lush backdrop for residential and recreational uses.

City Profile

 Population in Thousands

1980	536.7
1990	781.6
1992	816.3
1995 Estimate	850.0

 Socioeconomic Factors

Average Household Income

1980	$19,714
1991 Estimate	$37,513
% Change	90.3
1996 Projection	$45,744

Median Household Income

1980	$16,143
1991 Estimate	$30,031
% Change	86.0
1996 Projection	$36,595

 Labor Force & Employment

	1993
Total Number of Persons in the Labor Force (in 1000's)	471.5
Total Number of Persons Employed (in 1000's)	448.0
Average Unemployment Rate	5.0%

Total Employment in Thousands by Sector

	1980	1992
Construction	14.1	14.0
Manufacturing	31.2	52.9
Transportation/Utilities	7.4	13.4
Trade	52.1	83.4
F.I.R.E.	14.5	23.7
Services	45.1	107.5
Government	78.7	111.3

 Education

1992 Enrollment

Two Year College	18,340
Four Year Undergraduate	54,707
Four Year Graduate	15,674
Average SAT Score	1,037
Total Possible Score: 1600	
Average ACT Score	21.0
Total Possible Score: 36	

 Business Environment

Selected Major Employers

Texas Dept. of Transportation
University of Texas at Austin
City of Austin
IBM Corp.
Austin Ind. School District
Texas Dept. of Public Safety
Motorola Corp.
IRS/Austin Center
HEB Stores
Dell Computer Corp.

Media Profile

1 newspaper
22 radio stations
6 network television stations
1 cable television operator

% State Taxes[1]

Corporate Income/Franchise Tax	4.5%
Sales/Use Tax	8.25%
Individual Income Tax	0.0%
Unemployment Insurance Rate	2.70%

[1]*See the State Tax Notes on page 308.*

City Taxes[2]

County Tax	None
City Tax	1.00%
Other Taxes	.75%

Property Tax Rates [3,4]

$21.547 in $ per $1000

International Profile

Number of Foreign Banks	1
Number of Foreign-owned Businesses	23
Number of Persons Employed by Foreign-owned Businesses	481
Number of Daily International Flights	8

Real Estate

Occupancy Cost per Square Foot (Annual)

	Sq. Foot	Sq. Meters
Average Rental-Class A Office (Central Business District)	$14.44	$155.37
Average Rental-Class A Apartment	$7.67	$82.53
Average Rental- Warehouse	$4.21	$45.30

Construction Cost per Square Foot

	Sq. Foot	Sq. Meters
Excellent Class A Office	$109.11	$1,174.02
Class A Industrial/ Manufacturing	$66.56	$716.19

	Sq. Foot	Sq. Metres
Class A Distribution Warehouse	$46.89	$504.53
Excellent Class C Single Family Residential	$82.01	$882.43

Average Electric Cost (Cents per KwH)

	1992
Residential	$0.732
Commercial	$0.612
Industrial	$0.424
Average Price for a 3-bedroom Family House (in 1000's)	$125.0

Quality of Life

Climate

	Fahrenheit		Celsius	
	High	Low	High	Low
Winter	59	39	15	4
Spring	79	58	26	14
Summer	95	74	35	23
Autumn	81	59	27	15

Rainfall

	Inches	Millimeters
January	1.6	41
February	2.5	64
March	1.7	43
April	3.1	79
May	1.2	107
June	3.1	79
July	1.9	48
August	2.2	56
September	3.6	91
October	3.4	86
November	2.2	56
December	2.1	53

Cultural Highlights

Laguna Gloria Art Museum
Lyndon B. Johnson Presidential Library/Museum
Old Pecan St. Historical District

[2]See the State-Local General Sales Tax Notes on page 310.
[3]See the Property Tax Rate Notes on page 314.
[4]See the Classification of Real Property and Tangible Personal Property table on page 316.

Cultural Highlights (Continued)
 Texas Memorial Museum
 The French Legation Museum
 State Capitol Building

Leisure Highlights
 Bremond National Register District
 Zilker Park and Gardens

Crime

Rate per 100,000 Inhabitants	1991
Number of violent crimes	506.9
Number of property crimes	8,227.7

Average Wages for Selected Occupations

	Average Hiring Salary
Secretary (LR-3)	$17,524
Computer Systems Analyst III	$39,364
Computer Programmer III	$26,676
Engineer II	$32,812
Maintenance Machinist	$28,496

Birmingham

ALABAMA

now skiing in the South? That's one of the unexpected features of the Birmingham MSA, a five-county area of nearly one million. (Skiing is, in fact, a 2-hour drive from downtown Birmingham, and Gulf Coast beaches are 4 hours away.)

Founded at the intersection of two rail lines, Birmingham in the past was better known as a manufacturing and mining center than as a recreational or retail mecca. It hasn't left its industrial roots entirely, but its economy has diversified with growing employment in nonmanufacturing categories, most notably health care services, and telecommunications businesses. In fact, nonmanufacturing jobs increased by more than 20% between 1981 and 1991.

With nearly one-quarter of the state's population and an abundant transportation and distribution network consisting of air, rail, highway, and water facilities, Birmingham has drawn nearly half of the Fortune 500's leading industrial corporations for area operations. USX operates a $750 million seamless pipe mill here; its Fairfield Works is said to be the only fully integrated steel mill the manufacturer operates in the United States.

A $125 million airport expansion is under way; currently some 140 flights serving 65 cities arrive and depart from the airport, which is located within 5 miles of downtown.

Birmingham has also become Alabama's largest retail trade center and is home to Riverchase Galleria. This $300 million, 3.3-million-square-foot, mixed-use retail, hotel, and office project is the largest enclosed shopping mall in the South, with five anchor stores and 200 specialty stores. It draws an average of 300,000 shoppers per week.

City Profile

Population in Thousands

1980	883.9
1990	907.8
1992	926.4
1995 Estimate	934.0

Socioeconomic Factors

Average Household Income
1980	$18,866
1991 Estimate	$32,800
% Change	73.9
1996 Projection	$39,609

Median Household Income
1980	$15,533
1991 Estimate	$25,716
% Change	65.6
1996 Projection	$30,680

Labor Force & Employment

	1993
Total Number of Persons in the Labor Force (in 1000's)	452.2
Total Number of Persons Employed (in 1000's)	422.6
Average Unemployment Rate	6.5%

Total Employment in Thousands by Sector
	1980	1992
Construction	20.2	22.0
Manufacturing	64.4	54.3
Transportation/Utilities	29.0	30.9
Trade	82.8	103.1
F.I.R.E.	22.8	30.2
Services	66.7	112.9
Government	55.9	69.5

Education

1992 Enrollment
Two Year College	10,568
Four Year Undergraduate	17,199
Four Year Graduate	4,869
Average SAT Score	N/A
Total Possible Score: 1600	
Average ACT Score	17.8
Total Possible Score: 36	

Business Environment

Selected Major Employers
Alabama Power Company
AmSouth Bank
Baptist Medical Centers
Bellsouth Services
Drummond Company, Inc.
South Central Bell
SouthTrust Bank of Alabama
Birmingham Public Schools
City of Birmingham
Jefferson County Board of Education

Media Profile
2 newspapers
27 radio stations
6 network television stations
1 cable television operator

% State Taxes

Corporate Income/Franchise Tax	5.0%
Sales/Use Tax	9.5%
Individual Income Tax	5.0%
Unemployment Insurance Rate	2.70%

 City Taxes[1]

County Tax	1.00%
City Tax	3.00%
Other Taxes	None

 Property Tax Rates [2,3]

$69.50 in $ per $1000

International Profile

Number of Foreign Banks	0
Number of Foreign-owned Businesses	26
Number of Persons Employed by Foreign-owned Businesses	428
Number of Daily International Flights	1

Real Estate

Occupancy Cost per Square Foot (Annual)

	Sq. Foot	Sq. Meters
Average Rental-Class A Office (Central Business District)	$15.63	$168.18
Average Rental-Class A Apartment	$6.12	$65.85
Average Rental- Warehouse	$2.79	$30.02

Construction Cost per Square Foot

	Sq. Foot	Sq. Meters
Excellent Class A Office	$111.53	$168.18
Class A Industrial/ Manufacturing	$68.03	$732.00

	Sq. Foot	Sq. Meters
Class A Distribution Warehouse	$47.93	$515.73
Excellent Class C Single Family Residential	$84.81	$912.56

Average Electric Cost (Cents per KwH)

	1992
Residential	$0.701
Commercial	$0.683
Industrial	$0.438
Average Price for a 3-bedroom Family House (in 1000's)	$96.0

 Quality of Life

Climate

	Fahrenheit		Celsius	
	High	Low	High	Low
Winter	52	33	11	1
Spring	75	51	24	11
Summer	91	70	33	21
Autumn	74	51	23	11

Rainfall

	Inches	Millimeters
January	5.0	127
February	4.6	117
March	6.6	168
April	5.3	135
May	3.8	96
June	3.2	81
July	4.2	107
August	3.9	99
September	4.6	117
October	2.8	71
November	3.5	89
December	4.8	122

Cultural Highlights

Birmingham Museum of Art
Sloss Furnaces National Historic Landmark
Arlington Antebellum Home & Gardens

[1]See the State-Local General Sales Tax Notes on page 310.
[2]See the Property Tax Rate Notes on page 314.
See the Classification of Real Property and Tangible Personal Property table on page 316.

Cultural Highlights (Continued)
 Tannehill Historical State Park
 Birmingham Botanical Gardens

Leisure Highlights
 Birmingham Race Course
 Birmingham Zoo
 Riverchase Galleria
 Iron Man/Vulcan Statue
 Five Points South

Crime

Rate per 100,000 Inhabitants	1991
Number of violent crimes	1,127.7
Number of property crimes	5,532.4

Average Wages for Selected Occupations

	Average Hiring Salary
Secretary (LR-3)	$19,000
Computer Systems Analyst III	$40,000
Computer Programmer III	$29,000
Engineer II	$40,000
Maintenance Machinist	$25,000

Dallas

Life seems to proceed on a grander scale in Dallas. This MSA, covering six counties, is 4,471 square miles; the city of Dallas alone is 378 square miles. Seven of the nation's fastest-growing cities since 1980, with populations of more than 100,000, are in the Dallas-Fort Worth area. Dallas metro area has the fourth largest concentration of corporate headquarters in the United States. The Dallas Independent School District is the eighth largest in the country. Its airport is the second busiest in the world, accommodating more than 44 million passengers yearly. And its football team is a Super Bowl winner.

Although Dallas suffered economically in the 1980s and is still experiencing some corporate downsizing and consolidation (the most recent unemployment rate is 7.2%), the U.S. Department of Commerce projects that employment in Dallas will increase by 16.1% by the year 2000. The area has a well-diversified economy, with significant growth in the service sector and in distribution centers. Among the top 20 employers in the area are a temporary employment agency and an employee leasing firm.

Because of its proximity by air to Mexico City, Dallas is expected to reap economic benefits from NAFTA. International business is not new to Dallas; currently, more than 18,170 people work for 355 foreign-owned companies. Among the foreign-owned companies that have recently moved to the city are Santa Fe International, Fujitsu ICL, and Bridgestone.

The cost of living in Dallas is moderate, as compared with the East and West Coasts, and there is no corporate or personal income tax. Housing costs are roughly on a par with Atlanta's: the average cost for a new three-bedroom house is approximately $104,000. Plano, Richardson, and North Dallas are considered the prime middle-management residential areas.

Cultural and recreational attractions in Dallas exist on a grand scale too; on any given night, more than 100 live performances take place. The Dallas Arts District, a 60-acre development, is the largest downtown arts district in the country. Amusement parks, professional sports, 50,000 acres of parks, a zoo, an aquarium, and numerous museums contribute to Dallas's cultural and recreational diversity.

City Profile

Population in Thousands

1980	1,959.2
1990	2,553.4
1992	2,607.1
1995 Estimate	2,632.0

Socioeconomic Factors

Average Household Income

1980	$23,231
1991 Estimate	$43,444
% Change	87.0
1996 Projection	$52,394

Median Household Income

1980	$19,291
1991 Estimate	$33,275
% Change	72.5
1996 Projection	$41,046

Labor Force & Employment

	1993
Total Number of Persons in the Labor Force (in 1000's)	1,565.6
Total Number of Persons Employed (in 1000's)	1,452.9
Average Unemployment Rate	7.2%

Total Employment in Thousands by Sector

	1980	1992
Construction	60.2	47.7
Manufacturing	213.1	208.7
Transportation/Utilities	59.7	83.0
Trade	276.5	354.2
F.I.R.E.	88.2	122.4
Services	184.3	388.1
Government	124.5	169.2

Education

1992 Enrollment

Two Year College	49,237
Four Year Undergraduate	40,826
Four Year Graduate	15,837
Average SAT Score	827
Total Possible Score: 1600	
Average ACT Score	N/A
Total Possible Score: 36	

Business Environment

Selected Major Employers

American Airlines
Texas Instruments
U.S. Postal Service
Dallas ISD
Sears Roebuck Co.
The LTV Corp.
The City of Dallas
Electronic Data Systems Corp.
Callum Companies
E-Systems, Inc.

Media Profile

2 newspapers
39 radio stations
5 network television stations
1 cable television operator

State Taxes[1]

Corporate Income/Franchise Tax	4.5%
Sales/Use Tax	8.25%
Individual Income Tax	0.0%
Unemployment Insurance Rate	2.70%

[1]See the State Tax Notes on page 308.

 City Taxes[2]

County Tax	None
City Tax	1.00%
Other Taxes	1.00%

 Property Tax Rates [3,4]

$21.199 in $ per $1000

International Profile

Number of Foreign Banks	7
Number of Foreign-owned Businesses	355
Number of Persons Employed by Foreign-owned Businesses	18,170
Number of Daily International Flights	143

Real Estate

Occupancy Cost per Square Foot (Annual)

	Sq. Foot	Sq. Meters
Average Rental-Class A Office (Central Business District)	$16.75	$180.23
Average Rental-Class A Apartment	$7.26	$78.12
Average Rental-Warehouse	$3.92	$42.18

Construction Cost per Square Foot

	Sq. Foot	Sq. Meters
Excellent Class A Office	$109.11	$1,174.02
Class A Industrial/ Manufacturing	$66.56	$716.18

	Sq. Foot	Sq. Meters
Class A Distribution Warehouse	$46.89	$504.53
Excellent Class C Single Family Residential	$83.87	$902.44

Average Electric Cost (Cents per KwH)

	1992
Residential	$0.732
Commercial	$0.612
Industrial	$0.424
Average Price for a 3-bedroom Family House (in 1000's)	$103.8

 Quality of Life

Climate

	Fahrenheit		Celsius	
	High	Low	High	Low
Winter	54	34	12	1
Spring	77	55	25	13
Summer	98	75	37	24
Autumn	80	56	27	13

Rainfall

	Inches	Millimeters
January	1.7	43
February	1.9	48
March	2.4	61
April	3.6	91
May	4.3	109
June	2.6	66
July	2.0	51
August	1.8	46
September	3.3	84
October	2.5	64
November	1.8	46
December	1.7	43

Cultural Highlights

Biblical Arts Center
Dallas Museum of Art
Meadows Museum
The Sixth Floor Kennedy Exhibit
West End Historic District

[2]See the State-Local General Sales Tax Notes on page 310.
[3]See the Property Tax Rate Notes on page 314.
[4]See the Classification of Real Property and Tangible Personal Property table on page 316.

Leisure Highlights
Dallas Arboretum & Botanical Garden
Dallas Zoo
Fair Park
Old City Park
Dallas Market Hall

Crime

Rate per 100,000 Inhabitants	1991
Number of violent crimes	1,333.6
Number of property crimes	8,707.7

Average Wages for Selected Occupations

	Average Hiring Salary
Secretary (LR-3)	$24,856
Computer Systems Analyst III	$35,204
Computer Programmer III	$28,444
Engineer II	$32,812
Maintenance Machinist	$29,931

Fort Worth

TEXAS

Although Fort Worth is often considered together with Dallas (the two areas combined are referred to as the Metroplex and the cities do share an airport), Fort Worth is a market unto itself. It is growing most notably as a manufacturing and distribution center, with recent relocations including UPS, Nestle SA, and AloeCorp (distribution centers); and Sicpa Securink and GRID Systems (manufacturing). Employment in the services sector doubled between 1980 and 1992; services and wholesale/retail trade are the area's largest employers.

There is significant high-technology manufacturing located in the Fort Worth metro area, involved in plastics, electronics components, aircraft, medical and dental supplies, and more. The area has nine vocational/technical schools offering programs in business, computer science, and technical occupations. Local manufacturers can also work on process automation with the Automation and Robotics Research Institute, a research arm of the University of Texas at Arlington, which opened its facility in 1987.

The third most populous metro area in Texas, the Fort Worth–Arlington MSA covers three counties, whose population jumped from 973,000 in 1980 to 1.4 million in 1992. It is expected to grow by 100,000 by 1995. The area offers a broad mix of middle-management residential areas, including CandleRidge, Lake Country, Overton, Rivercrest, Colonial, Ridgelea, Woodhaven, Park Hill, and Tanglewood. The average price for a three-bedroom house is $85,000.

Area residents need not tap into Dallas's cultural and recreational resources for entertainment; Fort Worth has several of its own professional theater groups, a ballet, opera, and a chamber orchestra. Its Kimbell Art Museum has one of the largest acquisitions budgets in the United States. For devotees of country and western music, the Stockyards District (marking the last stop on the old Chisolm Trail) fills the bill.

City Profile

 Population
in Thousands

1980	973.0
1990	1,332.1
1992	1,400.0
1995 Estimate	1,500.0

 Socioeconomic
Factors

Average Household Income

1980	$21,727
1991 Estimate	$41,987
% Change	93.2
1996 Projection	$51,429

Median Household Income

1980	$18,784
1991 Estimate	$33,916
% Change	80.6
1996 Projection	$41,858

 Labor Force &
Employment

	1993
Total Number of Persons in the Labor Force (in 1000's)	735.2
Total Number of Persons Employed (in 1000's)	680.9
Average Unemployment Rate	7.4%

Total Employment in Thousands by Sector

	1980	1992
Construction	23.2	20.8
Manufacturing	106.3	100.1
Transportation/Utilities	33.2	61.6
Trade	106.9	149.7
F.I.R.E.	20.05	28.2
Services	69.5	148.2
Government	54.4	80.2

Education

1992 Enrollment

Two Year College	26,123
Four Year Undergraduate	29,691
Four Year Graduate	7,363
Average SAT Score	858
Total Possible Score: 1600	
Average ACT Score	N/A
Total Possible Score: 36	

Business Environment

Selected Major Employers

American Airlines
Lockheed-Fort Worth
Tandy Corporation
Bell Helicopter Textron
General Motors
Alcon Laboratories
Star Telegram
Electrocom Automation
Miller Brewing Company
Haliburton Logging

Media Profile

1 newspaper
29 radio stations
17 network television stations
1 cable television operator

State Taxes[1]

Corporate Income/Franchise Tax	4.5%
Sales/Use Tax	8.25%
Individual Income Tax	0.0%
Unemployment Insurance Rate	2.70%

[1]See the State Tax Notes on page 308.

City Taxes[2]

County Tax	None
City Tax	1.00%
Other Taxes	.50%

Property Tax Rates [3,4]

$24.14986 in $ per $1000

International Profile

Number of Foreign Banks	7
Number of Foreign-owned Businesses	355
Number of Persons Employed by Foreign-owned Businesses	18,170
Number of Daily International Flights	143

Real Estate

Occupancy Cost per Square Foot (Annual)

	Sq. Foot	Sq. Meters
Average Rental-Class A Office (Central Business District)	$16.75	$180.23
Average Rental-Class A Apartment	$7.26	$77.79
Average Rental- Warehouse	$3.92	$42.18

Construction Cost per Square Foot

	Sq. Foot	Sq. Meters
Excellent Class A Office	$109.11	$1,174.02
Class A Industrial/ Manufacturing	$66.56	$716.19

	Sq. Foot	Sq. Meters
Class A Distribution Warehouse	$46.89	$504.21
Excellent Class C Single Family Residential	$83.87	$902.44

Average Electric Cost (Cents per KwH)

	1992
Residential	$0.732
Commercial	$0.612
Industrial	$0.424
Average Price for a 3-bedroom Family House (in 1000's)	$85.0

Quality of Life

Climate

	Fahrenheit		Celsius	
	High	Low	High	Low
Winter	54	34	12	1
Spring	77	55	25	13
Summer	98	75	37	24
Autumn	80	56	27	13

Rainfall

	Inches	Millimeters
January	1.7	43
February	1.9	48
March	2.4	61
April	3.6	91
May	4.3	109
June	2.6	66
July	2.0	51
August	1.8	46
September	3.3	84
October	2.5	64
November	1.8	46
December	1.7	43

Cultural Highlights

Amon Carter Museum
Kimbell Art Museum
Sid Richardson Collection of Western Art
Sundance Square
Will Rogers Memorial Center

[2]See the State-Local General Sales Tax Notes on page 310.
[3]See the Property Tax Rate Notes on page 314.
[4]See the Classification of Real Property and Tangible Personal Property table on page 316.

Leisure Highlights
Fort Worth Zoo
Fort Worth Botanic Garden
White Elephant Saloon
Billy Bob's Texas
Arlington Convention Center

Crime

Rate per 100,000 Inhabitants	1991
Number of violent crimes	992.3
Number of property crimes	9,151.1

Average Wages for Selected Occupations

	Average Hiring Salary
Secretary (LR-3)	$20,200
Computer Systems Analyst III	$33,200
Computer Programmer III	$27,400
Engineer II	$42,600
Maintenance Machinist	$19,300

Houston

TEXAS

Having undergone the devastating effects of the oil and gas industry depression in the mid-1980s, when one out of seven jobs was lost, Houston has emerged strongly by cultivating a more diverse economy. Throughout the recession, in fact, employment in non-energy-related sectors grew by 9% per year. The current unemployment rate stands at 8.3%.

Much of the growth centers on health services, with the Texas Medical Center, employing some 51,000, as a catalyst. Business, legal, and professional services are also expanding. Job growth is expected to average 2.2% annually through 2011. But don't count out energy as a prime mover of the area's economy. The two largest employers in the area are Shell Oil and Exxon, and a half dozen petrochemical companies are among those that recently relocated to this area.

International trade comes naturally to Houston. The sixth largest port in the world, it leads all U.S. ports in foreign tonnage volume. Like Dallas-Fort Worth and San Antonio, it is poised to expand on NAFTA-inspired cross-border business opportunities.

Cultural and recreational life in this six-county area of more than 3.3 million caters to both sophisticated and frontier-town tastes and reflects the area's multicultural heritage. The average price for a three-bedroom house is approximately $101,300, and the variety of housing types and price ranges are as broad as might be expected in such a sprawling region. Middle-management residential communities include the Northwest, Clear Lake, Southwest (Bellaire, West University, Meyerland) and Southwest Montgomery County.

So persistent are images of highway gridlock that city promoters take pains to raise the issue and to defuse it. In fact, the Houston region has the most extensive freeway and toll road system in the Southwest, with more than 2,200 land miles of freeway and 280 lane miles of toll roads.

City Profile

Population in Thousands

1980	2,735.4
1990	3,301.9
1992	3,439.3
1995 Estimate	4,041.0

Socioeconomic Factors

Average Household Income

1980	$24,985
1991 Estimate	$36,662
% Change	46.7
1996 Projection	$42,346

Median Household Income

1980	$21,158
1991 Estimate	$30,704
% Change	45.1
1996 Projection	$35,245

Labor Force & Employment

	1993
Total Number of Persons in the Labor Force (in 1000's)	1,749.4
Total Number of Persons Employed (in 1000's)	1,604.8
Average Unemployment Rate	8.3%

Total Employment in Thousands by Sector

	1980	1992
Construction	131.6	108.7
Manufacturing	226.2	176.7
Transportation/Utilities	100.2	111.3
Trade	343.3	383.0
F.I.R.E.	86.6	69.6
Services	273.2	462.8
Government	154.8	219.8

Education

1992 Enrollment

Two Year College	69,952
Four Year Undergraduate	46,208
Four Year Graduate	21,096
Average SAT Score	841
Total Possible Score: 1600	
Average ACT Score	N/A
Total Possible Score: 36	

Business Environment

Selected Major Employers

Shell Oil Co.
Exxon Cos.
Continental Airlines
Kroger Co.
Houston Lighting & Power
Randall's Food Markets
Brown & Root
Southwestern Bell
Methodist Hospital
Cooper Industries

Media Profile

1 newspaper
38 radio stations
10 network television stations
3 cable television operators

State Taxes[1]

Corporate Income/Franchise Tax	4.5%
Sales/Use Tax	8.25%
Individual Income Tax	0.0%
Unemployment Insurance Rate	2.70%

[1]See the State Tax Notes on page 308.

City Taxes[2]

County Tax	None
City Tax	1.00%
Other Taxes	1.00%

Property Tax Rates [3,4]

$20.09 in $ per $1000

International Profile

Number of Foreign Banks	35
Number of Foreign-owned Businesses	686
Number of Persons Employed by Foreign-owned Businesses	20,356
Number of Daily International Flights	114

Real Estate

Occupancy Cost per Square Foot (Annual)

	Sq. Foot	Sq. Meters
Average Rental-Class A Office (Central Business District)	$14.15	$152.25
Average Rental-Class A Apartment	$6.92	$74.46
Average Rental-Warehouse	$3.33	$35.83

Construction Cost per Square Foot

	Sq. Foot	Sq. Meters
Excellent Class A Office	$113.96	$1,226.21
Class A Industrial/ Manufacturing	$69.51	$747.93

[2]See the State-Local General Sales Tax Notes on page 310.
[3]See the Property Tax Rate Notes on page 314.
[4]See the Classification of Real Property and Tangible Personal Property table on page 316.

	Sq. Foot	Sq. Meters
Class A Distribution Warehouse	$48.97	$526.92
Excellent Class C Single Family Residential	$87.60	$942.58

Average Electric Cost (Cents per KwH)

	1992
Residential	$0.916
Commercial	$0.750
Industrial	$0.423
Average Price for a 3-bedroom Family House (in 1000's)	$101.3

Quality of Life

Climate

	Fahrenheit		Celsius	
	High	Low	High	Low
Winter	62	41	17	5
Spring	79	58	26	14
Summer	94	73	34	23
Autumn	82	58	28	14

Rainfall

	Inches	Millimeters
January	3.0	76
February	3.0	76
March	3.0	76
April	4.0	102
May	5.0	127
June	4.0	102
July	3.0	76
August	4.0	102
September	5.0	127
October	4.0	102
November	3.0	76
December	4.0	102

Cultural Highlights

Bayou Bend Museum
Museum of Natural Science
San Jacinto Museum of History

Cultural Highlights (Continued)
 NASA/Johnson Space Center
 Texas Medical Center

Leisure Highlights
 AstroWorld
 WaterWorld
 Houston Zoo
 The Galleria
 Theatre District, Downtown

Crime

Rate per 100,000 Inhabitants	1991
Number of violent crimes	1,076.6
Number of property crimes	7,112.0

Average Wages for Selected Occupations

	Average Hiring Salary
Secretary (LR-3)	$27,144
Computer Systems Analyst III	$58,396
Computer Programmer III	$39,988
Engineer II	$38,844
Maintenance Machinist	$37,918

Little Rock

ARKANSAS

Best known now for the prominent former resident of the state governor's mansion, Little Rock covers four counties in central Arkansas. Its population of slightly more than 529,000 grew modestly from 474,000 in 1980 and is expected to increase modestly through 1995.

The two top employers are hospitals, but Little Rock has also made strides in telecommunications and information services. And although the area's nearest hub airport is via a 2-hour drive to Memphis, it has attracted foreign-owned companies such as Tokusen USA, Inc. (Japan) and America Bakels (Switzerland).

The cost of living in Little Rock is modest; the average price for a three-bedroom, 2,000-square-foot house is approximately $81,400. There are four prime middle-management residential areas: St. Charles, Hillcrest, and Pleasant Valley.

Area public schools have an enviable student-teacher ratio of 16 to 1. Nearly half the graduating high school seniors in Pulaski County attend college. The region also has five vocational/technical schools with a combined enrollment of more than 10,000.

Many of the area's recreational activities are water oriented: boating and fishing along the Arkansas River and Lake Maumelle, and the Riverfest annual festival featuring live music, food, and entertainment. Little Rock also offers jazz and blues festivals, ballet, opera, a symphony orchestra, two professional theater groups, and two museums.

City Profile

Population in Thousands

1980	474.0
1990	513.0
1992	529.3
1995 Estimate	533.0

Socioeconomic Factors

Average Household Income

1980	$18,761
1991 Estimate	$35,362
% Change	88.5
1996 Projection	$43,273

Median Household Income

1980	$15,596
1991 Estimate	$27,613
% Change	77.1
1996 Projection	$33,353

Labor Force & Employment

	1993
Total Number of Persons in the Labor Force (in 1000's)	266.6
Total Number of Persons Employed (in 1000's)	252.9
Average Unemployment Rate	5.3%

Total Employment in Thousands by Sector

	1980	1992
Construction	10.6	11.3
Manufacturing	37.6	33.2
Transportation/Utilities	14.6	17.2
Trade	45.7	61.9
F.I.R.E.	12.9	15.8
Services	36.2	72.5
Government	43.4	52.6

Education

1992 Enrollment

Two Year College	120
Four Year Undergraduate	11,560
Four Year Graduate	2,096
Average SAT Score	N/A
Total Possible Score: 1600	
Average ACT Score	19.8
Total Possible Score: 36	

Business Environment

Selected Major Employers

Arkansas Childrens Hospital
Baptist Medical Systems
Maybelline Products Company
Systematics Information Services
Arkansas Power & Light Company
Affiliated Food Stores Southwest
Dillard Department Stores
Nabholz Construction Company
Alltel Corporation

Media Profile

1 newspaper
19 radio stations
12 network television stations
1 cable television operator

State Taxes

Corporate Income/Franchise Tax	6.5%
Sales/Use Tax	7.5%
Individual Income Tax	7.0%
Unemployment Insurance Rate	4.10%

 City Taxes[1]

County Tax	1.00%
City Tax	None
Other Taxes	None

 Property Tax Rates [2]

$61.88 in $ per $1000

International Profile

Number of Foreign Banks	0
Number of Foreign-owned Businesses	5
Number of Persons Employed by Foreign-owned Businesses	11
Number of Daily International Flights	1

Real Estate

Occupancy Cost per Square Foot (Annual)

	Sq. Foot	Sq. Meters
Average Rental-Class A Office (Central Business District)	$11.00	$118.36
Average Rental-Class A Apartment	$7.20	$77.47
Average Rental- Warehouse	$1.75	$18.83

Construction Cost per Square Foot

	Sq. Foot	Sq. Meters
Excellent Class A Office	$107.89	$1,160.90
Class A Industrial/ Manufacturing	$65.82	$708.22

	Sq. Foot	Sq. Meters
Class A Distribution Warehouse	$46.37	$498.94
Excellent Class C Single Family Residential	$82.01	$882.43

Average Electric Cost (Cents per KwH)

	1992
Residential	$0.935
Commercial	$0.759
Industrial	$0.592
Average Price for a 3-bedroom Family House (in 1000's)	$81.4

Quality of Life

Climate

	Fahrenheit		Celsius	
	High	Low	High	Low
Winter	50	30	10	-1
Spring	74	51	23	11
Summer	93	71	34	22
Autumn	76	50	24	10

Rainfall

	Inches	Millimeters
January	3.9	99
February	3.8	96
March	4.7	119
April	5.4	137
May	5.3	135
June	3.7	94
July	3.6	91
August	3.1	79
September	4.3	109
October	2.8	71
November	4.4	112
December	4.2	107

Cultural Highlights

Arkansas Arts Center
Arkansas State Capitol
Arkansas Museum of Science & History

[1]See the State-Local General Sales Tax Notes on page 310.
[2]See the Classification of Real Property and Tangible Personal Property table on page 316.

Cultural Highlights (Continued)
 Old State House Museum
 The Arkansas Arts Center and Decorative
 Arts Museum

Leisure Highlights
 Little Rock Zoo
 Villa Marre
 Arkansas Territorial Restoration
 Marlsgate Plantation
 Statehouse Convention Center

Crime

Rate per 100,000 Inhabitants	1991
Number of violent crimes	1,408.9
Number of property crimes	7,943.3

Average Wages for Selected Occupations

	Average Hiring Salary
Secretary (LR-3)	$18,304
Computer Systems Analyst III	$46,852
Computer Programmer III	$34,684
Engineer II	$36,972
Maintenance Machinist	$30,056

Louisville

KENTUCKY

Located on the banks of the Ohio River, Greater Louisville comprises seven counties spanning two states: Kentucky and Indiana. The region offers a relatively low cost of living and affordable housing, with new three-bedroom, 2,000-square-foot houses selling for an average of $98,800. Well served by state and interstate highways, average commutation time from suburban residential areas to downtown is approximately 20 minutes.

Greater Louisville's economy has experienced a slow but steady transition from a manufacturing base to a service sector base. Health care and services now provide nearly a quarter of all jobs in the area. Rocked by economic cycles in the past, Louisville was one of only five major cities to add more than 10,000 jobs in 1992. Leading employers are General Electric, Humana, and United Parcel.

Recent relocations to the area include several companies from California, as well as from the Northeast, Canada, and France. (In fact, some 1,200 are employed by foreign-owned companies.) The community draws from a 29-county labor pool of more than 771,000 workers.

The area's educational system has improved over the past several years, and the dropout rate is a low 2.6 percent. Technical proficiency is considered key; the Jefferson County public school system has one computer terminal per every nine students.

Perhaps best known as the home of the Kentucky Derby, Louisville offers a wide variety of recreational opportunities, many of which are water oriented, such as boating, sports, and dining along the Ohio River. Louisville's 8,600-acre park system was designed by Frederick Law Olmsted, designer of New York City's Central Park.

City Profile

Population in Thousands

1980	956.8
1990	952.7
1992	960.5
1995 Estimate	962.1

Socioeconomic Factors

Average Household Income

1980	$19,737
1991 Estimate	$38,773
% Change	96.4
1996 Projection	$47,610

Median Household Income

1980	$17,094
1991 Estimate	$30,386
% Change	77.8
1996 Projection	$36,943

Labor Force & Employment

	1993
Total Number of Persons in the Labor Force (in 1000's)	512.0
Total Number of Persons Employed (in 1000's)	485.1
Average Unemployment Rate	5.3%

Total Employment in Thousands by Sector

	1980	1992
Construction	17.5	22.7
Manufacturing	100.3	87.9
Transportation/Utilities	24.3	32.6
Trade	89.0	119.7
F.I.R.E.	23.4	27.6
Services	76.5	133.9
Government	61.0	67.2

Education

1992 Enrollment

Two Year College	7,306
Four Year Undergraduate	24,633
Four Year Graduate	6,203
Average SAT Score	N/A
Total Possible Score: 1600	
Average ACT Score	18.4
Total Possible Score: 36	

Business Environment

Selected Major Employers

- U.S. Government
- General Electric Co.
- Jefferson County Public Schools
- United Parcel Service
- Galen
- The Kroger Company
- State of Kentucky
- Ford Motor Company
- Alliant Health System
- University of Louisville

Media Profile

- 1 newspaper
- 24 radio stations
- 9 network television stations
- 1 cable television operator

State Taxes

Corporate Income/Franchise Tax	8.25%
Sales/Use Tax	6.0%
Individual Income Tax	6.0%
Unemployment Insurance Rate	3.00%

 City Taxes

County Tax	None
City Tax	None
Other Taxes	None

 Property Tax Rates [1,2]

$11.51 in $ per $1000

 International Profile

Number of Foreign Banks	2
Number of Foreign-owned Businesses	31
Number of Persons Employed by Foreign-owned Businesses	1,233
Number of Daily International Flights	2

Real Estate

Occupancy Cost per Square Foot (Annual)

	Sq. Foot	Sq. Meters
Average Rental-Class A Office (Central Business District)	$17.50	$188.30
Average Rental-Class A Apartment	$5.00	$53.80
Average Rental-Warehouse	$3.50	$37.66

Construction Cost per Square Foot

	Sq. Foot	Sq. Meters
Excellent Class A Office	$116.38	$1,252.25
Class A Industrial/Manufacturing	$70.99	$763.85

[1]See the Property Tax Rate Notes on page 314.
[2]See the Classification of Real Property and Tangible Personal Property table on page 316.

	Sq. Foot	Sq. Meters
Class A Distribution Warehouse	$50.02	$538.22
Excellent Class C Single Family Residential	$87.60	$942.58

Average Electric Cost (Cents per KwH)

	1992
Residential	$0.596
Commercial	$0.540
Industrial	$0.381
Average Price for a 3-bedroom Family House (in 1000's)	$98.8

Quality of Life

Climate

	Fahrenheit		Celsius	
	High	Low	High	Low
Winter	41	24	5	-4
Spring	68	46	20	8
Summer	88	68	31	20
Autumn	69	46	21	8

Rainfall

	Inches	Millimeters
January	3.4	86
February	3.3	81
March	4.7	119
April	4.1	104
May	4.2	107
June	3.6	91
July	4.1	104
August	3.3	84
September	3.4	86
October	2.6	66
November	3.5	89
December	3.5	89

Cultural Highlights

Thomas Edison Historic House Museum
Hillerich & Bradsby
J.B. Speed Art Museum

Cultural Highlights (Continued)
 Kentucky Art & Craft Gallery
 Kentucky Derby Museum

Leisure Highlights
 Churchill Downs
 Historic Steamer Belle of Louisville
 Louisville Zoo
 Museum of History & Science/MAX Theater
 Kentucky Fair & Exposition Center

Crime

Rate per 100,000 Inhabitants	1991
Number of violent crimes	487.2
Number of property crimes	4,004.0

Average Wages for Selected Occupations

	Average Hiring Salary
Secretary (LR-3)	$23,608
Computer Systems Analyst III	$49,868
Computer Programmer III	$32,240
Engineer II	$35,500
Maintenance Machinist	$36,171

Memphis

TENNESSEE

In Memphis recording studios, the buzz words are "Beale Street," "Sun Studios," and "Graceland" . . . in Memphis business circles, the new buzz word is "Federal Express." Memphis's growth as a distribution center has been enhanced by such companies as Nike, Walt Disney Company, and Williams Sonoma, and now by Federal Express's decision to locate its headquarters here. Its international airport is less than a 15 minute drive from all major area business centers and handles more than 275 flights daily.

The Memphis metro area, which covers three counties in Tennessee, one county in Mississippi, and one county in Arkansas, has grown modestly, by slightly less than 10,000 people a year, since 1980. Currently, its population numbers more than one million, and its growth rate is expected to remain the same through 1997.

This MSA is notable for having posted gains in all nonagricultural industry sectors between 1980 and 1992, including major gains in wholesale/retail trade and services. There are 43 foreign-owned companies doing business in the Greater Memphis area, employing 1,343 people.

In addition to its rich musical heritage, Memphis offers a wide variety of cultural and recreational activities. It boasts 230 parks, totaling some 13,300 acres; 25 golf courses, 17 public swimming pools, 26 community centers, and 11 country clubs. The Pyramid, rising more than 300 feet just north of the convention center complex, houses a 20,000-seat sports arena, restaurants, and special attractions.

Housing is varied, too, ranging from modest homes in the $40,000 range in Midtown to Tudor-style mansions selling for $1 million and more. Average price for a three-bedroom, 2,000 sq. ft. house is $115,000. Apartments and condominiums downtown, some featuring views of the Mississippi river—both new and created by rehabilitating older buildings—have enlivened the downtown area.

City Profile

Population in Thousands

1980	913.5
1990	1,007.3
1992	1,027.3
1995 Estimate	1,073.3

Socioeconomic Factors

Average Household Income

1980	$18,801
1991 Estimate	$35,902
% Change	91.0
1996 Projection	$44,169

Median Household Income

1980	$15,240
1991 Estimate	$28,121
% Change	84.5
1996 Projection	$34,461

Labor Force & Employment

	1993
Total Number of Persons in the Labor Force (in 1000's)	470.8
Total Number of Persons Employed (in 1000's)	443.7
Average Unemployment Rate	5.8%

Total Employment in Thousands by Sector

	1980	1992
Construction	15.9	18.1
Manufacturing	59.6	60.2
Transportation/Utilities	27.5	47.3
Trade	97.1	126.5
F.I.R.E.	19.8	24.9
Services	73.6	126.9
Government	65.7	77.8

Education

1992 Enrollment

Two Year College	11,387
Four Year Undergraduate	21,359
Four Year Graduate	5,500
Average SAT Score	N/A
Total Possible Score: 1600	
Average ACT Score	18.7
Total Possible Score: 36	

Business Environment

Selected Major Employers

Federal Express
Naval Air Station
U.S. Government
Memphis City Board of Education
Memphis City Government
Baptist Memorial Hospital
Shelby County
Methodist
Kroger Company
University of Tennessee

Media Profile

1 newspaper
31 radio stations
9 network television stations
1 cable television operator

State Taxes[1]

Corporate Income/Franchise Tax	6.0%
Sales/Use Tax	8.75%
Individual Income Tax	0.0%
Unemployment Insurance Rate	2.70%

[1]See the State Tax Notes on page 308.

City Taxes[2]

County Tax	2.25%
City Tax	None
Other Taxes	None

Property Tax Rates [3,4]

$70.80 in $ per $1000

International Profile

Number of Foreign Banks	0
Number of Foreign-owned Businesses	43
Number of Persons Employed by Foreign-owned Businesses	1,343
Number of Daily International Flights	10

Real Estate

Occupancy Cost per Square Foot (Annual)

	Sq. Foot	Sq. Meters
Average Rental-Class A Office (Central Business District)	$10.00	$107.60
Average Rental-Class A Apartment	$6.00	$64.56
Average Rental-Warehouse	$1.50	$16.14

Construction Cost per Square Foot

	Sq. Foot	Sq. Meters
Excellent Class A Office	$111.53	$1,200.06
Class A Industrial/ Manufacturing	$68.03	$732.00

	Sq. Foot	Sq. Meters
Class A Distribution Warehouse	$47.93	$515.73
Excellent Class C Single Family Residential	$85.74	$922.56

Average Electric Cost (Cents per KwH)

	1992
Residential	$0.496
Commercial	$0.504
Industrial	$0.345
Average Price for a 3-bedroom Family House (in 1000's)	$115.0

Quality of Life

Climate

	Fahrenheit		Celsius	
	High	Low	High	Low
Winter	48	31	9	-1
Spring	73	52	23	11
Summer	92	73	33	23
Autumn	75	51	24	11

Rainfall

	Inches	Millimeters
January	4.6	117
February	4.3	109
March	5.4	137
April	5.8	147
May	5.1	129
June	3.6	91
July	4.0	102
August	3.7	94
September	3.6	91
October	2.4	61
November	4.3	107
December	4.9	124

Cultural Highlights

Beale Street Historical District
Dixon Gallery & Gardens
Graceland Mansion

[2]See the State-Local General Sales Tax Notes on page 310.
[3]See the Property Tax Rate Notes on page 314.
[4]See the Classification of Real Property and Tangible Personal Property table on page 316.

Cultural Highlights (Continued)
 National Civil Rights Museum
 Memphis Pink Palace & Planetarium

Leisure Highlights
 Great American Pyramid
 Memphis Queen Line
 Memphis Zoo & Aquarium
 Mud Island/Mississippi River Museum
 Memphis Cook Convention Center

Crime

Rate per 100,000 Inhabitants	1991
Number of violent crimes	1,083.0
Number of property crimes	6,759.7

Average Wages for Selected Occupations

	Average Hiring Salary
Secretary (LR-3)	$24,804
Computer Systems Analyst III	$52,260
Computer Programmer III	$31,356
Engineer II	$45,926
Maintenance Machinist	$32,988

Nashville

TENNESSEE

Although Opryland USA, a huge theme park/entertainment center/hotel complex, is Nashville's largest private employer, music is not this city's only business.

Located within 600 miles of half the U.S. population and more than 75% of the country's markets, this eight-county metro area has also become a hub for health care, financial, and business support services, while retaining its position as a manufacturing and distribution center. Its unemployment rate, at 4.6%, is lower than both the state and national averages.

Nashville's population grew dramatically to more than one million between 1980 and 1992, and its rate of growth through 1995 is expected to exceed that of the 1980s. Much of that growth is concentrated in Rutherford County, home of U.S. Nissan Motor Manufacturing, National Healthcorp, and Middle Tennessee State University. Williamson County is a close second to Rutherford County in growth, with a rise in upscale residential, retail, and commercial centers, and boasts 82% of its high school graduates continuing on to higher education.

One of Nashville's appealing features is its geography, located in a natural basin surrounded by rolling, wooded hills. The area's park system includes more than 6,650 acres and a host of natural and man-made lakes. Extensive recreational facilities also include 18 public and private golf courses, a Centennial Sportsplex for swimming and ice skating, soccer fields, tennis courts, and more.

Appealing, too, is Nashville's housing affordability—$95,000 is the average price for a three-bedroom, 2,000-square-foot house—coupled with average residential property taxes of slightly more than $1,100.

City Profile

 Population
in Thousands

1980	850.5
1990	985.0
1992	1,015.0
1995 Estimate	1,062.6

 Socioeconomic
Factors

Average Household Income

1980	$20,077
1991 Estimate	$37,803
% Change	88.3
1996 Projection	$46,078

Median Household Income

1980	$16,956
1991 Estimate	$29,932
% Change	76.5
1996 Projection	$36,157

Labor Force &
Employment

	1993
Total Number of Persons in the Labor Force (in 1000's)	538.5
Total Number of Persons Employed (in 1000's)	513.5
Average Unemployment Rate	4.6%

Total Employment in Thousands by Sector

	1980	1992
Construction	18.7	19.5
Manufacturing	80.8	90.3
Transportation/Utilities	19.5	30.3
Trade	82.0	125.8
F.I.R.E.	24.5	30.5
Services	71.9	150.2
Government	62.8	67.4

 Education

1992 Enrollment

Two Year College	8,956
Four Year Undergraduate	28,207
Four Year Graduate	6,962
Average SAT Score	N/A
Total Possible Score: 1600	
Average ACT Score	21.7
Total Possible Score: 36	

 Business
Environment

Selected Major Employers

Tenn. State Govt.
U.S. Govt.
Vanderbilt Univ. & Med. Ctr.
Metro. Nashville-Davidson Co. Govt.
Metro. Nashville-Davidson Co. Schools
Opryland USA
Kroger Co.
HCA. The Health Care Co.
Nissan Motor Mfg. USA
Shoney's Inc.

Media Profile

2 newspapers
25 radio stations
13 network television stations
1 cable television operator

% State Taxes[1]

Corporate Income/Franchise Tax	6.0%
Sales/Use Tax	8.75%
Individual Income Tax	0.0%
Unemployment Insurance Rate	2.70%

[1]See the State Tax Notes on page 310.

City Taxes[2]

County Tax	2.25%
City Tax	None
Other Taxes	None

Property Tax Rates [3,4]

$52.40 in $ per $1000

International Profile

Number of Foreign Banks	0
Number of Foreign-owned Businesses	64
Number of Persons Employed by Foreign-owned Businesses	6,310
Number of Daily International Flights	23

Real Estate

Occupancy Cost per Square Foot (Annual)

	Sq. Foot	Sq. Meters
Average Rental-Class A Office (Central Business District)	$17.84	$191.96
Average Rental-Class A Apartment	$7.65	$82.31
Average Rental-Warehouse	$2.91	$31.31

Construction Cost per Square Foot

	Sq. Foot	Sq. Meters
Excellent Class A Office	$107.89	$1,160.90
Class A Industrial/Manufacturing	$65.82	$708.22

	Sq. Foot	Sq. Meters
Class A Distribution Warehouse	$46.37	$498.94
Excellent Class C Single Family Residential	$82.01	$882.43

Average Electric Cost (Cents per KwH)

	1992
Residential	$0.496
Commercial	$0.504
Industrial	$0.345
Average Price for a 3-bedroom Family House (in 1000's)	$95.0

Quality of Life

Climate

	Fahrenheit		Celsius	
	High	Low	High	Low
Winter	46	28	8	-2
Spring	71	48	22	9
Summer	90	69	32	21
Autumn	72	48	22	9

Rainfall

	Inches	Millimeters
January	4.5	114
February	4.0	102
March	5.6	142
April	4.5	114
May	4.6	117
June	3.7	94
July	3.8	96
August	3.4	86
September	3.7	94
October	2.6	66
November	3.5	89
December	4.5	117

Cultural Highlights

Belle Meade Plantation
Country Music Hall of Fame & Museum
Cumberland Science Museum

[2]See the State-Local General Sales Tax Notes on page 310.
[3]See the Property Tax Rate Notes on page 314.
[4]See the Classification of Real Property and Tangible Personal Property table on page 316.

Cultural Highlights (Continued)
 State Capitol
 Tennessee State Museum

Leisure Highlights

 Grand Ole Opry
 Tennessee Botanical Gardens & Fine Arts
 Center
 Opryland USA
 Nashville Convention Center
 The Hermitage

Crime

Rate per 100,000 Inhabitants	1991
Number of violent crimes	1,014.5
Number of property crimes	5,412.9

Average Wages for Selected Occupations

	Average Hiring Salary
Secretary (LR-3)	$17,264
Computer Systems Analyst III	$45,344
Computer Programmer III	$30,836
Engineer II	$29,172
Maintenance Machinist	$24,024

New Orleans

LOUISIANA

The New Orleans MSA now covers eight parishes (counties), numbering some 1.3 million people; the parishes of St. James and Plaquemines were added in 1993. Although population growth has been modest, job growth has been steady and has diversified beyond the area's traditional oil and gas, tourism, port- and shipbuilding-related industries. Growing industries include health services, aerospace, and research and technology.

Behind the scenes of New Orleans's well-known charm and profuse cultural and recreational attractions has been, in recent years, an investment of more than a half billion dollars in infrastructure improvements. Once under way, riverboat gambling and casino gambling are expected to contribute long-term economic stability to the region.

Approximately 47 foreign-owned companies have operations in New Orleans, which has always been oriented toward international trade because of its location on the Mississippi River, upstream from the Gulf of Mexico. The Mississippi provides abundant natural resources and water access to markets in mid-America and around the globe. The River Region handles more than twice the amount of cargo tonnage that New York/New Jersey accommodates, and approximately three times that of Houston.

The cost of living is relatively modest, on a par with such cities as Houston, Kansas City, and Tampa. The average three-bedroom, 2,000-square-foot house sells for $96,000. Energy costs are even more modest, comparatively. According to a recent Department of Energy survey, for example New Orleans had the lowest electric rates among 40 large cities.

Education has gotten a boost from two initiatives at the state level. First, the 1988 Children First Act increased per-pupil spending by 8%, raised teacher pay 30%, and reduced class sizes. Louisiana also pays for all high achievers to attend college.

City Profile

Population in Thousands

1980	1,304.2
1990	1,285.3
1992	1,304.3
1995 Estimate	1,335.0

Socioeconomic Factors

Average Household Income
1980	$19,828
1991 Estimate	$34,834
% Change	75.7
1996 Projection	$42,059

Median Household Income
1980	$16,225
1991 Estimate	$27,016
% Change	66.5
1996 Projection	$32,298

Labor Force & Employment

	1993
Total Number of Persons in the Labor Force (in 1000's)	551.3
Total Number of Persons Employed (in 1000's)	516.8
Average Unemployment Rate	6.3%

Total Employment in Thousands by Sector

	1980	1992
Construction	38.3	23.0
Manufacturing	60.8	44.8
Transportation/Utilities	56.2	40.4
Trade	131.4	136.4
F.I.R.E.	30.8	29.2
Services	114.5	156.3
Government	84.0	93.9

Education

1992 Enrollment
Two Year College	7,942
Four Year Undergraduate	34,549
Four Year Graduate	8,194
Average SAT Score	N/A
Total Possible Score: 1600	
Average ACT Score	18.0
Total Possible Score: 36	

Business Environment

Selected Major Employers
Alton Ochsner Medical Foundation
Avondale Shipyards
Martin Marietta Manned Space Systems
National Supermarkets, Inc.
Schwegmann Bros. Giant Supermarkets
Shell Oil Co.
South Central Bell Telephone Co.
Tulane University
Wal-Mart Stores, Inc.
Winn Dixie of La., Inc.

Media Profile
1 newspaper
27 radio stations
9 network television stations
1 cable television operator

State Taxes

Corporate Income/Franchise Tax	8.0%
Sales/Use Tax	9.5%
Individual Income Tax	6.0%
Unemployment Insurance Rate	2.90%

 % City Taxes[1]

County Tax	5.00%
City Tax	None
Other Taxes	None

 % Property Tax Rates [2,3]

$143.68 in $ per $1000

⊕ International Profile

Number of Foreign Banks	0
Number of Foreign-owned Businesses	47
Number of Persons Employed by Foreign-owned Businesses	920
Number of Daily International Flights	36

🏠 Real Estate

Occupancy Cost per Square Foot (Annual)

	Sq. Foot	Sq. Meters
Average Rental-Class A Office (Central Business District)	$13.45	$144.72
Average Rental-Class A Apartment	$5.98	$64.34
Average Rental-Warehouse	$3.33	$35.83

Construction Cost per Square Foot

	Sq. Foot	Sq. Meters
Excellent Class A Office	$110.32	$1,187.04
Class A Industrial/ Manufacturing	$67.29	$724.04

	Sq. Foot	Sq. Meters
Class A Distribution Warehouse	$47.41	$510.13
Excellent Class C Single Family Residential	$85.74	$922.56

Average Electric Cost (Cents per KwH)

	1992
Residential	$0.762
Commercial	$0.810
Industrial	$0.522
Average Price for a 3-bedroom Family House (in 1000's)	$96.0

★ Quality of Life

Climate

	Fahrenheit		Celsius	
	High	Low	High	Low
Winter	62	43	17	6
Spring	79	59	26	15
Summer	91	74	33	23
Autumn	79	59	26	15

Rainfall

	Inches	Millimeters
January	5.0	127
February	5.2	132
March	4.7	119
April	4.5	114
May	5.1	129
June	4.6	117
July	6.7	170
August	6.2	157
September	5.9	150
October	2.7	69
November	4.1	104
December	5.3	135

Cultural Highlights

New Orleans Museum of Art
French Quarter
Garden District

[1]See the State-Local General Sales Tax Notes on page 310.
[2]See the Property Tax Rate Notes on page 314.
[3]See the Classification of Real Property and Tangible Personal Property table on page 316.

Cultural Highlights (Continued)
Jackson Square
Riverwalk Marketplace

Leisure Highlights
Aquarium of the Americas
Audubon Zoo
Jackson Brewery
French Quarter Festival Marketplace
Superdome

Crime

Rate per 100,000 Inhabitants	1991
Number of violent crimes	1,407.7
Number of property crimes	7,431.8

Average Wages for Selected Occupations

	Average Hiring Salary
Secretary (LR-3)	$19,604
Computer Systems Analyst III	$36,140
Computer Programmer III	$30,836
Engineer II	$30,000
Maintenance Machinist	$31,720

Oklahoma City

OKLAHOMA

Home of the National Cowboy Hall of Fame, Western Heritage Center, and numerous equine events, Oklahoma City mixes a fondness for the culture and lore of the Old West with a contemporary focus on expanding its position as a telecommunications center.

Its niche as a site for call center operations was given a recent boost with Hertz's decision to locate a worldwide reservation center here. Call centers depend on part-timers for shift operations, and the area's 17 colleges and universities provide a sizable pool of available labor.

Although the two largest employers in the area are the state government and Tinker Air Force Base, Oklahoma City's economy has diversified to include an almost equal number of jobs in services and wholesale/retail trade. AT&T and Southwestern Bell are among the top 25 local employers, and 90% of Southwestern Bell's telecommunications capacity is via fiber-optic cables.

Highway access enables delivery to any market in the United States within a day and a half, making Oklahoma City a distribution and trucking hub. Will Rogers Airport is served by seven carriers and 71 flights a day.

The metropolitan area's population is close to one million; nearly half live in Oklahoma City, the state capital. The area's per capita income level is higher than the national average, yet its housing costs are lower. The average selling price for a 2,000- to 2,500-square-foot home is less than $87,000.

City Profile

 Population in Thousands

1980	861.0
1990	959.0
1992	977.2
1995 Estimate	963.9

 Socioeconomic Factors

Average Household Income

1980	$20,256
1991 Estimate	$37,041
% Change	82.9
1996 Projection	$45,383

Median Household Income

1980	$16,877
1991 Estimate	$29,183
% Change	72.9
1996 Projection	$35,236

 Labor Force & Employment

	1993
Total Number of Persons in the Labor Force (in 1000's)	496.4
Total Number of Persons Employed (in 1000's)	472.6
Average Unemployment Rate	4.8%

Total Employment in Thousands by Sector

	1980	1992
Construction	19.8	13.8
Manufacturing	55.5	46.2
Transportation/Utilities	23.5	21.3
Trade	97.9	105.0
F.I.R.E.	24.9	25.1
Services	71.1	109.9
Government	89.1	103.6

 Education

1992 Enrollment

Two Year College	22,858
Four Year Undergraduate	37,764
Four Year Graduate	9,967
Average SAT Score	N/A
Total Possible Score: 1600	
Average ACT Score	19.6
Total Possible Score: 36	

 Business Environment

Selected Major Employers

Tinker Air Force Base
General Motors
Hertz Corp.
AT&T Network Systems
Fleming Companies, Inc.
American Fidelity Group
The Oklahoma Publishing Company
Dana Carriers, Inc.
Seagate Technology, Inc.
Kerr-McGee Corp.

Media Profile

2 newspapers
22 radio stations
10 network television stations
1 cable television operator

State Taxes[1]

Corporate Income/Franchise Tax	6.0%
Sales/Use Tax	9.5%
Individual Income Tax	10.0%
Unemployment Insurance Rate	3.40%

[1]See the State Tax Notes on page 308.

City Taxes

County Tax	None
City Tax	2.875%
Other Taxes	None

Property Tax Rates [2,3]

$94.58 in $ per $1000

International Profile

Number of Foreign Banks	0
Number of Foreign-owned Businesses	19
Number of Persons Employed by Foreign-owned Businesses	2,416
Number of Daily International Flights	0

Real Estate

Occupancy Cost per Square Foot (Annual)

	Sq. Foot	Sq. Meters
Average Rental-Class A Office (Central Business District)	$13.78	$148.27
Average Rental-Class A Apartment	$5.83	$62.73
Average Rental- Warehouse	$2.89	$31.10

Construction Cost per Square Foot

	Sq. Foot	Sq. Meters
Excellent Class A Office	$113.96	$1,226.21
Class A Industrial/ Manufacturing	$69.51	747.93

	Sq. Foot	Sq. Meters
Class A Distribution Warehouse	$48.97	$526.92
Excellent Class C Single Family Residential	$87.60	$942.58

Average Electric Cost (Cents per KwH)

	1992
Residential	$0.742
Commercial	$0.669
Industrial	$0.459
Average Price for a 3-bedroom Family House (in 1000's)	$85.00

Quality of Life

Climate

	Fahrenheit		Celsius	
	High	Low	High	Low
Winter	47	25	8	-4
Spring	72	49	22	9
Summer	94	71	34	22
Autumn	74	50	23	10

Rainfall

	Inches	Millimeters
January	1.0	25
February	1.3	33
March	2.1	53
April	2.9	74
May	5.5	140
June	3.9	99
July	3.0	76
August	2.4	61
September	3.4	86
October	2.7	69
November	1.5	38
December	1.2	31

Cultural Highlights

Harn Homestead
Kirkpatrick Center Museum Complex
National Cowboy Hall of Fame
National Softball Hall of Fame & Museum
State Capitol

[2]See the Property Tax Rate Notes on page 314.
[3]See the Classification of Real Property and Tangible Personal Property table on page 316.

Leisure Highlights
Frontier City Theme Park
Myriad Gardens
Crystal Bridge
Oklahoma City Zoo
Remington Park

Crime

Rate per 100,000 Inhabitants	1991
Number of violent crimes	723.9
Number of property crimes	7,324.1

Average Wages for Selected Occupations

	Average Hiring Salary
Secretary (LR-3)	$21,382
Computer Systems Analyst III	$44,803
Computer Programmer III	$34,694
Engineer II	$30,222
Maintenance Machinist	$28,849

San Antonio

TEXAS

Founded as a military garrison in 1718 by the Viceroy of Spain, San Antonio still has a formidable military presence, with four air force bases and one army post. San Antonio covers three counties, with an estimated 1992 population of nearly 1.3 million, growing from 1.07 million in 1980.

In addition to the military, services and wholesale/retail trade represent major job sources in San Antonio. Services, in fact, has been the fastest growing employment sector in the past decade, with an average annual growth of 6.4%. Recent relocations by companies from St. Louis and El Paso, as well as a significant expansion by an existing San Antonio-based company, underscore the area's strength in telecommunications.

In addition to telecommunications, public and private business leaders see more medical research, biotechnology, and distribution centers in San Antonio's future. Increasing trade with Mexico is expected to enhance the city's business role.

In 1992, San Antonio's cost of living ranked among the lowest of 25 MSAs with more than one million in population, according to the American Chamber of Commerce Researchers Association (ACCRA), and there is no corporate or personal income tax here. Average price of a three-bedroom, 2,000-square-foot house is approximately $87,000.

San Antonio has become a vibrant tourist destination. The Alamo is still a major draw, and The River Walk is one of San Antonio's better known recreational attractions. It consists of nearly two miles of shady walks with shops, dining and entertainment, and barges available for scenic tours. The newest attraction is Fiesta Texas, a $100 million, 201-acre musical and entertainment theme park developed by Opryland USA from Nashville and USAA, San Antonio's largest private employer.

City Profile

 Population in Thousands

1980	1,072.1
1990	1,302.1
1992	1,362.2
1995 Estimate	1,448.3

 Socioeconomic Factors

Average Household Income

1980	$18,482
1991 Estimate	$30,039
% Change	62.5
1996 Projection	$35,867

Median Household Income

1980	$15,192
1991 Estimate	$24,246
% Change	59.6
1996 Projection	$28,803

 Labor Force & Employment

	1993
Total Number of Persons in the Labor Force (in 1000's)	630.0
Total Number of Persons Employed (in 1000's)	588.0
Average Unemployment Rate	6.6%

Total Employment in Thousands by Sector

	1980	1992
Construction	27.0	23.5
Manufacturing	50.8	45.9
Transportation/Utilities	18.4	24.0
Trade	100.0	135.7
F.I.R.E.	26.5	38.6
Services	80.2	154.9
Government	93.2	123.6

 Education

1992 Enrollment

Two Year College	28,894
Four Year Undergraduate	17,629
Four Year Graduate	7,887
Average SAT Score	816
Total Possible Score: 1600	
Average ACT Score	N/A
Total Possible Score: 36	

 Business Environment

Selected Major Employers

Kelly Air Force Base
Fort Sam Houston
Lackland Air Force Base
USAA
HEB Grocery Co.
City of San Antonio
Randolph Air Force Base
San Antonio Independent School District
Northside ISD
Northeast ISD

Media Profile

2 newspapers
37 radio stations
6 network television stations
1 cable television operator

 State Taxes[1]

Corporate Income/Franchise Tax	4.5%
Sales/Use Tax	8.25%
Individual Income Tax	0.0%
Unemployment Insurance Rate	2.70%

[1]See the State Tax Notes on page 308.

City Taxes[2]

County Tax	None
City Tax	1.00%
Other Taxes	1.00%

Property Tax Rates [3,4]

$5.2835 in $ per $1000

International Profile

Number of Foreign Banks	1
Number of Foreign-owned Businesses	58
Number of Persons Employed by Foreign-owned Businesses	1,525
Number of Daily International Flights	41

Real Estate

Occupancy Cost per Square Foot (Annual)

	Sq. Foot	Sq. Meters
Average Rental-Class A Office (Central Business District)	$14.31	$153.98
Average Rental-Class A Apartment	$7.35	$79.09
Average Rental-Warehouse	$2.83	$30.45

Construction Cost per Square Foot

	Sq. Foot	Sq. Meters
Excellent Class A Office	$105.47	$1,134.86
Class A Industrial/Manufacturing	$64.34	$692.30

	Sq. Foot	Sq. Meters
Class A Distribution Warehouse	$45.33	$487.75
Excellent Class C Single Family Residential	$81.08	$872.42

Average Electric Cost (Cents per KwH)

	1992
Residential	$0.660
Commercial	$0.613
Industrial	$0.465
Average Price for a 3-bedroom Family House (in 1000's)	$86.9

Quality of Life

Climate

	Fahrenheit		Celsius	
	High	Low	High	Low
Winter	62	39	17	4
Spring	80	59	27	15
Summer	95	74	35	23
Autumn	82	59	28	15

Rainfall

	Inches	Millimeters
January	1.6	41
February	1.9	48
March	1.3	33
April	2.7	69
May	3.7	94
June	3.0	76
July	1.9	48
August	2.7	69
September	3.8	96
October	2.9	74
November	2.3	58
December	1.4	36

Cultural Highlights

Institute of Texan Cultures
The Alamo
Tower of the Americas/HemisFair Park
Fiesta Texas

[2]See the State-Local General Sales Tax Notes on page 310.
[3]See the Property Tax Rate Notes on page 314.
[4]See the Classification of Real Property and Tangible Personal Property table on page 316.

Leisure Highlights
IMAX Theater Rivercenter
Market Square Mexican Markets
San Antonio Botanical Gardens
San Antonio Missions National Historical
 Park
Sea World of Texas
The River Walk

Crime

Rate per 100,000 Inhabitants	1991
Number of violent crimes	712.2
Number of property crimes	9,740.8

Average Wages for Selected Occupations

	Average Hiring Salary
Secretary (LR-3)	$21,476
Computer Systems Analyst III	$30,846
Computer Programmer III	$33,696
Engineer II	$38,012
Maintenance Machinist	$24,086

MIDWEST

Overview

Whatever happened to smokestack industries? Along with agribusiness, they once dominated America's heartland. Many of the Midwest metro areas reviewed in this section, in fact, are still centers for heavy industrial production. However, the winds are shifting steadily toward high-tech manufacturing, distribution, international trade, and service businesses.

The Midwest areas experiencing growth in high-technology businesses are those, not surprisingly, that have a high concentration of vocational/technical schools and/or research-oriented universities and laboratories to support that growth, such as Minneapolis, Milwaukee, and Dayton.

One thing that has *not* changed about the midwest is the terminology consistently used to describe its work force. *Industriousness* is a word that keeps appearing, whether it is used to describe foundry workers or engineers and electronics pros. The Midwest exudes a certain no-nonsense approach to economic life. It balances a conservatism—perhaps resulting from the traditions of the nineteenth-century northern European immigrants who settled in the region—and the energy of its increasingly better-educated youth.

The Midwest's down-to-earth business style should not be confused with blandness in other areas. Indeed, the Midwest is full of surprises. You can find the most *avant* of avant garde art and theater in Cleveland, for example, or a traditional Japanese breakfast in a downtown Cincinnati hotel. Sculpture gardens, summer and winter arts and entertainment festivals, the biggest shopping mall in the United States, alternative music clubs, and riverboat gambling are just a few more of the attractions to be found in this region.

Nor should anyone think of the center of the country as being thoroughly landlocked. Many of the areas in this region are located along lakes and rivers, which accounts for their appeal not only as distribution centers (in part), but also as recreation centers. Water-oriented sports abound, as do opportunities for skiing, hiking, biking, and other forms of enjoying nature. In many of these communities, residents do have the time to enjoy their surroundings, in as much as commuting times are reasonable and relatively efficient.

The metro areas in this region are also well served by highways and by rail. Air service varies widely, and though all may refer to their airports as hubs, not all function that way. Facilities range from the busiest in the United States— Chicago's O'Hare—to the small but freight-intensive airport in Dayton. If proximity to markets is crucial, a Midwestern location provides excellent access, within 500 miles of a variety of key U.S. metropolitan areas.

One of the ironies of the metro areas reviewed in this section is that several straddle two or three states, and these states are engaged in very serious competition for new and expanding businesses. Economic incentives and training, the "weapons" in their respective arsenals, vary. Kentucky has been among the more aggressive in this area, which has helped promote its portion of the Cincinnati metro area.

The differences between the metro areas reviewed in this section are reflected in their approaches to their CBDs and educational systems. Some, like Cleveland, Minneapolis, and St. Louis have come far in terms of redeveloping older areas and bringing a new liveliness to them after business hours. Old warehouses, lofts, and historical homes have been renovated to add residential appeal to the urban mix. Other areas, such as Detroit, still have a long way to go.

In education, Indianapolis is emblematic of some of the changes taking place to prepare today's students for tomorrow's workplace. Among the public/private partnerships supporting these efforts are the following:

COMMIT, a coalition of the state's larger businesses dedicated to promoting better schools;

CLASS (Community Leaders Allied for Superior Schools), a group of corporate executives and professionals who, among other things, act as a clearinghouse for local, national, and international initiatives that focus on quality education.

Chicago

ILLINOIS

Chicago has traditionally been known as the "city of the big shoulders," and the 1990s have shown that it is also a city with a big reach.

Retailing, government, telecommunications, supermarketing, and food-related businesses are among the area's largest employers. Among them are Sears, Montgomery Ward, Ameritech, and Sara Lee, plus Navistar, Quaker Oats, USG, Borg-Warner, Bally Manufacturing, and Amoco. Many jobs are moving to the suburbs. Since 1972, employment in suburban Cook County has increased by 50%; overall employment in the suburban counties has increased by 120%, while jobs in the CBD have declined by 11%.

In addition to attracting U.S. corporations, the area has developed a strong international presence. Approximately 904 foreign-owned companies and 44 foreign banks are located in the area. Among the reasons for this presence is the city's strategic location in the center of the nation's heaviest concentration of rail lines, highways, and air routes (O'Hare International Airport is currently the busiest in the country). Lake Michigan also provides access to overseas shipping routes. Covering six counties in northeastern Illinois, the Chicago metro area now comprises 7.26 million people.

Chicagoans, transferees, and international visitors alike are also undoubtedly drawn to the area's considerable cultural and recreational activities. The Chicago Art Museum, one of dozens in the area, is perhaps most well known, as are the Steppenwolf Theatre Company, the Goodman Theatre, and, for the sports-minded, the Bears, the Bulls, the Blackhawks, the Cubs, and the White Sox.

Chicago's lakefront location offers 29 miles of usable beaches, with running paths, fishing piers, and yacht harbors. The city's extensive park system is connected by tree-lined boulevards, according to the master plan enacted following the Great Chicago Fire of 1871.

Housing opportunities are as varied as the area itself, from redeveloped old neighborhoods and elegant high-rises in the city to large-lot, executive-style suburban communities. The median price for a three-bedroom home is $148,100. Prime middle-management residential areas include Lincoln Park, Beverly, Chatham, and Irving Park.

City Profile

 ## Population in Thousands

1980	7,103.7
1990	7,261.2
1992	6,149.0
1995 Estimate	6,203.9

 ## Socioeconomic Factors

Average Household Income

1980	$23,705
1991 Estimate	$44,930
% Change	89.5
1996 Projection	$54,626

Median Household Income

1980	$20,278
1991 Estimate	$35,895
% Change	77.0
1996 Projection	$43,868

Labor Force & Employment

	1993
Total Number of Persons in the Labor Force (in 1000's)	3,196.7
Total Number of Persons Employed (in 1000's)	2,937.89
Average Unemployment Rate	8.1%

Total Employment in Thousands by Sector

	1980	1992
Construction	123.3	110.0
Manufacturing	812.2	509.2
Transportation/Utilities	194.8	199.2
Trade	770.9	726.8
F.I.R.E.	228.4	263.4
Services	667.5	897.9
Government	418.6	380.6

 ## Education

1992 Enrollment

Two Year College	190,542
Four Year Undergraduate	86,070
Four Year Graduate	58,839
Average SAT Score	N/A
Total Possible Score: 1600	
Average ACT Score	17.5
Total Possible Score: 36	

Business Environment

Selected Major Employers

Federal Govt.
City of Chicago
Sears Roebuck
Jewel Foods Stores
Cook County
State of Illinois
Ameritech Corp.
AT&T
Dominicks Finer Foods
UAL Corp.

Media Profile

5 newspapers
47 radio stations
12 network television stations
2 cable television operators

 ## State Taxes

Corporate Income/Franchise Tax	7.3%
Sales/Use Tax	8.75%
Individual Income Tax	3.0%
Unemployment Insurance Rate	2.70%

 City Taxes[1]

County Tax	.75%
City Tax	1.00%
Other Taxes	.75%

Property Tax Rates [2,3]

$99.64 in $ per $1000

International Profile

Number of Foreign Banks	44
Number of Foreign-owned Businesses	904
Number of Persons Employed by Foreign-owned Businesses	30,508
Number of Daily International Flights	257

Real Estate

Occupancy Cost per Square Foot (Annual)

	Sq. Foot	Sq. Meters
Average Rental-Class A Office (Central Business District)	$22.23	$239.84
Average Rental-Class A Apartment	$11.20	$120.51
Average Rental-Warehouse	$5.37	$57.78

Construction Cost per Square Foot

	Sq. Foot	Sq. Meters
Excellent Class A Office	$141.84	$1,526.20
Class A Industrial/ Manufacturing	$86.52	930.95

	Sq. Foot	Sq. Meters
Class A Distribution Warehouse	$60.96	$655.93
Excellent Class C Single Family Residential	$109.04	$1,173.27

Average Electric Cost (Cents per KwH)

	1992
Residential	$0.1114
Commercial	$0.827
Industrial	$0.620
Average Price for a 3-bedroom Family House (in 1000's)	$148.1

Quality of Life

Climate

	Fahrenheit		Celsius	
	High	Low	High	Low
Winter	29	14	-2	-10
Spring	59	39	15	4
Summer	83	63	28	17
Autumn	64	43	18	6

Rainfall

	Inches	Millimeters
January	1.6	41
February	1.3	33
March	2.6	66
April	3.7	94
May	3.2	81
June	4.1	104
July	3.6	91
August	3.5	89
September	3.4	86
October	2.3	58
November	2.1	52
December	3.1	53

Cultural Highlights

Adler Planetarium
Art Institute of Chicago
Chicago Historical Society
Field Museum of Natural history

[1]See the State-Local General Sales Tax Notes on page 310.
[2]See the Property Tax Rate Notes on page 314.
[3]See the Classification of Real Property and Tangible Personal Property table on page 316.

Cultural Highlights (Continued)
 Museum of Science & Industry

Leisure Highlights
 John G. Shedd Aquarium
 John Hancock Center
 Lake Michigan Waterfront
 Lincoln Park Zoological Gardens
 Sears Tower Skydeck

Crime

Rate per 100,000 Inhabitants	1991
Number of violent crimes	1,481.7
Number of property crimes	6,150.6

Average Wages for Selected Occupations

	Average Hiring Salary
Secretary (LR-3)	$26,676
Computer Systems Analyst III	$52,780
Computer Programmer III	$36,660
Engineer II	$39,832
Maintenance Machinist	$32,988

Cincinnati

OHIO

Greater Cincinnati may cover a dozen counties in three states (Ohio, Kentucky, and Indiana), but part of the area's appeal is its compactness; the farthest point in the metro area is a 45-minute drive from the CBD. The downtown area is compact too, and its various theaters, ballet, opera, and orchestras, as well as baseball and football at Riverfront Stadium, add up to an active life after business hours.

This metro area has grown modestly in population to approximately 1.8 million, from 1.66 million in 1980. The food, food-related, and consumer products industries are among the largest private employers in the area. Procter & Gamble, for example, is headquartered here, as are the Kroger Company and Chiquita Brands International. Service industries, distribution, retail, and data centers round out the economic picture, and manufacturing (particularly transportation equipment) is still strong.

Corporate downsizing has affected some of the larger employers, but unemployment is lower than the national average, at 6.0%. Approximately 2,666 people are employed by the 78 foreign-owned companies based in the area. Among the foreign-owned companies that have recently located here are Sachs Automotive, A-Mold, and Hoesch Suspensions. To accommodate growth, the area's airport has been expanded with a new runway and new gates. Nonstop service is available to London, Frankfurt, Paris, and Toronto, and direct service is available to more than 100 cities in the United States.

Cincinnati's location along the Ohio River contributes to its recreation and commerce alike. Numerous party boats (mobile and stationary restaurants) dot the river, and more than 46 million tons of goods pass through the Port of Cincinnati.

Outside the city, there is a variety of reasonably priced housing available. Prime middle-management areas include Montgomery/Loveland/Landen, Blue Ash, Hyde Park, and Western Hills/Delhi. The average price for an existing three-bedroom house is $83,000.

City Profile

 Population in Thousands

1980	1,660.2
1990	1,744.1
1992	1,817.6
1995 Estimate	1,889.0

 Socioeconomic Factors

Average Household Income

1980	$20,927
1991 Estimate	$39,722
% Change	89.8
1996 Projection	$48,271

Median Household Income

1980	$18,202
1991 Estimate	$32,044
% Change	76.0
1996 Projection	$38,977

 Labor Force & Employment

	1993
Total Number of Persons in the Labor Force (in 1000's)	784.7
Total Number of Persons Employed (in 1000's)	738.0
Average Unemployment Rate	6.0%

Total Employment in Thousands by Sector

	1980	1992
Construction	25.3	34.3
Manufacturing	162.4	141.9
Transportation/Utilities	33.7	40.1
Trade	140.7	189.6
F.I.R.E.	32.6	43.8
Services	121.7	198.6
Government	83.9	95.5

 Education

1992 Enrollment

Two Year College	12,408
Four Year Undergraduate	44,394
Four Year Graduate	11,237
Average SAT Score	N/A
Total Possible Score: 1600	
Average ACT Score	18.8
Total Possible Score: 36	

 Business Environment

Selected Major Employers
- U.S. Govt.
- GE Aircraft
- Procter & Gamble
- University of Cincinnati
- Kroger Co.
- City of Cincinnati
- Cincinnati Public Schools
- Hamilton County
- Armco
- Cincinnati Gas & Electric

Media Profile
- 2 newspapers
- 26 radio stations
- 6 network television stations
- 1 cable television operator

% State Taxes[1]

Corporate Income/Franchise Tax	8.9%
Sales/Use Tax	7.0%
Individual Income Tax	7.5%
Unemployment Insurance Rate	3.00%

[1]See the State Tax Notes on page 308.

 City Taxes[2]

County Tax	.50%
City Tax	None
Other Taxes	None

Property Tax Rates [3]

$68.78 in $ per $1000

International Profile

Number of Foreign Banks	0
Number of Foreign-owned Businesses	78
Number of Persons Employed by Foreign-owned Businesses	2,666
Number of Daily International Flights	30

Real Estate

Occupancy Cost per Square Foot (Annual)

	Sq. Foot	Sq. Meters
Average Rental-Class A Office (Central Business District)	$18.75	$201.75
Average Rental-Class A Apartment	$7.28	$78.33
Average Rental- Warehouse	$3.62	$38.95

Construction Cost per Square Foot

	Sq. Foot	Sq. Meters
Excellent Class A Office	$128.50	$1,382.66
Class A Industrial/ Manufacturing	$78.39	$843.48

	Sq. Foot	Sq. Meters
Class A Distribution Warehouse	$55.23	$594.27
Excellent Class C Single Family Residential	$99.72	$1,072.98

Average Electric Cost (Cents per KwH)

	1992
Residential	$0.670
Commercial	$0.632
Industrial	$0.443
Average Price for a 3-bedroom Family House (in 1000's)	$83.0

 Quality of Life

Climate

	Fahrenheit		Celsius	
	High	Low	High	Low
Winter	37	20	3	-7
Spring	64	42	18	6
Summer	85	64	29	18
Autumn	66	43	19	6

Rainfall

	Inches	Millimeters
January	3.2	81
February	2.9	74
March	3.9	99
April	3.5	89
May	4.0	102
June	3.9	99
July	4.2	107
August	3.1	79
September	2.8	71
October	2.8	71
November	3.4	86
December	3.1	79

Cultural Highlights
Contemporary Arts Center
Museum Center at Cincinnati Union Terminal
Oldenberg Brewery/Museum & Showplace

[2]See the State-Local General Sales Tax Notes on page 310.
[3]See the Classification of Real Property and Tangible Personal Property table on page 316.

Cultural Highlights (Continued)
 Taft Museum
 Covington Landing at Rivercenter

Leisure Highlights
 Cincinnati Zoo & Botanical Garden
 Turfway Park Race Course
 River Down Racetrack
 Kings Island Theme Park
 Meiers Wine Cellars

Crime

Rate per 100,000 Inhabitants	1991
Number of violent crimes	647.1
Number of property crimes	5,022.6

Average Wages for Selected Occupations

	Average Hiring Salary
Secretary (LR-3)	$23,504
Computer Systems Analyst III	$52,728
Computer Programmer III	$34,632
Engineer II	$38,636
Maintenance Machinist	$28,475

Cleveland

Cleveland is a metro area in transition. Located along the southern shore of the Ohio River, with a long history of manufacturing (particularly steel and transportation equipment), its economy is gradually shifting to more service-oriented industries, including health care and retail. Moreover, there has been considerable rebuilding downtown.

The area's business community is supported by myriad vocational schools that offer technical training. Enrollment at three area community colleges offering programs in business, computer sciences, and other technical occupations numbers approximately 40,000.

The Port of Cleveland, a foreign trade zone, serves more than 50 countries. In all, nearly 4,645 people work for 90 foreign-owned companies in the area. Among the foreign-owned companies that have located here more recently are Clestra Hauserman, Manior Electroalloys, and U.S. Protech.

The six-county area has declined in population to 2.2 million, from 2.27 million in 1980, and is projected to grow very modestly in the next few years. Not all counties in the area have experienced a lack of population growth, however. Geauga and Medina Counties, for example, have both experienced increases of more than 8% between 1980 and 1990. In the overall metro area, prime middle-management communities include Strongsville, Brecksville, Independence, and Shaker Heights. The average three-bedroom home sells for $109,800.

Not surprisingly, Lake Erie—with its 100 miles of shoreline— is the focal point for much of the area's recreational attractions. Pleasure boating and other water sports are the prime activities. Landlubbers, on the other hand, can avail themselves of Lakefront State Park, Huntington Beach, and Mentor Headlands State Park, as well as 150 golf courses, cross-country skiing and tobogganing throughout the 19,000-acre Metropark system.

The area also offers quality theater, dance, and ballet, symphony and jazz. The long-awaited Rock 'n Roll Hall of Fame is slated to be built in Cleveland. Special events in the area include the Budweiser Cleveland Grand Prix, the World Series of Golf, and the Soapbox Derby.

City Profile

Population in Thousands

1980	2,274.0
1990	2,202.0
1992	2,208.0
1995 Estimate	2,213.0

Socioeconomic Factors

Average Household Income

1980	$22,106
1991 Estimate	$39,481
% Change	78.6
1996 Projection	$47,581

Median Household Income

1980	$19,180
1991 Estimate	$31,481
% Change	62.8
1996 Projection	$37,538

Labor Force & Employment

	1993
Total Number of Persons in the Labor Force (in 1000's)	933.8
Total Number of Persons Employed (in 1000's)	865.2
Average Unemployment Rate	7.4%

Total Employment in Thousands by Sector

	1980	1992
Construction	29.8	30.8
Manufacturing	254.9	187.0
Transportation/Utilities	45.9	38.7
Trade	205.3	218.5
F.I.R.E.	48.2	60.3
Services	187.5	261.0
Government	122.6	120.7

Education

1992 Enrollment

Two Year College	32,094
Four Year Undergraduate	28,778
Four Year Graduate	11,610
Average SAT Score	N/A
Total Possible Score: 1600	
Average ACT Score	17.2
Total Possible Score: 36	

Business Environment

Selected Major Employers

Federal Govt.
Ford Motor Co.
Catholic Diocese
Cleveland Clinic
Cleveland Bd. of Education
MetroHealth Sys.
City of Cleveland
Univ. Hospitals
State of Ohio
LTV Steel

Media Profile

1 newspaper
27 radio stations
6 network television stations
1 cable television operator

State Taxes[1]

Corporate Income/Franchise Tax	8.9%
Sales/Use Tax	7.0%
Individual Income Tax	7.5%
Unemployment Insurance Rate	3.00%

[1]See the State Tax Notes on page 308.

 City Taxes[2]

County Tax	1.00%
City Tax	None
Other Taxes	1.00%

 Property Tax Rates [3]

$80.20 in $ per $1000

International Profile

Number of Foreign Banks	1
Number of Foreign-owned Businesses	90
Number of Persons Employed by Foreign-owned Businesses	4,645
Number of Daily International Flights	67

Real Estate

Occupancy Cost per Square Foot (Annual)

	Sq. Foot	Sq. Meters
Average Rental-Class A Office (Central Business District)	$17.78	$191.31
Average Rental-Class A Apartment	$8.22	$88.45
Average Rental-Warehouse	$3.96	$42.61

Construction Cost per Square Foot

	Sq. Foot	Sq. Meters
Excellent Class A Office	$134.57	$1,447.97
Class A Industrial/ Manufacturing	$82.08	$883.18

	Sq. Foot	Sq. Meters
Class A Distribution Warehouse	$57.83	$622.25
Excellent Class C Single Family Residential	$104.38	$1,123.13

Average Electric Cost (Cents per KwH)

	1992
Residential	$0.1094
Commercial	$0.971
Industrial	$0.663
Average Price for a 3-bedroom Family House (in 1000's)	$109.8

 Quality of Life

Climate

	Fahrenheit		Celsius	
	High	Low	High	Low
Winter	33	19	1	-7
Spring	58	38	14	3
Summer	82	61	28	16
Autumn	63	44	17	7

Rainfall

	Inches	Millimeters
January	2.5	64
February	2.2	56
March	3.0	76
April	3.3	84
May	3.3	84
June	3.5	89
July	3.4	86
August	3.4	86
September	2.9	74
October	2.5	64
November	2.8	71
December	2.8	71

Cultural Highlights

Cleveland Children's Museum
Cleveland Museum of Natural History
Playhouse Square Center

[2]See the State-Local General Sales Tax Notes on page 310.
[3]See the Classification of Real Property and Tangible Personal Property table on page 316.

Cultural Highlights (Continued)
The Cleveland Museum of Art
Tower City Center

Leisure Highlights
Cleveland Metroparks Zoo
Great Lakes Brewing Company
The Avenue at Tower City Center
The Galleria at Erieview
Visitor Center NASA Lewis Research Center

Crime

Rate per 100,000 Inhabitants	1991
Number of violent crimes	699.3
Number of property crimes	4,183.4

Average Wages for Selected Occupations

	Average Hiring Salary
Secretary (LR-3)	$21,396
Computer Systems Analyst III	$30,612
Computer Programmer III	$22,548
Engineer II	$32,760
Maintenance Machinist	$24,936

Columbus

Located in central Ohio, the state capital, Columbus, has come a long way since it was known in the late nineteenth century as the "Buggy Capital of the World" (for producing horse-drawn vehicles). More recently it has been referred to as the "Silicon Valley of retailing," thanks to the presence of major retail businesses such as The Limited, Sears, and J.C. Penney. It is also growing as a retail distribution center; for example, Spiegel recently relocated a catalog distribution center from Chicago to Groveport.

The metro area, which covers seven counties and comprises 1.4 million people, has also witnessed growth in insurance and banking, as well as research, information processing, and telecommunications. Ohio State University's Cary Y-MP supercomputer is used by researchers throughout the state. Manufacturing is an important component of the area's economy, too. For example, Anheuser-Busch maintains a large brewery in Columbus, McDonnell Douglas Corporation has an assembly plant for military cargo plane parts, and Honda of America has two auto plants in the area.

The population of Columbus is young; the median age is 29. Nearly three-quarters of the adult population are high school graduates, and more than one-fifth have college degrees. Columbus's "I Know I Can" program guarantees that every eligible high school graduate can attend college. Unemployment is below the national average, at 5.9%, and some 25,000 people work for more than 120 foreign-owned companies in the area

The Columbus metro area provides a cultural diversity and numerous recreational attractions. Annual events include the Ohio State Fair, summer evening concerts presented outdoors by the Columbus Symphony Orchestra, and the German Village Oktoberfest. Ohio State University is also the site of the Wexner Center for the Arts, which features modern art, theater, dance, and outdoor jazz concerts. Live music is also plentiful in a variety of clubs, and serious food enthusiasts can shop in farmers' markets or specialty groceries stores.

Housing choices are also diverse, ranging from new apartments, restored Victorian homes, and converted warehouse and industrial buildings downtown, to lush country club estates in Jefferson Township.

City Profile

Population in Thousands

1980	1,243.0
1990	1,377.0
1992	1,405.0
1995 Estimate	1,436.0

Socioeconomic Factors

Average Household Income

1980	$20,208
1991 Estimate	$39,318
% Change	94.6
1996 Projection	$48,340

Median Household Income

1980	$17,613
1991 Estimate	$31,746
% Change	80.2
1996 Projection	$39,031

Labor Force & Employment

	1993
Total Number of Persons in the Labor Force (in 1000's)	752.8
Total Number of Persons Employed (in 1000's)	708.7
Average Unemployment Rate	5.9%

Total Employment in Thousands by Sector

	1980	1992
Construction	21.2	27.6
Manufacturing	112.6	101.0
Transportation/Utilities	26.8	31.4
Trade	129.5	184.7
F.I.R.E.	40.1	59.6
Services	113.2	189.1
Government	115.4	133.5

Education

1992 Enrollment

Two Year College	9,085
Four Year Undergraduate	58,837
Four Year Graduate	13,723
Average SAT Score	N/A
Total Possible Score: 1600	
Average ACT Score	18.6
Total Possible Score: 36	

Business Environment

Selected Major Employers

The Ohio State University
State of Ohio
Honda of America Manufacturing
Columbus Public Schools
Limited, Inc.
U.S. Postal Service
Nationwide Insurance Companies
City of Columbus
Defense Construction Supply Center
Riverside Methodist Hospitals

Media Profile

1 newspaper
19 radio stations
5 network television stations
2 cable television operators

State Taxes[1]

Corporate Income/Franchise Tax	8.9%
Sales/Use Tax	7.0%
Individual Income Tax	7.5%
Unemployment Insurance Rate	7.00%

[1]See the State Tax Notes on page 308.

City Taxes[2]

County Tax	.50%
City Tax	None
Other Taxes	.25%

Property Tax Rates [3]

$59.73 in $ per $1000

International Profile

Number of Foreign Banks	1
Number of Foreign-owned Businesses	68
Number of Persons Employed by Foreign-owned Businesses	1,801
Number of Daily International Flights	3

Real Estate

Occupancy Cost per Square Foot (Annual)

	Sq. Foot	Sq. Meters
Average Rental-Class A Office (Central Business District)	$17.82	$191.74
Average Rental-Class A Apartment	$7.28	$78.33
Average Rental-Warehouse	$3.00	$32.28

Construction Cost per Square Foot

	Sq. Foot	Sq. Meters
Excellent Class A Office	$124.87	$1,343.60
Class A Industrial/ Manufacturing	$76.17	$819.59

	Sq. Foot	Sq. Meters
Class A Distribution Warehouse	$53.66	$577.38
Excellent Class C Single Family Residential	$95.06	$1,013.33

Average Electric Cost (Cents per KwH)

	1992
Residential	$0.680
Commercial	$0.574
Industrial	$0.443
Average Price for a 3-bedroom Family House (in 1000's)	$79.0

Quality of Life

Climate

	Fahrenheit		Celsius	
	High	Low	High	Low
Winter	35	19	2	-7
Spring	62	41	17	5
Summer	84	63	29	17
Autumn	65	43	18	6

Rainfall

	Inches	Millimeters
January	2.8	71
February	2.2	56
March	3.2	81
April	3.4	86
May	3.8	96
June	4.0	102
July	4.0	102
August	3.7	94
September	2.8	71
October	1.9	48
November	2.6	66
December	2.6	66

Cultural Highlights
Columbus City Center
Columbus Museum of Art
Ohio Historical Center

[2]See the State-Local General Sales Tax Notes on page 310.
[3]See the Classification of Real Property and Tangible Personal Property table on page 316.

Cultural Highlights (Continued)
 German Village Society
 Ohio Statehouse

Leisure Highlights
 Columbus Zoo
 Beulah Park Jockey Club
 Scioto Downs
 COSI, Ohio's Center of Science & Industry
 Veterans Memorial

Crime
Rate per 100,000 Inhabitants 1991
Number of violent crimes 720.8
Number of property crimes 6,263.6

Average Wages for Selected Occupations

	Average Hiring Salary
Secretary (LR-3)	$24,492
Computer Systems Analyst III	$48,256
Computer Programmer III	$35,776
Engineer II	$36,504
Maintenance Machinist	$35,193

Dayton

Although civic leaders stress Dayton's proximity to major markets, it has a decidedly high-tech heart. Wright Patterson Air Force Base, the area's largest employer, is the research and development arm of the U.S. Air Force. Technology developed here has spun off into nonmilitary uses, such as health care, fire-resistant fabrics, appliances, and automotive and aviation products. In addition to Wright Patterson, more than 830 high-technology companies are located in the area, including Mead Data Central, NCR/AT&T, and Systems Research Laboratories.

Covering four counties in southwest Ohio, Dayton's modest population growth is expected to continue to an estimated 984,600 residents by 1995. More than 75% of the adult population have a high school diploma or higher education, and nearly one-fifth have a bachelor's or higher degree. Nearly 15% of Ohio's engineers and engineering technicians are located in the Dayton area, and that percentage is expected to grow to more than 18% by the year 2000. Since 1990, an average of 1.4 patents per day have been issued to Dayton area inventors.

At the same time, much of the area's growth is expected to be in health care and business services. Distribution facilities are on the rise, partly because of Dayton's easy access to I-70 and I-75 (east-west and north-south corridors); and because Dayton is the global hub of Emery Worldwide, its airport is a busy cargo and freight facility.

Dayton offers a full complement of housing choices, including urban, rural, suburban, and historical neighborhoods. The cost of living in the area is comparable to that of Lexington, Kentucky, and the average price for a three-bedroom house is approximately $83,000.

A variety of recreational and cultural attractions are part of the area's appeal. It has more than 35,000 acres of parks, plus orchestras, dance and theater companies, and opera. Dayton is also home to the annual United States Air and Trade Show, Hamvention, Computerfest, and the Amateur Trapshooting Association Grand American Trapshoot.

City Profile

Population in Thousands

1980	942.1
1990	951.3
1992	954.1
1995 Estimate	984.6

Socioeconomic Factors

Average Household Income

1980	$20,397
1991 Estimate	$37,996
% Change	86.3
1996 Projection	$46,151

Median Household Income

1980	$18,070
1991 Estimate	$31,066
% Change	719
1996 Projection	$37,527

Labor Force & Employment

	1993
Total Number of Persons in the Labor Force (in 1000's)	469.6
Total Number of Persons Employed (in 1000's)	438.8
Average Unemployment Rate	6.6%

Total Employment in Thousands by Sector

	1980	1992
Construction	14.7	14.2
Manufacturing	110.9	95.6
Transportation/Utilities	15.6	17.6
Trade	83.0	101.2
F.I.R.E.	15.6	17.4
Services	82.3	119.9
Government	74.6	76.3

Education

1992 Enrollment

Two Year College	21,094
Four Year Undergraduate	28,232
Four Year Graduate	9,028
Average SAT Score	814
Total Possible Score: 1600	
Average ACT Score	18.7
Total Possible Score: 36	

Business Environment

Selected Major Employers

Wright Patterson Air Force Base
General Motors
Elder Breiman Stores
NAVISTAR
NCR/AT&T
Montgomery County
Emory Worldwide
Dayton Public Schools
U.S. Postal Service
The Mead Corporation

Media Profile

1 newspaper
16 radio stations
5 network television stations
2 cable television operators

State Taxes[1]

Corporate Income/Franchise Tax	8.9%
Sales/Use Tax	7.0%
Individual Income Tax	7.5%
Unemployment Insurance Rate	3.00%

[1]See the State Tax Notes on page 308.

% City Taxes[2]

County Tax	1.00%
City Tax	None
Other Taxes	.50%

% Property Tax Rates[3]

$75.90 in $ per $1000

⊕ International Profile

Number of Foreign Banks	0
Number of Foreign-owned Businesses	35
Number of Persons Employed by Foreign-owned Businesses	660
Number of Daily International Flights	2

⌂ Real Estate

Occupancy Cost per Square Foot (Annual)

	Sq. Foot	Sq. Meters
Average Rental-Class A Office (Central Business District)	$16.26	$174.96
Average Rental-Class A Apartment	$7.28	$78.33
Average Rental-Warehouse	$2.75	$29.59

Construction Cost per Square Foot

	Sq. Foot	Sq. Meters
Excellent Class A Office	$122.44	$1,317.45
Class A Industrial/Manufacturing	$74.69	$803.66

	Sq. Foot	Sq. Meters
Class A Distribution Warehouse	$52.62	$566.19
Excellent Class C Single Family Residential	$95.99	$1,032.85

Average Electric Cost (Cents per KwH)

	1992
Residential	$0.767
Commercial	$0.625
Industrial	$0.482
Average Price for a 3-bedroom Family House (in 1000's)	$82.8

★ Quality of Life

Climate

	Fahrenheit		Celsius	
	High	Low	High	Low
Winter	35	19	2	-7
Spring	62	41	17	5
Summer	85	64	29	18
Autumn	65	44	18	7

Rainfall

	Inches	Millimeters
January	2.6	66
February	2.1	53
March	3.1	79
April	3.4	86
May	3.7	94
June	3.8	96
July	3.4	86
August	3.1	79
September	2.4	61
October	2.0	51
November	2.6	66
December	2.5	64

Cultural Highlights

Dayton Art Institute
Dayton Museum of Natural History
International Women's Air & Space Museum

[2]*See the State-Local General Sales Tax Notes on page 310.*
[3]*See the Classification of Real Property and Tangible Personal Property table on page 316.*

Cultural Highlights (Continued)
 U.S. Air Force Museum
 Carriage Hill Farm

Leisure Highlights
 Aullwood Audubon Center & Farm
 Cox Arboretum
 Oregon District
 Sunwatch Archaeological Park
 Dayton Hara Complex

Crime

Rate per 100,000 Inhabitants	1991
Number of violent crimes	692.3
Number of property crimes	5,146.9

Average Wages for Selected Occupations

	Average Hiring Salary
Secretary (LR-3)	$23,000
Computer Systems Analyst III	$37,000
Computer Programmer III	$45,000
Engineer II	$40,000
Maintenance Machinist	N/A

Detroit

MICHIGAN

The Detroit metro area includes eight counties, covering 5,266 square miles in southeastern Michigan. Its population is 4.66 million, of which 77% are suburban residents. The area is best known as the home of General Motors, Chrysler, and Ford, and its economic life is closely tied to the fortunes of the auto industry.

Civic leaders expect that NAFTA will have a significantly positive effect on southern Michigan's economy. Currently, Michigan does more business with Canada than with any of the other states; 75% of its exports are in automotive products. Increased trade with Canada is expected to create 25,000 jobs in southern Michigan over the next 10 years.

Proximity to Canada is key—Detroit lies directly across the Detroit River from Ontario—but is not the only element of international trade. Michigan is also a top exporter to Mexico, with cars and automotive products representing the largest single export. Currently, some 390 foreign-owned companies, representing automotive, machinery, chemical, consumer goods, and service businesses are located here, employing more than 8,350 people. Extensive nonstop flights overseas are a help; service is available to Tokyo, Seoul, Amsterdam, Frankfort, Paris, and London.

Cars are not Detroit's only business, of course. Southeastern Michigan is also home to three-quarters of the more than 300 robotics companies in Michigan and has a number of industrial research and development laboratories, including the NASA Research and Development Center and the National Center for Manufacturing Sciences. Approximately one-third of the area's work force is employed in industrial and advanced manufacturing.

There are significant differences within the metro area in housing prices, educational attainment, median ages, and economic profiles, and suburban communities contrast sharply with the CBD. In Oakland County, EDS, Kmart, Dayton Hudson Corporation, and Michigan Bell are among the larger employers. More than 75% of the residents are high school graduates, and nearly 25% are college graduates. The median home selling price is in excess of $86,000.

Overall, the metro area encompasses 296 miles of Great Lakes shoreline, giving rise to an abundance of recreational opportunities, complemented by the presence of 3,000 inland lakes and rivers. In addition to its 20,000 acres of recreational land, Wayne County alone offers a variety of attractions, including Belle Isle (site of numerous festivals), Tiger Stadium, the Michigan State Fairgrounds, the Detroit Science Center, the Afro-American Museum, the Fox Theater, and Cobo Hall.

City Profile

 Population in Thousands

1980	4,488.0
1990	4,382.3
1992	4,421.2
1995 Estimate	4,450.4

 Socioeconomic Factors

Average Household Income

1980	$24,269
1991 Estimate	$43,647
% Change	79.8
1996 Projection	$52,483

Median Household Income

1980	$21,261
1991 Estimate	$36,023
% Change	69.4
1996 Projection	$43,573

 Labor Force & Employment

	1993
Total Number of Persons in the Labor Force (in 1000's)	2,121.3
Total Number of Persons Employed (in 1000's)	1,968.6
Average Unemployment Rate	7.2%

Total Employment in Thousands by Sector

	1980	1992
Construction	53.1	55.6
Manufacturing	498.5	416.7
Transportation/Utilities	83.5	85.6
Trade	369.1	452.3
F.I.R.E.	90.3	108.0
Services	351.0	521.0
Government	256.7	235.4

 Education

1992 Enrollment:

Two Year College	110,139
Four Year Undergraduate	47,418
Four Year Graduate	25,922
Average SAT Score	N/A
Total Possible Score: 1600	
Average ACT Score	17.4
Total Possible Score: 36	

 Business Environment

Selected Major Employers

General Motors Corp.
Chrysler Corp.
Detroit Medical Center
NBD Bancorp Inc.
Henry Ford Health System
Wayne State University
Detroit Edison Co.
Blue Cross & Blue Shield of Michigan
St. John Health Corp.
Michigan Bell Telephone Co.

Media Profile

2 newspapers
30 radio stations
7 network television stations
1 cable television operator

 State Taxes[1]

Corporate Income/Franchise Tax	2.35%
Sales/Use Tax	4.0%
Individual Income Tax	4.6%
Unemployment Insurance Rate	2.70%

[1]See the State Tax Notes on page 308.

 City Taxes

County Tax	None
City Tax	None
Other Taxes	None

 Property Tax Rates [2,3]

$88.2780 in $ per $1000

 International Profile

Number of Foreign Banks	1
Number of Foreign-owned Businesses	390
Number of Persons Employed by Foreign-owned Businesses	8,350
Number of Daily International Flights	98

Real Estate

Occupancy Cost per Square Foot (Annual)

	Sq. Foot	Sq. Meters
Average Rental-Class A Office (Central Business District)	$16.36	$169.49
Average Rental-Class A Apartment	$8.66	$931.80
Average Rental-Warehouse	$4.60	$49.50

Construction Cost per Square Foot

	Sq. Foot	Sq. Meters
Excellent Class A Office	$136.99	$1,474.01
Class A Industrial/ Manufacturing	$83.56	$899.11

[2]*See the Property Tax Rate Notes on page 314.*
[3]*See the Classification of Real Property and Tangible Personal Property table on page 316.*

	Sq. Foot	Sq. Meters
Class A Distribution Warehouse	$58.87	$633.44
Excellent Class C Single Family Residential	$105.31	$1,133.14

Average Electric Cost (Cents per KwH)

	1992
Residential	$0.971
Commercial	$0.1068
Industrial	$0.681
Average Price for a 3-bedroom Family House (in 1000's)	$86.0

Quality of Life

Climate

	Fahrenheit		Celsius	
	High	Low	High	Low
Winter	31	16	-1	-9
Spring	58	37	14	3
Summer	82	59	28	16
Autumn	63	41	17	5

Rainfall

	Inches	Millimeters
January	1.9	48
February	1.7	43
March	2.5	64
April	3.2	81
May	2.8	71
June	3.4	86
July	3.1	79
August	3.2	81
September	2.3	58
October	2.1	53
November	2.3	58
December	2.5	64

Cultural Highlights

Greektown
Henry Ford Museum & Greenfield Village
Historic Homes of the Auto Barons

Cultural Highlights (Continued)
 Motown Museum
 Detroit Institute of Arts

Leisure Highlights
 Fox Theatre
 Renaissance Center
 Belle Isle Park
 Detroit Zoological Park
 Cobo Hall

Crime

Rate per 100,000 Inhabitants	1991
Number of violent crimes	1,001.2
Number of property crimes	6,055.2

Average Wages for Selected Occupations

	Average Hiring Salary
Secretary (LR-3)	$28,288
Computer Systems Analyst III	$50,284
Computer Programmer III	$36,140
Engineer II	$37,128
Maintenance Machinist	$34,944

Indianapolis

INDIANA

Numerous metro areas in the Midwest like to refer to themselves as the "crossroads of the country," and Indianapolis can certainly advance a convincing argument as a contender. Seven spokes of four interstate highways intersect Indianapolis; the area has 30 motor freight carriers and is served by three freight railroads as well as by Amtrak. It is situated within 600 miles of half the U.S. population.

The status of Indianapolis as a business city has been boosted as a result of United Airlines' recent decision to build a $1 billion aircraft maintenance facility here. Other newcomers to the area include companies in businesses varying from video duplication to environmental testing to metal stamping, electric arc furnaces, windows, and seat belt/air bag production.

The largest employers in this nine-county central Indiana metro area of 1.4 million are government (federal and state, and public schools) and health care, but it also enjoys a balance of manufacturing, services, and wholesale/retail trade business activity. Nearly 17,000 residents work for 60 foreign-owned companies in the area, such as Veltri Stamping Corporation, Chemique Canada Ltd., and MacMillan Bloedel Bulk Packaging.

Housing choices in urban and suburban settings are varied, and residents enjoy a relatively short average commuting time (just over 20 minutes) to work. An average three-bedroom home sells for $84,600, and prime middle-management communities include Lockerbie, Eagle Creek, and Meridian-Kessler in the city, and Carmel, Geist, and Fishers in the suburbs.

Kids have an opportunity to participate in 34 organized sports in the area, with more than 300 sports opportunities offered by schools and community organizations. Other active recreational attractions include the 250-acre White River State Park, within walking distance from downtown; Brown County State Park; 113 city-owned parks; and 12 city-owned golf courses. Clubs have formed for bicycling, canoeing, and hiking enthusiasts. Among the better-known spectator sports here are the Indianapolis 500, the NFL Colts, and the NBA Indiana Pacers.

Dance, orchestral music, and theater are abundant in Indianapolis. One of its theater companies, the American Cabaret Theatre, in fact, relocated to Indianapolis from New York City. The Indianapolis Children's Museum is the world's largest, and the Eiteljorg Museum of American Indian & Western Art is one of the area's newest. For those yearning for a sense of Greenwich Village, the Broad Ripple neighborhood fills the bill with a variety of shops, clubs, cafes, and ethnic restaurants.

City Profile

Population in Thousands

1980	1,305.9
1990	1,380.5
1992	1,405.6
1995 Estimate	1,413.7

Socioeconomic Factors

Average Household Income

1980	$21,470
1991 Estimate	$36,873
% Change	71.7
1996 Projection	$44,310

Median Household Income

1980	$18,902
1991 Estimate	$30,262
% Change	60.1
1996 Projection	$35,872

Labor Force & Employment

	1993
Total Number of Persons in the Labor Force (in 1000's)	678.6
Total Number of Persons Employed (in 1000's)	642.6
Average Unemployment Rate	5.3%

Total Employment in Thousands by Sector

	1980	1992
Construction	23.4	33.4
Manufacturing	123.3	108.1
Transportation/Utilities	31.4	41.0
Trade	132.4	173.5
F.I.R.E.	38.4	53.6
Services	N/A	162.7
Government	89.4	102.7

Education

1992 Enrollment

Two Year College	4,155
Four Year Undergraduate	26,344
Four Year Graduate	6,263
Average SAT Score	N/A
Total Possible Score: 1600	
Average ACT Score	N/A
Total Possible Score: 36	

Business Environment

Selected Major Employers

Federal Government
State of Indiana
Eli Lilly and Co.
Indianapolis Public Schools
Allison Gas Turbine
Allison Transmission
Methodist Hospital
St. Vincent's
Community Hospitals

Media Profile

2 newspapers
26 radio stations
8 network television stations
2 cable television operators

State Taxes

Corporate Income/Franchise Tax	7.9%
Sales/Use Tax	5.0%
Individual Income Tax	3.4%
Unemployment Insurance Rate	2.70%

 City Taxes

County Tax	None
City Tax	None
Other Taxes	None

 Property Tax Rates [1,2]

$116.51 in $ per $1000

International Profile

Number of Foreign Banks	0
Number of Foreign-owned Businesses	54
Number of Persons Employed by Foreign-owned Businesses	7,278
Number of Daily International Flights	10

Real Estate

Occupancy Cost per Square Foot (Annual)

	Sq. Foot	Sq. Meters
Average Rental-Class A Office (Central Business District)	$15.85	$170.55
Average Rental-Class A Apartment	$6.94	$74.67
Average Rental-Warehouse	$3.65	$39.27

Construction Cost per Square Foot

	Sq. Foot	Sq. Meters
Excellent Class A Office	$123.65	$1,330.47
Class A Industrial/ Manufacturing	$75.43	$811.63

[1]See the Property Tax Rate Notes on page 314.
[2]See the Classification of Real Property and Tangible Personal Property table on page 316.

	Sq. Foot	Sq. Meters
Class A Distribution Warehouse	$53.14	$571.79
Excellent Class C Single Family Residential	$96.92	$1042.86

Average Electric Cost (Cents per KwH)

	1992
Residential	$0.579
Commercial	$0.583
Industrial	$0.417
Average Price for a 3-bedroom Family House (in 1000's)	$84.6

Quality of Life

Climate

	Fahrenheit		Celsius	
	High	Low	High	Low
Winter	34	18	1	-8
Spring	63	42	17	6
Summer	85	65	29	18
Autumn	66	43	19	6

Rainfall

	Inches	Millimeters
January	2.7	68
February	2.5	64
March	3.6	91
April	3.7	94
May	3.7	94
June	4.0	102
July	4.3	109
August	3.5	89
September	2.7	69
October	2.5	64
November	3.0	76
December	3.0	76

Cultural Highlights
Capitol Building
Conner Prairie Settlement
Eiteljorg Museum of American Indian & Western Art

Cultural Highlights (Continued)
 Indianapolis Museum of Art
 The Children's Museum of Indianapolis

Leisure Highlights
 Indianapolis City Center
 Indianapolis Motor Speedway &
 Indianapolis 500
 Indianapolis Zoo
 Madame Walker Urban Life Center
 Union Station

Crime

Rate per 100,000 Inhabitants	1991
Number of violent crimes	723.9
Number of property crimes	5,324.6

Average Wages for Selected Occupations

	Average Hiring Salary
Secretary (LR-3)	$24,170
Computer Systems Analyst III	$37,450
Computer Programmer III	$30,580
Engineer II	$27,580
Maintenance Machinist	$25,880

Kansas City

MISSOURI / KANSAS

It is not surprising that Kansas City, geographically located at the center of the United States, has grown as a transportation, manufacturing, warehousing, and distribution hub. The country's second largest rail center, Kansas City also has an extensive highway network, including eight federal, three interstate, and numerous state highways. In addition, 11 barge lines ship approximately 2 million tons of freight each year along the Missouri River.

This MSA covers five counties in Kansas and seven counties in Missouri. Its current population comprises 1.77 million and is expected to grow to 1.88 million by 1995.

Among the area's largest employers are Hallmark Cards, Inc., AT&T Microelectronics, Allied-Signal Aerospace, and Thomas J. Lipton Co. The service industry accounts for 25% of the area's nonagricultural jobs, and telemarketing has become an important element of Kansas City's economy. AT&T, Sprint, J.C. Penney Catalog Division, and Disney's Backstage Tele-Service Center are among the more prominent businesses in this group.

Approximately 2,191 people work for 71 foreign-owned companies here. Japan, Canada, and Germany are well represented among the newcomers to the area, including Pack America Corporation (from Osaka), Polytainers (from Toronto), and Hettich International GmbH (from Kirchlengern, Germany). Overall, unemployment is at a relatively low rate of 5.4%.

Housing prices vary from county to county in the area, largely because of differences in land costs. The average new house cost in Cass County, for example, is $70,000 to $80,000, whereas in Johnson County, strongest demand for new housing is in the $100,000 to $135,000 range.

Among Kansas City's extensive recreational facilities are Swope Park, the country's second largest urban park, which houses a theater, a zoo, two golf courses, and a braille trail. Numerous lakes and county and state parks are within a 60-minute drive from the city. In addition to offering dance, theater companies, and orchestral and chamber music, Kansas City is the home of the Nelson-Atkins Museum of Art, which has a comprehensive collection of Asian art.

City Profile

Population in Thousands

1980	1,589.0
1990	1,731.0
1992	1,774.0
1995 Estimate	1,881.0

Socioeconomic Factors

Average Household Income

1980	$21,667
1991 Estimate	$44,148
% Change	89.9
1996 Projection	$50,298

Median Household Income

1980	$18,968
1991 Estimate	$32,842
% Change	73.1
1996 Projection	$40,247

Labor Force & Employment

	1993
Total Number of Persons in the Labor Force (in 1000's)	886.9
Total Number of Persons Employed (in 1000's)	820.1
Average Unemployment Rate	5.4%

Total Employment in Thousands by Sector

	1980	1992
Construction	25.4	30.0
Manufacturing	119.8	104.3
Transportation/Utilities	52.6	64.1
Trade	161.7	196.5
F.I.R.E.	44.1	59.7
Services	129.9	203.1
Government	93.6	124.2

Education

1992 Enrollment:

Two Year College	27,654
Four Year Undergraduate	21,068
Four Year Graduate	8,572
Average SAT Score	979
Total Possible Score: 1600	
Average ACT Score	20.0
Total Possible Score: 36	

Business Environment

Selected Major Employers
Federal Government
United Telecom/Sprint
Hallmark Cards
State of Missouri
Kansas City Public Schools
Health Midwest
Trans World Airlines
University of Kansas Medical Center
Allied-Signal Aerospace
AT&T

Media Profile
1 newspaper
28 radio stations
7 network television stations
1 cable television operator

State Taxes[1]

Corporate Income/Franchise Tax	7.35%
Sales/Use Tax	6.9%
Individual Income Tax	7.75%
Unemployment Insurance Rate	3.51%

[1]See the State Tax Notes on page 308.

 City Taxes[2]

County Tax	1.00%
City Tax	.75%
Other Taxes	.50%

 Property Tax Rates [3,4]

$13.80 in $ per $1000

International Profile

Number of Foreign Banks	0
Number of Foreign-owned Businesses	71
Number of Persons Employed by Foreign-owned Businesses	2,191
Number of Daily International Flights	10

Real Estate

Occupancy Cost per Square Foot (Annual)

	Sq. Foot	Sq. Meters
Average Rental-Class A Office (Central Business District)	$14.67	$157.85
Average Rental-Class A Apartment	$7.51	$80.81
Average Rental-Warehouse	$3.90	$41.96

Construction Cost per Square Foot:

	Sq. Foot	Sq. Meters
Excellent Class A Office	$124.87	$1,343.60
Class A Industrial/ Manufacturing	$76.17	$819.59

	Sq. Foot	Sq. Meters
Class A Distribution Warehouse	$53.66	$577.38
Excellent Class C Single Family Residential	$95.99	$1,032.85

Average Electric Cost (Cents per KwH)

	1992
Residential	$0.866
Commercial	$0.692
Industrial	$0.550
Average Price for a 3-bedroom Family House (in 1000's)	$95.0

Quality of Life

Climate

	Fahrenheit		Celsius	
	High	Low	High	Low
Winter	37	19	3	-7
Spring	67	46	19	8
Summer	91	71	33	22
Autumn	71	49	22	9

Rainfall

	Inches	Millimeters
January	.9	23
February	1.1	28
March	2.1	53
April	2.7	69
May	3.4	86
June	4.1	104
July	3.5	89
August	3.2	81
September	3.3	84
October	2.5	64
November	1.2	31
December	1.1	28

Cultural Highlights
Arabia Steamboat Museum
Harry S. Truman Library
Kansas City Museum

[2]See the State-Local General Sales Tax Notes on page 310.
[3]See the Property Tax Rate Notes on page 314.
[4]See the Classification of Real Property and Tangible Personal Property table on page 316.

Cultural Highlights (Continued)
 Liberty Memorial Museum & Archives
 The Nelson-Atkins Museum of Art

Leisure Highlights
 Hallmark Visitors Center
 Kansas City Zoo
 Oceans of Fun
 The Woodlands Racetrack
 Worlds of Fun

Crime

Rate per 100,000 Inhabitants	1991
Number of violent crimes	1,175.0
Number of property crimes	6,303.5

Average Wages for Selected Occupations

	Average Hiring Salary
Secretary (LR-3)	$24,492
Computer Systems Analyst III	$49,712
Computer Programmer III	$36,556
Engineer II	$36,660
Maintenance Machinist	$32,198

Milwaukee

WISCONSIN

Beer may have made Milwaukee famous, but in reality breweries represent a very small segment of the area's economy. Machinery production, for example, constitutes one-third of manufacturing jobs, and high-tech production—including medical diagnostic instruments, computers, robotics, CAD/CAM processing, and advanced ceramics—has become central to Milwaukee's economic life.

Although still better known as a manufacturing center, Milwaukee's service businesses have been responsible for a higher percentage of recent job growth. In 1975 manufacturing employed one-third of Milwaukee's work force. By 1990 that segment had dropped to slightly under one-quarter, while services represented 27.5% of area jobs, a figure that is expected to increase to 31% by the year 2000.

This shift to services and the diversity of its industrial base have shielded Milwaukee from the magnitude of recessionary harm it suffered in the early 1980s. The current unemployment is 4.4%. Support for high-tech business is provided in numerous ways, including the efforts of a consortium dedicated to technology transfer, made up of the University of Wisconsin/Milwaukee, Marquette University, and the Milwaukee School of Engineering.

Located on the eastern shore of Lake Michigan, Milwaukee and the surrounding communities in this four-county MSA of 1.45 million residents offers a balance of cosmopolitan arts, culture, recreational opportunities, and an enlivened downtown with the convenience of relatively short commutes to work and affordably priced housing. The average price for a three-bedroom home is approximately $101,800.

Residents come from a variety of ethnic backgrounds (including German, Polish, Italian, African, Mexican, and Indian), which are celebrated during weekend ethnic festivals held in Maier Festival Park on Lake Michigan. Milwaukee also plays host to Summerfest and Winterfest, which present a variety of food, recreation, and entertainment.

Among the public/private partnership projects that have helped to renew the CBD are, The Grand Avenue, a shopping center; an exposition and convention center; the Milwaukee Center Theater District and other theater renovations; and several residential condominiums.

City Profile

 ## Population in Thousands

1980	1,397.0
1990	1,432.1
1992	1,452.9
1995 Estimate	1,475.0

 ## Socioeconomic Factors

Average Household Income

1980	$22,809
1991 Estimate	$46,387
% Change	103.4
1996 Projection	$56,546

Median Household Income

1980	$20,093
1991 Estimate	$37,654
% Change	87.4
1996 Projection	$45,888

 ## Labor Force & Employment

	1993
Total Number of Persons in the Labor Force (in 1000's)	775.3
Total Number of Persons Employed (in 1000's)	741.1
Average Unemployment Rate	4.4%

Total Employment in Thousands by Sector

	1980	1992
Construction	N/A	27.4
Manufacturing	206.7	164.5
Transportation/Utilities	34.5	36.4
Trade	144.3	169.4
F.I.R.E.	39.5	52.4
Services	N/A	220.6
Government	85.9	88.4

 ## Education

1992 Enrollment:

Two Year College	24,731
Four Year Undergraduate	39,683
Four Year Graduate	10,187
Average SAT Score	N/A
Total Possible Score: 1600	
Average ACT Score	19.3
Total Possible Score: 36	

 ## Business Environment

Selected Major Employers

Briggs & Stratton Corp.
WFSI-Milwaukee
Aurora Health Care Inc.
Wisconsin Bell Inc.
Allen-Bradley Co.
General Electric Co-Medical Systems & Other
A.O. Smith Corp.
Quad/Graphics Inc.
General Motors Corp.
Firstar Corp.

Media Profile

2 newspapers
28 radio stations
11 network television stations
1 cable television operator

 ## State Taxes[1]

Corporate Income/Franchise Tax	7.9%
Sales/Use Tax	5.5%
Individual Income Tax	6.93%
Unemployment Insurance Rate	3.05%

[1]See the State Tax Notes on page 308.

 City Taxes[2]

County Tax	.50%
City Tax	None
Other Taxes	None

 Property Tax Rates [3,4]

$38.35 in $ per $1000

 International Profile

Number of Foreign Banks	0
Number of Foreign-owned Businesses	72
Number of Persons Employed by Foreign-owned Businesses	4,513
Number of Daily International Flights	2

 Real Estate

Occupancy Cost per Square Foot (Annual)

	Sq. Foot	Sq. Meters
Average Rental-Class A Office (Central Business District)	$17.71	$190.56
Average Rental-Class A Apartment	$7.93	$85.33
Average Rental-Warehouse	$4.01	$43.15

Construction Cost per Square Foot

	Sq. Foot	Sq. Meters
Excellent Class A Office	$130.93	$1,408.81
Class A Industrial/Manufacturing	$79.87	$859.40

	Sq. Foot	Sq. Meters
Class A Distribution Warehouse	$56.27	$605.47
Excellent Class C Single Family Residential	$104.38	$1,123.13

Average Electric Cost (cents per KwH)

	1992
Residential	$0.711
Commercial	$0.605
Industrial	$0.411
Average Price for a 3-bedroom Family House (in 1000's)	$101.8

Quality of Life

Climate

	Fahrenheit		Celsius	
	High	Low	High	Low
Winter	26	11	-3	-12
Spring	54	36	12	2
Summer	80	61	27	16
Autumn	60	42	16	6

Rainfall

	Inches	Millimeters
January	1.6	41
February	1.3	33
March	2.6	66
April	3.4	86
May	2.7	69
June	3.6	91
July	3.5	89
August	3.1	79
September	2.9	74
October	2.3	58
November	1.9	48
December	2.0	51

Cultural Highlights

Discovery World Museum
Miller Brewing Company
Milwaukee Art Museum

[2]See the State-Local General Sales Tax Notes on page 310.
[3]See the Property Tax Rate Notes on page 314.
[4]See the Classification of Real Property and Tangible Personal Property table on page 316.

Cultural Highlights (Continued)
 Milwaukee Public Museum
 Mitchell Park Horticultural
 Conservatory/The Domes

Leisure Highlights
 Milwaukee County Zoo
 Pabst Mansion
 Sprecher Brewing Company
 Pabst Brewing Company

Crime

Rate per 100,000 Inhabitants	1991
Number of violent crimes	520.3
Number of property crimes	5,494.2

Average Wages for Selected Occupations

	Average Hiring Salary
Secretary (LR-3)	$25,168
Computer Systems Analyst III	$48,840
Computer Programmer III	$35,256
Engineer II	$37,700
Maintenance Machinist	$36,504

Minneapolis/St. Paul

MINNESOTA

Population growth in the Minneapolis/St. Paul metro area of 2.5 million residents (covering 11 counties in east-central Minnesota) may be modest by Sunbelt standards, but it is the fastest-growing area in the Midwest.

In addition to manufacturing (especially high tech—Minneapolis/St. Paul is the home of the first battery-powered heart pacemaker, as well as Cray Research's supercomputer business), this area's economy is balanced by health care, large retailers, banking and insurance companies, transportation, and utilities. Approximately 80% of residents over age 25 are high school graduates, and the area's unemployment rate is 5.3%.

Among the area's largest employers are 3M, Dayton Hudson, Health One, General Mills, Honeywell, Norwest, Unisys, U.S. West, and NWA. Smaller businesses are active here as well. Minneapolis/St. Paul ranks high in the nation in loans to small businesses and investments by venture capitalists. Minneapolis/St. Paul also has a tradition of corporate community-mindedness; many of the area's larger employers contribute 3% to 5% of their pretax earnings to charity.

Housing in the area ranges from luxury high-rise apartments and condominiums overlooking the Mississippi to restored historical mansions, renovated lofts, and lakeside and country club homes. Prime middle-management residential areas include Eden Prairie, Edina, Woodbury, and Eagan. The average price for a three-bedroom home is $110,200.

It is true that Minneapolis experiences long, snowy winters, but its annual snowfall rate is not the greatest in the United States, nor are its winter temperatures the coldest. The weather does allow for extensive winter sports activities, such as cross-country skiing, and the St. Paul Winter Carnival, featuring elaborately carved ice sculptures is much renowned. In warmer weather, the area's many lakes are focal points for boating and other water-oriented recreation.

The climate may also be a partial explanation for the growth of indoor retailing in the area, the most notable recently being the Mall of America, a 78-acre development large enough to house its own amusement park as well as a number of major anchor department stores. There is also a wealth of cultural activities available, ranging from the well-known Guthrie Theater and Walker Art Center to jazz and comedy clubs.

City Profile

Population in Thousands

1980	2,137.0
1990	2,464.0
1992	2,500.0
1995 Estimate	2,670.4

Socioeconomic Factors

Average Household Income

1980	$23,624
1991 Estimate	$45,538
% Change	92.8
1996 Projection	$55,485

Median Household Income

1980	$20,644
1991 Estimate	$37,448
% Change	81.4
1996 Projection	$45,617

Labor Force & Employment

	1993
Total Number of Persons in the Labor Force (in 1000's)	1,443.8
Total Number of Persons Employed (in 1000's)	1,367.2
Average Unemployment Rate	5.3%

Total Employment in Thousands by Sector

	1980	1992
Construction	46.0	46.6
Manufacturing	249.2	258.0
Transportation/Utilities	64.8	77.1
Trade	273.4	331.7
F.I.R.E.	70.8	101.3
Services	244.4	388.8
Government	161.2	191.8

Education

1992 Enrollment:

Two Year College	34,314
Four Year Undergraduate	75,453
Four Year Graduate	17,249
Average SAT Score	N/A
Total Possible Score: 1600	
Average ACT Score	20.8
Total Possible Score: 36	

Business Environment

Selected Major Employers

3M
Dayton Hudson
Health One
Honeywell
Lifespan
Norwest
Unisys
US West
Fairview Hospital
NWA

Media Profile

2 newspapers
36 radio stations
18 network television stations
1 cable television operator

State Taxes

Corporate Income/Franchise Tax	9.8%
Sales/Use Tax	7.5%
Individual Income Tax	8.5%
Unemployment Insurance Rate	2.00%

City Taxes[1]

County Tax	.50%
City Tax (Minneapolis Only)	.50%
Other Taxes	None

Property Tax Rates [2,3]

$101.68 in $ per $1000 Minneapolis
$109.00 in $ per $1000 St. Paul

International Profile

Number of Foreign Banks	1
Number of Foreign-owned Businesses	163
Number of Persons Employed by Foreign-owned Businesses	6,011
Number of Daily International Flights	36

Real Estate

Occupancy Cost per Square Foot (Annual)

	Sq. Foot	Sq. Meters
Average Rental-Class A Office (Central Business District)	$16.05	$172.70
Average Rental-Class A Apartment	$8.97	$96.52
Average Rental-Warehouse	$5.40	$58.10

Construction Cost per Square Foot

	Sq. Foot	Sq. Meters
Excellent Class A Office	$138.20	$1,487.03
Class A Industrial/ Manufacturing	$84.30	$907.07

	Sq. Foot	Sq. Meters
Class A Distribution Warehouse	$59.39	$639.04
Excellent Class C Single Family Residential	$107.17	$1,153.15

Average Electric Cost (Cents per KwH)

	1992
Residential	$0.691
Commercial	$0.589
Industrial	$0.428
Average Price for a 3-bedroom Family House (in 1000's)	$110.2

Quality of Life

Climate

	Fahrenheit		Celsius	
	High	Low	High	Low
Winter	20	2	-7	-17
Spring	56	36	13	2
Summer	83	63	28	17
Autumn	60	39	16	4

Rainfall

	Inches	Millimeters
January	.8	20
February	.9	23
March	1.7	43
April	2.1	53
May	3.2	81
June	4.1	104
July	3.5	89
August	3.6	91
September	2.5	64
October	1.9	48
November	1.3	33
December	.9	23

Cultural Highlights

Bell Museum of Natural History
Science Museum of Minnesota
Walker Art Center

[2]See the State-Local General Sales Tax Notes on page 310.
[3]See the Property Tax Rate Notes on page 314.
[4]See the Classification of Real Property and Tangible Personal Property table on page 316.

Cultural Highlights (Continued)
 Minneapolis Sculpture Garden
 State Capitol

Leisure Highlights
 Canterbury Downs Racetrack
 Ordway Music Theater
 Minneapolis Planetarium
 Minnesota Zoo
 The Guthrie Theater

Crime

Rate per 100,000 Inhabitants	1991
Number of violent crimes	470.0
Number of property crimes	5,102.9

Average Wages for Selected Occupations

	Average Hiring Salary
Secretary (LR-3)	$21,840
Computer Systems Analyst III	$42,120
Computer Programmer III	$31,616
Engineer II	$40,768
Maintenance Machinist	$28,600

St. Louis

MISSOURI

Although defense cutbacks have resulted in the loss of thousands of jobs at McDonnell Douglas, St. Louis's largest employer, the area has broadened its appeal sufficiently to withstand this turn of events. Service sector jobs (particularly health care), distribution facilities, auto parts manufacturing, regional corporate headquarters, and back office operations provide the area economy's current underpinning.

Home of Gateway Arch, the tallest monument in the United States, and located at the junction of the Missouri and Mississippi rivers, the St. Louis metro area covers 12 counties in eastern Missouri and western Illinois. Population is 2.5 million, which is estimated to grow by some 15,000 by 1995.

In addition to such Fortune 500 companies as Anheuser-Busch, Monsanto, Emerson Electric, and Ralston-Purina, many foreign-owned manufacturers are well represented in St. Louis. More than 2,800 people work for 68 foreign-owned companies in the area. Among those that have recently located here are the German companies MEMC and MG Industries Inc., and Bunge Corporation, a Dutch company.

Public/private partnerships have brought much new life to the CBD. Union Station, for example, a formerly closed train station, is now an active development, mixing hotels, restaurants, shops, and entertainment. A variety of urban housing is available, including high-rise apartments and renovated townhouses near the Mississippi. Prime suburban middle-management residential areas, such as Mehlville/Oakville, Kirkwood, University City/Olivette, and Sunset Hills, are within a 20- to 30-minute commute to the CBD. The average price for a three-bedroom home is $102,200.

Diversity in recreational attractions and events is the rule in St. Louis. Notable among them are the Six Flags amusement park, St. Louis Science Center, the Missouri Botanical Gardens (with the largest traditional Japanese garden in the United States), and Laumeier Sculpture Park, as well as the full gamut of cultural attractions. The area also offers a variety of riverboat cruises for dining and gambling.

City Profile

 ## Population in Thousands

1980	2,414.0
1990	2,492.0
1992	2,504.0
1995 Estimate	2,518.0

 ## Socioeconomic Factors

Average Household Income

1980	$21,373
1991 Estimate	$41,405
% Change	93.7
1996 Projection	$50,700

Median Household Income

1980	$18,654
1991 Estimate	$33,284
% Change	78.4
1996 Projection	$40,993

Labor Force & Employment

	1993
Total Number of Persons in the Labor Force (in 1000's)	1,249.3
Total Number of Persons Employed (in 1000's)	1,167.4
Average Unemployment Rate	6.6%

Total Employment in Thousands by Sector

	1980	1992
Construction	44.3	49.0
Manufacturing	239.0	200.4
Transportation/Utilities	72.7	77.2
Trade	229.2	276.3
F.I.R.E.	57.8	72.6
Services	217.8	333.6
Government	139.3	145.1

Education

1992 Enrollment:

Two Year College	53,047
Four Year Undergraduate	46,722
Four Year Graduate	18,372
Average SAT Score	801
Total Possible Score: 1600	
Average ACT Score	17.8
Total Possible Score: 36	

Business Environment

Selected Major Employers

McDonnell Douglas
Trans World Airlines
Schnuck Markets
Washington University
May Dept. Stores
St. Louis University
Anheuser-Busch
National Supermarkets
Monsanto

Media Profile

1 newspaper
27 radio stations
28 network television stations
4 cable television operators

State Taxes[1]

Corporate Income/Franchise Tax	5.0%
Sales/Use Tax	7.725%
Individual Income Tax	6.0%
Unemployment Insurance Rate	2.70%

[1]See the State Tax Notes on page 308.

City Taxes[2]

County Tax	None
City Tax	1.00%
Other Taxes	.50%

Property Tax Rates [3,4]

$60.28 in $ per $1000

International Profile

Number of Foreign Banks	0
Number of Foreign-owned Businesses	68
Number of Persons Employed by Foreign-owned Businesses	2,823
Number of Daily International Flights	16

Real Estate

Occupancy Cost per Square Foot (Annual)

	Sq. Foot	Sq. Meters
Average Rental-Class A Office (Central Business District)	$17.73	$190.77
Average Rental-Class A Apartment	$7.79	$83.82
Average Rental-Warehouse	$3.90	$41.85

Construction Cost per Square Foot

	Sq. Foot	Sq. Meters
Excellent Class A Office	$135.78	$1,460.99
Class A Industrial/ Manufacturing	$82.82	$891.14

[2]See the State-Local General Sales Tax Notes on page 310.
[3]See the Property Tax Rate Notes on page 314.
[4]See the Classification of Real Property and Tangible Personal Property table on page 316.

	Sq. Foot	Sq. Meters
Class A Distribution Warehouse	$58.35	$627.85
Excellent Class C Single Family Residential	$103.44	$1,113.01

Average Electric Cost (cents per KwH)

	1992
Residential	$0.778
Commercial	$0.646
Industrial	$0.523
Average Price for a 3-bedroom Family House (in 1000's)	$102.2

Quality of Life

Climate

	Fahrenheit		Celsius	
	High	Low	High	Low
Winter	38	20	3	-7
Spring	67	45	19	7
Summer	89	69	32	21
Autumn	69	47	21	8

Rainfall

	Inches	Millimeters
January	1.7	43
February	2.1	53
March	3.3	84
April	3.6	91
May	3.5	89
June	3.7	94
July	3.6	91
August	2.6	66
September	2.7	69
October	2.3	58
November	2.5	64
December	2.2	56

Cultural Highlights

Museum of Transportation
Saint Louis Art Museum
St. Louis Union Station

Cultural Highlights (Continued)
Missouri Botanical Garden
Jefferson National Expansion Memorial
Gateway Arch

Leisure Highlights
Anheuser-Busch Brewery Tour
Grant's Farm Tour
Six Flags Over Mid-America
Saint Louis Zoo

Crime

Rate per 100,000 Inhabitants	1991
Number of violent crimes	937.5
Number of property crimes	5,773.3

Average Wages for Selected Occupations

	Average Hiring Salary
Secretary (LR-3)	$25,428
Computer Systems Analyst III	$49,400
Computer Programmer III	$35,048
Engineer II	$35,932
Maintenance Machinist	$26,665

MOUNTAIN STATES

Overview

The metro areas of the Mountain States are as individualistic as the Old West itself. Their economies have proceeded along vastly different paths: from the dramatic, (formerly) energy-driven boom-and-bust cycles in Denver, to the sprawling, diverse growth of the Phoenix megalopolis, to the steady and methodical positioning of Salt Lake City as a high-tech center.

In many ways, California's losses have been the Mountain States' gain. The tremendous growth of the Las Vegas and Phoenix metro areas, for example, has been fueled in large measure by businesses and individuals seeking lower business occupancy and operating costs, as well as a lower cost of living than is currently available in some California markets.

The appeal of the Mountain States, however, is more complex than demographics. The grit, determination, and entrepreneurial spirit that founded the West is still very much in evidence. Mining—particularly for copper and silver—has long since been replaced as the region's key economic engine. The 1990s equivalent is high-tech industry. Computer software, biotechnology, and telecommunications have generated much of the job growth in several areas, such as Salt Lake City, Phoenix, Denver, and Colorado Springs.

At the same time, the burgeoning air, roadway, and rail transportation industries have generated growth for light manufacturing and distribution in these markets, particularly in Las Vegas, Phoenix, and Albuquerque. Many of these markets have free trade zones adjacent to their airports, and there is considerable airport expansion and construction under way to accommodate business and tourism growth. Denver's new airport, for example, will be larger than Disney World.

The Mountain States' almost relentlessly active style of life is another reason that the region continues to draw relatively young and well-educated people from other areas of the country. The expansiveness and uncommon natural beauty of the West is equalled by the quality and quantity of its recreational attractions: skiing, hiking, camping, river rafting, horseback riding, mountain biking, hunting, fishing, and more.

In fact, several of the metro areas covered in this section have been, and in some ways still are, perceived as destination resorts,

with an agreeable climate and an abundance of recreational and cultural attractions. These areas, however, have diversified beyond tourism; even Reno has been marketing itself as a regional hub for warehousing and distribution, within an overnight's reach of nearly 50 million people in the 11-state western region.

Two related factors are key to the Mountain States' future for business locations.

First, the region is not simply experiencing population growth; the population that is growing is young. Utah, for example, is projected to continue to have the youngest population in the United States, and its labor force is expected to grow at twice the national rate in the next decade. It is true that retirees have flocked to Las Vegas and Phoenix, but as a percentage of the total population in these markets, their numbers are no greater than the national average.

Second, many metro areas in this region are intensely focused on education. For the most part, test scores are higher than the national average and the percentage of students attending private school is low. Colorado, for example, ranks first in the number of adults with a college degree.

Several of these areas have significant additional resources to offer the business community. Sandia National Laboratories and Los Alamos National Laboratory, near Albuquerque, for example, can provide a range of cooperative efforts, including use of their facilities, personnel, and training. In the Phoenix metro area, Arizona State University, with an enrollment of 43,000, has had a strong impact on the area's economy. Cooperative efforts between the University and the business community can be established here too.

Housing costs in this region are generally lower than on the East and West Coasts, but there are significant differences within the region itself. As these markets wrestle with the issue of increasing infrastructure needs that accompany business and residential growth, the future of their tax rates remains an open question.

Albuquerque

NEW MEXICO

Albuquerque's history and culture are a unique mix of Indian, Spanish, and Anglo-American influences, and it has a long tradition as a center of trade and transportation—as a supply center, between 1850 and 1875 to the forts established in the Southwest, and as a key railroad stop after 1880.

Like its history and culture, Albuquerque's appeal is the result of a blend of disparate elements: the natural beauty of the Sandia mountains (offering hiking, camping, horseback riding, and skiing at the higher elevations); abundant artistic and cultural attractions in this city and in Santa Fe (an hour's drive away); hot air ballooning (the International Balloon Fiesta draws more than one million visitors over a 9-day period annually); extensive hunting and fishing (most fishing waters in the state are publicly owned); and access to many state and national parks and monuments.

Although Albuquerque's economy is dominated by government, military, and educational institutions, the wholesale/retail trade and service sectors have grown significantly since 1980. The rise in health care services has been the most dramatic; among the three largest employers in the area are Presbyterian Health Care, Lovelace Medical Care, and UNM Medical Center. Overall, unemployment is below the national average, at 4.6%.

At present there are signs that the economy is diversifying. Relocations and new businesses in the area include insurance, telemarketing, and an array of manufacturing firms involved in paper products, postal machines, optical instruments, scanning devices, and aircraft materials.

Industrial companies here have the benefit of two formidable resources: Sandia National Laboratories and Los Alamos National Laboratory, for whom technology transfer is a goal. Cooperative efforts range from use of their facilities, R&D agreements, personnel exchanges, on–and off-site training, and, in some instances, access to proprietary intellectual property.

City Profile

Population in Thousands

1980	420.2
1990	480.6
1992	526.4
1995 Estimate	538

Socioeconomic Factors

Average Household Income

1980	$19,670
1991 Estimate	$37,036
% Change	88.3
1996 Projection	$45,159

Median Household Income

1980	$16,460
1991 Estimate	$29,296
% Change	78.0
1996 Projection	$35,357

Labor Force & Employment

	1993
Total Number of Persons in the Labor Force (in 1000's)	275.2
Total Number of Persons Employed (in 1000's)	262.6
Average Unemployment Rate	4.6%

Total Employment in Thousands by Sector

	1980	1992
Construction	17.2	12.3
Manufacturing	12.6	20.0
Transportation/Utilities	11.5	12.2
Trade	33.6	61.0
Finance/Real Estate	10.6	14.3
Services	42.5	81.9
Government	42.0	51.3

Education

1992 Enrollment

Two Year College	13,117
Four Year Undergraduate	16,594
Four Year Graduate	7,530
Average SAT Score	N/A
Total Possible Score: 1600	
Average ACT Score	21.2
Total Possible Score: 36	

Business Environment

Selected Major Employers

University of New Mexico
Albuquerque Public School
Sandia Nat'l Labs
City of Albuquerque
Presbyterian Health Care
Lovelace Medical Center
Kirkland AFB
State of New Mexico
UNM Medical Center

Media Profile

2 newspapers
29 radio stations
9 network television stations
1 cable television operator

State Taxes

Corporate Income/Franchise Tax	7.6%
Sales/Use Tax	6.875%
Individual Income Tax	8.5%
Unemployment Insurance Rate	2.70%

City Taxes[1]

County Tax	.375%
City Tax	.4375%
Other Taxes	None

Property Tax Rates [2]

$29.165 in $ per $1000

International Profile

Number of Foreign Banks	0
Number of Foreign-owned Businesses	8
Number of Persons Employed by Foreign-owned Businesses	28
Number of Daily International Flights	2

Real Estate

Occupancy Cost per Square Foot (Annual)

	Sq. Foot	Sq. Meters
Average Rental-Class A Office (Central Business District)	$12.00	$129.12
Average Rental-Class A Apartment	$7.64	$82.21
Average Rental-Warehouse	$4.50	$48.42

Construction Cost per Square Foot

	Sq. Foot	Sq. Meters
Excellent Class A Office	$112.74	$1,213.08
Class A Industrial/ Manufacturing	$68.09	$732.65

	Sq. Foot	Sq. Meters
Class A Distribution Warehouse	$47.97	$516.16
Excellent Class C Single Family Residential	$87.60	$942.58

Average Electric Cost (Cents per KwH)

	1992
Residential	$0.958
Commercial	$0.897
Industrial	$0.640
Average Price for a 3-bedroom Family House (in 1000's)	$152.0

Quality of Life

Climate

	Fahrenheit		Celsius	
	High	Low	High	Low
Winter	51	26	8	-6
Spring	81	53	22	4
Summer	90	64	34	18
Autumn	68	40	22	6

Rainfall

	Inches	Millimeters
January	.4	10
February	.4	10
March	.5	13
April	.4	10
May	.5	13
June	.5	13
July	1.3	33
August	1.5	38
September	.9	23
October	.9	23
November	.4	10
December	.5	13

Cultural Highlights

Albuquerque Museum of Art, History & Science
New Mexico Ballet Company

[1]See the State-Local General Sales Tax Notes on page 310.
[2]See the Classification of Real Property and Tangible Personal Property Table on page 316.

Cultural Highlights (Continued)
Keller Hall-Fine Arts Center
Albuquerque Civic Light Opera
Association

Leisure Highlights
Old Town
Rio Grands Zoological Park
International Balloon Festival
Sandia Peak Aerial Tramway

Crime
Rate per 100,000 Inhabitants	1991
Number of violent crimes	1,198.2
Number of property crimes	7,786.6

Average Wages for Selected Occupations
	Average Hiring Salary
Secretary (LR-3)	$22,360
Computer Systems Analyst III	$50,793
Computer Programmer III	$35,360
Engineer II	$31,928
Maintenance Machinist	$27,851

Colorado Springs

COLORADO

Long known as a destination resort, with the Broadmoor Resort located here, Colorado Springs is within a few hours' drive of 35 ski resorts. The area also offers the full panoply of Mountain States recreational attractions: hiking, mountain biking, river rafting, horseback riding, hang gliding, hot air ballooning, rock climbing, hunting, and fishing. The U.S. Olympic Committee, U.S. Olympic Training Center, and numerous sports federations make their homes here.

This relatively small metro area—one county with fewer than 500,000 residents—is noted for its educational status as well as for its ample recreational attractions. For example, test scores are higher than the national average, fewer than 3% of students in the area attend private schools, and more than 80% of its high school graduates attend college.

Although Fort Carson, Peterson Air Force Base, and the Air Force Academy have been predominant economic forces in Colorado Springs, recent relocations by such companies as MCI, Apple Computer, and Future Call West are emblematic of the area's appeal as a high-tech and telecommunications center. Many companies relocating to the area have come from the Midwest.

Middle-management residential areas have experienced growth in the northwest and southwest areas, and the average three-bedroom house is priced at $93,000.

Colorado Springs' nearest hub airport is Denver, approximately an hour and a quarter, drive away. However, it has its own airport, too, with direct flights to Denver, Salt Lake City, Phoenix, Dallas, St. Louis, and Chicago.

Just as Fort Worth is establishing its own identity and cultural life apart from Dallas, Colorado Springs is doing much the same in relation to Denver. For example, it has two theater groups, its own opera company, orchestra, and museum.

City Profile

 ## Population in Thousands

1980	309.4
1990	397.0
1992	419.5
1995 Estimate	464.5

$ Socioeconomic Factors

Average Household Income

1980	$19,506
1991 Estimate	$38,795
% Change	98.9
1996 Projection	$48,034

Median Household Income

1980	$16,461
1991 Estimate	$30,476
% Change	85.1
1996 Projection	$37,631

 ## Labor Force & Employment

	1993
Total Number of Persons in the Labor Force (in 1000's)	190.5
Total Number of Persons Employed (in 1000's)	176.6
Average Unemployment Rate	7.3%

Total Employment in Thousands by Sector

	1980	1992
Construction	17.0	7.3
Manufacturing	6.2	21.6
Transportation/Utilities	4.7	6.5
Trade	25.7	37.8
Finance/Real Estate	5.6	8.6
Services	25.2	40.5
Government	23.4	38.1

Education

1992 Enrollment

Two Year College	5,435
Four Year Undergraduate	9,614
Four Year Graduate	2,555
Average SAT Score	1,007
Total Possible Score: 1600	
Average ACT Score	22.2
Total Possible Score: 36	

Business Environment

Selected Major Employers
Fort Carson
Peterson AFB
Air Force Academy
School District 11
Penrose Healthcare
D.E.C.
Memorial Hospital
MCI
Current Inc.
Hewlett Packard

Media Profile
1 newspaper
19 radio stations
6 network television stations
1 cable television operator

% State Taxes[1]

Corporate Income/Franchise Tax	5.1%
Sales/Use Tax	8.0%
Individual Income Tax	5.0%
Unemployment Insurance Rate	2.90%

[1]*See the State Tax Table Notes on page 308.*

City Taxes[2]

County Tax	1.00%
City Tax	2.50%
Other Taxes	None

Property Tax Rates [3]

$58.026 in $ per $1000

International Profile

Number of Foreign Banks	0
Number of Foreign-owned Businesses	9
Number of Persons Employed by Foreign-owned Businesses	62
Number of Daily International Flights	0

Real Estate

Occupancy Cost per Square Foot (Annual)

	Sq. Foot	Sq. Meters
Average Rental-Class A Office (Central Business District)	$12.50	$134.50
Average Rental-Class A Apartment	$5.64	$60.69
Average Rental-Warehouse	$4.00	$43.04

Construction Cost per Square Foot

	Sq. Foot	Sq. Meters
Excellent Class A Office	$120.02	$1,291.41
Class A Industrial/Manufacturing	$72.48	$779.88

	Sq. Foot	Sq. Meters
Class A Distribution Warehouse	$51.06	$549.40
Excellent Class C Single Family Residential	$88.53	$952.58

Average Electric Cost (Cents per KwH)

	1992
Residential	$0.507
Commercial	$0.490
Industrial	$0.400
Average Price for a 3-bedroom Family House (in 1000's)	$93.0

Quality of Life

Climate

	Fahrenheit		Celsius	
	High	Low	High	Low
Winter	43	16	6	-9
Spring	61	34	16	1
Summer	86	57	31	15
Autumn	67	37	19	3

Rainfall

	Inches	Millimeters
January	.5	13
February	.7	18
March	1.2	31
April	1.8	46
May	2.5	64
June	1.6	41
July	1.9	48
August	1.2	38
September	1.2	31
October	1.0	25
November	.8	20
December	.6	15

Cultural Highlights

Pro Rodeo Hall of Champions & Museum of the American Cowboy

Hall of Presidents

[2]See the State-Local General Sales Tax Notes on page 310.
[3]See the Classification of Real Property and Tangible Personal Property table on page 316.

Cultural Highlights (Continued)
 El Domar Carriage House Museum
 Colorado Springs Civic Theatre
 Colorado Springs Fine Art Center

Leisure Highlights
 Colorado Opera Festival
 Sport Festival
 The Fine Art Festival
 The Headquarter of the Professional
 Rodeo Cowboys Association (PRCA)

Crime

Rate per 100,000 Inhabitants	1991
Number of violent crimes	422.4
Number of property crimes	5,780.4

Average Wages for Selected Occupations

	Average Hiring Salary
Secretary (LR-3)	$19,448
Computer Systems Analyst III	$53,196
Computer Programmer III	$36,140
Engineer II	$38,948
Maintenance Machinist	$27,809

Denver

Denver is in the unique position of functioning, for many practical business purposes, like a Midwest city while offering the recreational benefits and life-style that Mountain States' residents relish. Although it is within a few hours' drive of camping, hiking, horseback riding, mountain biking, and what many believe is the best skiing in the United States, Denver's own high plains location protects it from very harsh weather.

Denver's location—literally 350 miles away from the center of the United States—also accounts for its position as a major airline hub and distribution center. That position will get a boost with the opening of the new Denver International Airport scheduled for opening in 1994-1995, some 24 miles from downtown, which will be larger than O'Hare and Dallas/Fort Worth combined.

Denver has become a significant telecommunications center, with U.S. West and AT&T among the top private employers in the area. Aerospace, technology, and manufacturing have a significant presence as well. Oil and gas, which were a major factor in the city's economy in the early 1980s, now account for about 1% of employment in the metro area.

Metro area residents take education and culture as seriously as they take recreation. Denver ranks second among large U.S. cities in the median number of school years completed by its residents, and Colorado itself ranks first in the number of adults with a college degree. Less than 10% of the school population attends private schools.

There are some 180 arts organizations in Scientific and Cultural Facilities District in the six-county area. The District is funded through a one-tenth of 1% sales tax. Its tradition of live theater dates back to touring companies in the 1880s and 1890s, and the Denver Performing Arts Complex is the second largest performing arts center in the country.

City Profile

 Population in Thousands

1980	1,618.5
1990	1,848.3
1992	1,901.9
1995 Estimate	1,974.6

 Socioeconomic Factors

Average Household Income

1980	$23,474
1991 Estimate	$40,721
% Change	73.5
1996 Projection	$49,069

Median Household Income

1980	$20,135
1991 Estimate	$33,555
% Change	66.7
1996 Projection	$40,778

 Labor Force & Employment

	1993
Total Number of Persons in the Labor Force (in 1000's)	894.8
Total Number of Persons Employed (in 1000's)	838.0
Average Unemployment Rate	6.4%

Total Employment in Thousands by Sector

	1980	1992
Construction	46.2	40.6
Manufacturing	124.3	90.6
Transportation/Utilities	55.5	71.5
Trade	192.4	211.0
Finance/Real Estate	54.0	66.8
Services	168.6	245.3
Government	138.2	136.4

 Education

1992 Enrollment

Two Year College	22,904
Four Year Undergraduate	29,948
Four Year Graduate	9,657
Average SAT Score	951
Total Possible Score: 1600	
Average ACT Score	20.0
Total Possible Score: 36	

 Business Environment

Selected Major Employers

US West
Martin Marietta
AT&T
Adolph Coors Co.
EG&G
Continental Airlines
United Airlines
Storage Tek
King Soopers
IBM

Media Profile

2 newspapers
32 radio stations
11 network television stations
1 cable television operator

 State Taxes[1]

Corporate Income/Franchise Tax	5.1%
Sales/Use Tax	8.0%
Individual Income Tax	5.0%
Unemployment Insurance Rate	2.70%

[1]See the State Tax Table Notes on page 308.

 City Taxes[2]

County Tax	None
City Tax	3.50%
Other Taxes	.80%

Property Tax Rates [3]

$67.375 in $ per $1000

International Profile

Number of Foreign Banks	1
Number of Foreign-owned Businesses	182
Number of Persons Employed by Foreign-owned Businesses	8,744
Number of Daily International Flights	50

Real Estate

Occupancy Cost per Square Foot (Annual)

	Sq. Foot	Sq. Meters
Average Rental-Class A Office (Central Business District)	$13.85	$149.03
Average Rental-Class A Apartment	$7.35	$79.09
Average Rental-Warehouse	$3.16	$34.00

Construction Cost per Square Foot

	Sq. Foot	Sq. Meters
Excellent Class A Office	$118.81	$1,278.39
Class A Industrial/Manufacturing	$71.75	$772.03

	Sq. Foot	Sq. Meters
Class A Distribution Warehouse	$50.55	$543.92
Excellent Class C Single Family Residential	$89.46	$962.59

Average Electric Cost (Cents per KwH)

	1992
Residential	$0.716
Commercial	$0.550
Industrial	$0.462
Average Price for a 3-bedroom Family House (in 1000's)	$130.0

 Quality of Life

Climate

	Fahrenheit		Celsius	
	High	Low	High	Low
Winter	43	16	6	-9
Spring	61	34	16	1
Summer	86	57	31	15
Autumn	67	37	19	3

Rainfall

	Inches	Millimeters
January	.5	13
February	.7	18
March	1.2	31
April	1.8	46
May	2.5	64
June	1.6	41
July	1.9	48
August	1.5	38
September	1.2	31
October	1.0	25
November	.8	20
December	.6	15

Cultural Highlights

Buffalo Bill's Memorial Museum & Gravesite
Colorado History Museum
Denver Museum of Natural History

[2]*See the State-Local General Sales Tax Notes on page 310.*
[3]*See the Classification of Real Property and Tangible Personal Property table on page 316.*

Cultural Highlights (Continued)
 U.S. Mint
 Colorado State Capitol Building

Leisure Highlights
 Red Rocks Amphitheatre
 Coors Brewery Tours
 Denver Center for the Performing Arts
 Larimer Square
 Denver Merchandise Mart Complex

Crime
Rate per 100,000 Inhabitants — **1991**

	1991
Number of violent crimes	730.1
Number of property crimes	5,890.7

Average Wages for Selected Occupations

	Average Hiring Salary
Secretary (LR-3)	$24,492
Computer Systems Analyst III	$49,556
Computer Programmer III	$36,348
Engineer II	$38,220
Maintenance Machinist	N/A

Las Vegas

NEVADA

Las Vegas has enjoyed a dramatic increase in population since 1980 (although the rate has slowed in the 1990s), giving the area something of a "boom town" feeling beyond the boundaries of its better-known casinos. Retirees have accounted for much of Las Vegas' in-migration, although as a group they comprise a lower percentage of its population than the national average. The largest age group is 25–34.

Without its stage makeup and glitz, Las Vegas emerges as a no-nonsense location for light manufacturing, which accounts for more than half of the new jobs in the area. Warehousing and distribution have grown, as has the motion picture and television production industry; Las Vegas accounts for some two-thirds of the revenues generated by this business in the state.

A perennial favorite for conventions and exhibitions, Las Vegas is closer to several major markets in Arizona and California than it is to Reno. Its hub airport, McCarran International, is in the midst of a $1 billion expansion plan, including roadway improvements and gate additions and construction of a 155-acre air cargo center. The Federal Aviation Administration has projected that McCarran will become the eleventh busiest airport in the United States by 2005.

Business and civic leaders have set their sights beyond the continental United States for business prospects. Statewide, exports have been increasing in the categories of primary metal products, scientific instruments, machinery, transportation equipment, and apparel. Las Vegas has become home to numerous international companies, including several Japanese-owned hotels and casinos, Canadian mining and manufacturing companies, and European manufacturing companies.

To accommodate the needs of a growing population, Clark County has seen the addition of nearly 50 new schools. College entrance exam scores are the same or higher than national averages, and about two-thirds of the district's graduates go on to higher education. There are also vocational/occupational programs in 24 areas of specialization.

City Profile

 ## Population in Thousands

1980	436.1
1990	741.5
1992	893.3
1995 Estimate	962.8

 ## Socioeconomic Factors

Average Household Income

1980	$21,822
1991 Estimate	$38,036
% Change	74.3
1996 Projection	$45,493

Median Household Income

1980	$18,444
1991 Estimate	$30,975
% Change	67.9
1996 Projection	$36,967

 ## Labor Force & Employment

	1993
Total Number of Persons in the Labor Force (in 1000's)	428.1
Total Number of Persons Employed (in 1000's)	399.5
Average Unemployment Rate	6.7%

Total Employment in Thousands by Sector

	1980	1992
Construction	14.1	27.0
Manufacturing	6.9	10.8
Transportation/Utilities	13.2	20.1
Trade	45.8	81.0
Finance/Real Estate	10.3	19.4
Services	104.5	188.5
Government	25.9	44.9

 ## Education

1992 Enrollment

Two Year College	11,069
Four Year Undergraduate	10,260
Four Year Graduate	2,587
Average SAT Score	924
Total Possible Score: 1600	
Average ACT Score	21.0
Total Possible Score: 36	

 ## Business Environment

Selected Major Employers

Circus Circus Enterprises
Hilton Nevada Corp.
Barbary Coast Hotels and Casino
El Rancho Hotel and Casino
Golden Gate Hotel Casino
Showboat, Inc.
Caesars Palace
ATI Medical
United Gaming

Media Profile

2 newspapers
29 radio stations
8 network television stations
1 cable television operator

 ## State Taxes

Corporate Income/Franchise Tax	0.0%
Sales/Use Tax	7.0%
Individual Income Tax	0.0%
Unemployment Insurance Rate	2.95%

City Taxes[1]

County Tax	.50%
City Tax	None
Other Taxes	None

Property Tax Rates [2,3]

$29.227 in $ per $1000

International Profile

Number of Foreign Banks	0
Number of Foreign-owned Businesses	32
Number of Persons Employed by Foreign-owned Businesses	525
Number of Daily International Flights	4

Real Estate

Occupancy Cost per Square Foot (Annual)

	Sq. Foot	Sq. Meters
Average Rental-Class A Office (Central Business District)	$14.75	$158.71
Average Rental-Class A Apartment	$7.75	$83.39
Average Rental-Warehouse	$4.39	$47.23

Construction Cost per Square Foot

	Sq. Foot	Sq. Meters
Excellent Class A Office	$135.78	$1,460.99
Class A Industrial/Manufacturing	$82.00	$882.23

[1]See the State-Local General Sales Tax Notes on page 310.
[2]See the Property Tax Rate Notes on page 314.
[3]See the Classification of Real Property and Tangible Personal Property table on page 316.

	Sq. Foot	Sq. Meters
Class A Distribution Warehouse	$57.77	621.61
Excellent Class C Single Family Residential	$102.51	$1,103.01

Average Electric Cost (Cents per KwH)

	1992
Residential	$0.557
Commercial	$0.622
Industrial	$0.586
Average Price for a 3-bedroom Family House (in 1000's)	$127.0

Quality of Life

Climate

	Fahrenheit		Celsius	
	High	Low	High	Low
Winter	56	33	13	1
Spring	77	50	25	10
Summer	105	76	41	24
Autumn	82	54	28	12

Rainfall

	Inches	Millimeters
January	.5	13
February	.5	13
March	.4	10
April	.2	5
May	.2	5
June	.1	3
July	.5	13
August	.5	13
September	.3	8
October	.3	8
November	.4	10
December	.3	8

Cultural Highlights

Las Vegas Strip
LasVegas Art Museum
Las Vegas Natural History Museum

Cultural Highlights (Continued)
Liberace Museum
Ripley's Believe It or Not Museum

Leisure Highlights
Bally's Casino Resort
Guinness World of Records Museum
Ceasars Palace
Cashman Field Center

Crime

Rate per 100,000 Inhabitants	1991
Number of violent crimes	788.1
Number of property crimes	6,235.5

Average Wages for Selected Occupations

	Average Hiring Salary
Secretary (LR-3)	$23,920
Computer Systems Analyst III	$45,084
Computer Programmer III	$32,916
Engineer II	N/A
Maintenance Machinist	$34,902

Phoenix

ARIZONA

Like Las Vegas, Phoenix has experienced a population boom since 1970; between 1970 and 1990, it has jumped, in population, from thirty-third to twentieth largest metro area in the United States. Although much of the population growth is fueled by retirees, the percentage of people over 65 in Phoenix is comparable to the national average.

In stark contrast to the agelessness of its surrounding desert and mountains, the Phoenix area's rapid growth has meant that much of its housing, infrastructure, and commercial facilities are relatively new. About one-third of the housing in Maricopa County, for example, has been built in the past 10 years.

The area's amenable climate and proximity to the Grand Canyon and other singular natural attractions, as well as abundant sports and recreational attractions, have made Phoenix an international destination resort. These elements, and a reasonable cost of living (home prices are roughly comparable to the Denver area), have also drawn relatively young and well-educated people to the area. The presence of Arizona State University, the third largest university in the United States, is also key to the area's economy.

Maricopa County's economy is diverse; in addition to travel and tourism, it is based on manufacturing, government, wholesaling and distribution (markets with a total population of more than 10 million are within overnight service, and Sky Harbor International Airport is a regional hub), services, and construction. Nearly half of all manufacturing employment in Maricopa County is in computers, components, aerospace, instrumentation, and telecommunications.

Maricopa County is also growing as a regional financial services center. It has recently attracted several large credit card and data centers such as Bank America, Security Pacific Bankcard, and Chase Manhattan Bank. Popular with Japanese tourists, Phoenix is emerging as an international business center. Nearly one hundred and forty foreign-owned companies are located in the area, including dozens of high-tech firms.

City Profile

Population in Thousands

1980	1,509.2
1990	2,122.1
1992	2,212.0
1995 Estimate	2,431.0

Socioeconomic Factors

Average Household Income

1980	$21,193
1991 Estimate	$42,158
% Change	98.9
1996 Projection	$51,468

Median Household Income

1980	$18,063
1991 Estimate	$33,254
% Change	84.1
1996 Projection	$40,923

Labor Force & Employment

	1993
Total Number of Persons in the Labor Force (in 1000's)	1,038.1
Total Number of Persons Employed (in 1000's)	972.9
Average Unemployment Rate	6.3%

Total Employment in Thousands by Sector

	1980	1992
Construction	50.6	53.2
Manufacturing	114.0	127.7
Transportation/Utilities	30.7	56.5
Trade	162.0	247.0
Finance/Real Estate	44.9	74.4
Services	132.8	286.6
Government	100.8	143.1

Education

1992 Enrollment:

Two Year College	70,894
Four Year Undergraduate	32,021
Four Year Graduate	14,943
Average SAT Score	917
Total Possible Score: 1600	
Average ACT Score	17.3
Total Possible Score: 36	

Business Environment

Selected Major Employers

State of Arizona
Motorola
Samaritan Health Systems
City of Phoenix
Maricopa County
Allied-Signal
Honeywell
America West
Mesa Public Schools
American Express

Media Profile

2 newspapers
38 radio stations
11 network television stations
2 cable television operators

% State Taxes

Corporate Income/Franchise Tax	9.3%
Sales/Use Tax	8.5%
Individual Income Tax	7.0%
Unemployment Insurance Rate	2.70%

 City Taxes[1]

County Tax	.50%
City Tax	1.20%
Other Taxes	None

Property Tax Rates [2,3]

$130.80 in $ per $1000

International Profile

Number of Foreign Banks	1
Number of Foreign-owned Businesses	134
Number of Persons Employed by Foreign-owned Businesses	2,299
Number of Daily International Flights	22

Real Estate

Occupancy Cost per Square Foot (Annual)

	Sq. Foot	Sq. Meters
Average Rental-Class A Office (Central Business District)	$16.13	$173.56
Average Rental-Class A Apartment	$6.85	$73.71
Average Rental-Warehouse	$3.27	$35.19

Construction Cost per Square Foot

	Sq. Foot	Sq. Meters
Excellent Class A Office	$113.96	$1,226.21
Class A Industrial/ Manufacturing	$68.82	$740.50

	Sq. Foot	Sq. Meters
Class A Distribution Warehouse	$48.48	$521.64
Excellent Class C Single Family Residential	$86.67	$932.57

Average Electric Cost (Cents per KwH)

	1992
Residential	$0.1069
Commercial	$0.915
Industrial	$0.622
Average Price for a 3-bedroom Family House (in 1000's)	$93.5

 Quality of Life

Climate

	Fahrenheit		Celsius	
	High	Low	High	Low
Winter	65	39	18	4
Spring	83	53	28	12
Summer	105	80	41	27
Autumn	88	59	31	15

Rainfall

	Inches	Millimeters
January	.7	18
February	.6	15
March	.8	20
April	.3	8
May	.1	3
June	.1	3
July	.8	20
August	1.2	31
September	.7	18
October	.5	13
November	.5	13
December	.8	20

Cultural Highlights
Desert Botanical Garden
Frank Lloyd Wright's Taliesin West
Heritage Square

[1]See the State-Local General Sales Tax Notes on page 310.
[2]See the Property Tax Rate Notes on page 314.
[3]See the Classification of Real Property and Tangible Personal Property table on page 316.

Cultural Highlights (Continued)
 Pueblo Grande Museum & Cultural Park
 The Heard Museum

Leisure Highlights
 Fiesta Bowl
 Phoenix International Raceway

Crime

Rate per 100,000 Inhabitants	1991
Number of violent crimes	771.4
Number of property crimes	7,408.0

Average Wages for Selected Occupations

	Average Hiring Salary
Secretary (LR-3)	$20,000
Computer Systems Analyst III	$44,700
Computer Programmer III	$38,400
Engineer II	$38,500
Maintenance Machinist	$24,300

Reno

NEVADA

The one-county Reno MSA is home to Lake Tahoe, Squaw Valley, more than a dozen other ski resorts, and numerous historic sites, including Virginia City, now a ghost town and site of what was the richest mining strike of the nineteenth century.

Added to these attractions in Reno are several well-known gaming casinos. Gaming represents Reno's largest private employer, but as it has become more widespread in other parts of the country, Reno has made a concerted effort to broaden its own economic and life-style appeal by sponsoring a variety of special events, such as an annual hot air balloon race, rodeos, a country/western music festival and a Cinco de Mayo festival.

In the past few years, the downtown area has undergone considerable revitalization, and a $100 million National Bowling Stadium is slated to begin hosting national bowling tournaments in 1995.

Reno has also become increasingly attractive as a manufacturing, warehousing, and distribution center. Freight can be shipped overnight to 80% of the western states, and next-day service is available to the others. Infrastructure improvements include an airport expansion, which will add a new runway to Reno Cannon International Airport.

Other area infrastructure improvements have focused on schools, with the addition of eight new elementary schools, one new middle school, and one new high school in the district. Students scores on college board exams are higher than the national average, and 4% or fewer students attend private schools.

A "Partners in Education" program has resulted in more than $1 million in contributions, through 600 partnerships with local businesses, corporations, individuals, clubs, and foundations. A new districtwide occupational center provides training in a number of areas in which Reno-based businesses have employee needs.

City Profile

 Population in Thousands

1980	193.8
1990	257.1
1992	266.5
1995 Estimate	283.0

 Socioeconomic Factors

Average Household Income

1980	$23,589
1991 Estimate	$41,040
% Change	74.0
1996 Projection	$49,266

Median Household Income

1980	$19,855
1991 Estimate	$33,149
% Change	67.0
1996 Projection	$40,067

 Labor Force & Employment

	1993
Total Number of Persons in the Labor Force (in 1000's)	141.6
Total Number of Persons Employed (in 1000's)	131.0
Average Unemployment Rate	7.5%

Total Employment in Thousands by Sector

	1980	1992
Construction	7.2	7.0
Manufacturing	8.1	9.0
Transportation/Utilities	8.1	9.5
Trade	24.6	33.6
Finance/Real Estate	6.1	7.1
Services	43.2	58.0
Government	16.1	19.7

Education

1992 Enrollment:

Two Year College	7,688
Four Year Undergraduate	7,720
Four Year Graduate	2,229
Average SAT Score	972
Total Possible Score: 1600	
Average ACT Score	21.4
Total Possible Score: 36	

Business Environment

Selected Major Employers
Washoe Co. Schools
Washoe Med. Cntr.
John Ascuaga's Nugget
Univ. of Nevada
Harrah's Reno
Reno Hilton
Eldorado Hotel
Circus Circus
County of Washoe
St. Mary's Hosp.

Media Profile
1 newspaper
27 radio stations
7 network television stations
1 cable television operator

State Taxes

Corporate Income/Franchise Tax	0.0%
Sales/Use Tax	7.0%
Individual Income Tax	0.0%
Unemployment Insurance Rate	3.00%

City Taxes[1]

County Tax	.50%
City Tax	None
Other Taxes	None

Property Tax Rates [2,3]

$26.944 in $ per $1000

International Profile

Number of Foreign Banks	0
Number of Foreign-owned Businesses	38
Number of Persons Employed by Foreign-owned Businesses	373
Number of Daily International Flights	1

Real Estate

Occupancy Cost per Square Foot (Annual)

	Sq. Foot	Sq. Meters
Average Rental-Class A Office (Central Business District)	$16.20	$174.31
Average Rental-Class A Apartment	$7.16	$77.02
Average Rental- Warehouse	$3.96	$42.61

Construction Cost per Square Foot:

	Sq. Foot	Sq. Meters
Excellent Class A Office	$139.41	$1,500.5
Class A Industrial/ Manufacturing	$84.19	$905.88

	Sq. Foot	Sq. Meters
Class A Distribution Warehouse	$59.32	$638.28
Excellent Class C Single Family Residential	$105.31	$1,133.14

Average Electric Cost (Cents per KwH)

	1992
Residential	$0.557
Commercial	$0.622
Industrial	$0.589
Average Price for a 3-bedroom Family House (in 1000's)	$118.0

Quality of Life

Climate

	Fahrenheit		Celsius	
	High	Low	High	Low
Winter	45	20	7	-7
Spring	63	29	17	-2
Summer	91	48	33	9
Autumn	70	31	21	-1

Rainfall

	Inches	Millimeters
January	1.2	31
February	1.0	25
March	.7	18
April	.5	13
May	.7	18
June	.3	8
July	.3	8
August	.3	8
September	.3	8
October	.3	8
November	.6	15
December	1.2	31

Cultural Highlights

E.L. Weigand Art Museum
National Automobile Museum
Nevada Museum of Art
Victorian Square

[1]See the State-Local General Sales Tax Notes on page 310.
[2]See the Property Tax Rate Notes on page 314.
[3]See the Classification of Real Property and Tangible Personal Property table on page 316.

Leisure Highlights

Fleischman Planetarium,
 University of Nevada
Harolds Club Gun Collection & Museum
Reno-Tahoe Gaming Academy
Wilbur D. May Great Basin Adventure Park
Wilbur D. May Museum &
 Arboretum/Botanical Gardens

Crime

Rate per 100,000 Inhabitants	1991
Number of violent crimes	673.7
Number of property crimes	6,247.7

Average Wages for Selected Occupations

	Average Hiring Salary
Secretary (LR-3)	$20,800
Computer Systems Analyst III	$36,966
Computer Programmer III	$33,228
Engineer II	$35,597
Maintenance Machinist	$27,892

Salt Lake City

UTAH

Founded in 1847 by Brigham Young, Salt Lake City is still influenced by the Mormon faith and culture; the tallest structure downtown is the Church of Jesus Christ of Latter-day Saints (LDS) office building. LDS members comprise approximately 40% of the population, but many other faiths and cultures are represented here as well.

Although civic leaders like to point to Salt Lake City's unhurried and uncrowded quality of life, the city has taken on a higher profile as a business and recreational center in recent years. Surrounded by outstanding skiing areas, it has been selected by the U.S. Olympic Committee as the United States bid city for the 2002 Winter Olympics. The city's new Delta Center provides 20,000 seats for Jazz basketball and 12,000 seats for Eagles hockey games.

Telecommunications, high-tech, health care, and biomedical businesses have been drawn to Salt Lake City, as have other service companies and small manufacturers. Of more than 40 companies moving to the area in 1993, nearly one-third came from California.

One of the MSA's attractions is a growing young population. Approximately 80% of Utah's population resides along an 80-mile corridor, called the Wasatch Front, comprising two MSAs. Since 1980, Utah has been the fastest-growing state and is projected to continue to have the youngest population in the country. Its labor force is expected to grow at twice the national rate in the next decade.

Utah spends more than 40% of its annual budget on education, the largest percentage in the U.S. Students score above the national average on SAT and ACT scores with strong skills in the language arts. The state also ranks high in the percentage of high school graduates qualified to take Advance Placement college exams. In the Salt Lake City/Ogden MSA, two percent of the school-age population attends private school.

City Profile

 ## Population in Thousands

1980	910.2
1990	1,072.2
1992	1,104.3
1995 Estimate	1,168.2

 ## Socioeconomic Factors

Average Household Income

1980	$21,277
1991 Estimate	$40,568
% Change	90.7
1996 Projection	$49,187

Median Household Income

1980	$18,825
1991 Estimate	$33,115
% Change	75.9
1996 Projection	$40,453

Labor Force & Employment

	1993
Total Number of Persons in the Labor Force (in 1000's)	527.3
Total Number of Persons Employed (in 1000's)	507.0
Average Unemployment Rate	3.9%

Total Employment in Thousands by Sector

	1980	1992
Construction	21.6	22.9
Manufacturing	60.1	69.1
Transportation/Utilities	27.0	34.5
Trade	95.9	128.3
Finance/Real Estate	20.8	30.6
Services	N/A	130.7
Government	88.8	102.8

Education

1992 Enrollment:

Two Year College	9,526
Four Year Undergraduate	31,916
Four Year Graduate	5,600
Average SAT Score	N/A
Total Possible Score: 1600	
Average ACT Score	21.8
Total Possible Score: 36	

Business Environment

Selected Major Employers

Hill Air Force Base
Intermountain Health Care
State of Utah
Brigham Young University
University of Utah
Thiokol Corporation
Smith's Food and Drug Centers
Granite School District
Jordan School District
Utah State University

Media Profile

2 newspapers
29 radio stations
12 network television stations
1 cable television operator

 ## State Taxes

Corporate Income/Franchise Tax	5.0%
Sales/Use Tax	8.25%
Individual Income Tax	7.2%
Unemployment Insurance Rate	1.40%

% City Taxes[1]

County Tax	1.00%
City Tax	None
Other Taxes	.25%

% Property Tax Rates [2]

$19.003 in $ per $1000

International Profile

Number of Foreign Banks	0
Number of Foreign-owned Businesses	40
Number of Persons Employed by Foreign-owned Businesses	1,392
Number of Daily International Flights	28

Real Estate

Occupancy Cost per Square Foot (Annual)

	Sq. Foot	Sq. Meters
Average Rental-Class A Office (Central Business District)	$14.31	$153.98
Average Rental-Class A Apartment	$7.03	$75.64
Average Rental- Warehouse	$3.80	$40.89

Construction Cost per Square Foot

	Sq. Foot	Sq. Meters
Excellent Class A Office	$118.81	$1,278.40
Class A Industrial/ Manufacturing	$71.75	$772.03

[1]See the State-Local General Sales Tax Notes on page 310.
[2]See the Classification of Real Property and Tangible Personal Property table on page 316.

	Sq. Foot	Sq. Meters
Class A Distribution Warehouse	$50.55	$543.92
Excellent Class C Single Family Residential	$90.40	$972.70

Average Electric Cost (Cents per KwH)

	1992
Residential	$0.709
Commercial	$0.589
Industrial	$0.363
Average Price for a 3-bedroom Family House (in 1000's)	$100.0

Quality of Life

Climate

	Fahrenheit		Celsius	
	High	Low	High	Low
Winter	37	20	3	-7
Spring	61	37	16	3
Summer	93	62	34	17
Autumn	67	39	19	4

Rainfall

	Inches	Millimeters
January	1.4	36
February	1.3	33
March	1.7	43
April	2.2	56
May	1.5	38
June	1.0	25
July	.7	18
August	.9	23
September	.9	23
October	1.1	28
November	1.2	31
December	1.4	36

Cultural Highlights
Family History Library
Hansen Planetarium
Historic Temple Square

Cultural Highlights (Continued)
 Museum of Church History & Art
 Utah Museum of Natural History

Leisure Highlights
 Beehive House
 Kennecott Copper Mine
 The Church of Latter-day Saints Office
 Building
 Trolley Square
 State Capitol

Crime

Rate per 100,000 Inhabitants	1991
Number of violent crimes	373.7
Number of property crimes	6,404.4

Average Wages for Selected Occupations

	Average Hiring Salary
Secretary (LR-3)	$23,140
Computer Systems Analyst III	$42,016
Computer Programmer III	$32,448
Engineer II	$36,504
Maintenance Machinist	$29,307

WEST COAST

Overview

The West is a study in contrasts. Agriculture, logging, and aerospace are still crucial to the region's economy, but high-tech industries, trade, and health care have become predominant in many of the metro areas reviewed in this section. California, Oregon, and Washington have also become increasingly important as gateways to the Pacific Rim. Rather than being perceived as the outer edge of the U.S. frontier, they are now seen as centrally located between Asia and Europe, two mega-markets of the global economy.

The western region is not a homogenous one, nor is it above competing with itself for business. Many newcomers to Oregon and Washington have come from California, for example, as well as from Asia and Europe. Californians acknowledge that their living costs are high, but their rejoinder is that family incomes and professional attainment are among the highest in the country.

Throughout the 1980s most of these areas experienced growth that ranged from the merely robust to the spectacular. The reason is that for the high-tech and biomedical companies establishing a foothold in the nation's economy, these areas represented fertile ground because of their well-educated work force, trained by the region's science and technology-oriented institutions.

For the young, bright, ambitious, and entrepreneurial, the West has been seen simply, as a great place in which to live. And the West draws an abundance of such people, as evidenced by Microsoft, Intel, Apple Computer, Esprit, Levi-Strauss, Nike, Genentech, and Lucasfilm, among others.

The region's quality of life, in short, has fueled the synergy between business and population growth. The West offers some of the country's most stunning natural attractions, vistas, and recreational opportunities. The coast, rolling hillsides, expansive valleys, forests, and mountains provide a geographic diversity that matches the region's diverse economic life. With easy access to beaches and mountains, residents also have an enviable choice of sunning, swimming, or snow skiing during the same season. Most of these areas enjoy a moderate climate, making outdoor activities possible throughout the year.

The 1990s, however, have been a more subdued period. The recession, coupled with cutbacks in defense spending, has affected areas that once considered themselves recession-proof. The Northwest's economic fate, for example, is strongly linked to the

fate of the aerospace industry, and civic leaders in Washington state heaved a collective sigh of relief when Boeing decided to build a large airplane parts manufacturing facility in Pierce County, rather than move out of the region.

At the same time, the region has been something of a victim of its own success. With growth comes a potential strain on infrastructure, and some West Coast areas are experiencing more pressures than others in terms of traffic congestion, high housing prices, and strains on local school systems.

Some metro areas are responding to this dilemma by developing growth management plans that call for concentrating economic development in already built-up areas and keeping rural areas rural. Others are beefing up infrastructure improvement plans— highway and airport expansions and a variety of mass transit alternatives, including light rail. Concerns about air quality and traffic congestion in California make access to mass transit key for larger employers.

Limitations on growth can also result from facing time-consuming regulatory issues and approvals. Boeing's decision to locate its plant in Pierce County rather than in Seattle itself, for example, was due in part to the perceived differences in the approval process involved, as well as to the availability of property. Some areas are addressing this issue by establishing "one-stop shops" to guide prospective businesses through the regulatory process, whereas others seem to regard the issue with something akin to benign neglect.

The good news in the West is that many of the areas reviewed in this section have vital urban cores as well as growing suburban and rural hubs of growth. They attract after-business-hours activity because of lively recreational, cultural, and retail opportunities, as well as special events. A certain loopy charm coexists with cosmopolitan sophistication. Proud of their heritage, several cities have turned large sections of their downtown historical districts into attractions catering to residents and tourists alike.

Future growth in the region will depend to a great extent on these areas' ability to sustain all the advantages they have—natural beauty, abundant recreation and culture, job opportunities, and living costs in line with family incomes—without becoming overcongested, crowded, and costly for businesses and residents.

Anaheim/Santa Ana

CALIFORNIA

In addition to its year-round pleasant climate (punctuated by the occasional smog alert), the Anaheim-Santa Ana area is blessed with geographical diversity: 20 miles from its coastline, ocean, and sandy beaches are mountains and pine trees. In between are rolling hills, deserts, and valleys. In all, there are close to 600 public parks and a national forest that straddles Orange and Riverside Counties. Bike and trail systems link most parts of the county. The metro area's current population is more than 2.3 million, which is expected to grow to approximately 2.6 million by the year 2000.

Housing choices are as diverse as the county's geography and recreational activities, ranging from Victorian homes in Tustin, to expansive new homes and planned communities in Mission Viejo and Laguna Hills, to dramatic condominiums overlooking the Pacific along the coast. The median price for new sale housing (including both attached and detached single-family homes) is $248,000.

Of the more than 60,000 businesses that call the area home, the majority are local operations; while 20% are branches of companies based elsewhere. The overwhelming majority employ 20 people or fewer. Services represent the largest group of businesses, with wholesale and retail trade a distant second and manufacturing representing less than 10% of the business category mix. Businesses are fairly equally distributed between the north (Buena Park, Anaheim, Orange), the south (Newport Beach, Costa Mesa, Irvine, Tustin, and points south), and central regions (the communities in between).

Those looking for man-made recreational attractions have broad choices, including Disneyland, Knott's Berry Farm, and the Queen Mary, as well as the Laguna Art Museum, the Performing Arts Center for opera, symphony, and dance, and Anaheim Stadium, home of the Angels and the Rams.

City Profile

Population in Thousands

1980	1,932.7
1990	2,411.0
1992	2,485.2
1995 Estimate	2,643.0

Socioeconomic Factors

Average Household Income

1980	$26,714
1991 Estimate	$53,485
% Change	100.2
1996 Projection	$64,754

Median Household Income

1980	$22,788
1991 Estimate	$42,392
% Change	86.0
1996 Projection	$51,578

Labor Force & Employment

	1993
Total Number of Persons in the Labor Force (in 1000's)	1,385.9
Total Number of Persons Employed (in 1000's)	1,295.4
Average Unemployment Rate	6.5%

Total Employment in Thousands by Sector

	1980	1992
Construction	222.1	222.1
Manufacturing	50.4	50.7
Transportation/Utilities	27.9	37.9
Trade	203.4	271.6
Finance/Real Estate	57.0	95.1
Services	174.5	322.8
Government	99.7	128.5

Education

1992 Enrollment

Two Year College	44,543
Four Year Undergraduate	26,796
Four Year Graduate	5,251
Average SAT Score	980
Total Possible Score: 1600	
Average ACT Score	N/A
Total Possible Score: 36	

Business Environment

Selected Major Employers

County of Orange
Santa Ana Unified School District
The Register
Tarbell Relocation Services
Baxter Healthcare Corporation
UCI Medical Center
City of Santa Ana
ITT Electromechanical Components
Western Medical Center
Ricoh Electronics

Media Profile

1 newspaper
5 radio stations
2 network television stations
2 cable television operators

State Taxes[1]

Corporate Income/Franchise Tax	9.3%
Sales/Use Tax	8.5%
Individual Income Tax	11.0%
Unemployment Insurance Rate	3.40%

[1]See the State Tax Table Notes on page 308.

City Taxes[2]

County Tax	1.25%
City Tax	None
Other Taxes	.50%

Property Tax Rates [3,4]

$10.3269 in $ per $1000

International Profile

Number of Foreign Banks	N/A
Number of Foreign-owned Businesses	N/A
Number of Persons Employed by Foreign-owned Businesses	N/A
Number of Daily International Flights	N/A

Real Estate

Occupancy Cost per Square Foot (Annual)

	Sq. Foot	Sq. Meters
Average Rental-Class A Office (Central Business District)	$18.21	$195.94
Average Rental-Class A Apartment	$12.80	$137.73
Average Rental-Warehouse	$4.89	$52.62

Construction Cost per Square Foot

	Sq. Foot	Sq. Meters
Excellent Class A Office	$145.48	$1,565.36
Class A Industrial/Manufacturing	$87.85	$945.27

[2]See the State-Local General Sales Tax Notes on page 310.
[3]See the Property Tax Rate Notes on page 314.
[4]See the Classification of Real Property and Tangible Personal Property table on page 316.

	Sq. Foot	Sq. Meters
Class A Distribution Warehouse	$61.89	$665.94
Excellent Class C Single Family Residential	$111.83	$1,203.29

Average Electric Cost (Cents per KwH)

	1992
Residential	$0.1066
Commercial	$0.996
Industrial	$0.604
Average Price for a 3-bedroom Family House (in 1000's)	$209.0

Quality of Life

Climate

	Fahrenheit		Celsius	
	High	Low	High	Low
Winter	66	44	19	7
Spring	71	51	22	11
Summer	83	63	28	17
Autumn	78	57	26	14

Rainfall

	Inches	Millimeters
January	3.0	76
February	2.5	64
March	1.7	43
April	.8	20
May	.2	5
June	.1	3
July	.1	3
August	.1	3
September	.2	5
October	.2	5
November	1.4	36
December	1.6	41

Cultural Highlights
Crystal Cathedral
Festival of Arts of Laguna Beach
Huntington Beach
Mission San Juan Capistrano
Richard Nixon Library

Leisure Highlights
Disneyland
Knott's Berry Farm
Newport Beach

Crime
Rate per 100,000 Inhabitants 1991

Number of violent crimes	412.9
Number of property crimes	3,237.2

Average Wages for Selected Occupations

	Average Hiring Salary
Secretary (LR-3)	$28,600
Computer Systems Analyst III	$53,924
Computer Programmer III	$38,532
Engineer II	$49,712
Maintenance Machinist	$42,827

Fresno

CALIFORNIA

Once an arid desert in central California, Fresno is now a formidable agricultural and manufacturing center. It averages more than $2.6 billion annually in the production of some 200 crops, livestock, and poultry, and it has been dubbed "the raisin capital of the world." Among the largest food-related private employers are Zacky Farms, Foster Farms, Fleming Foods, and the Harris Ranch Beef Company. Larger manufacturing companies include Champion Parts Rebuilders, Inc., Sunrise Medical, Grundfos Pumps, and Guardian Industries.

However, agriculture and manufacturing are not the only engines driving Fresno's economy. Since the early 1980s employment in service businesses has increased more than 50%, and this sector now comprises approximately one-fifth of the jobs in the county. Insurance and health care are dominant in this group.

Almost equidistant from Los Angeles and San Francisco, Fresno is mindful of the importance of congestion free roadways to its economy. An ongoing Metropolitan Area Freeway Plan has included widening of Freeway 99 (which runs north-south), expansion of Freeways 180 (east–west) and 168, and an extension of Freeway 41 (north–south).

This metro area covers one county— Fresno County— but it is one of the state's largest, encompassing 6,000 square miles that mix urban and rural ambiance. Population has grown steadily, from 658,000 in 1980 to a current 799,800, and it is young, with a median age of 29. Population is projected to grow to 875,000 by 1995. The unemployment rate is 17.9%, resulting in part from employment swings in agriculture. The average home selling price is $105,000. Prime middle-management areas include Woodward Park, Bluffs/Van Ness, New Fig Garden, and Northeast Clovis.

Located within a 2 hours' drive to three national parks— Yosemite, Kings Canyon, and Sequoia—Fresno also offers recreational activities ranging from skiing, sailing, fishing, camping, and river rafting to High Sierra horse-pack trips and four-wheel drive excursions. Fresno's performing arts include theater, dance, contemporary musical performances, and an orchestra; a key attraction is the Tower Theatre, a rehabilitated theater in Fresno's historical Tower District, which is also dotted with restored homes, antique and specialty shops, and restaurants.

City Profile

Population in Thousands

1980	658.0
1990	713.0
1992	799.8
1995 Estimate	875.0

Socioeconomic Factors

Average Household Income

1980	$19,786
1991 Estimate	$43,128
% Change	118.0
1996 Projection	$53,338

Median Household Income

1980	$15,830
1991 Estimate	$31,645
% Change	99.9
1996 Projection	$39,324

Labor Force & Employment

	1993
Total Number of Persons in the Labor Force (in 1000's)	340.8
Total Number of Persons Employed (in 1000's)	279.7
Average Unemployment Rate	17.9%

Total Employment in Thousands by Sector

	1980	1992
Construction	11.2	11.4
Manufacturing	23.4	25.1
Transportation/Utilities	11.0	12.2
Trade	48.6	56.8
F.I.R.E.	11.0	13.2
Services	36.0	55.6
Government	40.9	52.4

Education

1992 Enrollment

Two Year College	19,914
Four Year Undergraduate	14,726
Four Year Graduate	4,374
Average SAT Score	881
Total Possible Score: 1600	
Average ACT Score	N/A
Total Possible Score: 36	

Business Environment

Selected Major Employers

Fresno Unified School District
Fresno County
Internal Revenue Service
Community Hospital
City of Fresno
Clovis Unified School District
St. Agnes Medical Center
California State Univ.-Fresno
Valley Childrens Hospital
Bank of America

Media Profile

1 newspaper
31 radio stations
8 network television stations
1 cable television operator

State Taxes[1]

Corporate Income/Franchise Tax	9.3%
Sales/Use Tax	8.5%
Individual Income Tax	11.0%
Unemployment Insurance Rate	3.40%

[1]See the State Tax Table Notes on page 308.

 City Taxes[2]

County Tax	1.25%
City Tax	None
Other Taxes	.50%

 Property Tax Rates [3,4]

$10.8399 in $ per $1000

 International Profile

Number of Foreign Banks	0
Number of Foreign-owned Businesses	28
Number of Persons Employed by Foreign-owned Businesses	1,362
Number of Daily International Flights	6

 Real Estate

Occupancy Cost per Square Foot (Annual)

	Sq. Foot	Sq. Meters
Average Rental-Class A Office (Central Business District)	$18.00	$193.68
Average Rental-Class A Apartment	$11.29	$121.48
Average Rental- Warehouse	$4.80	$51.64

Construction Cost per Square Foot

	Sq. Foot	Sq. Meters
Excellent Class A Office	$144.26	$1,552.24
Class A Industrial/ Manufacturing	$87.12	$937.41

[2]See the State-Local General Sales Tax Notes on page 310.
[3]See the Property Tax Rate Notes on page 314.
[4]See the Classification of Real Property and Tangible Personal Property table on page 316.

	Sq. Foot	Sq. Meters
Class A Distribution Warehouse	$61.38	$660.45
Excellent Class C Single Family Residential	$111.83	$1,203.29

Average Electric Cost (Cents per KwH)

	1992
Residential	$0.1179
Commercial	$0.1096
Industrial	$0.730
Average Price for a 3-bedroom Family House (in 1000's)	$105.0

 Quality of Life

Climate

	Fahrenheit		Celsius	
	High	Low	High	Low
Winter	54	37	36	3
Spring	74	48	23	9
Summer	99	65	37	18
Autumn	79	51	26	11

Rainfall

	Inches	Millimeters
January	3.7	94
February	3.0	76
March	2.4	61
April	1.2	31
May	.2	5
June	.3	8
July	0	0
August	.1	3
September	.3	8
October	.2	5
November	1.9	48
December	2.0	51

Cultural Highlights
Discovery Center
Fresno Arts Center
Fresno Metropolitan Museum

Cultural Highlights (Continued)
 Museum of Fresno City and County
 Historical Society
 Roeding Park Zoo

Leisure Highlights
 Oban-Odor Festival

Crime

Rate per 100,000 Inhabitants	1991
Number of violent crimes	1,021.3
Number of property crimes	8,078.4

Average Wages for Selected Occupations

	Average Hiring Salary
Secretary (LR-3)	$24,128
Computer Systems Analyst III	$46,800
Computer Programmer III	$35,204
Engineer II	$24,190
Maintenance Machinist	$33,425

Los Angeles

CALIFORNIA

Economic restructuring in major industries—financial institutions, aerospace and defense among the most dramatic—has hit Los Angeles County, whose unemployment rate is currently above 10%. But the near-term economic picture here is not universally grim. Among the brighter spots are the entertainment industry and international trade, which is on the rise. The combined seaports of Los Angeles-Long Beach are among the busiest in the world, handling twice the number of containers as Seattle and Tacoma. The area continues to be a major tourist center, thanks in part to the presence of Hollywood and several of the nation's top ten amusement/theme parks.

Infrastructure improvements are on the horizon as well. School choice, decentralized decision-making, and business involvement have been introduced in the city's school system. More than $2 billion has been earmarked for public transit projects in the coming years in greater Los Angeles, and a $1.3 billion project has been approved which will link the docks by below-grade railway lines to three major railroad terminals.

The county's population now stands at over 9 million, representing growth of approximately 20% since 1980. Births and immigration account for the lion's share of the growth. Culturally diverse, Los Angeles is home to more Latino and Asian-owned businesses than any other city in the country. The number of African-American-owned companies is second only to New York City.

In an area as vast as Los Angeles County, it seems inevitable that growth in some areas comes at the expense of other areas. For example, the San Gabriel Valley has attracted warehousing and distribution facilities relocating from more congested areas of the country, while new retail development is underway in the Santa Clarita and Antelope Valleys north of the San Gabriel mountains.

In addition to the county's famed beaches and boating facilities, Los Angeles offers diversity in cultural attractions, such as the Museum of Contemporary Art, the Los Angeles County Museum of Art, and the Music Center Opera Company. Living in Los Angeles is not inexpensive, but home prices, while still among the highest in the country, have declined significantly over the past few years. Current median home price is $182,000.

City Profile

Population in Thousands

1980	7,477.2
1990	8,863.2
1992	9,127.6
1995 Estimate	9,524.3

Socioeconomic Factors

Average Household Income

1980	$22,480
1991 Estimate	$44,862
% Change	99.6
1996 Projection	$54,343

Median Household Income

1980	$17,935
1991 Estimate	$33,786
% Change	88.4
1996 Projection	$41,272

Labor Force & Employment

	1993
Total Number of Persons in the Labor Force (in 1000's)	4,540.0
Total Number of Persons Employed (in 1000's)	4,031.0
Average Unemployment Rate	11.2%

Total Employment in Thousands by Sector

	1980	1992
Construction	119.1	106.6
Manufacturing	912.1	717.0
Transportation/Utilities	200.8	203.2
Trade	816.9	855.8
Finance/Real Estate	234.6	254.1
Services	831.0	1133.7
Government	482.9	539.0

Education

1992 Enrollment

Two Year College	275,752
Four Year Undergraduate	142,302
Four Year Graduate	78,385
Average SAT Score	803
Total Possible Score: 1600	
Average ACT Score	N/A
Total Possible Score: 36	

Business Environment

Selected Major Employers

California Federal Bank
Transamerican. Life & Annuity
Coast Savings Financial
Sanwa Bank California
Atlantic Richfield
Unocal
Occidental Petroleum
Northrop
Times Mirror

Media Profile

3 newspapers
46 radio stations
26 network television stations
3 cable television operators

State Taxes[1]

Corporate Income/Franchise Tax	9.35%
Sales/Use Tax	8.5%
Individual Income Tax	11.0%
Unemployment Insurance Rate	3.40%

[1]See the State Tax Table Notes on page 308.

City Taxes[2]

County Tax	1.25%
City Tax	None
Other Taxes	1.00%

Property Tax Rates [3,4]

$10.30 in $ per $1000

International Profile

Number of Foreign Banks	82
Number of Foreign-owned Businesses	1,653
Number of Persons Employed by Foreign-owned Businesses	47,414
Number of Daily International Flights	373

Real Estate

Occupancy Cost per Square Foot (Annual)

	Sq. Foot	Sq. Meters
Average Rental-Class A Office (Central Business District)	$21.62	$232.63
Average Rental-Class A Apartment	$10.73	$115.45
Average Rental- Warehouse	$4.56	$49.07

Construction Cost per Square Foot

	Sq. Foot	Sq. Meters
Excellent Class A Office	$145.48	$1,565.36
Class A Industrial/ Manufacturing	$87.85	$945.27

	Sq. Foot	Sq. Meters
Class A Distribution Warehouse	$61.89	$665.94
Excellent Class C Single Family Residential	$113.70	$1,223.41

Average Electric Cost (Cents per KwH)

	1992
Residential	$0.918
Commercial	$0.858
Industrial	$0.778
Average Price for a 3-bedroom Family House (in 1000's)	$182.0

Quality of Life

Climate

	Fahrenheit		Celsius	
	High	Low	High	Low
Winter	67	48	19	9
Spring	71	53	22	12
Summer	84	64	29	18
Autumn	79	59	26	15

Rainfall

	Inches	Millimeters
January	3.7	94
February	3.0	76
March	2.4	61
April	1.2	31
May	.2	5
June	.3	8
July	0	0
August	.1	3
September	.3	8
October	.2	5
November	1.9	48
December	2.0	51

Cultural Highlights

George C. Page Museum of La Brea Disoveries
Los Angeles County Museum of Art
Mann's Chinese Theatre

[2]*See the State-Local General Sales Tax Notes on page 310.*
[3]*See the Property Tax Rate Notes on page 314.*
[4]*See the Classification of Real Property and Tangible Personal Property table on page 316.*

Cultural Highlights (Continued)
 Music Center of Los Angeles County
 Natural History Museum of Los Angeles Co.

Leisure Highlights
 CBS Television City
 Hollywood
 Universal Studios Hollywood
 Hollywood Palladium
 Farmers Market

Crime

Rate per 100,000 Inhabitants	1991
Number of violent crimes	1,795.9
Number of property crimes	5,826.6

Average Wages for Selected Occupations

	Average Hiring Salary
Secretary (LR-3)	$29,692
Computer Systems Analyst III	$51,584
Computer Programmer III	$37,700
Engineer II	$39,468
Maintenance Machinist	$36,816

Oakland

CALIFORNIA

One of the ironies of the Oakland metro area is that population and job growth are not expected to take place within the same areas. For example, Concord, San Ramon, and Walnut Creek are major business centers that accounted for nearly three-quarters of new jobs in Contra Costa County between 1985 and 1990. Although that rate is expected to slow down through 2010, residential growth is projected elsewhere in the central and eastern parts of the county. Civic leaders expect this to strain the county's transportation system and affect other infrastructure issues.

Covering Alameda and Contra Costa counties in northern California, the Oakland metro area comprises 2.17 million people, of whom approximately 372,000 live in Oakland itself. The population is expected to grow to 2.23 million by 1995, with Oakland's growing to nearly 381,000. The current unemployment is 6.8%.

The largest employers in area are in the transportation, food and food-related businesses, and health care, such as Kaiser Permanente, a health maintenance organization. Recent relocations into the area have included Crowley Maritime, in the marine transportation and oil spill cleanup business, United Airlines, for airplane repairs and maintenance, and Smart & Final, a discount food business.

With access to several universities nearby, as well as electronic access to higher education institutions statewide, the area has also attracted numerous high-tech companies whose growth can be readily accommodated in planned business parks.

The average home price in the county is $226,000. Prime middle-management areas include Montclair, Rockridge, Glenwood, Grand/Lake Shore, Skyline Boulevard, and Broadway Terrace.

Oakland's recreational attractions include the Jack London Waterfront, Children's Fairyland, and the Festival at the Lake, held at Lake Merritt. Performing arts include theater, ballet, opera, and a symphony orchestra. The sports-minded are fans of the Oakland Athletics and the Golden State Warriors. And, of course, San Francisco's abundant cultural attractions are just across the bay.

City Profile

 Population in Thousands

1980	1,761.0
1990	2,117.0
1992	2,176.0
1995 Estimate	2,232.0

Socioeconomic Factors

Average Household Income

1980	$23,493
1991 Estimate	$47,768
% Change	103.3
1996 Projection	$57,956

Median Household Income

1980	$20,311
1991 Estimate	$38,290
% Change	88.5
1996 Projection	$46,654

Labor Force & Employment

	1993
Total Number of Persons in the Labor Force (in 1000's)	1,130.8
Total Number of Persons Employed (in 1000's)	1,053.9
Average Unemployment Rate	6.8%

Total Employment in Thousands by Sector

	1980	1992
Construction	36.6	40.9
Manufacturing	110.8	109.3
Transportation/Utilities	43.3	54.2
Trade	164.1	203.4
Finance/Real Estate	37.1	57.4
Services	136.0	228.6
Government	154.4	169.0

 Education

1992 Enrollment

Two Year College	79,132
Four Year Undergraduate	34,336
Four Year Graduate	24,558
Average SAT Score	813
Total Possible Score: 1600	
Average ACT Score	N/A
Total Possible Score: 36	

 Business Environment

Selected Major Employers
Safeway, Inc.
Kaiser Permanente
American Protective Services
Kaiser Aluminum
Clorox Co.
City of Oakland
Crowley Maritime
American Presidents Companies
Port of Oakland
GF Industries

Media Profile
1 newspaper
4 radio stations
23 network television stations
1 cable television operator

 State Taxes[1]

Corporate Income/Franchise Tax	9.3%
Sales/Use Tax	8.5%
Individual Income Tax	11.0%
Unemployment Insurance Rate	3.40%

[1]See the State Tax Table Notes on page 308.

% City Taxes[2]

County Tax	1.25%
City Tax	None
Other Taxes	1.0%

Property Tax Rates [3,4]

$12.397 in $ per $1000

International Profile

Number of Foreign Banks	N/A
Number of Foreign-owned Businesses	N/A
Number of Persons Employed by Foreign-owned Businesses	N/A
Number of Daily International Flights	N/A

Real Estate

Occupancy Cost per Square Foot (Annual)

	Sq. Foot	Sq. Meters
Average Rental-Class A Office (Central Business District)	$19.66	$211.52
Average Rental-Class A Apartment	$12.54	$134.93
Average Rental-Warehouse	$4.45	$47.88

Construction Cost per Square Foot

	Sq. Foot	Sq. Meters
Excellent Class A Office	$157.60	$1,695.78
Class A Industrial/ Manufacturing	$95.17	$1,024.03

	Sq. Foot	Sq. Meters
Class A Distribution Warehouse	$67.05	$721.46
Excellent Class C Single Family Residential	$124.88	$1,343.71

Average Electric Cost (Cents per KwH)

	1992
Residential	$0.1179
Commercial	$0.1096
Industrial	$0.730
Average Price for a 3-bedroom Family House (in 1000's)	$226.0

☆ Quality of Life

Climate

	Fahrenheit		Celsius	
	High	Low	High	Low
Winter	59	46	15	8
Spring	61	49	16	9
Summer	64	53	18	12
Autumn	68	55	20	13

Rainfall

	Inches	Millimeters
January	4.5	114
February	2.8	71
March	2.6	66
April	1.5	38
May	.4	10
June	.2	5
July	.1	3
August	.1	3
September	.2	5
October	1.1	28
November	2.5	64
December	3.5	89

Cultural Highlights

Camron-Stanford House
The Oakland Museum
Dunsmuir House & Gardens
Jack London Waterfront
Old Oakland

[2]See the State-Local General Sales Tax Notes on page 310.
[3]See the Property Tax Rate Notes on page 314.
[4]See the Classification of Real Property and Tangible Personal Property table on page 316.

Leisure Highlights
 Chinatown
 Lake Merritt
 Tilden Park

Crime
Rate per 100,000 Inhabitants | 1991
Number of violent crimes | 1,037.3
Number of property crimes | 6,421.1

Average Wages for Selected Occupations

	Average Hiring Salary
Secretary (LR-3)	$28,340
Computer Systems Analyst III	$57,616
Computer Programmer III	$38,064
Engineer II	$43,108
Maintenance Machinist	$36,857

Portland

OREGON

If California has its Silicon Valley, then Oregon has a Silicon Forest. Portland's pedigree as a high-tech center dates back to the post-World War II period, with the establishment of Tektronix. Today, Intel, Wacker Siltronic, NEC, Epson, Fujitsu, Mentor Graphics, NCUBE, and Sequent are among the some 500 high-tech companies that have operations here. However, the economy is not dependent on electronics alone; retailing, finance, manufacturing, and service businesses balance the economy, the predominant industries being aerospace, transportation, apparel, wood products, printing and publishing, and food manufacturing/processing.

No longer considered "frontier" territory, this four-county area in northwest Oregon is becoming a trade and distribution center for the Pacific Rim, thanks not only to its location, but also to its World Trade Center, Foreign Trade Zone, freshwater port facilities, and direct passenger and cargo flights to Japan and Korea.

To support high-tech industry growth, colleges and universities are expanding research facilities, and more than 80 companies have used area community colleges for training and classes. A JobNet program links employers to the area's labor force, matching workers to jobs and community training resources.

Business newcomers to the area have come primarily from California, representing a mix of service and manufacturing companies. At least 30 foreign-owned companies are located here, including STC Submarine Systems, Oki Semiconductor, and Granpac Foods. Foreign-owned local manufacturing plants employ about 4,700 people.

The area's appeal blends the rustic and the cosmopolitan. Extensive parks, fishing, water-skiing, sailing, windsurfing on the Columbia River, and hiking and skiing on the slopes of Mt. Hood are among the recreational attractions. Downtown Portland is a vibrant business, cultural, and retailing center—the Pacific Northwest's first Saks Fifth Avenue is located here, for example—with investment and growth guided by a Downtown Plan adopted more than 20 years ago.

Portland is attracting considerable migration, and the metro area has grown by some 200,000 residents since 1980 to a current population of 1.3 million. The average home price here is approximately $147,800. Prime middle-management areas include West Linn, Beaverton, Westmoreland, and Oak Hills. Businesses and residents alike will find that utility costs are moderated by the area's hydroelectric power base, and its water, which is plentiful, needs minimal treatment.

City Profile

 ## Population in Thousands

1980	1,105.8
1990	1,239.8
1992	1,308.7
1995 Estimate	1,348.2

 ## Socioeconomic Factors

Average Household Income

1980	$21,522
1991 Estimate	$42,240
% Change	96.3
1996 Projection	$51,731

Median Household Income

1980	$18,494
1991 Estimate	$33,434
% Change	80.8
1996 Projection	$41,035

 ## Labor Force & Employment

	1993
Total Number of Persons in the Labor Force (in 1000's)	719.2
Total Number of Persons Employed (in 1000's)	621.9
Average Unemployment Rate	6.6%

Total Employment in Thousands by Sector

	1980	1992
Construction	24.9	26.4
Manufacturing	113.9	101.5
Transportation/Utilities	36.6	38.7
Trade	142.3	167.1
Finance/Real Estate	45.7	55.8
Services	95.6	170.3
Government	84.9	89.2

 ## Education

1992 Enrollment

Two Year College	31,626
Four Year Undergraduate	22,808
Four Year Graduate	8,714
Average SAT Score	928
Total Possible Score: 1600	
Average ACT Score	N/A
Total Possible Score: 36	

 ## Business Environment

Selected Major Employers
Fred Meyer, Inc.
U.S. Bancorp
Tektronix, Inc.
Kaiser Permanente
Legacy Health System
Sisters of Providence Health Care System
Intel Cop.
Safeway, Inc.
Precision Castparts
US West

Media Profile
1 newspaper
34 radio stations
11 network television stations
2 cable television operators

% State Taxes

Corporate Income/Franchise Tax	6.6%
Sales/Use Tax	0.0%
Individual Income Tax	9.0%
Unemployment Insurance Rate	3.50%

 City Taxes

County Tax	None
City Tax	None
Other Taxes	None

 Property Tax Rates [1,2]

$33.5048 in $ per $1000

International Profile

Number of Foreign Banks	3
Number of Foreign-owned Businesses	137
Number of Persons Employed by Foreign-owned Businesses	4,654
Number of Daily International Flights	28

Real Estate

Occupancy Cost per Square Foot (Annual)

	Sq. Foot	Sq. Meters
Average Rental-Class A Office (Central Business District)	$18.43	$198.31
Average Rental-Class A Apartment	$8.62	$92.75
Average Rental-Warehouse	$4.05	$43.58

Construction Cost per Square Foot

	Sq. Foot	Sq. Meters
Excellent Class A Office	$133.35	$1,434.85
Class A Industrial/ Manufacturing	$80.53	$866.50

[1]See the Property Tax Rate Notes on page 314.
[2]See the Classification of Real Property and Tangible Personal Property table on page 316.

	Sq. Foot	Sq. Meters
Class A Distribution Warehouse	$56.74	$610.52
Excellent Class C Single Family Residential	$103.44	$1,113.01

Average Electric Cost (Cents per KwH)

	1992
Residential	$0.520
Commercial	$0.507
Industrial	$0.385
Average Price for a 3-bedroom Family House (in 1000's)	$147.8

 Quality of Life

Climate

	Fahrenheit		Celsius	
	High	Low	High	Low
Winter	47	34	8	1
Spring	61	41	16	5
Summer	76	54	24	12
Autumn	63	45	17	7

Rainfall

	Inches	Millimeters
January	7.1	180
February	4.6	117
March	4.3	109
April	2.4	61
May	2.0	51
June	1.2	31
July	.4	10
August	.8	20
September	1.6	41
October	3.3	84
November	5.7	145
December	7.1	180

Cultural Highlights
Oregon Art Institute
Oregon Historical Society
Pittock Mansion

Cultural Highlights (Continued)
 The American Advertising Museum
 The Grotto

Leisure Highlights
 International Rose Test Garden
 Japanese Gardens
 World Forestry Center
 Metro Washington Park Zoo

Crime

Rate per 100,000 Inhabitants	1991
Number of violent crimes	276.1
Number of property crimes	5,421.3

Average Wages for Selected Occupations

	Average Hiring Salary
Secretary (LR-3)	$21,674
Computer Systems Analyst III	$40,392
Computer Programmer III	$32,760
Engineer II	$42,744
Maintenance Machinist	$25,854

Riverside/San Bernardino

CALIFORNIA

Also known as the Inland Empire, this area of southern California has grown most rapidly in the past few years. Population grew more than 70% since 1980, to a current level of 2.7 million. Among the reasons for the Inland Empire's growth are affordable housing and land for both commercial and industrial development, plus an ample highway network and an international airport in Ontario. Median household income in this area is slightly lower than that in Los Angeles, but median home prices are considerably lower, at $127,000.

Like Los Angeles, the Inland Empire's economy is fueled largely by services and trade. Among the largest employers in the area are Marriott Corp. (with resort hotels at Rancho Mirage and Palm Desert), Rohr Industries (an aerospace/aircraft subcontractor), Dayton Hudson Corp., Kmart, GTE California, Sun World International (growers/packers) and several large supermarketing companies. The area has attracted manufacturing, warehousing and distribution facilities from Los Angeles County. The area's labor force is growing more quickly than local employment, however, and the unemployment rate stands at 11.6%.

Home to several colleges and universities, the Inland Empire also has more than 50,000 students enrolled in vocational/technical schools and two-year colleges that offer programs in business, computer science, and other technical occupations.

Among the area's special events are a Renaissance Faire and annual date festival. Recreational attractions include downhill and cross-country skiing, fishing, and camping.

City Profile

 Population in Thousands

1980	1,558.2
1990	2,588.7
1992	2,823.7
1995 Estimate	3,169.1

 Socioeconomic Factors

Average Household Income

1980	$20,247
1991 Estimate	$43,001
% Change	112.4
1996 Projection	$52,921

Median Household Income

1980	$17,060
1991 Estimate	$32,729
% Change	91.8
1996 Projection	$40,603

 Labor Force & Employment

	1993
Total Number of Persons in the Labor Force (in 1000's)	1,145.5
Total Number of Persons Employed (in 1000's)	1,012.6
Average Unemployment Rate	11.6%

Total Employment in Thousands by Sector

	1980	1992
Construction	26.1	40.1
Manufacturing	63.8	86.6
Transportation/Utilities	25.6	36.3
Trade	106.3	186.3
Finance/Real Estate	18.9	31.0
Services	89.7	184.7
Government	101.3	156.9

 Education

1992 Enrollment

Two Year College	54,226
Four Year Undergraduate	13,185
Four Year Graduate	7,839
Average SAT Score	882
Total Possible Score: 1600	
Average ACT Score	N/A
Total Possible Score: 36	

 Business Environment

Selected Major Employers
Marriott Corp.
Rohr Industries, Inc.
Landmark Land Co.
Dayton Hudson Corp.
The VMS Co.
American Stores
Stater Bros.
Kmart
GTE California
Sun World International

Media Profile
1 newspaper
8 radio stations
26 network television stations
1 cable television operator

 State Taxes[1]

Corporate Income/Franchise Tax	9.3%
Sales/Use Tax	8.5%
Individual Income Tax	11.0%
Unemployment Insurance Rate	3.40%

[1]See the State Tax Table Notes on page 308.

 % City Taxes[2]

County Tax	1.25%
City Tax	None
Other Taxes	.50%

 % Property Tax Rates [3,4]

$10.5642 in $ per $1000

International Profile

Number of Foreign Banks	0
Number of Foreign-owned Businesses	113
Number of Persons Employed by Foreign-owned Businesses	2,206
Number of Daily International Flights	0

Real Estate

Occupancy Cost per Square Foot (Annual)

	Sq. Foot	Sq. Meters
Average Rental-Class A Office (Central Business District)	$16.75	$180.23
Average Rental-Class A Apartment	$8.45	$90.92
Average Rental-Warehouse	$4.79	$51.54

Construction Cost per Square Foot

	Sq. Foot	Sq. Meters
Excellent Class A Office	$144.26	$1,552.24
Class A Industrial/ Manufacturing	$87.12	$937.41

	Sq. Foot	Sq. Meters
Class A Distribution Warehouse	$61.38	$660.45
Excellent Class C Single Family Residential	$110.90	$1,193.28

Average Electric Cost (Cents per KwH)

	1992
Residential	$0.1212
Commercial	$0.1136
Industrial	$0.795
Average Price for a 3-bedroom Family House (in 1000's)	$127.0

 ## Quality of Life

Climate

	Fahrenheit		Celsius	
	High	Low	High	Low
Winter	67	41	19	5
Spring	74	47	23	8
Summer	92	58	33	14
Autumn	82	51	28	11

Rainfall

	Inches	Millimeters
January	3.7	94
February	3.0	76
March	2.4	61
April	1.2	31
May	.2	5
June	.3	8
July	0	0
August	.1	3
September	.3	8
October	.2	5
November	1.9	48
December	2.0	51

Cultural Highlights

Book of Life Museum
California Museum of Photography
Jurupa Mountains Cultural Center
Riverside Art Center and Museum
Western Camera Museum

[2]*See the State-Local General Sales Tax Notes on page 310.*
[3]*See the Property Tax Rate Notes on page 314.*
[4]*See the Classification of Real Property and Tangible Personal Property table on page 316.*

Leisure Highlights

Jazz Festival
Riverside Community Players
July 4th Celebration
Mayor's Ball for the Arts
Riverside Philharmonic

Crime

Rate per 100,000 Inhabitants	1991
Number of violent crimes	414.9
Number of property crimes	2,673.2

Average Wages for Selected Occupations

	Average Hiring Salary
Secretary (LR-3)	$27,144
Computer Systems Analyst III	$50,908
Computer Programmer III	$37,804
Engineer II	$38,792
Maintenance Machinist	$31,449

Sacramento

CALIFORNIA

The five-county Sacramento metro area has outpaced the state in manufacturing sector growth over the past decade. Manufacturers are a diverse mix of high-tech (for example, Hewlett-Packard, Intel, and NEC Electronics), food-related (for example, Blue Diamond Growers, Campbell Soup, Rainbo Earth Grains and Sunsweet Growers), and health care (for example, Baxter-Microscan) industries.

Sacramento, California's capital, is located in the north central part of the state, with an extensive transportation network that combines four major highways, a deep-water port, railroads, and light transit. Improvements are planned to be made over the next 20 years, including construction currently under way to add 10 more gates and to more than double the existing terminal space at Sacramento Metro Airport.

In addition to two large universities and five community colleges, business support is provided by more than 160 vocational and training programs in the area, and county offices of education offer technical and vocational training for high school students through Regional Occupational Programs. The Port of Sacramento Japanese School currently offers a dozen classes for Japanese children.

Mild climate (which changes dramatically in the Sierra Nevada mountain range), strategic location, and abundant historic attractions have helped to draw people to the area. Sacramento's population has also experienced robust growth—more than 30% since 1980. Total population is approximately 1.64 million, up from 1.15 million in 1980. Relatively affordable housing costs are a factor too. The median price for an existing three-bedroom home is $135,000.

Tourism is an important element of the area's economy. In addition to the State Capitol, Sacramento offers an eclectic mix of attractions, ranging from the nation's largest railroad museum in the heart of a restored historical district along the Sacramento River and a museum displaying a large collection of antique Fords, to riverboat cruises and the Crocker Art Museum, the oldest public art museum in the West.

Within a day's drive are the Sierra Nevada mountains, winery tours, Lake Tahoe, and Yosemite National Park. Sacramento is also home to the California State Fair, an annual Jazz Jubilee, and the relatively new Sacramento Kings basketball team.

City Profile

 Population
in Thousands

1980	1,152.1
1990	1,497.7
1992	1,641.4
1995 Estimate	1,744.0

 Socioeconomic
Factors

Average Household Income

1980	$20,629
1991 Estimate	$40,014
% Change	94.0
1996 Projection	$48,694

Median Household Income

1980	$17,559
1991 Estimate	$31,697
% Change	80.5
1996 Projection	$38,551

 Labor Force &
Employment

	1993
Total Number of Persons in the Labor Force (in 1000's)	792.9
Total Number of Persons Employed (in 1000's)	723.6
Average Unemployment Rate	8.7%

Total Employment in Thousands by Sector

	1980	1992
Construction	20.9	29.5
Manufacturing	28.5	42.6
Transportation/Utilities	22.7	29.1
Trade	98.3	142.6
Finance/Real Estate	23.2	42.4
Services	77.9	150.1
Government	145.8	185.4

 Education

1992 Enrollment

Two Year College	52,682
Four Year Undergraduate	31,068
Four Year Graduate	12,414
Average SAT Score	903
Total Possible Score: 1600	
Average ACT Score	N/A
Total Possible Score: 36	

 Business
Environment

Selected Major Employers

State of California
UC Davis
McClellan AFB
County of Sacramento
Sac. Metro Airport
US Postal Service
San Juan School District
Sac. City School District
CSUS
Pacific Bell

Media Profile

1 newspaper
29 radio stations
10 network television stations
1 cable television operator

% State Taxes[1]

Corporate Income/Franchise Tax	9.3%
Sales/Use Tax	8.5%
Individual Income Tax	11.0%
Unemployment Insurance Rate	3.40%

[1]See the State Tax Table Notes on page 308.

City Taxes[2]

County Tax	1.25%
City Tax	None
Other Taxes	.50%

Property Tax Rates [3,4]

$10.321 in $ per $1000

International Profile

Number of Foreign Banks	0
Number of Foreign-owned Businesses	41
Number of Persons Employed by Foreign-owned Businesses	183
Number of Daily International Flights	2

Real Estate

Occupancy Cost per Square Foot (Annual)

	Sq. Foot	Sq. Meters
Average Rental-Class A Office (Central Business District)	$20.67	$222.41
Average Rental-Class A Apartment	$7.64	$82.20
Average Rental-Warehouse	$3.60	$38.74

Construction Cost per Square Foot

	Sq. Foot	Sq. Meters
Excellent Class A Office	$146.69	$1,578.38
Class A Industrial/ Manufacturing	$88.58	$953.12

	Sq. Foot	Sq. Meters
Class A Distribution Warehouse	$62.41	$671.53
Excellent Class C Single Family Residential	$114.63	$1,233.42

Average Electric Cost (Cents per KwH)

	1992
Residential	$0.818
Commercial	$0.847
Industrial	$0.731
Average Price for a 3-bedroom Family House (in 1000's)	$135.0

★ Quality of Life

Climate

	Fahrenheit		Celsius	
	High	Low	High	Low
Winter	53	38	12	3
Spring	71	45	22	7
Summer	93	58	34	14
Autumn	78	50	26	10

Rainfall

	Inches	Millimeters
January	4.0	102
February	2.9	74
March	2.1	53
April	1.3	33
May	.3	8
June	.1	3
July	.1	3
August	.1	3
September	.3	8
October	.9	23
November	2.2	56
December	3.0	76

Cultural Highlights

California State Indian Museum
California State Railroad Museum
Crocker Art Museum

[2]See the State-Local General Sales Tax Notes on page 310.
[3]See the Property Tax Rate Notes on page 314.
[4]See the Classification of Real Property and Tangible Personal Property table on page 316.

Cultural Highlights (Continued)
 Sacramento History Museum
 Towe Ford Museum

Leisure Highlights
 Blue Diamond Visitors Center
 Delta King Riverboat
 Governor's Mansion
 State Capitol
 Sutter's Fort State Historic Park

Crime

Rate per 100,000 Inhabitants	1991
Number of violent crimes	794.4
Number of property crimes	6,415.6

Average Wages for Selected Occupations

	Average Hiring Salary
Secretary (LR-3)	$26,156
Computer Systems Analyst III	$47,736
Computer Programmer III	$35,724
Engineer II	$38,324
Maintenance Machinist	$32,136

San Diego

CALIFORNIA

The defense and aerospace industries based in San Diego have been undergoing significant downsizing, and the county's unemployment rate is 7.9%, but the area's economy has other strengths to rely on. With access to prominent research facilities—including the University of California, San Diego, School of Medicine, the Scripps Institutions of Science and Medicine, and the Salk Institute of Biotechnology/Industrial Associates—high-tech and biotechnology companies have found San Diego an amenable place to call home.

This county, roughly the size of Connecticut, has witnessed dramatic growth since 1980, from 1.86 million to 2.6 million in population, and is expected to grow still more to nearly 3 million by the year 2000. San Diego was one of only 30 metro areas with 30% or more growth in the 1980s, and one of four larger metro areas (with populations of two million or more) that achieved such growth.

Recently, San Diego has drawn manufacturing, recycling, and biotechnology firms from locations as diverse as Germany, France, Michigan, Tennessee, Missouri, and Minneapolis. Its mild and usually sunny climate has made tourism a big business; most recent figures show that tourists account for more than $3 million in revenue annually and that nearly 125,000 people are employed by tourism-related businesses.

San Diego's uniformly pleasant climate also makes for plentiful outdoor recreational opportunities. The county's coastline covers 70 miles, and there are more than 175 public parks, 78 golf courses, and 1,200 public tennis courts to choose from. In addition to the famous San Diego Zoo, there are other animal attractions: Wild Animal Park, Sea World, and the Steven Birch Aquarium. Cultural and architectural attractions abound; Cabrillo National Monument is one of more than a dozen museums and galleries in San Diego. The county is also home to more than a dozen theater groups, ballet, opera, and a symphony orchestra.

By California standards, San Diego is reasonably affordable. The average price for a three-bedroom house is $175,000, with prime middle-management areas clustered along the I-15 corridor as well as in Eastlake in Chula Vista.

City Profile

Population in Thousands

1980	1,861.8
1990	2,498.0
1992	2,602.2
1995 Estimate	2,695.2

Socioeconomic Factors

Average Household Income

1980	$21,230
1991 Estimate	$44,797
% Change	111.0
1996 Projection	$54,953

Median Household Income

1980	$17,436
1991 Estimate	$33,707
% Change	93.3
1996 Projection	$41,869

Labor Force & Employment

	1993
Total Number of Persons in the Labor Force (in 1000's)	1,201.1
Total Number of Persons Employed (in 1000's)	1,106.0
Average Unemployment Rate	7.9%

Total Employment in Thousands by Sector

	1980	1992
Construction	36.0	43.3
Manufacturing	108.1	124.0
Transportation/Utilities	28.7	34.7
Trade	148.8	219.7
Finance/Real Estate	38.7	60.9
Services	148.2	282.8
Government	141.2	179.1

Education

1992 Enrollment

Two Year College	85,772
Four Year Undergraduate	52,057
Four Year Graduate	24,113
Average SAT Score	894
Total Possible Score: 1600	
Average ACT Score	N/A
Total Possible Score: 36	

Business Environment

Selected Major Employers

U.S. Active Duty
U.S. Civilian
UCSD
County of San Diego
San Diego Unified Schools
City of San Diego
Sharp Healthcare
Scripps Inst.
State of California
U.S. Postal System

Media Profile

2 newspapers
28 radio stations
7 network television stations
2 cable television operators

State Taxes[1]

Corporate Income/Franchise Tax	9.3%
Sales/Use Tax	8.5%
Individual Income Tax	11.0%
Unemployment Insurance Rate	3.40%

[1]See the State Tax Table Notes on page 308.

 % City Taxes[2]

County Tax	1.25%
City Tax	None
Other Taxes	.50%

Property Tax Rates [3,4]

$10.3659 in $ per $1000

International Profile

Number of Foreign Banks	1
Number of Foreign-owned Businesses	245
Number of Persons Employed by Foreign-owned Businesses	6,727
Number of Daily International Flights	27

Real Estate

Occupancy Cost per Square Foot (Annual)

	Sq. Foot	Sq. Meters
Average Rental-Class A Office (Central Business District)	$18.41	$198.09
Average Rental-Class A Apartment	$11.58	$124.60
Average Rental-Warehouse	$4.95	$53.26

Construction Cost per Square Foot

	Sq. Foot	Sq. Meters
Excellent Class A Office	$141.84	$1,526.20
Class A Industrial/Manufacturing	$85.66	$921.70

	Sq. Foot	Sq. Meters
Class A Distribution Warehouse	$60.35	$649.37
Excellent Class C Single Family Residential	$109.04	$1,173.27

Average Electric Cost (Cents per KwH)

	1992
Residential	$0.1078
Commercial	$0.903
Industrial	$0.736
Average Price for a 3-bedroom Family House (in 1000's)	$175.0

 ★ Quality of Life

Climate

	Fahrenheit		Celsius	
	High	Low	High	Low
Winter	65	48	18	9
Spring	68	55	20	13
Summer	76	65	24	18
Autumn	75	60	24	16

Rainfall

	Inches	Millimeters
January	2.0	51
February	1.0	25
March	2.0	51
April	1.0	25
May	.2	5
June	.1	3
July	.1	3
August	.1	3
September	.2	5
October	.3	8
November	1.0	25
December	1.0	25

Cultural Highlights

Cabrillo National Monument
Old Town San Diego State Historic Park
Stephen Birch Aquarium/Museum

[2]See the State-Local General Sales Tax Notes on page 310.
[3]See the Property Tax Rate Notes on page 314.
[4]See the Classification of Real Property and Tangible Personal Property table on page 316.

Cultural Highlights (Continued)
 Del Coronado Hotel

Leisure Highlights

 San Diego Wild Animal Park
 San Diego Zoo
 Seaport Village
 La Costa Resort & Spa
 San Diego Sports Arena
 Sea World, Mission Bay Park

Crime

Rate per 100,000 Inhabitants	1991
Number of violent crimes	966.8
Number of property crimes	5,853.7

Average Wages for Selected Occupations

	Average Hiring Salary
Secretary (LR-3)	$26,832
Computer Systems Analyst III	$40,000
Computer Programmer III	$35,620
Engineer II	$39,416
Maintenance Machinist	$39,644

San Francisco

CALIFORNIA

San Francisco's unique vistas, natural beauty, renowned cultural attractions, and urban charm should not overshadow its role as the financial heart of the West Coast. San Francisco is the home of the Pacific Stock Exchange and West Coast headquarters for the Federal Reserve Bank and Federal Home Loan Bank. Bank America, the Bank of California, Transamerica, Union Bank, and Wells Fargo are also based in San Francisco. Financing of a different sort is clustered in the area as well: one-fifth of the larger venture capital firms in the United States are located in Menlo Park, in San Mateo County.

Among the larger employers are Bechtel, Chevron, Levi-Strauss, McKesson, and Pacific Telesis. With traditional links to Asia, the San Francisco metro area—comprising San Francisco, Marin, and San Mateo Counties—has experienced significant growth in Pacific Rim-headquartered companies located here. San Francisco's port has increased its tonnage in recent years, owing mainly to the addition of Nedlloyd Shipping Lines, which uses San Francisco as a hub for shipping between South America and Asia. Both Tokyo and London are within a 10-hour flight, further reinforcing the city's potential as an international center.

Medical sciences are important to San Francisco. For example, one of the city's larger employers is the University of California, San Francisco, a medical research institution. UCSF receives more research funding from the National Institute of Health than any other medical school. It has been at the forefront of developing transplant techniques, neonatal intensive care, and in cancer, AIDS, arthritis and sickle cell anemia research.

San Francisco county's population of some 730,000 people, living within one of the world's best known, 47-square-mile urban regions, has grown less than 10% since 1980. Despite its density, though, San Francisco offers more acres of park land per resident than other city in the country, including Golden Gate Park and the Golden Gate Recreation Area. An additional 891,000 people live in San Mateo and Marin counties, whose population is growing at a rate higher than the national average.

Within the city are a dozen distinct residential areas. About two-thirds of San Francisco's housing is renter occupied, with rents ranging from $1,000 to $1,500 for two- and three-bedroom apartments and houses. Most recent statistics show the median price for a new home to be $276,000. More than one-third of the people who work in San Francisco live outside the city.

City Profile

Population in Thousands

1980	1,488.9
1990	1,603.7
1992	1,642.9
1995 Estimate	1,703.6

Socioeconomic Factors

Average Household Income

1980	$24,628
1991 Estimate	$53,121
% Change	115.7
1996 Projection	$64,942

Median Household Income

1980	$19,927
1991 Estimate	$40,202
% Change	101.7
1996 Projection	$49,330

Labor Force & Employment

	1993
Total Number of Persons in the Labor Force (in 1000's)	884.9
Total Number of Persons Employed (in 1000's)	829.5
Average Unemployment Rate	6.3%

Total Employment in Thousands by Sector

	1980	1992
Construction	30.1	28.0
Manufacturing	91.5	75.6
Transportation/Utilities	86.8	77.8
Trade	194.8	196.0
Finance/Real Estate	107.3	102.0
Services	225.9	303.0
Government	136.8	133.2

Education

1992 Enrollment

Two Year College	60,924
Four Year Undergraduate	28,545
Four Year Graduate	22,722
Average SAT Score	855
Total Possible Score: 1600	
Average ACT Score	N/A
Total Possible Score: 36	

Business Environment

Selected Major Employers

Bankamerica Corp.
Wells Fargo & Co.
Transamerica
Pacific Gas & Electric
Pacific Telesis Group
Chevron
Levi-Strauss Associates
Del Monte Foods
Potlach
Tri Valley Growers

Media Profile

2 newspapers
40 radio stations
23 network television stations
1 cable television operator

% State Taxes[1]

Corporate Income/Franchise Tax	9.3%
Sales/Use Tax	8.5%
Individual Income Tax	11.0%
Unemployment Insurance Rate	3.40%

[1]See the State Tax Table Notes on page 308.

 City Taxes[2]

County Tax	1.25%
City Tax	None
Other Taxes	1.25%

Property Tax Rates [3,4]

$10.9 in $ per $1000

International Profile

Number of Foreign Banks	24
Number of Foreign-owned Businesses	670
Number of Persons Employed by Foreign-owned Businesses	16,354
Number of Daily International Flights	244

Real Estate

Occupancy Cost per Square Foot (Annual)

	Sq. Foot	Sq. Meters
Average Rental-Class A Office (Central Business District)	$20.79	$223.70
Average Rental-Class A Apartment	$14.20	$152.79
Average Rental-Warehouse	$5.12	$55.09

Construction Cost per Square Foot

	Sq. Foot	Sq. Meters
Excellent Class A Office	$164.87	$1,774.00
Class A Industrial/ Manufacturing	$99.57	$1,071.37

	Sq. Foot	Sq. Meters
Class A Distribution Warehouse	$70.15	$754.81
Excellent Class C Single Family Residential	$131.40	$1,413.86

Average Electric Cost (Cents per KwH)

	1992
Residential	$0.1179
Commercial	$0.1096
Industrial	$0.730
Average Price for a 3-bedroom Family House (in 1000's)	$276.0

Quality of Life

Climate

	Fahrenheit		Celsius	
	High	Low	High	Low
Winter	56	46	13	8
Spring	61	49	16	9
Summer	64	53	18	12
Autumn	68	55	20	13

Rainfall

	Inches	Millimeters
January	4.5	114
February	2.8	71
March	2.6	66
April	1.5	38
May	.4	10
June	.2	5
July	0	0
August	.1	3
September	.2	5
October	1.1	28
November	2.5	64
December	3.5	89

Cultural Highlights

Cable Car Museum
Chinatown
Fisherman's Wharf

[2]See the State-Local General Sales Tax Notes on page 310.
[3]See the Property Tax Rate Notes on page 314.
[4]See the Classification of Real Property and Tangible Personal Property table on page 316.

Cultural Highlights (Continued)
 Union Square
 Golden Gate Bridge & Park

Leisure Highlights

 Alcatraz, San Francisco Bay
 Broadway/North Beach
 Japantown
 Pier 39
 The Cannery

Crime

Rate per 100,000 Inhabitants	1991
Number of violent crimes	983.7
Number of property crimes	5,806.9

Average Wages for Selected Occupations

	Average Hiring Salary
Secretary (LR-3)	$29,068
Computer Systems Analyst III	$52,808
Computer Programmer III	$35,100
Engineer II	$40,300
Maintenance Machinist	$39,374

San Jose

CALIFORNIA

Although dominated earlier in the twentieth century by agriculture, fruit and vegetable packing, and canning, San Jose's chief harvest quickly turned to electronics following World War II, when technical advances designed for the military, and spearheaded by teachers at Stanford University, were turned to private use. Presently, San Jose is the nerve center of Silicon Valley, home to more than 3,000 high-technology companies that are responsible for producing nearly one-quarter of the nations's electron tubes, semiconductors, and computer storage devices.

With the exception of Lockheed Missiles, all of the largest employers in the area are high-tech companies, including Hewlett-Packard, IBM, Sun Microsystems, Intel, and Apple Computer. So are companies relocating or expanding in the area, such as Cisco Systems, Xerox Engineering, and Sony Corporation of America. Approximately 300 of the companies located here are foreign-owned—such as Toshiba America, Hitachi Instruments, and Fujitsu America—employing more than 15,000 people. Training for the computer sciences and other technical occupations is provided by six 2-year colleges and nine vocational/technical schools.

This metro area comprises one county, Santa Clara County, in north-central California. Its population has grown steadily, from nearly 1.3 million in 1980, to a current 1.5 million. Nearly half the population resides in the city of San Jose. The median age is 32, with 35 to 49 year-olds representing the largest group. The unemployment rate is 7.2%.

Because the area ranks high in the number of families with annual incomes over $50,000, it is not surprising to find that housing costs are proportionate; the median sales price in the county is $228,000.

Located 25 miles from the Pacific Ocean, San Jose offers a panoply of beaches and water-oriented recreation activities. Music festivals, the boardwalk in Santa Cruz, Raging Waters Park, and nearby wine country tours round out the recreational picture. San Jose also has two theater groups, ballet, opera, a symphony orchestra, and at least two science and technology museums, one of which is for the children who presumably will join the ranks of the next generation of "techies."

City Profile

Population in Thousands

1980	1,295.1
1990	1,497.6
1992	1,531.8
1995 Estimate	1,588.8

Socioeconomic Factors

Average Household Income

1980	$26,589
1991 Estimate	$57,647
% Change	116.8
1996 Projection	$69,665

Median Household Income

1980	$23,446
1991 Estimate	$46,627
% Change	98.9
1996 Projection	$58,019

Labor Force & Employment

	1993
Total Number of Persons in the Labor Force (in 1000's)	830.4
Total Number of Persons Employed (in 1000's)	770.7
Average Unemployment Rate	7.2%

Total Employment in Thousands by Sector

	1980	1992
Construction	26.1	27.2
Manufacturing	248.3	234.9
Transportation/Utilities	21.7	22.2
Trade	125.2	157.9
Finance/Real Estate	27.6	31.5
Services	146.4	223.4
Government	79.9	88.6

Education

1992 Enrollment

Two Year College	81,073
Four Year Undergraduate	24,128
Four Year Graduate	24,705
Average SAT Score	990
Total Possible Score: 1600	
Average ACT Score	N/A
Total Possible Score: 36	

Business Environment

Selected Major Employers

Lockheed Missiles
Hewlett-Packard
Stanford University
Santa Clara County
IBM Corporation
Sun Microsystems
Apple Computers
National Semiconductor
Amdahl Corp.
City of San Jose

Media Profile

1 newspaper
18 radio stations
23 network television stations
1 cable television operator

State Taxes[1]

Corporate Income/Franchise Tax	9.3%
Sales/Use Tax	8.5%
Individual Income Tax	11.0%
Unemployment Insurance Rate	3.40%

[1]See the State Tax Table Notes on page 308.

% City Taxes[2]

County Tax	1.25%
City Tax	None
Other Taxes	1.00%

% Property Tax Rates [3,4]

$11.4990 in $ per $1000

International Profile

Number of Foreign Banks	3
Number of Foreign-owned Businesses	330
Number of Persons Employed by Foreign-owned Businesses	11,829
Number of Daily International Flights	19

Real Estate

Occupancy Cost per Square Foot (Annual)

	Sq. Foot	Sq. Meters
Average Rental-Class A Office (Central Business District)	$21.64	$232.85
Average Rental-Class A Apartment	$12.67	$136.33
Average Rental-Warehouse	$4.54	$48.85

Construction Cost per Square Foot

	Sq. Foot	Sq. Meters
Excellent Class A Office	$156.39	$1,682.76
Class A Industrial/ Manufacturing	$94.44	$1,016.17

	Sq. Foot	Sq. Meters
Class A Distribution Warehouse	$66.54	$715.97
Excellent Class C Single Family Residential	$122.08	$1,313.58

Average Electric Cost (Cents per KwH)

	1992
Residential	$0.1179
Commercial	$0.1096
Industrial	$0.730
Average Price for a 3-bedroom Family House (in 1000's)	$225.0

Quality of Life

Climate

	Fahrenheit		Celsius	
	High	Low	High	Low
Winter	59	46	15	8
Spring	61	49	16	9
Summer	64	53	18	12
Autumn	68	55	20	13

Rainfall

	Inches	Millimeters
January	4.5	114
February	2.8	71
March	2.6	66
April	1.5	38
May	.4	10
June	.2	5
July	.1	3
August	.1	3
September	.2	5
October	1.1	28
November	2.5	64
December	3.5	89

Cultural Highlights

Children's Discovery Museum of San Jose
Japanese Friendship Gardens
Chinese Cultural Gardens

[2]See the State-Local General Sales Tax Notes on page 310.
[3]See the Property Tax Rate Notes on page 314.
[4]See the Classification of Real Property and Tangible Personal Property table on page 316.

Cultural Highlights (Continued)
 Rosicrucian Egyptian Museum
 San Jose Museum of Art

Leisure Highlights
 Winchester Mystery House
 Happy Hollow Park & Zoo
 The Tech Museum of Innovation
 San Jose McEnery Convention Center
 Santa Clara County Fairgrounds

Crime

Rate per 100,000 Inhabitants	1991
Number of violent crimes	522.4
Number of property crimes	4,515.0

Average Wages for Selected Occupations

	Average Hiring Salary
Secretary (LR-3)	$30,212
Computer Systems Analyst III	$54,392
Computer Programmer III	$41,236
Engineer II	$48,412
Maintenance Machinist	$39,228

Seattle

WASHINGTON

Located in the center of western Washington state, on the eastern shore of Puget Sound, Seattle lies between two mountain ranges: the Olympics and the Cascades. The Seattle MSA, comprising King and Snohomish Counties, experienced tremendous growth in the 1980s and now comprises more than two million residents. However, its economic and population growth was subsequently dampened by the national recession and cutbacks in defense spending.

Yet the slowdown in the area's economy is not without a silver lining. Housing prices have receded somewhat from their boom-time highs. The average price for a three-bedroom home in Snohomish County is approximately $145,000. Civic leaders also have something of a breather, during which they can address issues of growth management, rapid transit, and the regulatory climate. Moreover, while acknowledging the critical role of both the forest products industry and aerospace (Boeing in particular) in the area's economic life, they are seeking new avenues to growth, encouraging high-tech, biotech, and service businesses, as well as the Pacific Rim connection.

Aiding the Pacific Rim connection is the Port of Seattle, one of the largest in the United States. Its facilities include a Foreign Trade Zone (incorporating port marine and airport facilities). Japan is Seattle's biggest trading partner, and several Japanese companies have recently relocated to the area, including U.S. Hayakawa, an aircraft parts manufacturer; Sanken, a plastics manufacturer; and Japan Ace, an aerospace company.

Contrary to popular belief, it does not rain continuously in Seattle; the rainy season lasts from late fall to early spring, averaging a total annual rainfall of 39 inches, which is less than that of New York, Houston, or Atlanta. Nevertheless, the area has been an incubator for a number of leading-edge indoor leisure trends, including drinking specialty coffee and enjoying alternative rock music.

Seattle also offers nearly a dozen professional theater groups, three symphony orchestras, ballet, opera, and more than a dozen museums and art galleries. Special attractions include the Seattle Center and Spaceneedle, the Seattle Aquarium, and the Pacific Science Center. Football, baseball, and basketball fans follow the Seahawks, Mariners, and Supersonics.

City Profile

 Population
in Thousands

1980	337.7
1990	465.6
1992	502.4
1995 Estimate	545.0

Socioeconomic
Factors

Average Household Income

1980	$23,882
1991 Estimate	$51,559
% Change	115.9
1996 Projection	$63,348

Median Household Income

1980	$20,735
1991 Estimate	$41,149
% Change	98.5
1996 Projection	$50,578

Labor Force &
Employment

	1993
Total Number of Persons in the Labor Force (in 1000's)	1,175.6
Total Number of Persons Employed (in 1000's)	1,095.7
Average Unemployment Rate	6.8%

Total Employment in Thousands by Sector

	1980	1992
Construction	N/A	60.7
Manufacturing	N/A	211.2
Transportation/Utilities	N/A	69.6
Trade	N/A	264.8
Finance/Real Estate	N/A	73.5
Services	N/A	286.3
Government	N/A	158.7

 Education

1992 Enrollment

Two Year College	56,445
Four Year Undergraduate	30,640
Four Year Graduate	14,247
Average SAT Score	918
Total Possible Score: 1600	
Average ACT Score	N/A
Total Possible Score: 36	

 Business
Environment

Selected Major Employers
The Boeing Co.
Edmonds School District
GTE Northwest
Advanced Tech. Labs.
Snohomish Cty. Govmnt.
John Fluke Mfg. Co.
Olson's Foods
Blue Cross
Tramco
Everett School District

Media Profile
3 newspapers
34 radio stations
17 network television stations
1 cable television operator

 State Taxes

Corporate Income/Franchise Tax	0.0%
Sales/Use Tax	8.2%
Individual Income Tax	0.0%
Unemployment Insurance Rate	1.90%

 City Taxes[1]

County Tax	None
City Tax	1.70%
Other Taxes	None

 Property Tax Rates [2,3]

$13.586 in $ per $1000

International Profile

Number of Foreign Banks	6
Number of Foreign-owned Businesses	392
Number of Persons Employed by Foreign-owned Businesses	7,893
Number of Daily International Flights	99

 Real Estate

Occupancy Cost per Square Foot (Annual)

	Sq. Foot	Sq. Meters
Average Rental-Class A Office (Central Business District)	$20.99	$225.85
Average Rental-Class A Apartment	$9.72	$104.59
Average Rental- Warehouse	$5.11	$54.98

Construction Cost per Square Foot

	Sq. Foot	Sq. Meters
Excellent Class A Office	$145.48	$1,565.36
Class A Industrial/ Manufacturing	$87.85	$945.26

	Sq. Foot	Sq. Meters
Class A Distribution Warehouse	$61.89	$665.94
Excellent Class C Single Family Residential	$112.76	$1,213.30

Average Electric Cost (Cents per KwH)

	1992
Residential	$0.448
Commercial	$0.470
Industrial	$0.377
Average Price for a 3-bedroom Family House (in 1000's)	$145.0

 Quality of Life

Climate

	Fahrenheit		Celsius	
	High	Low	High	Low
Winter	45	36	7	2
Spring	58	42	14	6
Summer	75	56	24	13
Autumn	60	47	16	8

Rainfall

	Inches	Millimeters
January	6.0	152
February	4.0	102
March	4.0	102
April	2.0	51
May	2.0	51
June	2.0	51
July	1.0	25
August	1.0	25
September	2.0	51
October	3.0	76
November	5.0	127
December	6.0	152

Cultural Highlights

Museum of Flight
Pacific Science Center
Seattle Art Museum

[1]See the State-Local General Sales Tax Notes on page 310.
[2]See the Property Tax Rate Notes on page 314.
[3]See the Classification of Real Property and Tangible Personal Property table on page 316.

Cultural Highlights (Continued)
 Space Needle
 Pioneer Square

Leisure Highlights
 Hiram M. Chittenden (Ballard) Locks
 Pike Place Market
 Tillicum Village & Tours
 Woodland Park Zoological Gardens
 Seattle Aquarium

Crime

Rate per 100,000 Inhabitants	1991
Number of violent crimes	596.4
Number of property crimes	6,557.4

Average Wages for Selected Occupations

	Average Hiring Salary
Secretary (LR-3)	$18,647
Computer Systems Analyst III	$39,770
Computer Programmer III	$26,928
Engineer II	$39,768
Maintenance Machinist	$23,379

Tacoma

Just 36 miles south of Seattle, on Commencement Bay by the southeastern shore of Puget Sound, Tacoma is Washington's third largest city and a regional center for shipping, shipbuilding, forest products, metal refining, and chemical industries. It has also carved out a niche for itself by focusing on trade and health care.

Central to the area's efforts to strengthen its links with the Pacific Rim is the Port of Tacoma on Puget Sound, which features on-dock intermodal transportation, allowing containers to be moved directly from ships onto trains and vice versa. The area's economy has also gotten a boost from Boeing's decision to build an 850,000-square-foot airplane parts manufacturing plant in Frederickson.

Pierce County's population has grown by 22% since 1980, to a current population of 624,000 people, one-quarter of whom are in the 25-to-34 age group. The biggest gains were in South Prairie, Roy, and Sumner. The average sale price of a single-family home here is $129,000. Neighborhoods offer a choice of urban, suburban, and rural ambiance. Military households comprise nearly one-third of the population, reflecting the considerable military presence in Tacoma, including the Army's Fort Lewis and Madigan Army Medical Center and the Air Force's McCord Air Force Base. The economic impact of the military is said to be about $1.5 billion annually.

The heart of Tacoma's cultural life is the Pantages Centre for the Performing Arts, a restored vaudeville theater and historical landmark that is the site for music, dance, and drama. Tacoma also offers numerous theater groups, symphony orchestras, and ballet. It is home to the Bing Crosby Historical Society and the Camp Six Logging Museum.

Extensive recreational facilities are water- and mountain-oriented, including camping and hiking in Mount Rainier National Park and Olympic National Park and through state and city parks, plus skiing, cycling, river rafting, fishing, and hunting. The annual Western Washington State Fair takes place here in the fall. The Tacoma Dome, catalyst for downtown revival when it opened in 1983, is the site of numerous sports and entertainment events.

City Profile

Population in Thousands

1980	485.6
1990	586.2
1992	623.6
1995 Estimate	N/A

Socioeconomic Factors

Average Household Income

1980	$20,063
1991 Estimate	$36,980
% Change	84.3
1996 Projection	$44,794

Median Household Income

1980	$17,380
1991 Estimate	$29,968
% Change	72.4
1996 Projection	$35,899

Labor Force & Employment

	1993
Total Number of Persons in the Labor Force (in 1000's)	267.2
Total Number of Persons Employed (in 1000's)	243.6
Average Unemployment Rate	8.8%

Total Employment in Thousands by Sector

	1980	1992
Construction	7.3	10.9
Manufacturing	22.0	20.2
Transportation/Utilities	6.7	9.3
Trade	32.9	51.3
Finance/Real Estate	7.0	10.5
Services	31.3	53.1
Government	34.6	43.4

Education

1992 Enrollment

Two Year College	11,985
Four Year Undergraduate	5,492
Four Year Graduate	2,155
Average SAT Score	910
Total Possible Score: 1600	
Average ACT Score	N/A
Total Possible Score: 36	

Business Environment

Selected Major Employers

Boeing
Multicare Medical Center
Puget Sound Bankcorp
St. Joseph Hospital
Good Samaritan Hospital
Group Health Co-op of Puget Sound
Nalley's Fine Foods
West Coast Grocery Company
University of Puget Sound

Media Profile

1 newspaper
10 radio stations
17 network television stations
2 cable television operators

State Taxes

Corporate Income/Franchise Tax	0.0%
Sales/Use Tax	8.2%
Individual Income Tax	0.0%
Unemployment Insurance Rate	1.90%

City Taxes[1]

County Tax	None
City Tax	1.30%
Other Taxes	None

Property Tax Rates [2,3]

$12.46 in $ per $1000

International Profile

Number of Foreign Banks	0
Number of Foreign-owned Businesses	24
Number of Persons Employed by Foreign-owned Businesses	520
Number of Daily International Flights	99

Real Estate

Occupancy Cost per Square Foot (Annual)

	Sq. Foot	Sq. Meters
Average Rental-Class A Office (Central Business District)	$20.99	$225.82
Average Rental-Class A Apartment	$9.72	$104.59
Average Rental-Warehouse	$5.11	$54.98

Construction Cost per Square Foot

	Sq. Foot	Sq. Meters
Excellent Class A Office	$143.05	$1,539.22
Class A Industrial/Manufacturing	$86.39	$929.56

	Sq. Foot	Sq. Meters
Class A Distribution Warehouse	$60.86	$654.85
Excellent Class C Single Family Residential	$110.90	$1,193.28

Average Electric Cost (Cents per KwH)

	1992
Residential	$0.448
Commercial	$0.470
Industrial	$0.377
Average Price for a 3-bedroom Family House (in 1000's)	$116.5

Quality of Life

Climate

	Fahrenheit		Celsius	
	High	Low	High	Low
Winter	45	36	7	2
Spring	58	42	14	6
Summer	75	56	24	13
Autumn	60	47	16	8

Rainfall

	Inches	Millimeters
January	6.0	152
February	4.0	102
March	4.0	102
April	2.0	51
May	2.0	51
June	2.0	51
July	1.0	25
August	1.0	25
September	2.0	51
October	3.0	76
November	5.0	127
December	6.0	152

Cultural Highlights

Gig Harbor
Ruston Way Waterfront Parks
Tacoma Art Museum

[1]See the State-Local General Sales Tax Notes on page 310.
[2]See the Property Tax Rate Notes on page 314.
[3]See the Classification of Real Property and Tangible Personal Property table on page 316.

Leisure Highlights

Point Defiance Zoo & Aquarium
Tacoma Mall
Wright Park/Seymour Botanical
Conservatory
Tacoma Dome Exhibition Hall

Crime

Rate per 100,000 Inhabitants	1991
Number of violent crimes	947.5
Number of property crimes	6,032.1

Average Wages for Selected Occupations

	Average Hiring Salary
Secretary (LR-3)	$16,782
Computer Systems Analyst III	$35,793
Computer Programmer III	$24,235
Engineer II	$35,791
Maintenance Machinist	$21,041

PART *II*

Destination America:

An In-Depth Look at Location Opportunities in America's Regions and Cities

The Strategic Planning Process for American Site Selection

In today's complex corporate real estate environment, strategic planning is essential in providing a conceptual framework to test alternative uses, to maximize underutilized land assets, and to properly evaluate a location for a new corporate facility. The cost of occupancy, always an important factor for companies, is increasingly significant. Today's business environment is experiencing ever-greater financial performance pressures, and corporate real estate departments must reexamine facility operations, searching for operational and locational cost economies.

For a typical corporation, next to payroll costs, occupancy costs are the second largest expense. Head count reductions through attrition, early retirement, or elimination of support services are usually the first round of a cost-cutting review. Occupancy cost reductions—including a search for alternative locations that offer more competitive and productive environments—should be the second round in the review.

Unfortunately, for most corporate entities, systematic personnel reduction is analogous to cutting production in manufacturing. Consequently, reducing occupancy costs becomes even more important.

Therefore, a Corporate Real Estate Strategic Plan is required in order to balance conflicting demands to manage facility requirements and capital resources, and the need to minimize operations.

Before any corporate entity begins to look at occupancy costs, a Corporate Real Estate Strategic Plan, including its desired "position" in major markets, should be formulated and approved.

The strategic planning process establishes a clear method for determining the "best fit" of the corporate facility to a given location. Strategic planning can be seen as a search for the most

competitive and "best fit" real estate for a specific property or site—one that can carry the highest residual land and property value, while achieving the least occupancy cost. The Corporate Real Estate Strategic Plan should identify facility objectives and goals, but not specify program implementation, as the lease-versus-buy decision is frequently best made in the local area market, particularly in today's very competitive real estate environment.

Six Steps in the Corporate Location Analysis Process

Six steps are involved in a Corporate Location Analysis. Strategic planning and Quality of Life indexing, along with predevelopment financial feasibility testing are critical considerations to a "best fit." These steps do not heavily involve design activities; rather, they should identify the crucial user/facility programming requirements that must be accommodated, explicit location criteria, and financing parameters by which design and project scenarios are evaluated.

These components closely resemble the "product development cycle" of the consumer industry, in which a perceived "market need" proceeds to conceptualization and is then refined by specific evaluation of financial realities and the product's intended market position.

1. The Corporate Real Estate Strategic Plan
The first step is to establish a Corporate Real Estate Strategic Plan, which emulates the commercial "product development cycle," particularly in identifying future space needs, anticipating market position, accommodating the desired corporate image, and repositioning services or production for greatest cost-competitive advantages.

Creating a Corporate Real Estate Strategic Plan is much like a repositioning campaign for a consumer product, intended as a broad goal list to increase market share, pump up sales velocity, or rejuvenate a stalled product line. The Corporate Real Estate Strategic Plan is thus a digest of the corporate goals, comprising the product or services position desired for each major market, and the facility requirements for target users projected 5 years into the future. The creation of such a plan includes these action steps:

- Conduct potential user group surveys.
- Forecast absorption and occupancy rates.
- For each target market in the Strategic Plan, establish a "ground test" of comparables, including consideration of building amenities and capture rates that better-performing, or "preferred" projects have achieved.

• Conduct opinion leader interviews of knowledgeable local sources in the brokerage, business, and civic communities to establish a "best of" list in each target market.

Establish a base case analysis of current operating costs, specific to type of facility in the current corporate real estate inventory. Use this base case analysis to evaluate all other occupancy costs for any projected new facilities.

2. Establish Location Criteria

In advance of actual site evaluation or project predevelopment feasibility testing, general Location Criteria must be established—and certain demographic data collected—into a conceptual framework that will allow evaluation of specific sites. Today's location analysis must include information on a given area's Quality of Life (QOL), as well as Employer/Business Preference Criteria related to taxation, productivity, and other operational concerns.

Potential disposable income, job formation, employment trends, residential growth, and other softer QOL criteria must be assembled and used in a rational way within the facility location analysis process.

QOL indexing has remained a controversial subject for demographers and sociologists. There can be little argument that the criteria that might be contained in a QOL analysis can be a valuable tool in assessing locational attributes. The weight to be assigned to each QOL line item is worthy of debate, as each can be skewed depending on the bias of the observer. However, in combination with an Employer/Business Preference Criteria, in which more empirically measured data can be compared by location, the QOL index can serve to overcome some of the limitations of the Employer/Business Preference Criteria.

Corporate Location Criteria

Quality of Life Index

1. Housing Quality/Neighborhood Integrity
2. Education Quality and Placement Record
3. Employment Security and Choice
4. Police Services/Perception of Security
5. Shoppers' Goods/Availability and Choice
6. Medical Services/Depth of Expertise
7. Regional Recreational Offerings
8. Cultural Opportunities
9. Transportation System/Ease of Access
10. Taxation Levels/Service Provided
11. Integrity of Political System
12. Climate/Landscape Quality

Employer/Business Preference Criteria

1. QOL Index
2. Area Work Ethic
3. Area Tax Considerations
4. Available Labor/Clerical Pool
5. Political/Business Coalition
6. Advance Growth Planning
7. Regional Economic Outlook
8. Financial Assistance
9. University R&D Capabilities
10. Gateway Airport/Transportation
11. Incubator Opportunities
12. Foreign/Domestic Market Access

The Quality of Life Index, which includes residential, cultural, and civic stability, is integral to the Corporate Location Analysis process, as the QOL Index is the first component of typical Preference Criteria used in Facility Location Analyses.

For example, if a relatively young but stable work force is required, housing quality, neighborhood integrity, and primary and secondary education are paramount considerations, along with housing affordability. These attributes, particularly with respect to housing affordability in the early child-rearing years, are frequently a crucial determinant in recruiting and retaining an effective work force.

3. Site Capacity Testing

The third step in the corporate location analysis is to test specific sites for their full development capacity, or to decide which properties may be surplus in a given corporate portfolio. The following are key steps in Site Capacity tests:

- Classify the site within the corporate portfolio of similarly owned or leased facilities and rank the site in its existing form against other, more attractive properties in its submarket area.
- Identify all major advantages and limitations to vehicular access.
- Investigate site utility infrastructure and the capacity of systems to handle upgrades or conversions.
- Assess the site context.
- Identify current zoning constraints.

The result of the Site Capacity analysis is to establish a "design envelope" program of facility zoning, site capacity, bulk coverage, and access and circulation, including pre-identification of environmental constraints. Clearly, a target user program can best be utilized for a given site only after such an exercise has been completed.

4. Predevelopment Feasibility

In tandem with the development of various scenarios for the acquisition of new facilities, a simultaneous testing of predevelopment feasibility through detailed financial pro forma modeling must occur. Fundamental to a new facility decision is the lease-versus-buy analysis, which evaluates fully loaded development costs and the commitment of corporate capital resources against similar out-leased premises. This is one component of the Corporate Real Estate Management Decision Matrix (discussed in the following section).

List all financing assumptions, including interest rates, secondary financing, and return on investment objectives or hurdle rates for corporate equity. Perform risk and sensitivity analyses at 10% and 15% increments on all assumptions.

- Run alternative assumptions on density and coverage, particularly for multiphase projects on which significant residual value for later phases exists.
- Project realistic 11-year pro forma scenarios.
- Establish a "lease-versus-own" evaluative model, based on internal corporate capital requirements and alternative financing sources.
- Identify and list alternative public/private financing opportunities, including special public funds eligible for infrastructure and site access improvements.
- The financial analysis must move in tandem with the physical design process for site location evaluation, including planning sketches, schematic site plans, and user-specific space plan designs.
- The predevelopment financial review should provide feedback, in work sessions, on significant cost reductions that may be required in planning the new facilities, or in user negotiations for out-leased premises.

5. Management Decision Matrix

Given the "target user" facility requirements, and identification of a tentative location, the next step is to evaluate both the location and the facility according to an established set of Management Criteria. Elements of this "Management Decision Matrix" should consider all aspects of the project and include the following criteria topics:

- Evaluate "lease-versus-own" and "internal-versus-external" development management team.
- Weigh perceived reaction of targeted user and potential of various specific locations to induce additional outside tenant interest, particularly for a site that may have solid residual value.
- Evaluate potential for attracting a joint venture developer to share risks.

- Evaluate location for availability of public funds for portions of project improvements, along with potential for spin-off of parcels, with proceeds to fund additional development costs.

6. Adopt an Implementation Plan

The final step in the corporate location analysis process is to devise an action agenda to implement the project.

An action agenda should address all the necessary steps for implementation, including the following:

- Create an overall development schedule, including approval process, target user move-in constraints, design and major equipment lead time horizons, and tenant completion/occupancy dates.
- Identify joint venture alternatives and the steps required to encourage interest, and negotiate a development agreement with an outside entity or financial institution.
- List and identify all professional team requirements, including specialists needed to execute the project master plan and each consultant's current availability and work load.
- Identify and focus on the Public Approval Process and those who could or would oppose or support such a project.

Conclusion

Relocation decisions are among the most important long-range choices a company will make. Management must weigh all options carefully, using all available information and outside specialists with expertise in real estate, strategic planning, taxation, and accounting. Such decisions affect every aspect of the company, from the bottom line to the corporate culture.

The results of the Corporate Location Analysis process are modified by each successive component activity to produce a preferred scheme and location. By using QOL indexes and site-specific Employer Preference Criteria in tandem with predevelopment financial feasibility studies, an action agenda can be established to evaluate and implement the investment decision.

Site Selection Criteria: Human Resources, Technology, and Locational Alternatives

Directors of corporate real estate are now working to anticipate the changing needs of their corporations, produced by the long-term structural changes occurring in the national and international business environments.

Corporate real estate directors are under pressure to reduce the costs of managing and maintaining their staffs and associated functions of the real estate department, while still meeting multiscope internal user group demands. As a result, real estate directors are using outside companies to assist in many areas of corporate real estate planning and management.

A function often out-sourced is the analysis of locations for corporate facilities. Facilities location analysis requires an objective, multidisciplinary approach in order to provide the total quality management and control demanded by corporate user groups. Finance, operations, human resources, marketing, transportation/distribution, telecommunications, tax, and legal, as well as real estate issues, must be understood and integrated. The requirements and objectives of the various corporate operations must be balanced into a strategic plan for the future. Information flow and decision processing are critical elements of a location study.

These complex issues must be addressed in the context of multilocation decision making, which may include national and international alternatives. Few corporate real estate departments are equipped to handle the magnitude of data collection, synthesis, and evaluation required to address the issues of multisite, multilocation analyses through a comprehensive program. Internal pressures, organizational hierarchy, and reporting requirements often complicate the real estate department's ability to address all client issues.

Consultants specializing in corporate location decisions can provide the corporate real estate director with a cost-effective,

experienced, multidisciplinary team and an objective methodology for conducting a comprehensive location study. The successful outsourcing of these services, however, requires that the consultant have a sound understanding of corporate objectives and a proven approach to managing the myriad of issues that will arise during the course of the assignment.

What drives a corporation's decision in selecting a site for expansion of an existing business, to start a new operation, or as part of a consolidation strategy? Some may be surprised to learn that real estate costs alone are not foremost, nor is the lure of significant economic incentives.

Human resources' needs come first; in short, the current and projected labor force must be of sufficient quality, availability, cost, and stability to support the corporation's goals and objectives. Site decisions must not only support the corporation's long-term business strategy; they must also enable that strategy to succeed.

It is no secret that corporate America faces intense pressure to become more competitive, more flexible, and swifter in its response to changing market demand. Reengineering business processes and downsizing have become facts of corporate life, and many corporations are seeking to consolidate or centralize their operations. In the realm of site selection and relocation, the new corporate reality often translates into the need to contain or reduce occupancy costs while improving the quality of labor and productivity.

In this business environment, the site selection and relocation decision-making process has become ever more complex. First, companies are becoming increasingly diversified, which means that different operations within those companies have differing elements of personnel needs. For example, a community that might serve a data processing division may well be inappropriate for a marketing or customer support division.

Second, the choice of locations has also become more diverse. Business truly has become global, and the current state of telecommunications allows a business to function just as well in Dublin or Glasgow as it might in Phoenix or Seattle.

With so much at stake, locational decisions must be supported by reliable and comprehensive data. Fortunately, there is no scarcity of information available regarding every area's population, prevailing wages/benefits, housing, schools, taxes, and other key ingredients (or factors). But data alone does not create an obvious area "profile" or present a readily discernible ideal choice for a corporation. What matters is what the data means to the corporation, or what might be termed "qualitative objectivity" in interpreting the data.

Labor Force Issues

Typically, a corporate location study team will include the CFO, COO, and corporate real estate and human resources executives. Their collective responsibility is to examine closely the demographic labor force, financial/economic information, and education and quality of life/business climate to determine location suitability.

Whether or not a corporation is planning to relocate personnel from an existing site to a new location, its strategic plan will depend on hiring a considerable number of workers from the selected new location. There are a number of key questions regarding an area's labor force: What is the existing level of demand for workers who have the skills sought by the corporation? How extensive is the available pool of workers? What are the prevailing wages and benefits? What is the level of salary inflation? What is the turnover rate in the corporation's industry? What is the unemployment rate? Is the 18-to-44-year-old population stable, growing, or declining? What are the most productive methods of recruitment? How long does it take to fill different positions in the geographic area? Do local, regional, or state economic development agencies provide assistance with training (or retraining), screening, and hiring?

Statistics alone do not yield obvious solutions. One community, for example, was rated very high in a recent study on QOL issues, in which the belief in "family values" was evident. However, further inquiry showed that certain industries in this community found it exceedingly difficult to find workers for second- and third-shift slots, as the timing interfered with traditional family activities. Thus, this area may not be an ideal choice for those industries with unconventional work shifts.

Education Issues

The quality of an area's labor force is largely dependent on the quality of its education system. Corporate America's focus on educational issues has become increasingly intense. In a site selection or relocation decision, educational requirements will vary, depending on the types of jobs the corporation seeks to fill. Generally, however, there are a number of issues that must be analyzed: curriculum, facilities, pupil/teacher ratios in elementary and secondary schools, SAT scores, percentage of students graduating from high school, and the percentage of students moving on to higher education. Information on metropolitan areas should cover both urban and suburban systems.

A detailed analysis of an area's colleges and universities may also be important. Many corporations seek communities where

the presence of colleges and universities attracts good students who may stay in the community after graduation to pursue their careers.

Quality and Availability of Vocational Schools

It is not enough to know that, yes, a community does have a vocational education program. It is also important to know what type of curriculum is offered. Does it cover business issues, and how current is the technology used? (These questions are particularly important for financial service companies and institutions). Are robotics and automation offered? Is there a dynamic working relationship between the Vo-Tech schools and the economic development agencies in the area, region, or state?

The art of "qualitative objectivity" is key in analyzing educational issues. For example, one community we have examined, which has consistently had a very well educated labor force and which has also had desirable traits such as a high teacher/pupil ratio, currently suffers from inadequate educational facilities. This will ultimately translate into significant tax increases as the community upgrades its facilities. Such issues must be factored into decision making by any company considering a move to this community.

Housing, Quality of Life, Business Climate/Political Issues

More difficult to quantify than labor and education statistics, but paramount in importance, are issues of "quality of life." They will largely determine how sound the long-term match between a corporation and a community will be. Analyzing these issues requires a thorough understanding of a corporation's unique culture. The following questions must be addressed: How receptive is the community to incoming businesses? Does it maintain a policy of growth management, and is it actively seeking to diversify its economic and industrial base? How does its regulatory environment (including zoning and site review, if appropriate) compare with that of other communities? Where will workers live? Key to a pleasant quality of life in a community is the availability of different types of housing at price levels affordable to the target work force. Equally important are commute patterns; attractive and affordable housing seems less appealing when going from home to work and back takes a long time. Long commutes, perpetual gridlock, problematic public transportation systems—all are major drawbacks to living in many communities.

What types of recreational facilities and activities does the community offer? How healthful is the air quality and the general

environment? A vibrant community that can keep its existing population base and expand it by attracting people from other parts of the country is a desirable one for business.

Area Analyses: A Case Example

The impact of human resource needs was evident in a recent study we did for a large service sector company. The company was seeking to establish a major regional operations center and projected that approximately 500 employees would be relocated and another 1,500 would be hired locally.

The initial phase of our analysis covered all Metropolitan Statistical Areas (MSAs) across the United States, ranging from a population of 250,000 to 2.5 million. We chose these parameters because previous studies had shown that an operation of this size in a community with a population of less than 250,000 will strain the corporate relationship with the community. We had also found that significant costs and economic benefits may not be achieved in the largest MSAs.

After the initial phase of the study, the list of possibilities was reduced from 155 to 25. Here we began to focus in greater detail on issues of labor cost and availability, population growth, unemployment rates, the 18-to-44-year-old age group, and industry-specific labor forces.

Several different scenarios were analyzed through an interactive computerized model; the "what ifs?" were addressed by changing the weighting and ranking of key issues. What became clear was that no matter what the scenario, certain communities consistently clustered at the top of the list. The analysis of the top 25 candidates was presented to the company's executive committee.

During the subsequent phase of the study, more detailed information was provided by appropriate economic development agencies, and the list was further narrowed to 12 metro areas. Then we conducted interviews with about a half dozen major employers in each area for specific information about their respective communities, labor forces, turnover rates, hiring experiences, and possible union problems. These interviews, as always, were conducted in confidence.

To narrow the choice to four possibilities, the communities were visited with the various user groups involved, including managers, telecommunications directors, and operations staff. We also examined the availability of various sites, performed analyses of buying versus building versus leasing facilities, and entered into preliminary negotiations.

Locational Trends

In making locational decisions, it is important to be aware that communities are in a constant state of evolution. Past performance should be examined, but the future is more important. Although cities in a period of transition can be a more difficult "sell" to corporate executives, many have hidden attributes or have retooled; these should be brought to the corporation's attention.

Currently, the so-called second-tier cities are becoming more popular as they retool and diversify. Even in strong communities, however, the downtown areas are typically less robust than the suburbs. Thus, we expect to see more suburban-to-suburban relocations.

We also find that more companies are interested in obtaining training assistance from municipal, regional, or state sources, rather than outright grants for their relocation. Financial incentives based on hiring—that is, offsetting taxes based on hiring a certain number of people over a certain period of time—have been introduced, and we expect that more states will begin similar programs in order to remain competitive.

Corporations embarking on location studies will undoubtedly find that the information provided by the various municipal, regional, and state economic development entities may not be uniform in scope. A key role of the location consultant, therefore, is to make sure that the information received from these sources is timely, comprehensive, and lends itself to "apples-to-apples" comparisons.

One of the misconceptions about the location consulting business is that the consultant's only role is to recommend a specific community to the corporation based on all its findings. Rather, the consultant's role is to advise the corporation on what all the statistics mean to its ability to do business. The consultant cannot make the location decision for the corporation.

Corporate executives can fall prey to preconceived notions based on what they see or read in the media. They may also tend to focus initially on the "top five" business locations in vogue at the time. The consultant's role, then, is to try to prevent such prejudices from affecting decision making. Guidance in structuring the location study is key; better-focused issues and questions lead to the "qualitative objectivity" that enables better decision making.

Housing Affordability: A Ranking of American Cities by Housing Costs Relative to Income

Ernst & Young, through the National Real Estate Index, analyzed the housing costs in 70 U.S. markets and have ranked relative housing affordability based on current mortgage interest rates, household incomes, home prices, and rental rates. Markets are ranked from most to least affordable, based on the cost of single family homes and apartments relative to local market household income.

Key Findings in the United States

The most affordable and the least affordable major housing markets, of the 70 metropolitan markets analyzed in this study, are shown below.

Most Affordable Housing Markets In the United States		Least Affordable Housing Markets in the United States	
Metropolitan Market	Composite Housing Costs Relative to Income[1]	Metropolitan Market	Composite Housing Costs Relative to Income[1]
Kansas City, MO	18.1	San Francisco, CA	49.6
Omaha, NE	18.4	Honolulu, HI	48.6
Houston, TX	19.0	Los Angeles, CA	40.6
Dallas-Fort Worth, TX	19.5	New York City, NY	36.2
Denver, CO	20.0	Oakland-East Bay, CA	35.0
Grand Rapids, MI	20.0	San Diego, CA	34.8
St. Louis, MO	20.2	Orange County, CA	34.3
Birmingham, AL	20.6	San Jose, CA	34.0
Columbus, OH	20.8	Boston, MA	31.4
Charlotte, NC	20.8	Miami, FL	30.7

[1]*As a precentage of disposable median household income. The composite figure is a simple average of the single family home and rental components. These components are shown in the chart on pages 292-294.*

Sources: *Coldwell Banker Residential Real Estate Group and the National Real Estate Index provided the bulk of the home price and rental rates data, respectively, on which this study was based. See page 295 for a complete explanation of the methodology and sources.*

U.S. Market Composite Housing Costs
All Markets

Metropolitan Market	1993 Affordability Ranking[1]	Single Family Home Cost Relative to Income	Rental Cost Relative to Income	Composite Housing Costs Relative to Income
Albuquerque, NM	48	24.8	27.8	26.3
Atlanta, GA	11	20.4	21.4	20.9
Austin, TX	18	21.7	22.1	21.9
Bakersfield, CA	55	29.6	27.4	28.5
Baltimore, MD	46	29.2	23.0	26.1
Birmingham, AL	8	20.3	21.0	20.6
Boston, MA	62	36.6	26.1	31.4
Buffalo, NY	40	23.1	26.3	24.7
Central New Jersey	15	22.4	20.6	21.5
Charleston, SC	41	22.9	27.0	25.0
Charlotte, NC	10	20.6	21.0	20.8
Chicago, IL	56	30.3	27.3	28.8
Cincinnati, OH	34	27.2	20.8	24.0
Cleveland, OH	42	25.6	25.0	25.3
Columbus, OH	9	21.1	20.5	20.8
Dallas-Fort Worth, TX	4	17.6	19.1	19.5
Denver, CO	5	19.8	20.3	20.0
Detroit, MI	35	23.7	24.3	24.0
El Paso, TX	37	24.2	24.3	24.4
Fort Lauderdale, FL	49	25.0	28.0	26.5
Fresno, CA	59	31.6	28.6	30.1
Grand Rapids, MI	6	20.0	20.0	20.0
Greensboro/ Winston-Salem, NC	47	29.6	22.7	26.2
Greenville/ Spartanburg, SC	22	21.0	23.9	22.5
Hartford, CT	45	26.9	24.9	25.9
Honolulu, HI	69	62.9	34.2	48.6
Houston, TX	3	18.9	19.1	19.0
Indianapolis, IN	17	24.5	19.1	21.8
Jacksonville, FL	19	19.8	24.2	22.0
Kansas City, MO	1	15.9	20.3	18.1
Knoxville, TN	25	21.8	23.7	22.8
Las Vegas, NV	28	21.8	24.6	23.2
Los Angeles, CA	68	52.0	29.2	40.6
Memphis, TN	20	21.2	23.2	22.2
Miami, FL	61	28.4	33.0	30.7
Milwaukee, WI	23	22.1	23.3	22.7

[1]Markets are rated in descending order from the most affordable (low numbers) to the least affordable (higher numbers). Although the figures in columns 2-4 are rounded, markets are ranked based on actual, rather than rounded, affordability numbers.

Note About the Study Methodology: In a study of this nature, there are almost always some inherent shortcomings related to the underlying data employed. We recognize, for instance, that the employment of amenitized four-bedroom houses and fully-amenitized, two-bedroom apartments as the proxy for home ownership and rental costs, respectively, may not be as representative in some markets as others. The purpose of this study, however, was to analyze, in as systematic a fashion as possible, housing conditions in a wide cross section of urban areas across the United States, and we believe that this methodology best achieves that objective.

U.S. Market Composite Housing Costs
All Markets (Continued)

Metropolitan Market	1993 Affordability Ranking[1]	Single Family Home Cost Relative to Income	Rental Cost Relative to Income	Composite Housing Costs Relative to Income
Minneapolis/ St. Paul, MN	24	22.4	23.1	22.8
Nashville, TN	12	19.6	22.2	20.9
Nassau/Suffolk, NY	30	23.2	23.6	23.4
New Orleans, LA	14	21.4	20.8	21.1
New York, NY	67	36.4	36.1	36.2
Northern New Jersey	50	28.2	25.3	26.8
Norfolk, VA	29	22.5	23.9	23.2
Oakland/ East Bay, CA	66	40.2	29.7	35.0
Omaha, NE	2	17.3	19.4	18.4
Orange County, CA	64	41.9	26.7	34.3
Orlando, FL	32	23.0	24.2	23.6
Philadelphia, PA	51	28.2	25.6	26.9
Phoenix, AZ	31	22.6	24.4	23.5
Pittsburgh, PA	57	25.6	31.9	28.8
Portland, OR	38	23.1	25.9	24.5
Providence, RI	58	34.1	23.8	29.0
Raleigh/Durham, NC	26	21.7	24.2	23.0
Richmond, VA	27	21.8	24.2	23.0
Riverside/ San Bernardino, CA	54	31.6	25.2	28.4
Rochester, NY	33	26.2	21.0	23.6
Sacramento, CA	52	33.2	22.6	27.9
Salt Lake City, UT	13	22.0	20.2	21.1
San Antonio, TX	16	19.1	24.0	21.6
San Diego, CA	65	37.2	32.4	34.8
San Francisco, CA	70	65.1	34.1	49.6
San Jose, CA	63	41.8	26.1	34.0
Sarasota/Bradenton, FL	53	27.8	28.0	27.9
Seattle, WA	36	24.7	24.1	24.4
St. Louis, MO	7	19.0	21.4	20.2
Tampa/St. Petersburg/ Clearwater, FL	44	23.7	27.2	25.4
Tucson, AZ	60	29.6	31.6	30.6
Tulsa, OK	21	18.2	26.1	22.2
Washington, DC	43	26.6	24.2	25.4
West Palm Beach, FL	39	22.2	26.8	24.5

Sources: The Local Market Composite Housing Cost Index combines effective gross rents for high-quality multifamily properties, as reported by the National Real Estate Index, and mortgage payments calculated for existing single family homes, based on average home prices, as compiled by Coldwell Banker's Residential Real Estate Group for four-bedroom, single family homes. The monthly rental and mortgage payments are compared with local household income to derive the ranking. The household income data is as reported in Sales & Marketing Management's 1992 Survey of Buying Power.

U.S. Market Population and Household Income

Metropolitan Market	% 1990–1991 Population	Median Household Income[2] (in dollars)	Metropolitan Market	% 1990–1991 Population	Median Household Income[2] (in dollars)
Albuquerque, NM	2.3	29,145	Nashville, TN	1.8	32,568
Atlanta, GA	3.1	35,536	Nassau-		
Austin, TX	3.3	31,835	Suffolk, NY	0.2[1]	53,425
Bakersfield, CA	4.3	30,139	New Orleans, LA	0.8	28,757
Baltimore, MD	1.3	36,520	New York, NY	0.2[1]	32,417
Birmingham, AL	1.1	29,003	Northern NJ	0.2[1]	48,648
Boston, MA	(0.4)	42,278	Norfolk, VA	1.5	31,853
Buffalo, NY	0.3	29,594	Oakland/East Bay, CA	1.3	42,048
Central New Jersey	0.2[1]	55,212	Omaha, NE	1.5	34,898
Charleston, SC	3.3	29,356	Orange County, CA	1.3	46,655
Charlotte, NC	2.4	32,316	Orlando, FL	3.6	32,102
Chicago, IL	1.2	39,440	Philadelphia, PA	0.4	39,012
Cincinnati, OH	1.2	33,563	Phoenix, AZ	2.2	30,162
Cleveland, OH	0.5	32,543	Pittsburgh, PA	0.4	29,540
Columbus, OH	1.8	33,529	Portland, OR	3.6	32,961
Dallas/Fort Worth, TX	2.4	36,569	Providence, RI	0.1	31,744
Denver, CO	2.8	35,408	Raleigh-		
Detroit, MI	0.4	36,150	Durham, NC	3.2	35,116
El Paso, TX	3.4	25,059	Richmond, VA	1.8	34,244
Fort Lauderdale, FL	2.5	31,839	Riverside/		
Fresno, CA	3.4	27,901	San Bernardino, CA	5.1	34,542
Grand Rapids, MI	1.6	35,647	Rochester, NY	1.0	35,735
Greensboro/			Sacramento, CA	3.4	34,689
Winston-Salem, NC	1.5	29,843	Salt Lake City, UT	2.9	33,194
Greenville/			San Antonio, TX	1.8	28,316
Spartanburg, SC	1.5	29,662	San Diego, CA	2.0	35,776
Hartford, CT	0.1	43,379	San Francisco, CA	1.4	41,307
Honolulu, HI	1.7	45,406	San Jose, CA	0.5	49,087
Houston, TX	3.5	35,648	Sarasota/		
Indianapolis, IN	1.8	34,263	Bradenton, FL	2.4	29,715
Jacksonville, FL	3.0	30,051	Seattle, WA	2.2	39,065
Kansas City, MO	1.2	35,208	St. Louis, MO	0.6	35,125
Knoxville, TN	2.4	27,281	Tampa/St Petersburg/		
Las Vegas, NV	8.5	31,025	Clearwater, FL	1.6	26,703
Los Angeles, CA	1.3	36,039	Tucson, AZ	1.5	24,663
Memphis, TN	1.3	29,706	Tulsa, OK	1.9	27,318
Miami, FL	2.1	27,401	Washington, DC	1.6	47,347
Milwaukee, WI	0.9	35,476	West Palm		
Minneapolis/			Beach, FL	2.7	32,926
St. Paul, MN	1.7	37,580			

[1]The Census Bureau is no longer providing population figures for these jurisdictions within the greater New York-New Jersey-Long Island metropolitan area. This 0.2% figure represents the figure for the entire metropolitan area. In all likelihood, growth in Central New Jersey exceeded the growth rate in the greater metropolitan area.

[2]As reported in Sales & Marketing Management's 1992 Survey of Buying Power, page B-19.

Methodology

The 1993 Study of Housing Costs compares housing expenditures in 70 major metropolitan markets in the United States. The markets were selected on the basis of size. All urban areas having more than one million residents in their respective metropolitan areas (as defined by the Census Bureau) were included, as well as select, rapidly growing smaller markets, as reflected in recently released population growth estimates by the Census Bureau. Generally, all markets included in the study have at least 500,000 residents.

Home ownership costs and rents were compared with median household income in each respective local market. As before, we have employed standard mortgage costs (i.e., this year, 7.5% for 30-year fixed-rate financing, down from 8% last year) and, except for Canadian markets, standard tax deductions across all metropolitan areas (25% of total monthly mortgage payments).

The comprehensive market rankings shown represent a "benchmark" approximation of relative housing affordability. Actual housing costs will vary, depending on the mortgage terms, property taxes, and insurance rates available in local markets, as well as on the individual's tax bracket and the prevailing tax rates within respective states. In addition, as noted earlier, the study ranks metropolitan areas as defined by the Census Bureau, not individual cities.

U.S. Corporate Relocation Survey: Where American Firms Plan to Relocate During the Next Decade

Ernst & Young's Real Estate Advisory Services, The National Real Estate Index, and the International Association of Corporate Real Estate Executives conducted a survey of corporate America to determine the impact of corporate relocation, expansion, and consolidation on the nation's investment real estate sector. Corporate real estate executives were asked to report their preferred location sites and factors. Specifically, they were asked to identify those markets nationwide preferred for the location of three types of facilities—office, distribution, and manufacturing—and to indicate the site selection factors that were most important in their decision making.

Preferred Site Selection Factors

Introduction and Key Findings

The majority of questions asked of the nation's leading corporate real estate professionals in the survey pertained to the most important economic, political, and social factors that determine the location decisions for major private and public organizations. Specifically, survey respondents were asked to rank the relative significance of 28 selection factors employed in making location decisions in the United States. These individual site selection factors were clustered in six broad categories, including real estate-related costs, market/corporate/supplier accessibility, taxes/regulatory environment, quality of life, labor quality/availability, and infrastructure considerations.

Real Estate-Related Costs—Most Critical Category

Of the six broad category factors, real estate-related costs were the most important, overall, to the survey respondents. In fact, more than 58% of the study participants rated the three real estate-related criteria (i.e., low lease rates, low construction costs, and up-front rent concessions), overall, as "very important" site selection factors. Another 38% of the respondents indicated that these three factors were, overall, at least moderately important.

Taxes/Regulatory Factors—Second Most Important Category

Nearly half of the study participants rated taxes and the regulatory environment as "very important," and nearly 84% rated them as at least moderately important. In addition, the broad category of infrastructure factors was also assigned a high priority by the study participants.

Low Lease Rates, Educated Labor Force, and Access to Major Highways—Most Important Individual Factors

As can be seen in Fig. 1-1, the most important individual site selection factor, by a wide margin, was low lease rates. Virtually all of the survey respondents (98%) rated this as at least moderately important in their site selection calculus.

The next two most important factors were the availability of an educated labor force and access to major highways. Nineteen in 20 survey respondents indicated that an educated labor force was at least moderately important in their site selection decision making. Approximately 93% of the survey respondents rated access to major highway arteries as at least moderately important.

Surprisingly, personal income taxes and affordable housing did not rate in the top tier of factors, despite the wide publicity they garner in the media. Perhaps most surprising, however, was that tax relocation/start-up incentives were not named in the top tier of important individual site selection factors. Factors that scored relatively low included access to rail, climate, recreational/cultural amenities, access to corporate/division headquarters, and the availability of industry-specific skills.

A complete listing of the individual site selection factors discussed in the study and their relative ranking can be seen in Fig. 1-2.

Figure 1-1: Top Ten Site Selection Factors

Factor	Weighted Average Score*
1. Low lease rates	2.81
2. Educated labor force	2.48
3. Access to major highways	2.48
4. Low construction costs	2.47
5. Access to primary consumer markets	2.41
6. Well-developed energy/telecommunications systems	2.37
7. Favorable local government attitude toward business	2.34
8. Low property tax rates	2.28
9. Low crime rate	2.26
10. Low corporate and business taxes	2.18

Study participants were asked to rate the site selection factors on a continuum from 1 (not important) to 3 (very important).

Real Estate Costs

Real estate-related costs constituted the single most important overall category in the site selection calculus of corporate real estate decision makers. Nearly three-fifths of the survey respondents rated this category as very important in location decision making, and 96% viewed it as at least moderately important.

As shown in Figure 1-2, the single most important site selection factor was low lease rates, rated as very important by more than 80% of the study participants. Approximately 93% indicated that low construction costs were at least moderately important.

The availability of up-front rent concessions (weighted average score of 2.13) was viewed as only moderately important by survey respondents.

Figure 1-2: Preferred Site Selection Factors

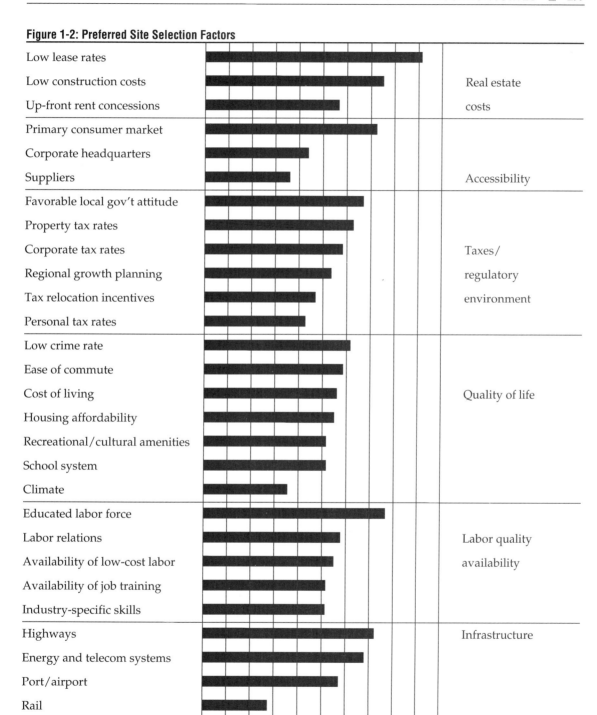

Accessibility to Market/Suppliers/Corporate Headquarters

A far lower proportion of study participants—approximately only two-thirds—rated accessibility, overall, as at least moderately important. Nevertheless, as seen in Figure 1-2, one accessibility-related factor, "access to primary consumer markets," ranked among the five most important individual site selection factors. Interestingly, as discussed in greater depth in Chapter 6, this was named by study participants as the single most important factor in deciding to locate in a foreign country. Approximately 85% of the study participants rated access to consumer markets as at least moderately important in their location decision making.

The other accessibility-related site selection factors, however, were rated as among the least important in the study. For instance, fewer than three in ten study participants rated proximity to corporate/division headquarters, and only one in six named access to suppliers, as very important site selection factors.

Taxation/Regulatory Environment

Perhaps the site selection category most highly publicized by the media is the tax and regulatory environment. Descriptions of the incentive programs offered major firms considering an expansion or new location frequently occupy the front pages of local newspapers, and the appropriate degree of cooperation between local government and respective local business communities is the focus of many an op-ed article.

The study participants offered mixed views on this broad criterion. Although two individual site selection factors—a favorable local government attitude toward business and low property tax rates—were viewed as ranking among the most important site selection factors, a number of other factors that many analysts might have intuitively assumed to be important did not fare as well. For instance, personal income tax levels ranked near the bottom of individual site location factors. And, perhaps most surprising of all, tax relocation/start-up incentives were named by relatively few study participants (only 27%) as constituting a very important site selection factor. In fact, it ranked only 23rd among the 28 individual site selection factors included in the study.

Specifically, as can be seen in Figure 1-2, the highest ranking factor in this category was the relationship between local government and business. Clearly, the nation's leading corporate real estate professionals believe that a favorable working relationship between local government and the business community is an important factor in site selection. In fact, more than half of the

study participants indicated that this factor was very important to them. In addition, the property tax rate level (which could have been considered a real estate-related factor as well) was viewed as very important to four in ten study participants and, overall, received the eighth highest-weighted average ranking of all individual site selection factors.

The other tax-related factor viewed as important by the nation's corporate real estate executives was corporate and business taxes, though perhaps not ranked as high as some might have anticipated. More than four-fifths of the study participants believed that corporate/business taxation levels are at least moderately important, enough to rank this factor as the tenth most important overall.

As noted earlier, perhaps the greatest surprise here was the comparative little importance attached to personal income taxes. In fact, although approximately two-thirds of the study participants viewed the rate of personal income taxes as moderately important, fewer than one in five identified it as a "very important" site selection factor. Consequently, of the individual factors included in the study, only access to rail arteries, access to suppliers, and favorable climate received a lower-weighted average score.

Quality of Life Characteristics

The broad criterion "quality of life" received the lowest rating, overall, of the six broad site selection categories. In fact, only one of the seven individual QOL factors ranked in the top ten individual factors.

Whereas a low crime rate was viewed as very important by nearly four in ten study participants and at least moderately important by a total of nine in ten (thereby achieving the rank of ninth most important factor), such factors as recreational/cultural amenities, climate, and even the quality of school systems, received a relatively low rating.

As seen in Figure 1-2, even the affordability of housing, a factor that garners considerable attention in the press, was considered to be of only midlevel significance by study participants. Two other factors that ranked in the upper half of the 28 site selection factors in importance were the overall cost of living and the ease of commute.

Labor Costs, Quality, and Availability

Another broad category that might have been expected to achieve an overall higher rating was labor. Although an educated labor force ranked behind only low lease rates as an important site selection factor, each of the other four individual labor-related factors, including (perhaps surprisingly) labor costs, was

rated, at best, only in the midlevel tier of individual factors.

As seen in Figure 1-2, more than half of the study participants viewed the availability of a well-educated labor force as a "very important" site selection factor. A full 19 in 20 rated it to be of at least moderate significance. All other labor-related factors paled in comparison with this individual factor. For instance, the availability of low-cost labor, which has been widely cited as one of the most important objections to the proposed free trade treaty with Mexico, received only a midlevel ranking. In fact, it ranked behind "labor relations" in the pecking order of significant factors. A full one-third of study participants rated good labor relations as a very important site selection factor.

In addition, the availability of continuing education and job training programs at the local level did not garner as much support as might have been anticipated (a 2.03 weighted average score), and the availability of industry-specific skills received approximately the same response as the availability of continuing education. One possible interpretation of this data is that what the nation's corporations are calling for, first and foremost, is a reemphasis on the "basics" of education, such as literacy, communication skills, mathematics, and, increasingly in this age, fundamental computer skills, rather than more specific job skills. In addition, a nonadversarial workplace environment is ostensibly more important than merely low labor costs.

Infrastructure

Infrastructure rated as one of the most significant broad criteria. Two of the four individual infrastructural-related site selection factors ranked among the ten most important overall.

As seen in Figure 1-2, the most important infrastructural factor (and a commentary of sorts on the current transportation priorities in the United States) was favorable access to major highways. The only factors to achieve a higher or comparable rating in the study were low lease rates and the availability of an educated labor force.

The second infrastructural-related factor viewed as highly important by the study participants was the availability of advanced energy and telecommunications systems. Approximately 46% of the study participants rated this as a very important criterion, and more than nine in ten viewed it as at least moderately important. Its 2.37 weighted average score made it the sixth most important site selection factor.

The other infrastructural factors were not considered nearly as important by the study participants, however. In fact, access to rail ranked last of all 28 site selection factors included in the study.

Accessibility to a port and/or major airport was not as important as might have been expected. Still, 37% of the survey respondents viewed this criterion as very important, and 77% viewed it as at least moderately important.

Figure ES-1: Preferred Site Selection Factors

Site Selection Factors	Moderately Important %	% of Survey Respondents Top 10 Individually Important or Very Important	Weighted Average*	Factor Rating**
1. Real Estate-Related Costs				
Low lease rates	82	98	2.81	1
Low construction costs	54	93	2.47	4
Up-front rent concessions	35	78	2.13	
2. Market/Corporate Accessibility				
Primary consumer markets	56	85	2.41	5
Suppliers	16	59	1.75	
Corporate/division headquarters	28	60	1.88	
3. Taxes/Regulatory Environment				
Property tax rates	40	87	2.88	8
Corporate and business taxes	36	82	2.18	10
Personal income taxes	19	66	1.86	
Favorable local government attitude towards business	52	82	2.34	7
Tax relocation/startup incentives	27	69	1.97	
Regional growth planning	25	83	2.08	
4. Quality of Life				
Housing affordability	26	86	2.12	
Cost of living	27	86	2.12	
Recreational/cultural amenities	21	76	2.02	
Climate	14	56	1.70	
Ease of commute	28	86	2.14	
Low crime rate	38	88	2.26	9
School system	25	75	2.01	
5. Labor Quality/Availability				
Educated labor force	52	95	2.48	2
Availability of low-cost labor	29	79	2.09	
Availability of continuing education/ job-training programs	26	78	2.03	
Labor relations	33	79	2.12	
Industry-specific skills	23	79	.02	
6. Infrastructure				
Port/airport	37	77	2.14	
Rail	13	41	1.54	
Major highways	55	93	2.48	3
Energy and telecommunications systems	46	92	2.37	6

*Study participants were asked to rate the site selection factors on a continuum from 1 (not important) to 3 (very important).

**Ten factors receiving highest weighted average response.

Prospects for Relocation/Expansion/Consolidation

In order to evaluate the prospective impact of the survey respondents' preferred location markets and site selection factors, study participants were asked to report the prospects for relocation, expansion, or consolidation at their firms and their preferences for fulfilling their firms' future real estate requirements.

The most basic question concerned prospects for firm relocation, expansion, or consolidation. The responses of the study participants indicate that the restructuring of the nation's economy is far from over. In fact, as can be seen in Figure ES-3, 53% of the study participants indicated that their firms were currently considering consolidating office facilities. Only 33%, by contrast, were considering expansions. A sizable proportion—upward of two-fifths—expected to relocate.

Almost 80% of all respondents are planning a relocation or expansion of one or more of their corporate facilities. More than 36% were preparing to relocate or expand within a year. Nearly one-quarter (23%) expected to expand or relocate within 1 to 3 years. For those planning to expand, the average anticipated additional space requirement was approximately 215,000 square feet.

Figure ES-3: Relocation/Expansion/Consolidation Plans

	Relocation	Expansion	Consolidation
Manufacturing	10%	10%	13%
Distribution	15	16	20
Office	42	33	53
R&D	5	5	7

Fulfillment of Space Requirements

In order to determine the prospective impact of the location and site selection factor preferences, study participants were asked to report how they anticipated meeting their future needs for space. As seen in Figure ES-4, the most popular option, by a wide margin, remains leasing. Half of the survey respondents indicated that they would likely use a traditional lease format.

The second preferred fulfillment method, named by 22% of the study participants, was to contract for build-to-suit space. Perhaps the most surprising result, in light of plummeting property prices, was that only 4% of the study participants chose an outright purchase of an existing property as the preferred fulfillment mode.

Preferred Property Types

Office facilities, overall, remain the preferred property type to meet corporate relocation/expansion needs through 1995. As seen in Figure ES-5, approximately seven in ten study participants indicated that office space, either suburban office, campus,

or CBD (central business district) office, would be the property type in greatest demand. What is surprising, perhaps, is the comparatively low proportion of respondents who preferred a traditional downtown location. Only 12% of respondents selected CBD office space; approximately 58% selected a suburban midrise or campus location.

Nearly 17% of the respondents expected to require light industrial space in a business park setting. Approximately one in ten expected to need bulk distribution space. Only 3.3% would need R&D space. Overall, industrial space figured in the future plans of approximately three in ten of the study participants.

Impact on Economy and Commercial Real Estate

Taking into account the site and real estate preferences expressed by the study participants, it appears that demand from major corporations will stimulate improvement in the nation's suburban office, bulk warehouse, and light industrial park sectors.

Although suburban office space currently is greatly overbuilt, vacancy rates are already falling in many prime suburban office markets nationwide as a result of the dramatic decline in construction. In fact, vacancy in higher quality space has fallen to the low or mid teens or, in exceptional instances, single digits, in a number of important suburban submarkets. As shown in Figure ES-5, because study participants overwhelmingly preferred suburban space, the recovery of the suburban office sector should accelerate as the economy rebounds, and more corporations consider expansion (albeit cautiously), rather than consolidation. Consequently, a number of prime suburban submarkets could see dramatic improvement in the next 12 to 24 months.

In the industrial sector, study participants expressed a strong preference for light industrial park space. This sector, currently oversupplied, has seen construction decline to the point that a rebound is imminent. Therefore, the strong preference expressed by study participants will likely accelerate this improvement as the economy rebounds.

The results of the study indicate dreary prospects for two important sectors, however. First, for the nation's badly oversupplied and still deteriorating CBD office sector, the weak preference expressed by study participants means that major corporate users will likely absorb very little CBD office space in the foreseeable future. In the flex/R&D category, the story is much the same, despite the dramatic decline in construction.

With respect to individual markets—although locales such as north suburban Atlanta, Dallas's far north suburbs, Charlotte, and Salt Lake City still have overbuilt office and industrial sectors—market conditions, particularly in the suburbs, have

improved. Such markets can expect an additional shot in the arm, both in the absorption of existing space and in build-to-suit construction, as the economy rebounds.

These market areas will benefit not only from the jobs created directly by corporate relocations and expansions, but also from the construction jobs created by those firms who choose to build space, rather than lease or purchase existing space. Because a number of markets nationwide have seen construction plunge in this recession, new construction jobs could have a major local economic impact in some markets.

Figure ES-4: Preferred Space Fulfillment Method

Method	% of Respondents
Traditional lease	50
Contract for build-to-suit	22
Joint venture	10
Sale lease-back	7
Other	7
Purchase of existing property	4

Figure ES-5: Property Category Preferences

Property Type	% of Respondents
Suburban midrise office	33
Campus	25
Light industrial park	17
CBD office	12
Bulk warehouse	10
R&D	3

Appendices & Notes

State Tax Notes

California: Corporations electing a water's-edge method of apportioning income must pay an additional tax.

Colorado: The 5.1% maximum rate applies for tax years beginning on or after July 1, 1992, but before July 1, 1993. The corporate income tax rate decreases to 5% for tax years beginning on or after July 1, 1993.

Connecticut: Beginning January 1, 1995, the rate is reduced to 11.25% and is further reduced over the next 3 years, becoming 10% beginning January 1, 1998.

Maine: The sales tax rate decreases to 5% as of July 1, 1993.

Massachusetts: Certain interest, dividends, and 50% of net capital gains are taxed at 12%. Unemployment compensation, alimony, Massachusetts bank interest, rental income, pension and annuity income, and IRA/Keogh distributions are taxed at 5.95%.

Michigan: A modified value-added tax called the *single business tax* is imposed. The tax base is much broader than a general net income tax base.

Missouri: For tax years beginning on or after September 1, 1993, the flat tax rate increases from 5% to 6.25%, and the federal income tax deduction is limited to 50%.

Montana: Effective July 1, 1993, but retroactive to January 1, 1993, the tax rate is 6.7%. In addition to the tax rate change, the individual tax scheme is changed. These changes are currently being challenged.

Montana: A corporation that makes a water's-edge election is subject to tax at a rate of 7%.

New Hampshire: Interest and dividends are taxed at 5%.

New Jersey and Pennsylvania: The taxes are basically taxes on gross income with few deductions allowed.

New York: The income tax rate is scheduled to decrease to 7.59375% for 1994.

New York: The corporate income tax rate includes a 15% surtax that is set to expire July 1, 1995. An additional surcharge of 17% is imposed on business activity carried on in New York City and certain surrounding counties.

North Carolina: The corporate tax rate is scheduled to decrease to 7.8275% for tax years beginning on or after January 1, 1994.

North Dakota, Rhode Island, and Vermont: The states' taxes are based on federal tax liability. The rate indicated assumes taxpayer is subject to a maximum effective federal tax rate of 31%.

Ohio: The corporate income tax rate does not include the .22% Tier 1 litter tax. The Tier 1 litter tax cannot exceed $5,000 for a corporation or a combined group of corporations.

Oklahoma: The personal income tax rate assumes the taxpayer is deducting federal income taxes. If the taxpayer is not deducting federal income taxes, the maximum rate is 7%.

Pennsylvania: In addition to the income tax, all corporate taxpayers pay a capital stock/franchise tax of .01275% of the corporation's taxable value.

Tennessee: Interest and dividends can be taxed at rates as high as 6%.

Texas: A corporation franchise tax is imposed at the greater of 4.5% of net taxable earned surplus or 0.25% of net taxable capital.

Wisconsin: Wisconsin imposes a "Temporary Surcharge" equal to 0.4345% in addition to the regular income tax rate. The Temporary

Surcharge is imposed only on business income. The rate of 0.4345% is applicable for tax years ending on or before April 30, 1993.

Wisconsin: Wisconsin imposes a "Temporary Surcharge" equal to 5.5% of the gross income or franchise tax (before applicable credits) in addition to the regular income or franchise tax. The rate of 5.5% is applicable for tax years ending on or before April 30, 1993.

Wyoming: A 5% rate is in effect until June 30, 1993; thereafter, the rate is 6%.

State-Local General Sales Tax Notes: Combined Rates, Selected Cities, November 1992

Alabama: Other tax is rate imposed in police jurisdictions.

Alaska: Boroughs may levy a sales and use tax not to exceed 6%. Cities outside boroughs may levy a tax not to exceed 3%. Cities within boroughs may levy a sales or use tax on all source taxes by the borough in the manner provided for boroughs, but may not exceed 6%. City sales taxes are in addition to borough sales taxes.

Arizona: Subject to voter approval, various counties are authorized to impose the following taxes: a public transportation excise tax at a rate not to exceed 10% of the state tax; a general excise tax not to exceed 10% of the state tax to support countywide services; a stadium district transaction privilege tax, if a major league baseball franchise is awarded within the district, at a rate not to exceed 5% of the state tax; a tax not more than 2% of the state rate to finance major league baseball spring training operations; a transaction tax not to exceed 10% of the state sales tax rate to finance a county jail district. The board of directors of any recreation center is authorized to levy a transaction privilege tax on the gross proceeds of retail sales, based on the amount or volume of business transacted by persons on account of their business activities in the district. The tax rate cannot exceed 1% in the first year and 0.5% for the remaining life of the district. Until June 30, 1994, any county having a county hospital that has an occupancy rate for licensed hospital beds, except psychiatric beds, of less than 20% is authorized to levy a tax equal to 10% of the sales tax applicable to each person engaging in or continuing in the county in a taxable business for the purposes of retiring county hospital warrants. Once approved by the board of supervisors, the tax is imposed for 48 months, unless the warrants are retired before 48 months.

Arkansas: Subject to voter approval, counties are authorized to levy local sales and use taxes for the following purposes: repaying capital improvement bonds at 0.25%–2%, in 0.25% increments; public mass transportation systems at 0.25%; financing capital improvements at 0.25%–1%; financing an airport or riverport jointly owned and operated by a county and by one or more other counties or by a metropolitan port authority, a regional airport commission or other instrumentality, for up to 48 months, at 1%. Specified municipalities may impose a sales and use tax, subject to voter approval, for the following purposes: to finance capital improvements at 0.25%–71%; to finance park and recreation facilities at 0.5%–71%; to fund public mass transportation not to exceed 0.25%. Any city with 3,000 or fewer inhabitants that is located in a county that borders on the state line, that contains a historic district included in the National Registry of Historic Places, and that is certified by the State Parks, Recreation, and Travel Commission as having tourism as the majority industry, may impose, with voter approval, a tax from 0.25% to 1% to finance capital improvements.

California: All counties have adopted a 1.25% sales tax. Cities may levy a conforming 1.0% tax (80% of the total local tax), and counties must allow a credit of 1.0% against the county rate. The board of any county may levy a transactions and use tax at a rate of 0.25% or 0.5%, or establish an authority for specific purposes, which may levy a 0.25% or 0.5% sales and use tax, subject to voter approval. The Local Transportation Authority and Improvement Act authorizes

the imposition of a voter-approved retail transactions and use tax applicable both in the incorporated and unincorporated territory of a county by any local transportation authority created or designated by the county board of supervisors to carry out the provisions of the act. The tax rate may be 0.25%, 0.5%, 0.75%, or 1.00% and must not remain in effect for more than 20 years. Several districts are authorized to impose a transaction and use tax to fund public mass transit, transportation and traffic, public education, libraries, justice facilities, drug abuse prevention, crime prevention, health care services, etc.

Colorado: The regional transportation district, consisting of the City and County of Denver and portions of Adams, Arapahoe, Jefferson, Boulder, and Douglas counties, levies a 0.6% sales tax. Other authorized taxes include the following: Incorporated cities and towns may levy sales and/or use taxes, with voter approval. Public highway authorities may levy sales and use taxes not to exceed 0.4%. Local improvement district tax board of county having a population greater than 100,000 may fund all or a portion of the cost of specified local improvements by levying a sales tax not to exceed 0.5% through the local improvement district, with voter approval. A 0.1% tax applies to all sales that are subject to the transportation tax for the Denver Metropolitan Scientific and Cultural Facilities District, and an additional 0.1% tax applies for the Denver Metropolitan Baseball Stadium District.

Florida: The governing body in each county may levy a local government (sales) surtax that may be in the form of (1) a charter county transit system surtax at a rate not to exceed 1%, (2) a local government infrastructure surtax for up to 15 years at the rate of 0.5% or 1%, (3) a small-county surtax of 0.5% or 1%, (4) an indigent care surtax not to exceed 0.5% (may not be imposed after 10/1/98 or if (5) or (6) below are imposed),

(5) a county public hospital surtax of 0.5%, or (6) a small-county indigent care surtax of 0.5%. County taxes imposed under (2), (3), (4), (5), and (6) may not exceed 1%.

Georgia: The general assembly has authorized the imposition of joint county and municipal sales and use taxes. It created special districts, based on county lines, which may impose a 1% tax. Specified counties are authorized to impose a local sales and use tax for educational purposes. Governing bodies (Fulton, DeKalb, Cobb, Clayton or Gwinnett counties and the City of Atlanta) that enter into rapid transit contracts with the Metropolitan Atlanta Rapid Transit Authority may levy sales and use taxes at the rate of 1% until June 30, 2032, and 0.5% thereafter. No tax may be levied unless the tax is imposed in Fulton and DeKalb counties.

Hawaii: Hawaii counties (except Kalawao County) may impose a 0.5% general excise (sales) and use tax surcharge to provide funds for public mass transit projects from January 1, 1993, through December 31, 2002.

Idaho: Cities that derive a major portion of their economic well-being from tourism may impose a sales tax on all sales subject to taxation under the state Sales and Use Tax Act if approved by 60% of the cities' voters.

Illinois: Home rule cities are able to impose sales taxes at 0.25% increments, which will be collected by the state Department of Revenue. Counties and municipalities may impose a sales tax not to exceed 1%. City sales taxes are in addition to any county and transit sales taxes. Two transit districts levy an additional sales tax of 0.25% or 0.75%. Chicago imposes its own sales and use tax of 1%. Beginning September 1, 1991, local taxes may not be imposed on sales of food to be consumed off premises.

Iowa: Counties are authorized to levy a local sales and service tax at a rate not to exceed 1%, with voter approval.

Kansas: If approved by the voters, Class A and Class C cities may levy 0.25%, 0.5%, 0.75%, or 1% retailers' sales taxes, Class B cities may levy retailers' sales taxes at rates ranging from 0.25% to 2% in 0.25% increments, and Class D cities may levy retailers' sales taxes at rates ranging from 0.25% to 1.75% in 0.25% increments. In addition, Class D cities, with voter approval, may impose an additional 0.5% or 0.75% sales tax. A board of county commissioners may levy the tax at 0.5% or 1%, although certain counties may levy the tax at 0.25%, 1.5%, or 2%. The rate of county-imposed tax may be equal to the sum of the rate allowed to be imposed by a board of county commissioners on July 1, 1992, plus 0.25%, 0.5%, 0.75%, or 1%. After voter approval, a city or county may impose an additional 0.25%, 0.5%, 0.75%, or 1% retailers' sales tax to fund health care services. Any county that is part of the Kansas and Missouri culture district must impose a countywide sales tax not to exceed 0.25%, subject to voter approval.

Louisiana: City sales taxes are in addition to any parish sales taxes. Any school board taxes are included in parish sales taxes. Any local government subdivision or school board is authorized to levy a sales tax not to exceed 3%, unless specifically approved in a special election.

Minnesota: Counties are authorized to impose a 0.5% local option general sales and use tax. Specified cities are authorized to impose a general sales tax.

Missouri: Cities may impose a 0.5%, 0.875%, or 1% sales tax, except St. Louis, which may impose a 1.375% tax. Municipalities, except for that part of the municipality located in whole or in part within any first-class county having a charter form of government and not containing any part of a city with a population of 400,000 or more and adjacent to a city not within a county, are authorized to impose an additional sales (capital improve-

ments) tax of 0.125%, 0.25%, 0.0375%, or 0.5%, subject to voter approval. Up to a 0.5% sales tax may be imposed for transportation purposes by specified local governments. Transportation development districts may impose a sales tax at an unspecified rate if approved by local voters. Counties are authorized to impose local sales taxes under several statutes, all subject to voter approval.

Nebraska: Metropolitan class, primary class, and first and second class cities may increase an existing tax by an amount not to exceed 0.5%, subject to voter approval.

Nevada: The state sales tax of 6.5% includes 4.5% for local school support and city-county relief. These taxes are mandatory in all 17 counties. Counties may levy an additional tax for public transportation, road construction, or tourism.

New Mexico: Municipalities may impose an excise tax at the rate of up to 1.25% and, until July 1, 1996, a special municipal gross receipts tax may be imposed at a rate not to exceed 0.25%. Municipalities are authorized to levy an excise tax (infrastructure gross receipts tax) on any person engaging in business at a rate not to exceed 0.125%. A county fire protection excise tax may be imposed at 0.125% or 0.25% of gross receipts. Counties that meet certain property tax rate requirements are authorized to impose a 0.375% gross receipts tax. Subject to voter approval, counties that meet certain population, property tax, and severance tax requirements are authorized to impose a 0.5% local hospital gross receipts tax and a 0.125% special county hospital gross receipts tax for up to 10 years. The majority of the members of the governing body of any county may enact an ordinance imposing a county health care gross receipts tax at a rate of 1/16 of 1%. The governing bodies of municipalities and counties may impose an environmental services gross receipts tax at

a municipal rate of 0.0625% and a county rate of 0.125%.

New York: An additional 0.25% sales tax for the Metropolitan Commuter Transit District is imposed in New York City and the counties of Dutchess, Nassau, Orange, Putnam, Rockland, Suffolk, and Westchester. Yonkers preempts a portion of the county tax.

Ohio: Counties may impose a sales tax not to exceed 1.5%. An additional transit tax is imposed in several counties, but may not exceed 1.5%.

Tennessee: If a county levies a tax less than one-half of the state rate, a city may levy only the difference. If a city or county adopts a local option base, then the sales tax may not exceed $5 on the sale of any single item of personal property if the local tax rate does not exceed 1%, and may not exceed $7.50 whenever the tax rate exceeds 1%.

Texas: A county that is not located within a rapid transit authority or a regional transportation authority may adopt a county sales or use tax, subject to voter approval, to reduce property taxes. Qualified cities may levy an additional 0.5% local sales tax to reduce city property taxes or, if no property tax is imposed, may impose this additional tax, with voter approval. Cities located in a county with a population of more than 750,000 are authorized to levy an additional 0.5% tax, if approved by voters, not to exceed a combined state-local rate of 7.25%.

Utah: Cities and counties may impose a sales tax of 0.75% or 1%. Presently, all 29 counties levy the tax. Cities within the counties that impose the tax receive a portion of the revenues. Cities and counties are also authorized to levy a 0.25% transit tax. Resort communities may include an additional sales tax of up to 1%. City and county taxes do not overlap.

Virginia: Cities are independent of counties in Virginia. Every city and county imposes a 1% sales tax; total combined statewide sales tax is 4.5%.

Washington: Cities and counties may levy a local sales and use tax of 0.5%. They are also authorized to levy an additional sales tax not to exceed 0.6% for transportation. Counties must allow a credit for the full amount of any city sales and use taxes. If the county in which the city is located imposes a sales and use tax, the city tax rate may not exceed .425%. Counties and cities may levy an additional 0.5% if approved by voters.

Wisconsin: The county sales and use taxes may be imposed only for the purpose of directly reducing the property tax levy.

Wyoming: Counties may levy an additional capital improvement tax not to exceed 1%, subject to voter approval.

Source: ACIR staff compilation from Commerce Clearing House, State Tax Reporter *(Chicago, 1992).*

Property Tax Rate Notes, Selected Cities, 1990— State Taxes

Alabama: Rates are combined state, county, city, and school tax rates.

Alaska: Rates are the total property tax levies for municipal and school purposes.

Arizona: Rates are based on state, county, city, junior college, and primary and secondary school levies, but do not include special or improvement district levies.

California: The following cities have additional rates for land only: Concord (.112), Fremont (.026), Hayward (.004), Ventura Code 03001 (.02322).

Delaware: The following cities and counties give discounts on property taxes if the taxes are paid by certain deadlines: Harrington, Laurel, Lewes, and Milford.

Florida: Rates are combined city, county, and school tax levies except for Sarasota, which includes only the city and county rate.

Georgia: Rates are combined state, county, and city tax rates. The city of Gainesville has a different ratio to assessed value of 100%.

Hawaii: The first rate in the column is the tax rate per $1,000 net taxable building, and the second rate is the tax rate per $1,000 net taxable land.

Idaho: The rate is the composite of state, county, city, and school district levies.

Illinois: The rates are a composite of the county, city, school, sanitary district, and park district levies.

Indiana: The rates are the composite of state, county, city, school, and other district levies.

Iowa: The rates are the composite of state, county, city, school, agricultural extension, hospital, and others. Where more than one

rate prevails in a city, the highest rate is used in the composite.

Kansas: Rates include state, county, city, and school taxes.

Kentucky: Rates include state ($1.89 per $1,000), county, city, and school districts for cities with populations of 7,000 and more.

Louisiana: The rate is the aggregate of all levies for parish, municipal, and district purposes. Special districts, such as road, school, and levee districts, are organized to cover parts of a parish and, in some cases, parts of more than one parish.

Maine: Rates include state, county, and city or town taxes.

Maryland: Rates are the combined state ($2.10), county, and city tax rates. For tax years beginning after June 30, 1991, assessment is 40% of phased-in value.

Massachusetts: Rates are the residential property tax rates for fiscal year 1991. Rates for open spaces, commercial, industrial, and personal property are not reflected.

Michigan: Rates reflect the total county, city, and school levies for each city. Certain other assessments (e.g., local transportation facilities, drainage systems, jails) are not reflected.

Mississippi: Rates are the combined rates for cities and counties for fiscal year 1989.

Missouri: Rates are the composite of several levies, including state, county, city, school, and other districts. The rates for Kansas City and Rolla are city only.

Montana: Rates include the state, county, city, school district, and, where applicable, the university millage fund, vo-tech, accredited high school fund, and special district tax rates.

Nebraska: The rates listed are the aggregate rates (rounded to the nearest hundredth) for county, city, school district, and miscellaneous levies.

Nevada: Rates include state, county, city, and school district levies.

New Jersey: The Cherry Hill rate excludes the fire districts. The Edison rate is for the non-trash district.

New Mexico: Rates are for New Mexico residents. Rates for nonresidents range from 15.359% to 40.780%.

New York: The following cities have higher nonhomestead tax rates: Johnstown, Newburgh, Niagara Falls, North Tonawanda, Kingston, Lackawanna, and Rochester.

North Carolina: Listed are the aggregate rates of tax payable to the county collector and the rate of tax payable to the city collector.

North Dakota: The rates are the total property tax rates for state, county, city, and school district purposes for 1989.

Oklahoma: Rates include county, city, and school district levies.

Oregon: Rates include county, city, school district, and other levies.

Pennsylvania: Rates are a composite of county, city, and school taxes. County rates include levies for institution districts where applicable.

South Dakota: Rates include county, city, and school taxes.

Tennessee: Rates include county, city, and special districts for 1988. The city of Nashville is served by an Urban Services District with taxing authority, and no other city or county taxes apply.

Texas: Rates contain county, city, and school levies. The Port Arthur rate does not include the school district levy.

Virginia: Rates are the county and city tax rates combined, where applicable.

Washington: Rates include state, county, city, and school levies.

West Virginia: Rates include state, county, and municipal levies.

Wisconsin: Rates include state, county, local, and school tax levies.

Wyoming: Rates include state, county, city, and school levies. The state rate of $12 per $1,000 is for the state school foundation.

Source: Commerce Clearing House, State Tax Reporter *(Chicago, 1991).*

Classification of Real Property and Tangible Personal Property, 1991

State	Number of Classes Real	Number of Classes Personal	Residential Real	Residential Personal	Commercial/ Industrial Real	Commercial/ Industrial Personal	Telecommunications Utility Real	Telecommunications Utility Personal
Alabama	3	3	10%	10%	20%	20%	30%	30%
Alaska	1	1	100	X	100	100	100	100
Arizona	9	9	10	10	25	25	30	30
Arkansas	1	1	20	20	20	20	20	20
California	2	1	100	X	100	100	100	100
Colorado	6	1	14.34	X	29	29	29	29
Connecticut	1	1	70	70	70	70	X	X
Delaware	1	X	100	X	100	X	100	X
District of Columbia	5	1	100	X	100	100	100	X
Florida	1	1	100	X	100	100	Local	Local
Georgia	2	1	40	X	40	40	40	40
Hawaii	1	X	100	X	100	X	100	X
Idaho	1	1	50	X	100	100	100	100
Illinois	1	X	33.33	33.33	33.33	X	33.33	X
Indiana	1	1	33.33	X	33.33	33.33	33.33	33.33
Iowa	4	X	79	X	100	X	100	X
Kansas	4	5	12	X	30	20	30	30
Kentucky	1	1	100	X	100	100	100	100
Louisiana	5	5	10	X	51	15	10/25	25
Maine	1	1	100	X	100	100	100	X
Maryland	1	1	100	X	100	100	100	100
Massachusetts	4	4	100	X	100	100	100	100
Michigan	6	5	50	X	50	50	50	50
Minnesota	12	1	1/2/3	X	3.2/4.95	X	4.95	X
Mississippi	3	2	10	X	15	15	30	30
Missouri	3	9	19	X	32	33.33	32	33.33
Montana	11	13	3.86	X	3.86	3.86	12	12
Nebraska	1	1	100	X	100	100	100	100
Nevada	1	1	35	X	35	35	35	35
New Hampshire	1	X	100	X	100	X	X	X
New Jersey	1	1	100	X	100	50	100	50
New Mexico	1	1	33.33	X	33.33	33.33	33.33	33.33
New York	2	X	100	X	100	X	100	X
North Carolina	1	1	100	100	100	100	100	100
North Dakota	4	X	9	X	10	X	10	10
Ohio	2	3	35	X	35	27	35	100
Oklahoma	1	1	Max 35	Max 35	Max 35	Max 35	Max 35	Max 35
Oregon	1	1	100	X	100	100	100	100
Pennsylvania	1	X	Max 100	X	Max 100	X	Max 100	X
Rhode Island	1	1	Max 100	Max 100	Max 100	Max 100	Max 100	Max 100
South Carolina	6	4	4	X	6	10.5	10.5	10.5
South Dakota	2	X	100	X	100	X	100	100
Tennessee	4	3	25	5	40	30	55	55
Texas	1	1	100	X	100	100	100	100
Utah	5	1	66.9	X	95	100	100	100
Vermont	1	2	100	X	100	50	100	50
Virginia	1	1	100	100	100	100	100	100
Washington	1	1	100	X	100	100	100	100
West Virginia	3	3	60	60	60	60	60	60
Wisconsin	1	1	100	X	100	100	X	X
Wyoming	3	1	9.5	X	11.5	11.5	11.5	11.5

MV—market value

X—exempt

Classification of Real Property and Tangible Personal Property, 1991—State Notes

Alabama: Tangible personal property consists of passenger cars and noncommercial pickup trucks weighting 8,000 lbs. or less. Owner-occupied, single family property is assessed at 10%. Other residential property is assessed at 20%.

Arizona: Basis is "limited property value" for primary taxes (i.e., taxes imposed for maintenance and operators of counties, cities, school districts, community college districts, and the state) and the "full cash value" for secondary taxes (i.e., taxes imposed for debt retirement, voter-approved budget overrides, and the maintenance and operation of special service districts, such as sanitation, fire, and road improvement). "Limited property value" is defined as the limited property value in the prior year plus 10% of such value, or 25% of the difference between the full cash value of the property in the current tax year and the limited property value of the parcel in the prior tax year.

California: The 1975–76 assessed value of property is the base value. Property may be reassessed only after new construction on, transfer of, or sale of property after the 1975 assessment. The fair market value base may reflect the inflationary rate, not to exceed or decrease by 2% for any year.

Colorado: Residential real property must be valued for assessment at 15% of actual value, but the legislature must determine the percentage of aggregate statewide valuation for assessment attributable to residential realty. If there is a change in the level of value used to determine actual value, the legislature must adjust the ratio of valuation for assessing residential realty to ensure that the percentage of the aggregate statewide value for assessment attributable to residen-

tial realty remains the same as the preceding year.

Connecticut: Regulated telecommunications companies are exempt. Nonregulated telecommunications companies providing long-distance services are subject to local assessment.

District of Columbia: A telecommunications company is given a credit, for at least the property tax due, against toll telecommunication taxes paid for the year in question.

Delaware: The following are the basic years selected by the three counties: Kent, 1987; New Castle, 1983; and Sussex, 1974.

Florida: Telecommunications companies are subject to real and personal property assessment by their respective county property appraisers.

Hawaii: Counties may classify by differential rates both on the basis of use (three counties) and land v. improvements (one county).

Idaho: The first $50,000 of the market value for assessment purposes of residential improvements, or 50% of the market value for assessment purposes of residential improvements, whichever is less, is exempt.

Illinois: Any county with a population of 200,000 or more may classify. Only Cook County does. The assessment level of its highest class cannot exceed 2 times the level of its lowest class. Cook County has 11 assessment levels.

Louisiana: Telecommunications property is assessed at 10% for land and 25% for improvements.

Maine: Personal property of telecommunications is subject to a state tax of 27 mils, and is exempt from ordinary property taxes.

Maryland: Real property is assessed at its full cash value, except that for tax years beginning after June 30, 1991, the assessment of real property is 40% of its phased-in value.

Michigan: The state equalizes totals separately for the 6 classes.

Minnesota: Actually, there are 12 classes of property, but Class 5 property includes both real and personal property. The property tax is based on a tax capacity system for all classes and subclasses of property. Each county auditor must compute the net tax capacity for each parcel according to the rates specified in the classification provisions. The net tax capacity is the appropriate rate multiplied by the parcel's market value. Residential homesteads are assessed at 1% of market value on the first $68,000 of market, 2% on the amount over $68,000 but not exceeding $110,000, and 3% on the amount over $110,000. Lower assessment rates apply for residential homesteads by blind persons, permanently and totally disabled veterans, any person permanently and totally disabled and receiving public aid constituting at least 90% of the total income, and any person whose household income is 150% or less of the federal poverty level. Commercial, industrial, and public utility real property has a class rate of 3.3% on the first $100,000 of market value and 5.06% of the market value over $100,000.

New Hampshire: Assessment ratios are determined by towns and cities and varied from 17% to 123% in 1990. Effective March 1, 1990, telephone and telegraph companies pay a communication source tax to the state.

New Jersey: Property is assessed at "taxable value," which each county board establishes for its county. The percentage may not be less than 20% or greater than 100%. Personal property is assessed in each taxing jurisdiction. The following are exempt from the personal property tax: inventories, motor vehicles, personal property held for use in the business of farming, and personal property of life insurance companies.

Ohio: Real property is assessed at a level not to exceed 35% of market value. The taxable value of a telephone or telegraph company with more than 15,000 access lines and an interexchange telecommunications company is assessed at 88%, and a telephone and telegraph company is assessed at 100%.

Pennsylvania: In fourth to eighth class counties, real property is assessed at a predetermined ratio not to exceed 75%. County commissioners in second to eighth class counties and city councils have the power to levy a personal property tax on certain intangibles.

South Dakota: Real and personal property of telephone companies subject to the gross receipts tax are exempt from the property tax. Personal property not centrally assessed is tax exempt.

Tennessee: Household goods, furnishings, wearing apparel, and other tangible personal property to $7,500 ($15,000 if jointly owned by a husband and wife) are exempt.

Utah: Land of more than one acre per residential unit is assessed at 100%.

Virginia: Machinery and tools used in specified businesses, manufacturing, or mining activities are valued on the basis of depreciated cost or percentages of original total capitalized cost. Assessments of transportation personal property are apportioned on the basis of miles traveled in Virginia.

Wisconsin: For tax years 1989 through 1992, the assessed value of property may not be adjusted by more than 25% of the previous year's value, unless property did not exist in the same form as at present, or was not taxed during the preceding year.

Wyoming: Industrial property is assessed at 11.5%. Commercial property is assessed at

9.5%. Telecommunications companies are subject to a state-levied tax based on gross revenues, in lieu of a property tax. Manufacturing machinery and equipment and merchants and manufacturers stocks are exempt.

Source: ACIR staff compilation based on information from state departments of revenue (Fall 1991) and Commerce Clearing House, State Tax Guide *(Chicago, 1991).*

Index